THE CAMBRIDGE COMPANION TO
DIETRICH BONHOEFFER

This *Companion* serves as a guide for readers wanting to explore the thought
and legacy of the great German theologian Dietrich Bonhoeffer (1906–45).
The book shows why Bonhoeffer remains such an attractive figure to so
many people of diverse backgrounds. Its chapters, written by authors from
differing national, theological and church contexts, provide a helpful introduction to, and commentary on, Bonhoeffer's life, work and writing and so
guide the reader along the complex paths of his thought. Experts set out
comprehensively Bonhoeffer's political, social and cultural contexts, and
offer biographical information which is indispensable for the understanding of his theology. Major themes arising from the theology, and different
interpretations of it, lead the reader into a dialogue with this most influential of thinkers, who remains both fascinating and challenging. There are a
chronology, a glossary and an index.

CAMBRIDGE COMPANIONS TO RELIGION
A series of companions to major topics and key figures in
theology and religious studies. Each volume contains specially
commissioned essays by international scholars which provide
an accessible and stimulating introduction to the subject for new
readers and non-specialists.

Other titles published

THE CAMBRIDGE COMPANION TO CHRISTIAN DOCTRINE
edited by Colin Gunton

THE CAMBRIDGE COMPANION TO BIBLICAL INTERPRETATION
edited by John Barton

THE CAMBRIDGE COMPANION TO LIBERATION THEOLOGY
edited by Christopher Rowland

Forthcoming

THE CAMBRIDGE COMPANION TO ST PAUL
edited by J. D. G. Dunn

THE CAMBRIDGE COMPANION TO MEDIEVAL JEWISH THOUGHT
edited by Daniel H. Frank and Oliver Leaman

THE CAMBRIDGE COMPANION TO KARL BARTH
edited by John Webster

THE CAMBRIDGE COMPANION TO CHRISTIAN ETHICS
edited by Robin Gill

THE CAMBRIDGE COMPANION TO POSTMODERN THEOLOGY
edited by Kevin Vanhoozer

THE CAMBRIDGE COMPANION TO FEMINIST THEOLOGY
edited by Susan Frank Parsons

THE CAMBRIDGE COMPANION TO

DIETRICH BONHOEFFER

Edited by John W. de Gruchy

Robert Selby Taylor Professor of Christian Studies, University of Cape Town

CAMBRIDGE
UNIVERSITY PRESS

PUBLISHED BY THE PRESS SYNDICATE OF THE UNIVERSITY OF CAMBRIDGE
The Pitt Building, Trumpington Street, Cambridge CB2 1RP, United Kingdom

CAMBRIDGE UNIVERSITY PRESS
The Edinburgh Building, Cambridge CB2 2RU, UK   http://www.cup.cam.ac.uk
40 West 20th Street, New York, NY 10011-4211, USA   http://www.cup.org
10 Stamford Road, Oakleigh, Melbourne 3166, Australia

First published 1999

Printed in the United Kingdom at the University Press, Cambridge

Typeset in Severin 10/13 pt [VN]

A catalogue record for this book is available from the British Library

Library of Congress Cataloguing in Publication data

The Cambridge companion to Dietrich Bonhoeffer / edited by John W. de Gruchy.
    p.   cm. – (Cambridge companions to religion)
    Includes bibliographical references and index.
    ISBN 0 521 58258 X (hardback). – ISBN 0 521 58781 6 (paperback)
    1. Bonhoeffer, Dietrich, 1906–1945.   I. De Gruchy, John W.
II. Series
BX4827.B57C36   1999
230'.044'092–dc21   98–35990   CIP

ISBN 0 521 58258 X hardback
ISBN 0 521 58781 6 paperback

To
Eberhard and Renate Bethge
with gratitude

Contents

Notes on contributors

John de Gruchy is Robert Selby Taylor Professor of Christian Studies and Director of the Research Institute on Christianity in South Africa at the University of Cape Town, where he has taught since 1973. He is also the Founding Editor of the *Journal of Theology for Southern Africa*. His publications include *The Church Struggle in South Africa* (Grand Rapids: Eerdmans, 1986); *Bonhoeffer and South Africa* (Grand Rapids: Eerdmans, 1986); *Liberating Reformed Theology: The 1990 Warfield Lectures* (Grand Rapids: Eerdmans, 1991); *Bonhoeffer: Witness to Jesus Christ* (Minneapolis: Fortress Press, 1988); and *Christianity and Democracy: A Theology for a Just World Order* (Cambridge: Cambridge University Press, 1995). Most recently he edited *Bonhoeffer for a New Day* (Grand Rapids: Eerdmans, 1997), and *Creation and Fall*, volume III of the new English translation of Dietrich Bonhoeffer's *Works* (Minneapolis: Fortress Press, 1997).

Keith Clements has been General Secretary of the Conference of European Churches (Geneva) since 1997. His publications include *A Patriotism for Today: Love of Country in Dialogue with the Witness of Dietrich Bonhoeffer* (Collins, 1986), *What Freedom? The Persistent Challenge of Dietrich Bonhoeffer* (Bristol Baptist College, 1990) and *Learning to Speak: The Church's Voice in Public Affairs* (T. & T. Clark, 1995). He has also broadcast and contributed to a number of symposia on Bonhoeffer and other modern theologians, and is now completing a biography of the ecumenical pioneer J. H. Oldham.

Wayne Whitson Floyd, Jr is the Director of the Bonhoeffer Center at the Lutheran Theological Seminary at Philadelphia, USA, and General Editor and Project Director of the *Dietrich Bonhoeffer Works* (*DBW*) English Edition (1995–　). He also serves as Canon Theologian of the Episcopal Cathedral of St Stephen in Harrisburg, Pennsylvania; as Dean of the School of Christian Studies of the Episcopal Diocese of Central Pennsylvania; and as an Associate Fellow in the Department of Religion of Dickinson College, Carlisle,

Pennsylvania. His publications on Dietrich Bonhoeffer include *Theology and the Dialectics of Otherness: On Reading Bonhoeffer and Adorno* (1988); *Bonhoeffer Bibliography: Primary Sources and Secondary Literature in English* (co-author with Clifford Green, 1992); *Theology and the Practice of Responsibility* (co-editor with Charles Marsh, 1994); and the new *DBW* edition of Bonhoeffer's *Act and Being* (editor, 1996).

Clifford Green is Professor of Theology at Hartford Seminary, Hartford, Connecticut, and Executive Director of the *Dietrich Bonhoeffer Works* translation project. He is the author of *Bonhoeffer: A Theology of Sociality* (Eerdmans, 1999), editor of several volumes in the German and English editions of Bonhoeffer's works, and author of numerous articles on Bonhoeffer. He also edited and contributed to *Karl Barth: Theologian of Freedom* (Fortress Press, 1991), and *Churches, Cities, and Human Community* (Eerdmans, 1996), and contributed chapters on Marx, Tillich, Gutierrez and Cone to *Critical Issues in Modern Religion* (Prentice-Hall, 1990).

Geffrey B. Kelly, STD, LLD, is Professor of Systematic Theology, Chairman of the Department of Religion, and Director of the Lassallian Leadership Institute at La Salle University, Philadelphia, Pennsylvania. He is also President of the International Bonhoeffer Society, English Language Section, having been recently re-elected to a second four-year term in 1996. He served as Secretary of the Society from its founding in 1974 until 1992. Dr Kelly is the author of *Liberating Faith: Bonhoeffer's Message for Today* and co-author with F. Burton Nelson of *A Testament to Freedom: The Essential Writing of Dietrich Bonhoeffer.* He is co-editor with John D. Godsey of *Ethical Responsibility: Bonhoeffer's Legacy to the Churches*, a collection of the papers delivered at the Second International Bonhoeffer Congress held in Oxford, England, in 1980. Dr Kelly has written numerous articles on Bonhoeffer's theology and spirituality and given conferences, workshops and retreats around the United States on the theme of Bonhoeffer's Christocentric Spirituality. He has also presented scholarly papers at the international Bonhoeffer conferences held every four years beginning with the Second International Bonhoeffer Congress in 1976 at the World Council of Churches Headquarters in Geneva.

John Moses is an Anglican priest and taught German History at the University of Queensland for twenty-eight years. Since June 1997 he has been Adjunct Professor in History at the University of New England, Armidale, New South Wales, Australia. He has written extensively on German labour history (*Trade Unionism in Germany from Bismarck to Hitler 1869–1933* (2 vols., London/New York: George Prior/Barnes & Noble, 1982); *Trade Union Theory from Marx to Walesa* (Oxford; Berg Publishers, 1990)). He is currently investigating the part played by the churches in East Germany in undermining the rule of 'real existing socialism' in that former communist state.

F. Burton Nelson is Research Professor of Christian Ethics of North Park Theological Seminary, Chicago, Illinois, having taught theology and ethics there since 1960. He is also a Senior Associate at Oxford University, associated with the Oxford Centre for Hebrew and Jewish Studies and as adjunct faculty for the Holocaust Memorial Foundation of Illinois. His books include *The Story of the People of God* (Covenant Press, 1971); *A Testament to Freedom: The Essential Writings of Dietrich Bonhoeffer* (edited and written with Geffrey B. Kelly (Harper & Row, 1990, 1995)); he is the editor of *The Bonhoeffers: Portrait of a Family*, by Sabine Leibholz-Bonhoeffer (Covenant Publications, 1994). He is currently working on volumes relating Bonhoeffer to spirituality and to parish ministry. He has served for over ten years as the Vice-President of the International Bonhoeffer Society, English Language Section. He is a member of the Church Relations Committee of the Holocaust Memorial Museum in Washington, D.C. His degrees are from Brown University (BA); Yale University (M.Div.); and Northwestern University (Ph.D.).

Andreas Pangritz is Privatdozent (outside lecturer) of Systematic Theology at Freie Universität Berlin, Germany. He is author of *Dietrich Bonhoeffers Forderung einer Arkandisziplin* (Cologne: Pahl-Rugenstein, 1988); *Karl Barth in der Theologie Dietrich Bonhoeffers* (Berlin: Alektor, 1989; English translation forthcoming, Grand Rapids: Eerdmans); *Polyphonie des Lebens: Zu Dietrich Bonhoeffers 'Theologie der Musik'* (Berlin: Alektor, 1994); *Vom Kleiner- und Unsichtbarwerden der Theologie: Zum Projekt einer 'impliziten Theologie' bei Barth, Tillich, Bonhoeffer, Benjamin, Horkheimer und Adorno* (Tübingen: Theologischer Verlag, 1996); 'Sharing the Destiny of his People', in *Bonhoeffer for a New Day*, ed. John W. de Gruchy (Grand Rapids: Eerdmans, 1997) and '"Mystery and Commandment" in Leo Baeck's and Dietrich Bonhoeffer's Thinking', *European Judaism*, 30 (2) (1997).

Larry Rasmussen has been Reinhold Niebuhr Professor of Social Ethics at Union Theological Seminary in the City of New York since 1986. He is the recipient of the 1997 Grawemeyer Award in Religion for one of his most recent books, *Earth Community, Earth Ethics* (Orbis Books, 1996). (The chapter in this volume entitled 'Song of Songs' features Bonhoeffer as a source for eco-theology.) Rasmussen is also the author of *Moral Fragments and Moral Community: A Proposal for Church in Society* (Fortress Press, 1993) and, with Daniel C. Maguire, *Ethics for a Small Planet: New Horizons on Population, Consumption, and Ecology* (State University of New York Press, 1998).

Martin Rumscheidt is Professor of Historical and Doctrinal Studies at Atlantic School of Theology in Halifax, Nova Scotia. He has published and edited books on Karl Barth. He is the translator of the new edition of Bonhoeffer's *Act and Being* (*DBWE* ii) and of *The Theology of Dietrich Bonhoeffer* by Ernst Feil. He has been designated, with Wayne W. Floyd, Jr, to produce the new translation and edition of *Letters and Papers from Prison* for the *Dietrich Bonhoeffer Works in English* Edition. He is a member of the *DBWE* Editorial Board.

Peter Selby is an Anglican, currently serving as Bishop of Worcester, England. After seven years as Area Bishop of Kingston upon Thames he held the William Leech Professorial Fellowship in Applied Christian Theology at Durham University. Recent publications include: *Rescue: Jesus and Salvation Today* (SPCK, 1996) and *Grace and Mortgage: The Language of Faith and the Debt of the World* (Darton, Longman & Todd, 1997), which seeks to examine Bonhoeffer's Christology in relation to the economy of credit and debt.

Haddon Willmer retired in 1998 as Professor of Theology at the University of Leeds, where he has taught Christian history and theology since 1966. He has special interests in forgiveness and politics, in the relation between Christianity and European civilisation and in contemporary realisations of Christianity in mission and development. He studied in Tübingen in 1973–4, seeking to understand Bonhoeffer by investigating some of his less noticed contemporaries, such as Heinrich Vogel (*Studies in Church History*, Subsidia 7, pp. 327–46) and Otto Dibelius (*Studies in Church History*, 15, pp. 443–51).

Ruth Zerner, Associate Professor of History at Lehman College of the City University of New York, is the author of the commentary in Dietrich Bonhoeffer, *Fiction from Prison: Gathering up the Past* (Philadelphia: Fortress Press, 1981) and of 'Dietrich Bonhoeffer and the Jews: Thoughts and

Actions, 1933–1945', *Jewish Social Studies*, 37 (1975). In addition to writing numerous articles on Bonhoeffer, the German Church Struggle and the Holocaust and teaching German history and human rights courses, she has served as chair of two of the annual scholars' conferences on 'The Church Struggle and the Holocaust', as well as Protestant co-convenor of The Rainbow Group, a New York City scholars' seminar of Jewish–Christian dialogue.

Preface

The decision by Cambridge University Press to publish this *Companion to Dietrich Bonhoeffer* is indicative of Bonhoeffer's stature at the end of the twentieth century. It also suggests that his significance will continue to be recognised well into the next. This assessment is reinforced by the recently completed publication of the new sixteen-volume German critical edition of all Bonhoeffer's writings, and by the decision to translate all these volumes, some of considerable size, into English. If further evidence were needed to stake Bonhoeffer's claim to continuing relevance, we could also refer to the vitality of the International Bonhoeffer Society, whose seventh Congress was held in Cape Town in 1996, with the next about to take place in Berlin in the year 2000.

The purpose of this *Companion* is to provide a guide for those who wish to explore the legacy of this remarkable pastor, theologian and martyr, and to discover some of the reasons why he has such an attraction for many people in many different contemporary contexts. Numbered amongst them are people from different walks of life, different Christian and other religious traditions, different cultures and different academic disciplines. We hope that this volume will further their interest in Bonhoeffer and deepen their understanding of his legacy and challenge. However, in preparing this volume we have been conscious of another possible constituency, namely a new generation who, even if they are already familiar with Bonhoeffer by name and have some acquaintance with his life and work, would like to enter into a deeper dialogue. Of course, such a volume should not become a substitute for exploring Bonhoeffer's legacy at first hand. Yet, given the diverse nature of his writings (which include everything from theological tomes to poetry, from sermons and tracts for the times to love letters), the almost frenetic character of his relatively short life, and the complex historical environment within which he lived, this volume will prove to be a useful companion along the way both for those starting out and those already further along the road.

The authors of the chapters come from a variety of different national, theological and ecclesial backgrounds. Some have been selected primarily because of their life-long dedication to Bonhoeffer research; others because they bring particular insights to the study of Bonhoeffer which arise more out of their own long-standing existential response to the challenge of Bonhoeffer's legacy. Of course, it is not possible to separate the authors neatly into two such groups, for all would fit into both. Few if any Bonhoeffer scholars have been untouched by his existential demands. So most essays, depending on their specific theme, combine both elements in varying degrees. But some more clearly demonstrate a detailed knowledge of the sources and the debates that have informed Bonhoeffer scholarship, while others reflect more the wrestling of soul which inevitably accompanies those who encounter Bonhoeffer amidst the struggles and demands of life.

The *Companion* is simply structured. In the first part we introduce the reader to Bonhoeffer's historical context, his multi-faceted life, the theological and intellectual influences which shaped his thought, the publication of his written works, and the way in which his legacy has been received and interpreted during the past fifty years. In the second part we focus more specifically on the major themes of his theology as these are expressed in his books and other writings. While this has generally followed the chronological order of his publications, beginning with his doctoral dissertation *Sanctorum Communio* and ending with his posthumously published *Letters and Papers from Prison*, the essays have invariably explored their respective themes more broadly. This has inevitably meant that there is some overlapping in the material covered. We have sought to prevent excessive repetition, but we have also recognised the validity of different perspectives on the same themes. We have also included a glossary of some of the terms used in the volume which might need more explanation than is given in the text itself, as well as a chronology of Bonhoeffer's life and times.

Although there is a broad consensus amongst Bonhoeffer scholars on many issues, there is also diversity of approach and interpretation. Part of Bonhoeffer's attraction is the fact that while his theology has remarkable continuity and coherence, it is also an unfinished symphony (a metaphor appropriate to Bonhoeffer as an accomplished musician) which invites others to participate and take the discussion further in relation to their own interests and contexts. Bonhoeffer would have shunned any attempt to enclose his theology within some rigid orthodoxy, either traditional or in terms of a school of thought. He would also have shunned any attempt to turn theology into a trendy exercise which showed little respect for Christian tradition or which misused it in the pursuit of unfaithful 'relevance'.

What attracts most of us to Bonhoeffer is precisely his endeavour to be faithful to the past and yet take risks for the future, his commitment to the gospel and yet his creativity in expressing its meaning, his passionate interest in theology and yet his love of learning in all its variety, and his being rooted in German culture while seeking to be a citizen of the world.

In concluding this Preface I should like to express my gratitude to various people. First of all, I have dedicated the volume to Eberhard and Renate Bethge. Their role in handing on and interpreting the Bonhoeffer legacy has been indispensable. This will be evident at many points in the chapters that follow. But above and beyond this role has been their remarkable friendship, hospitality and personal interest in the lives and endeavours of so many of us who have had the privilege of being part of the international network of Bonhoeffer scholarship. Secondly, my thanks must go to those who have contributed chapters to this *Companion*. All readily agreed to participate in the project, kept to the schedule, and produced chapters worthy of the subject. They also represent the wider international Bonhoeffer community of scholars upon whom we are all mutually dependent. It has been one of the great pleasures of my life and academic career to be part of this circle, a circle which is always open to include others with the same interest irrespective of their background, expertise or vocation. Thirdly, I am most grateful to Gillian Walters, whose assistance, knowledge of Bonhoeffer's legacy and dedication to the project made my task far more manageable than it would otherwise have been. Finally, a word of thanks to Ruth Parr and Cambridge University Press for the invitation to prepare the *Companion to Dietrich Bonhoeffer*, and to Kevin Taylor for his role in its publication.

John W. de Gruchy
Cape Town

Glossary

Abwehr
This was the counterintelligence agency of the armed forces in Nazi Germany. The *Abwehr* became a centre for the resistance movement against Adolf Hitler and his Nazi government. Bonhoeffer became a civilian member of the *Abwehr* in 1939 through the connection of his brother-in-law, Hans von Dohnanyi.

Arcani disciplina (Arkandisziplin)
The 'discipline of the secret', or arcane discipline, describes the practice in the early church of protecting the mysteries of the faith against their profanation. This became necessary especially after the Constantinian Settlement in the fourth century made Christianity a legitimate religion in the Roman Empire, a process that led many people to join the church without strong commitment. The 'discipline of the secret' meant that only those instructed in the Christian faith (catechumens) and willing to make a Christian commitment through baptism were to be admitted to the eucharistic celebration.

Aryan clause (*Arierparagraph*)
This refers to Paragraph 7 of the Law for the Reconstruction of the Professional Civil Service passed by the German Reichstag on 7 April 1933, banning Jews and anyone of Jewish descent from any appointment to any public office. This also applied to clergy in the German Evangelical (Protestant) Church. The Aryan clause became an important issue in the Church Struggle of the 1930s, when the Brown Synod of the Evangelical Church formally adopted it as a condition for acceptance into the ordained ministry.

Barmen Confession
This is the six-point declaration adopted by Evangelical (Protestant) Church leaders opposed to the German Reich Church at their first synod held in Barmen, Westphalia, from 29 to 31 May 1934. Without mentioning Nazism, the Barmen Confession or Declaration categorically rejected any ideological

addition to the revelation of the word of God in Jesus Christ. It did not, however, directly address the 'Jewish question'.

Barmen Synod

This event formally constituted the Confessing Synod of the Evangelical Church in Germany, usually referred to as the Confessing Church. The synod was attended by 139 delegates from twenty-six provincial churches (*Landeskirchen*) of the Evangelical Church.

Brown Synod

The Prussian General Synod, or the 'Brown Synod', which took place in September 1933, was so named because of the brown uniform worn by the overwhelming majority of representatives at the synod who supported Nazi policy. It was at this synod that the oath of allegiance to Hitler and the Aryan clause were adopted and the national bishop, Ludwig Müller, was elected.

Cantus firmus

This musical term refers to the recurring melody line which holds in tension and holds together the counterpoint (*Kontrapunkt*). Speculating about the 'polyphony in music' in his letters from prison, Bonhoeffer uses *cantus firmus* and counterpoint as metaphors to propose his understanding of the 'polyphony of life'. The love of God and of his eternity '*genitivus objectivus*' are seen as the *cantus firmus* to which – as contrapuntal themes – 'the other melodies of life' are related and yet of which they are independent.

Church Struggle (*Kirchenkampf*)

This refers to the conflict within the German Evangelical Church between the Confessing Church and the official Reichskirche, which accepted the ecclesiastical policies of the National Socialist Party (Nazis). Hitler used these policies in his attempt to dominate and control the Evangelical Church by integrating it into the Nazi bureaucratic structure. At stake in the struggle were the authenticity and integrity of the Protestant Church to be faithful to Scripture and its historic confessions of faith.

Confessing Church (Bekennende Kirche)

The Confessing Church came into being at the Barmen Synod in May 1934. At this synod, a fourth of the German Protestant pastors elected to oppose the Nazi policies of Ludwig Müller (national bishop) of the German Reich Church. They resisted the adoption of the Aryan clause, choosing to remain separate from the Reich Church, which they felt was compromising the word of God in favour of Nazi ideology. For the next few years, the Confessing Church became a place of resistance within Nazi Germany.

Crystal Night (*Kristallnacht*)
This refers to the night of November 9 1938 when the Nazi Party instigated the systematic destruction of Jewish property and places of worship. Some 7,500 shops were vandalised and 171 Jewish synagogues were burnt to the ground. This night, which is also known as 'the night of broken glass', is referred to in Bonhoeffer's bible by an underlining of the text from Psalm 74, 'they burned all the meeting places of God in the land'.

The Evangelical Church in Germany (Evangelische Kirchen in Deutschland)
The Evangelical (Protestant) Church in Germany was historically divided after the Protestant Reformation in the sixteenth century into autonomous provincial churches (*Landeskirchen*). While predominantly Lutheran, the Evangelical Church also included Reformed churches, and the large and influential Prussian Church of the Union, a united Lutheran and Reformed Church.

'German Christians' (Deutsche Christen)
This is the name chosen by those Protestants who supported Adolf Hitler and Nazi ideology. The 'German Christians' represented a movement within the Evangelical Church that supported the process of assimilating the church into the ideology of the Nazi state. The 'German Christians' believed that Christianity found its appropriate expression in Germany through German culture, and that Hitler was completing the work begun at the Reformation by Martin Luther.

'The Jewish question' or 'The Jewish problem' (*Judenfrage*)
This refers to the Nazi policy towards people of Jewish descent within Germany and German-occupied countries. The propaganda of the 'Jewish question' led to policies of slanderous and brutal anti-Semitism and to the widespread hatred of Jews, including those who were baptised Christians. Under Nazi policy, Jewish citizens were denied access to the civil service, their shops were boycotted, their property was confiscated, and they were forced to live in ghettos. The ultimate end of this policy was referred to as the 'final solution', which was a systematic plan for the annihilation of all European Jews. Six million Jews died in concentration camps during the Second World War as a result of this policy.

National bishop (*Reichsbischof*)
A national bishop was proposed by the 'German Christians' in April 1933. Their aim was the formation of a single German Reich Church based upon Nazi doctrine, thus uniting the twenty-eight *Landeskirchen* under one authority. Ludwig Müller, Hitler's favoured candidate, was elected *Reichsbischof*

at the German National Synod of September 1933, the infamous Brown Synod. The plan to introduce the office of *Reichsbischof* was one of the main reasons for the convening of the Barmen Synod, and it was implicitly condemned in the Barmen Declaration.

Reich Church (Reichskirche)
The name given to the official Protestant Church in Germany dominated by the 'German Christians' and supportive of Nazi policy.

Synod of Dahlem
Held in October 1934, this synod further entrenched the Confessing Church in opposition to the German Christians and the Reich Church, by the formation of its own, separate church government and structures, including ordination training centres, and the ultimate declaration that the Confessing Church represented the only legal church within Germany.

Status confessionis
This term, which was used by the Protestant Reformers in the sixteenth century in their struggle against Roman Catholicism, was adopted by Karl Barth, Dietrich Bonhoeffer and others to describe the situation which had arisen as a result of the challenge of Nazi ideology to the Christian faith and church. The situation demanded that the Evangelical Church confess its faith anew in response to the issues which now confronted it. The Barmen Declaration was such a confession.

Chronology

A brief outline of Bonhoeffer's life and times

1906   4 February, Dietrich Bonhoeffer born in Breslau, Germany
1912   Family moves to Berlin, where Karl Bonhoeffer, Dietrich's father, takes up a position at Berlin University
1913   Dietrich Bonhoeffer begins gymnasium studies
1916   Family moves to the suburb of Grunewald
1918   Walter Bonhoeffer, Dietrich's brother, dies on the western front
1921   Dietrich and twin sister, Sabine, are confirmed
1923   Begins theological studies at Tübingen
1924   Continues theological studies at Berlin; travels to Rome and north Africa with elder brother Klaus
1927   Qualifies for licentiate with his doctoral dissertation, *Sanctorum Communio*
1928   Curate in Barcelona
1929   Summer lectures in systematic theology, Berlin; assistant pastor in Berlin
1930   Completes second dissertation, later published as *Act and Being*; Sloane Fellow at Union Theological Seminary, New York (1930–1)
1931   July: first meeting with Karl Barth
       August: lecturer in theological faculty, Berlin
       September: appointed Youth Secretary of World Alliance for Promoting International Friendship through the Churches Conference, Cambridge
       October: chaplain at Technical College, Berlin
       November: takes confirmation class in Berlin-Wedding
1932   Winter lecture course on 'Creation and Sin' (later published as *Creation and Fall*)
1933   January: Hitler becomes Chancellor

February: The Reichstag is burnt

April: Aryan civil-service legislation is passed, dismissing Jews from public office

Ludwig Müller appointed *Reichsbischof*

Summer lectures in Berlin, on Christology

September: Pastors' Emergency League organised, with aid of Martin Niemöller; Brown Synod dominated by German Christians is held

October: Bonhoeffer moves to London to take up pastorate of two German-speaking churches

1934 May: first synod of the Confessing Church is held at Barmen

Adoption of Barmen Declaration

August: Ecumenical Conference, Fanö

1935 April: becomes director of Preachers' Seminary, Zingst

June: seminary moves to Finkenwalde

September: Nuremberg Laws are passed

October: family moves to Charlottenberg, Berlin

December: Confessing Church seminaries declared illegal

1936 February: members from Finkenwalde visit Denmark and Sweden

August: authorisation to teach at Berlin University is withdrawn

1937 September: Finkenwalde is closed down by Gestapo

November: *The Cost of Discipleship* is published

December: begins collective pastorate in Köslin and Gross-Schlönwitz

1938 January: expulsion from Berlin

February: makes first contact with leaders of the resistance movement

April: all pastors required to take the oath of allegiance to Hitler

September: writes *Life Together* while in Göttingen

November: Crystal Night

1939 June: travels to America for the second time; returns to Berlin in July

August: becomes a civilian agent of the *Abwehr* (military intelligence)

September: German troops invade Poland; formal Allied Declaration of War

1940 March: illegal seminary in Köslin and Gross-Schlönwitz closed down by the Gestapo

Begins to write his *Ethics*

November: becomes member of *Abwehr* staff in Munich

Stays at Benedictine monastery in Ettal; continues work on the *Ethics*

1941   February–March: travels to Switzerland to meet with Karl Barth and Visser't Hooft

August: second visit to Switzerland

October: under 'Operation 7' the first Jews are deported from Berlin

1942   April: travels to Norway and Sweden

May: visits Switzerland for third visit

May/June: meets Bishop George Bell in Sweden

1943   January: becomes engaged to Maria von Wedemeyer

April: arrested, placed in Tegel Prison, Berlin

December: writes Christmas essay, 'Ten Years After'

1944   April: first of the 'theological letters' from prison

July: assassination attempt on Hitler

September: incriminating evidence on the *Abwehr* is uncovered by the Gestapo

1945   February: moved to Buchenwald concentration camp

April: moved to Regensburg and then Schönberg and finally to Flossenbürg

8 April: court-martialled

9 April: executed at Flossenbürg

Part one

Bonhoeffer's life and legacy

1 Bonhoeffer's Germany: the political context

JOHN A. MOSES

The Germany of Dietrich Bonhoeffer's lifetime (1906–45) experienced three radical constitutional changes, all of which were to affect Bonhoeffer's formation in crucial ways. His first twelve years saw the Wilhelmine Empire (Kaiserreich), founded under Otto von Bismarck in 1871, reach the zenith of its power and then virtually self-destruct at the end of the First World War in 1918. The Kaiserreich was followed by Germany's first experiment in parliamentary democracy, the ill-fated Weimar Republic. It lasted from 1919 until 1933 when it also collapsed, or more accurately, was destroyed by a combination of hostile attacks from the anti-democratic forces of both the extreme left and the extreme right, on the one hand, and the political inexperience of the supporters of the constitution on the other. Then, out of the political and economic chaos of the end-phase of the Weimar years (1929–33), arose the National Socialist dictatorship of Adolf Hitler, the Third Reich. It was this latter manifestation of the German spirit which Bonhoeffer judged as essentially evil and which left him no alternative but to resist to the death.

These three Germanies were not discrete political entities. They were linked by strong elements of continuity. Of central importance among these were the industrialist and commercial elites, the military, especially the officer corps, the educated middle classes (the *Bildungsbürgertum*) including the various professions, in short, people who had originally identified themselves strongly with the Bismarckian system. They considered themselves as comprising the *Nation*, as the custodians of the 'true' national values, monarchist and conservative. Opposed to these were the broad mass of the industrial working class who, during the Kaiserreich, had aligned themselves behind the Social Democratic Party (SPD) and the socialist-oriented Free Trade Unions. After having been outlawed by Bismarck in 1878 the socialists had regrouped in 1891, and by 1912 were the largest single party in the German national parliament, the Reichstag. The SPD had been a *de facto* national opposition in the Kaiserreich, but German domestic political life was further complicated by the existence of a strong Roman Catholic party, the Zentrum or Centre Party, which also represented the Roman Catholic population's opposition to the Protestant (*Evangelisch*) and Prussian hegemony in the united Germany. The Centre Party also fostered a Christian trade union movement distinct from the larger Free Trade Unions. So there were at least two strong elements in German society which perceived themselves, in varying degrees, to have been marginalised in the Wilhelmine Empire.

In the Weimar Republic it appeared at first as though the moderate forces of social democracy, the Roman Catholic Centre Party and liberals, could collaborate on the basis of the new constitution, designed to safeguard basic rights for the long-term political and economic stability of the nation. Their praiseworthy aims, however, were frustrated by the continued presence of old-fashioned right-wing conservatives. Added to these was the new Nazi Party, which attracted many disgruntled elements even more hostile to the Weimar system. The German Communist Party, the largest outside the Soviet Union, also functioned to undermine the parliamentary state.

When, as a consequence of the world economic crisis in 1930, the Nazis under Adolf Hitler suddenly mobilised sufficient votes to win 112 seats in the Reichstag, compared to their previous 12, the possibility of the Nazis combining forces with other extreme right-wing forces to form a government was realised. Hitler became Chancellor in January 1933. He was widely regarded as the leader (Führer) who would rid Germany of the chaotic politics of the Weimar era and the concomitant threat of a communist take-over, restore Germany's international prestige, repudiate the provisions of the Versailles *Diktat*, which was seen to restrict Germany's economic recovery as well as military power, and thus set Germany on the path to 'glorious times', as promised by Kaiser Wilhelm early in his reign, in 1894.[1] The consequences of Hitler's seizure of power, apart from the ruthless elimination of all sources of opposition both inside the Nazi Party and without, were first, economic recovery, largely through rearmament and massive public works, but secondly the implementation of a radical anti-Jewish policy in accordance with Nazi ideology. All this led to the serious preparation for war, the refusal to pay off international debts, and the beginning of actual physical persecution of citizens of Jewish ancestry and belief.

A perceptive foreign observer of Germany in 1936[2] remarked that Hitler had not only successfully duped the German people, but had through his pre-war foreign policy temporarily held in check both the former enemy nations of France and Britain, as well as the Soviet Union. By the end of summer 1939, Hitler had judged the time right for the implementation of his long-term objectives, and so the Second World War began and the fateful steps towards the 'final solution to the Jewish question' were taken.

One of the great tragedies of German history is that the opposition to these disastrous policies from Germans themselves was notoriously weak. The army, the church and the representatives of the former political parties, with few notable exceptions, were either unable to mount a sustained critique of the Nazi regime or, least of all, engage in conspiratorial action against it. Dietrich Bonhoeffer must be counted among the most outstanding of these exceptions. This chapter will proceed by commenting on each of the 'three Germanies' of Bonhoeffer's lifetime with a view to highlighting those features which affected his development.

THE KAISERREICH

The examination of imperial Germany, both its domestic politics and its foreign policy has become a veritable industry since 1945. International scholarship has been at pains to discover the elements of continuity between the Kaiserreich and the Third Reich.[3] Had German history taken an ominously different path to modernity from the Western nations, a *Sonderweg*, which was so flawed that it could produce such barbaric outcomes as the Second World War and the Holocaust? What were the reasons for this? What was the role of the First World War which seemed to be the fatal turning point? If the Kaiserreich bore the chief responsibility for this, as the 'Fischer School' in Hamburg has persuasively argued, then Germany was indeed under the control of men who provoked the civilised world to resist all their efforts to impose their will over Europe and much of the then colonial world.[4] That Prussia-Germany actually attempted from 1914 to 1918 to do so is beyond dispute. What is still puzzling to some is why the German power-elite believed it had no alternative but to plunge the world into the 'murderous anarchy' of the First World War.

At the time of Bonhoeffer's birth the German Empire was at the peak of its military and industrial power and was fast becoming the world's second naval power, much to the disquiet of Britain. It was the era of intensifying Anglo-German antagonism.[5] This was characterised by the burgeoning 'naval race' between Britain and Germany whereby the German intention had been to break Britain's two-power-standard of naval armament, not necessarily for an armed confrontation with the Royal Navy, but to have a 'fleet-in-being' so large that it constituted a risk to Britain and thus would force her to acknowledge Germany's right to be counted as a major world power.[6] All this emerged from the fertile mind of Grand Admiral Alfred von Tirpitz (1849–1930).

The 'Tirpitz Plan', more than colonial rivalry in Africa and the Pacific, was responsible for the ultimately fatal estrangement of Britain and Germany. Indeed, the 'Tirpitz Plan' and the British response, namely to design even bigger and faster battleships called 'dreadnoughts', symbolised not only the irreconcilable naval policies of the two nations but also their respective self-perceptions as Great Powers. For Britain the maintenance of a large navy was the major existential issue, and so she conceived of it in purely defensive terms. It was never designed to land armies in central Europe or elsewhere for the purposes of conquest. But the Germans perceived that the possession of a mighty navy was an absolute necessity to ensure the Great Power status to which most educated Germans believed destiny had called her. So, whereas Britain's navy was the end result of pragmatic considerations, the German navy was an 'instrument' of *Weltpolitik*, indeed the key to the future.

It is vitally important to understand what Germans meant by *Weltpolitik*. It was not simply overseas expansion to secure markets for developing industries as John A. Hobson (1858–1940) had criticised in 1902.[7] Rather, *Weltpolitik* was the implementation of a doctrine of history. The most-quoted expression of it was formulated by Professor Max Weber in his famous Freiburg inaugural address of May 1895, when he said:

> We must grasp that the unification of Germany was a youthful spree, indulged in by the nation in its old age; it would have been better had it never taken place, since it would have been a costly extravagance, if it was the conclusion rather than the starting-point for German power politics on a global scale.[8]

For Max Weber and for virtually all of the academic elite of Germany this view of national history was paradigmatic. The Prussian national spirit, *Volksgeist*, had effected the unification of Germany under Bismarck in 1871, and the essence of that spirit was the drive to expand. Prussia had absorbed 'Germany'; now Prussia-Germany's future role in history was to further expansion in the world by being vigorously competitive with the other Powers. This, indeed, was how the world was constituted, as many leading German thinkers averred. The philosopher G. W. F. Hegel (1770–1831) had earlier provided the intellectual framework for such a view of world history. Indeed, the purpose or vocation of each of the peoples on the earth was to become a state, and this could only be accomplished through the use of force because the expansionist drive that resides in every people, to a greater or lesser degree, could not be expressed otherwise. The course of world history revealed a constant struggle between peoples for hegemony; warfare was the natural order of things. So Hegel had laid the foundation for a latter-day Machiavellianism which was taken up most eloquently by the historian Heinrich von Treitschke (1825–96), the doyen of the 'Prussian School of History', who stressed that if a nation was not expanding it was dying.

Other leading German social scientists of the Wilhelmine era echoed these convictions, some more forthrightly than others. The more significant of these were the Neo-Rankeans named after Leopold von Ranke (1795–1886), who had in a seminal essay of 1833, *The Great Powers*, observed that nations were concentrations of 'moral energy' bent upon expansion and establishing their hegemony, as the behaviour of the nation-states in the Napoleonic era so graphically illustrated. Ranke's admirers at the turn of the century, especially Erich Marcks and Max Lenz, restated Ranke's ideas to apply to the then existing world empires, and came to the judgement that whereas the other World Powers, especially Britain, were showing signs of decay, Prussia-Germany was restless with creative energy in every sphere, industrially, commercially, militarily and intellectually. She was the culturally supreme nation, and it was thus her God-given vocation to hasten the decline of the moribund Powers and assume the leading world-political position.

The point is that Wilhelmine imperialism, in contrast to the imperialism of the other Powers at the time, was strongly ideologically driven, and apart from the Social Democratic Party and elements within the Roman Catholic Centre Party, there was virtually no opposition to it. Indeed, among its staunchest advocates were German Protestant theologians. Prominent among these were Bonhoeffer's Berlin teachers, particularly Adolf von Harnack (1851–1930) and Reinhold Seeberg (1859–1935). As leaders in the theological discipline, these men not only shared the dominant Neo-Rankean paradigm concerning the need for the nation to expand, but also provided it with a persuasive theological justification.

Harnack and Seeberg's point of departure was essentially that of Hegel and von Ranke, namely that peoples were 'ideas of God' and that it was in their nature to compete with each other for domination of the earth. Force was a given in the life of nations; eternal peace, say, as envisaged by the philosopher Immanuel Kant (1724–1804) was certainly not a possibility in this world. Theologically speaking, most German Protestant theologians of the Wilhelmine era were more concerned with the existing world as the venue of Almighty God's self-revelation than with the Bible as the source of revelation. This meant that their theological orientation was determined by their understanding of world history. In a word, it was not so much the activity of God in the Bible that claimed their attention as God's tangible and visible accomplishments with and for the German people between 1870 and 1914. God, Hegel claimed, 'had been dissolved into history'. The author of the universe could only be conceived of in relation to divine self-revelation, indeed God's Reich on earth. For the German theologians, this Reich was without doubt the Prusso-German Empire.

Given this mind-set there was a general mental preparedness for war among the German educated elite, not least within the theological faculties of the universities. Consequently, when the war came in August 1914, there was not so much surprise expressed as indignation that the Western nations actually blamed Germany for it. Although warfare was regarded as endemic to the human condition, and indeed, as part of the history of salvation, there was a great concern to repudiate Western accusations of German barbarism and war-guilt generally. The reasons for this are most instructive and need to be understood if any sense is to be made of the behaviour of the Protestant Church towards the Weimar Republic and later, the Third Reich.

In the first place, if the God of history employed war to work out God's purpose for humankind, then there could be no question of allocating 'guilt'; wars have to happen in the same way as storms occur in nature. Following from this, the German intellectual elite, especially, were indignant that their Western counterparts could accuse them of moral turpitude and apostasy for endorsing the war and the behaviour of the German army in Belgium. This the German academic community did in a series of notorious manifestos which were designed for foreign consumption. German war sermons interpreted the war as an entirely righteous one of self-defence against a circle of uncivilised enemies who were jealous of Germany's superior industrial and scientific as well as cultural achievements. It was entirely correct that Germany, as the land of true, purified (Protestant) Christianity, should assume her role as the 'Hammer of God'. The war was judgement on disobedient and errant nations, indeed the 'tribunal of the world'. As such the war was a form of the 'last judgement' in which Germany, as champion of the right cause, would punish the decadent and morally inferior Powers, and emerge victorious.

The German scholar Klaus Vondung has investigated the mentality of many of Germany's leading writers, poets, philosophers, historians and theologians and has concluded that in Germany, more than in other belligerent countries, this apocalyptic understanding of the war was very widely spread.[9] Individual theologians such as Adolf von Harnack, who enjoyed the confidence of political leaders including the Kaiser himself, were equally convinced that God was on the German side, and that a victorious outcome was a foregone conclusion. However, as the march of events was to show, God deserted the Germans and delivered them up to their despised enemies.

These views were, of course, also those of most Protestant *Bildungsbür-ger*, the educated classes. The working class and their political representatives had either always opposed the idea of war or, in so far as they were convinced that it was a war of defence, believed in fighting it only to preserve the *status quo ante bellum*; there ought not to be any annexations of foreign territory. Consequently, when it appeared by all human reckoning that the war was really unwinnable, the rank and file of the armed forces, as well as industrial labour, began a series of strikes which led to the so-called November Revolution at the end of 1918. What they opposed was the pointless continuation of the conflict, contrary to the manipulations of the military and naval chiefs who, even *after the armistice of 11 November 1918 had been signed*, believed that it was necessary to fight to save the honour of their class.[10]

The circumstances surrounding Germany's military defeat in the last months of 1918 gave rise to the legend of the *stab-in-the-back*. Right-wing officers and their supporters claimed that the army was still capable of holding the western front, despite the superiority of Allied forces, but was crippled in its efforts by the left-wing inspired strikes on the home front as well as by the earlier demands for a liberalisation of the constitution from the SPD, the Centre Party and the liberals. This proved to be a fateful legacy for the Weimar Republic because the new democratic Germany was associated in the mind of conservatives and radical right-wing people with the betrayal of the Fatherland to the enemy.

The Kaiserreich had, indeed, been dominated by an elite of very anti-democratic elements, the aristocracy, the army, and particularly the state bureaucracies, as well as the commercial/industrialist groups. They were aided and abetted by the churches, especially the Protestant Church, and the universities. The working class had been at best 'negatively integrated' in a society whose masters were deeply opposed to amending the Bismarckian constitution to allow responsible government. This would have meant admitting the representatives of organised labour into the corridors of power. But the 'vagabonds without a fatherland', as the Kaiser once designated the socialists, were never really considered part of the nation; the anti-socialist elements would have preferred to outlaw them again as did Bismarck during 1878–91. The idea of 'negative integration' simply meant that organised labour, party and trade unions, had become too large for the government to risk confronting but were still too small to initiate strikes on a sufficiently large scale in order to force the constitutional changes they desired. The relationship between the forces of conservatism and labour was analogous to an armed truce. Consequently, one speaks of a negatively integrated working class in imperial Germany.

The First World War had been initially seen by some more liberal-minded thinkers as an opportunity for a genuinely positive integration of labour into the monarchical state. But the euphoria of the 'August days' and the 'Ideas of 1914' about a unifying spirit infusing all Germans regardless of party affiliation soon gave way to disillusionment. It is crucial to understand what Germans imagined they were fighting for. The 'power elite' and their national supporters believed that they were defending two things. First, they wanted to secure Germany's monarchical constitution from the democratic reforms demanded in particular by organised labour. Secondly, they wanted to ensure Germany's 'rightful' status as the dominant power in Europe, that is, the right to annex those foreign territories needed for Germany's future power base in Europe. All this was in accordance with the conviction that this was how Germany must pursue her pre-ordained course in world history. Thus, when the war broke out the government adopted a war-aims programme of annexation in East and West to protect 'legitimate' German interests for 'imaginable time'.[11]

Organised labour supported the war effort, however, for very different reasons. They were given to understand first that the war was one of national self-defence, and secondly that in recognition of their support there would be a series of constitutional reforms in labour's interests. There were, then, two distinct and mutually exclusive sets of German war aims. Failure to appreciate this fact will confuse our understanding of the underlying problem of the Weimar Republic.

WEIMAR GERMANY

A reading of Hitler's *Mein Kampf*, together with subsequent scholarly studies, confirms that the anti-Semitic radical right and conservatives in Germany shared essentially the same revulsion for the democratic republic which was founded after the November Revolution, through the collaboration of moderate Social Democrats, the Roman Catholic Centre Party and smaller groupings of liberals. All of these were united in their desire to make a parliamentary system, without the monarchy, work for Germany. The Protestant Churches must be counted among those conservative Germans who had traditionally seen the union of 'throne and altar' to be a fundamental requirement for a state under Almighty God. The monarchs of the various Protestant German states had been, by virtue of their office, also the chief overseers of their territorial churches. The Kaiser, for example, had been *summus episcopus* of the state church of Prussia. Now that he had abdicated and the monarchies had all been abolished, the churches had to rethink their position within the new state. It was a tentative readjustment at best. Not all pastors and theologians could follow the example of Adolf von Harnack or leading historians such as Friedrich Meinecke, and endorse the republic to become *Vernunftrepublikaner*, meaning republicans by rational choice while at heart they remained monarchists (*Herzensmonarchisten*). The advent of the republic demanded from church people a fundamental change in their world view.

However, the republic had more than a fighting chance of survival, as research has now confirmed. It was not a foregone conclusion that it would fail. The disparate elements which strove to effect the transition from monarchy to republic and from a war-time to a peace-time economy were motivated by rational considerations even though they were technically 'class enemies'. Had the basis for their initial collaboration remained viable, there is no reason to believe that the republic had to collapse. In the first weeks of November 1918, when left-wing-motivated strikes and demonstrations in the major industrial cities gave every indication that a Soviet-style revolution could eventuate, the leaders of industrial labour and of industry negotiated an agreement for the peaceful transition from a war-time to a peace-time economy. This was known as the 'November Pact' or the Stinnes–Legien agreement (15 November 1918), after the leader of the industrialists and the chairman of the Free Trade unions respectively.[12] Neither Stinnes nor Legien had any interest in allowing a disruption of the German economy which would have resulted in a Soviet outcome of the November turbulence. Both men wanted a compromise that would preserve the crucial interests of capital and simultaneously guarantee organised labour a range of improvements in working conditions such as an eight-hour day and binding wage agreements. Factory councils were also set up, consisting equally of management and labour representatives.

These agreements between capital and labour constituted a major extra-governmental initiative to stabilise the situation. A further and, in the event, crucial stabilising arrangement had been made between the new government and the old army. The leader of the Social Democrats, Fritz Ebert, who had been elected chairman of the Commissars of the People when the last imperial government of Prince Max of Baden had voluntarily stepped down, the Kaiser having abdicated, gained the support of the senior general officer then commanding the German army, Wilhelm Groener. Ebert was well known as a moderate, anti-revolutionary democrat who had finally won the confidence of the officer corps for his anti-Soviet stand during the last weeks of 1918 and January 1919. Groener, then, guaranteed to keep the army loyal to the new government and use it to stamp out all Soviet-like revolutionary activity. So the Stinnes–Legien agreement and the Ebert–Groener arrangements created conditions in which a national election could be held on 19 January 1919.

The outcome of the election was the coalition of the majority Social Democrats, the Centre Party and the new German Liberal Party, known henceforth as the 'Weimar Coalition'. It was through their collaboration and compromises that the Weimar constitution was forged and became law by August 1919. The fortunes of the new republic really then rested on the possibility of a continuation, in the first place, of the good working relationship that had been built up between the trade unions, who had achieved in 1919/20 their greatest numerical strength ever (8,000,000), and German industry. Secondly, of course, the continued loyalty of the army to the republican government was also crucial. However, neither of these twin prerequisites for the stability and continued existence of the republic could be guaranteed.

Already on 13 March 1920 the first test of army loyalty came. The overthrow of the government was planned by disgruntled monarchist officials and disloyal sections of the army who wished to protest at the disbandment of their regiments as stipulated by the Treaty of Versailles. This attempt was known as the Kapp Putsch after its chief conspirator, Wolfgang Kapp (1858–1922). Army units succeeded in occupying Berlin, forcing the government to flee to Stuttgart. A new government with Kapp as Chancellor was proclaimed, but this provoked a massive general strike engineered by the leader of the unions, Carl Legien.

It was the most successful strike in German history to that point, firstly because of the total solidarity of all unions, including the white-collar unions. Their aim was solely to restore the constitutional government and to get legislation enacted which would henceforth guarantee the informal achievements won by organised labour in previous negotiations with industry. Within fourteen days the Kapp regime collapsed since no services could be implemented; indeed, no public servants could be paid on account of the strike. The strike had saved the republic and in so doing gave rise to the legend of the 'emergency button' (*Knopfdruck*) of the general strike which could be pressed to protect the republic from any future right-wing assaults upon it.

However, when the legal government required the army to deal with the disloyal units that had occupied Berlin, the commanding general, Hans von Seeckt (1866–1936), flatly refused all assistance under the thinly veiled pretext of maintaining a strict neutrality. The old deep-seated hostility on the part of the officer corps to democratic institutions was re-emerging and became more intense as the republic lurched from one economic crisis to another. Events such as the occupation of the Ruhr by French and Belgian troops to enforce German reparation payments under the requirements of the Treaty of Versailles led to an increasing polarisation of German politics, a tendency which was even further exacerbated by the ensuing great inflation that became unmanageable by the end of 1923. The latter episode also had disastrous long-term consequences because at the time the middle class, having lost all their savings, became very suspicious of any inflationary economic policy to cure national financial problems. A milder form of inflationary policy during the great economic crisis of 1929–33 may have contributed to political stability, but the then Chancellor, Heinrich Brüning of the Centre Party, would not venture to experiment, and the results were a total breakdown of all government social services and public-sector spending.

In retrospect, the Kapp Putsch and the Great Inflation at the beginning of the republic adumbrated its collapse over a decade later. The former showed that the culture of the military in Germany could not accommodate to the new constitution. The latter illustrated that the stability of the republic would depend on the satisfactory resolution of the economic needs of the German middle classes, or more precisely, how these needs were actually met. How to combat inflation and at the same time protect the living standards of citizens became the major political economic preoccupation of the republic. Inflation, however, had been already present in the German economy *prior* to the foundation of the republic in 1919. This was due to the fact that the war had been financed by deficit spending virtually from the outset. So rampant inflation had not been caused by the reparations payments made obligatory for Germany through the Treaty of Versailles, as opponents of fulfilling the Treaty obligations liked to argue. The fact, however, that reparations could be so easily blamed in the minds of the general public for Germany's chronic balance-of-payments problems played into the hands of the right-wing opponents of the republic.

Of course, the Great Inflation and the Ruhr occupation also caused the total breakdown of the arrangements established to facilitate co-operation between industry and labour. Whereas initially the trade unions and industry had agreed to consultation on a range of issues such as the eight-hour day and wage agreements, all these had broken down by 1924, and so industrial relations had been set back to the pre-war confrontational mode. The unions, however, were in a much better bargaining position than at that time. Now, their right to exist was guaranteed in the constitution, and so at the trade union congress in 1925 they determined to use their power base to work towards what they called *Wirtschaftsdemokratie* (economic democracy). In practice this meant that they, as the main representatives of the work force, would seek to negotiate with management not only to win better wages and conditions but also to effect a more equitable distribution of national wealth.

When, after the chaos of the Great Inflation, the international community, led by the United States, extended to Germany massive loans (the Dawes Plan), the economy once again picked up significantly and in a few years real wages had reached the 1913 level. So, for a time it seemed that organised labour and organised capital in Germany were able to pursue their respective goals without imposing undue stress on the existing constitutional framework. Capital tolerated the Weimar 'system' so long as it enabled business as usual, but organised labour wanted the new Germany to be a state which guaranteed the basic right to work and a *menschenwürdiges Dasein* for all citizens, that is a standard of living commensurate with human dignity. This was the thinking behind the national unemployment insurance bill which was passed through the Reichstag in 1926.

The moderate left, the Centre Party and liberals conceived of the new republic as a progressive welfare state and so favoured the extension of *Sozialpolitik*, that is welfare legislation which would give expression to the principles set down in the constitution. This was very much the commitment of the Social Democrats in particular, supported by the socialist-orientated trade unions. The latter at their 1928 congress at Hamburg reiterated their goals of economic democracy by issuing a detailed manifesto prepared by a leading trade union theorist, Fritz Naphtali. It virtually demanded that industrial management be compelled by law to manage the economy in consultation with the elected representatives of organised labour. Indeed, the purpose of the economy was to be no longer the production of surplus value but the fulfilment of the needs of the population.

To the ears of Germany's industrial leaders in 1928, just when business was starting to flourish, the ideology of economic democracy sounded ominously like Marxism by stealth. Not surprisingly, industry unanimously rejected such forms of economic management, preferring the tried and tested system of *Herr-im-eigenen-Hause*, that is being 'master in one's own house'. The notion of *Mitbestimmung*, or co-determination, was totally alien to them. So, the two pillars upon which the Weimar Republic rested, namely organised labour and organised capital, represented two distinctly and mutually exclusive conceptions of the state. For labour the state had to be proactively interventionist in the economy for the well-being primarily of the wage earner; for capital, the state was there to create the best possible conditions for business. As indicated, these two concepts could co-exist so long as the 'system' was not subjected to excessive strains. Unfortunately, however, in October 1929 the greatest of imaginable strains eventuated with the beginning of the world economic crisis, the Great Depression.

Germany was most severely affected because the foreign loans made available under the Dawes Plan were called in, thus imposing on Germany the virtually impossible task of servicing international debts, making regular reparations payments, and at the same time sustaining the elaborate welfare system that had been built up. The world economic crisis thus confronted Germany's politicians with the agonising choice between abandoning the welfare system and saving the 'economy' and trying to maintain some semblance of welfare provision, particularly unemployment benefits, and experimenting with job-creation schemes at the expense of the 'economy'.

These were crucial political choices which polarised the representatives of labour on the one hand and of big business on the other. And after the September 1930 elections, when unemployment was becoming unmanageable, this polarisation was reflected in the election results. Both the extremists of the left and the right made significant gains. From then on, the formation of a coalition government which could rely on a firm parliamentary majority proved impossible, and the emergency powers provision of the constitution which permitted the President to appoint a Chancellor loyal to him were invoked. From September 1930 until January 1933, when Adolf Hitler was summoned to form a coalition, none of the series of three Chancellors (Brüning, 1930–2, von Papen, June to November 1932, and Schleicher, to January 1933) had been able to govern without resort to the emergency powers provision. To all intents and purposes, parliamentary government had ceased in Germany from 1930 because no consensus could be arrived at as to how to manage the economy. And Hitler's brief in January 1933 had been specifically to return the economy to a 'healthy' footing. This task he undertook by first eliminating all political parties except his own, the NSDAP, and getting the Reichstag to pass the so-called Enabling Bill (23 March 1933). Thereby, the new Chancellor had virtually unrestricted powers to make any changes he liked, quite unchallenged. And one of the great ironies of history was that Hitler used in principle the job-creation plans devised by the trade unions and rejected by the Brüning administration to begin to overcome the massive unemployment problem. The notorious Third Reich had been inaugurated and the 'Nazi Revolution' begun.

THE THIRD REICH

Although Hitler had harvested spectacular successes at the national elections, his party never achieved an absolute majority. Millions of Germans had reservations about the Nazis and their open contempt for the rule of law, but they had no political answers to Nazi terrorist tactics, especially when Hitler enjoyed the support of both the army and the police forces of the major German states as well as that of the Nazi para-military organisation, the *Sturm-Abteilung* (SA). The latter was virtually a 'brown army', and its presence was a major factor in implementing Hitler's seizure of power. It was the sheer unpredictable force available to Hitler that intimidated his conservative and aristocratic erstwhile supporters, who had mistakenly believed that by 'jobbing Hitler into office' (Alan Bullock) they could control him to do their bidding. These elements within German society, who considered themselves the representatives of the 'real' Germany, had just as little conception of who Hitler was and what his movement was about as the communists or the Social Democrats. Indeed, Hitler's style surprised everyone; he was a unique political phenomenon when compared to the leaders of other one-party states such as Mussolini's Italy or Franco's Spain.

The so-called *Führerstaat* or leader state, as conceived by Hitler, was totally unprecedented. It could not be compared with the absolutist monarchies of the past since these at least acknowledged some universally recognisable legal principles. In Germany, the absolutist state was a *Rechtsstaat*, a state with a codified legal system, even though the monarch was 'above' the law. In Nazi Germany, the law was ultimately the capricious will of the Führer, and was the product of Hitler's personal values as these had been formed throughout his unique experience in his home town Braunau, in imperial Vienna and as a soldier at the front during the First World War. His political ideas are spelt out in his autobiography *Mein Kampf*, which he composed while in gaol at Landsberg, Bavaria during 1923 after the abortive *putsch* of that year in Munich. The views expressed in that book are those of a partially educated crank, but the curious thing is that they were shared by millions of other Germans and Austrians. As the American historian David Schoenbaum has observed,

That Hitler, whether in his weakness for pastry, for shepherd dogs, for national self-glorification, or for continental expansion, was in the main stream of German history is no less obvious. However eccentric his interpretations, his sympathies and antipathies were of the stuff of German life, whether they affected art or politics. Of his millions of voters before 1933 and delirious mass audiences afterward, very few were consciously endorsing his originality.[13]

Hitler's rise to become the unchallenged dictator of a great cultural nation and industrial power was not inevitable. The circumstances created by the world economic crisis which ultimately crippled the ability of 'civic society to reproduce itself' in Germany (T. W. Mason), prepared the population to accept the services of a 'strong man' to restore both Germany's economic viability and international respect. There is no doubt that once appointed to office, Hitler exerted an unprecedented magnetism over the German people in their despair. They wanted to believe that the ills from which the country was suffering could be remedied by stern measures. Parliamentary democracy Western style had clearly not been able to deliver. So the German people were persuaded that Hitler represented a return to the familiar authoritarianism and truly Teutonic values of the Bismarckian and Wilhelmine eras. Indeed, the *Day of Potsdam* (21 March 1933), when the Reich President Hindenburg officially greeted the newly elected Reichstag and the first Hitler cabinet, had been a major propaganda *coup* on behalf of the Nazis. It was a virtual confirmation for the German people that National Socialism was a legitimate expression of the spirit of Prussian-German history. This explains in part why there was so little effective resistance to Nazism. It appeared to represent the resurrection and continuation of a political culture that distinguished Prussia-Germany from the barbarous East (communism) and the decadent West (liberalism). This, of course, was a delusion which Hitler and his staff were pleased to sustain. But Hitler was not a reincarnation of Bismarck; he was a totally new phenomenon which has challenged historians, political scientists, sociologists and psychologists to advance a satisfactory explanation. Formerly, the official Marxist view that Nazism was the most grotesque expression of finance capital in its final stages of development enjoyed widespread support. However, T. W. Mason exploded this thesis by pointing out that while he may have been greatly assisted into power by big business Hitler began pursuing political goals (expulsion and then extermination of the Jews and grandiose expansion) which ran counter to the essential interests of business; indeed, they were exclusively political goals which derived from the will of the Führer and for which he was able to gain the endorsement of both the Nazi Party *and the German masses.* Hitler represented an 'autonomous' political programme unrelated to the socio-economic structure of Germany.

How Hitler succeeded in gaining the endorsement for his destructive objectives is a complex issue. The above quotation from David Schoenbaum illustrates the susceptibility of the Germans for Hitler's oft-stated aim to free Germany from the shackles of Versailles and restore national greatness. However, this endorsement was only the first fateful step in giving Hitler a blank cheque to carry out his other agenda, especially the *final solution* to the 'Jewish question', about which there was a veil of semi-secrecy and much misinformation.

The Third Reich was Hitler's fiefdom. He surrounded himself with sycophants, in some cases brilliant men such as the architect Albert Speer, in others, men who were psychologically aberrant, such as Heinrich Himmler, head of the infamous SS (*Schutz-Staffel*). They all gave their loyal service to the person of Hitler, without which his policies could not have been implemented. What is incontrovertible is the fact that Hitler could not have seized power or carried out his subsequent criminal aims had it not been for the loyalty of the army. Only a handful of officers had sufficient reservations to consider deposing Hitler on the grounds that he was incompetent as a military planner and would lead Germany to destruction. This was the rationale for the conspiracy of officers against Hitler that led to the ill-fated assassination attempt of 20 July 1944, with which Dietrich Bonhoeffer was associated.

Much has been written about the German resistance to Hitler and the failure of the conspiracy on 20 July. There has also been considerable discussion about Bonhoeffer's own role in the conspiracy.[14] We cannot deal here with any of this in detail, but it is important to note that Bonhoeffer's motivation as a theologian was different in principle from those whose chief priority was to salvage the honour of the German nation and to gain favourable peace conditions. It is in contrasting Bonhoeffer's reasons for participating in the anti-Hitler plot with those of the officers that a great deal can be learnt about the political culture of 'Bonhoeffer's Germany', and the extent to which he had distanced himself from his nationalist contemporaries.

If we look back at Bonhoeffer's mentors, the theologians of Wilhelmine and Weimar Germany, we see for the most part men who were not simply fervent patriots but an estate of intellectuals who perceived themselves as the custodians of the national cultural heritage. They had incorporated the history of the state into their theology to such an extent that they could virtually equate the foreign policy of the Reich with the kingdom of God on earth. The Harnacks, Seebergs and Deissmanns stand as representatives of their estate. They elevated a version of Luther's doctrine of the two kingdoms to dogmatic status. According to this the *Machtstaat*, the power state, was the instrument of God in history, destined to realise God's will for humankind. As indicated, this presumed not only Luther, but also the teachings of G. W. F. Hegel, Leopold von Ranke and the so-called Neo-Rankeans, who exerted a virtual monopoly over historical training at German universities in the Wilhelmine period. At that time, the historians and theologians shared the same *Weltanschauung*, and their understanding about the evolution of the Prussian-German Empire consisting of a federation of principalities, i.e. of monarchies by the grace of God, and its destiny in the world (imperialism), was mutually reinforcing.

It is, therefore, not surprising that Bonhoeffer, too, accorded a very high status to the function of the state in the history of salvation.[15] This, however, came to be radically modified by his experience of Christianity in other countries (Italy, Spain, the United States and England), with the growing ecumenical movement, and not least by his encounter with the theology of his Swiss friend and theological mentor, Karl Barth. All this combined to enable Bonhoeffer to critique the Hitler regime in ways not possible for the majority of his co-religionists. These continued to see the state as an autonomous entity distinct from the society over which it ruled; indeed, an entity operating in a sphere above the people in its charge, following its own laws of existence which had been prescribed by Almighty God. The subjects of the state had no prior right to criticise or judge it in any way; their role was always to obey no matter how unjust or destructive the laws and decisions of the state might appear to be. Ultimately everything that happened was in accordance with the inscrutable will of the Almighty.

There was, however, another side to the Lutheran doctrine of the two kingdoms. The state may not interfere with the proclamation of the gospel. So when the Nazi racial law to exclude persons of Jewish ancestry from the public service was applied to the church, legislating in effect who may or may not be baptised, a *status confessionis* was given, meaning that the church was confronted with a crisis of conscience and had to declare its position in order to remain true to the gospel. Nazi Jewish policy, then, was a violation by the state of the doctrine of the two kingdoms, and here the Confessing Church felt that it had no alternative but to take a stand if it was to continue to represent the true identity of the Christian faith.

Up to 1933 Bonhoeffer had been willing to accord the state its traditional right to be solely responsible for the secular world. He was, after all, profoundly influenced by the long-established Lutheran-dominated political culture, just as he was sceptical of the ability of liberal democracy to govern Germany.[16] However, Bonhoeffer, in contrast to the vast majority of his co-religionists in the Confessing Church, which even admitted an oath of loyalty to the Führer, was not content merely to declare before the state that it had no right to interfere in the affairs of the church: he was prepared to make the second step into conspiratorial resistance. As he had stated in 1933 in reference to the state's persecution of Jewish citizens, one must consider whether to 'put a spoke in the wheel' (of the state).[17]

Bonhoeffer is unique among the active opponents of the Nazi regime because he was able to develop a theology of resistance, indeed an ethics of responsible action.[18] Shortly after his arrest, Bonhoeffer shared some of his deepest thoughts with his fellow conspirators on their role. As yet, the abortive assassination attempt was still in the future, but Bonhoeffer's insights have even greater significance in hindsight:

> Civil courage, in fact, can grow out of the free responsibility of free men. Only now are the Germans beginning to discover the meaning of free responsibility. It depends on a God who demands responsible action in a bold venture of faith, and who promises forgiveness and consolation to the man who becomes a sinner in that venture.[19]

Notes

1 E. Johann, *Reden des Kaisers*, ed. E. Johann (Munich: Deutscher Taschenbuch Verlag, 1966), p. 58.
2 S. H. Roberts, *The House That Hitler Built* (London: Methuen, 1937), p. 362.
3 F. Fischer, *From Kaiserreich to Third Reich: Elements of Continuity in German History 1871–1945* (London: Allen & Unwin, 1986), pp. 97–9.
4 For an outline of the debate initiated in 1961 by Professor Fritz Fischer, see J. A. Moses, *The Politics of Illusion: The Fischer Controversy in German Historiography* (London: George Prior, 1978).
5 P. M. Kennedy, *The Rise of the Anglo-German Antagonism 1860–1914* (London: Allen & Unwin, 1980).
6 V. R. Berghahn, *Germany and the Approach of War in 1914*, vol. II (London: Macmillan, 1993), pp. 49–55.
7 Hobson attacked the idea that colonies were necessary for creating markets for the industrial products of the imperial power. Competition for colonies was a 'constant menace to peace' and should be abandoned for free trade, which would be much more conducive to maintaining international peace. J. A. Hobson, *Imperialism: A Study*, vol. III (London: Allen & Unwin), p. 152.
8 W. J. Mommsen, *Max Weber and German Politics 1890–1920* (Chicago:

University of Chicago Press, 1984), p. 69.

9 K. Vondung, *Die Apokalypse in Deutschland* (Munich: Deutscher Taschenbuch Verlag, 1988), p. 133.

10 G. Ritter, *The Sword and the Sceptre: The Problem of Militarism in Germany* (Florida: University of Miami Press, 1972), pp. 378–80.

11 F. Fischer, *Griff nach der Weltmacht – die Kriegszielpolitik des kaiserlichen Deutschland 1914/18* (Düsseldorf: Droste Verlag, 1961), p. 110.

12 J. A. Moses, *Trade Unionism in Germany from Bismarck to Hitler* (London: George Prior, 1982).

13 D. Schoenbaum, *Hitler's Social Revolution: Class and Status in Nazi Germany 1933–1939* (London: Weidenfeld & Nicolson, 1967), p. xii.

14 E. Bethge, *Dietrich Bonhoeffer: Theologian, Christian, Contemporary* (London: Collins, 1970), pp. 626–92.

15 See, for example, his essay on 'State and Church' published in 1941, in D. Bonhoeffer, *Ethics* (New York: Macmillan, 1941), pp. 332–53.

16 J. de Gruchy, 'Dietrich Bonhoeffer and the Transition to Democracy in the German Democratic Republic and South Africa', *Modern Theology*, 12 (3) (July 1996).

17 D. Bonhoeffer, *No Rusty Swords: Letters, Lectures and Notes, 1928–1936, Collected Works of Dietrich Bonhoeffer*, vol. 1 (London: Collins, 1977), p. 221.

18 D. Bonhoeffer, *Ethics* (New York: Macmillan, 1965), p. 224.

19 'After Ten Years', in D. Bonhoeffer, *Letters and Papers from Prison: The Enlarged Edition* (New York: Macmillan, 1972), p. 6.

2 The life of Dietrich Bonhoeffer

F. BURTON NELSON

Shortly after Dietrich Bonhoeffer's abrupt and tragic death on 9 April 1945, one of his long-standing friends, Reinhold Niebuhr, paid him the ultimate tribute in an article entitled 'The Death of a Martyr'. 'The story of Bonhoeffer', Niebuhr wrote, 'is worth recording. It belongs to the modern acts of the apostles.'[1] Niebuhr went on to predict that

> Bonhoeffer, less known than Martin Niemöller, will become better known. Not only his martyr's death, but also his actions and precepts contain within them the hope of a revitalised Protestant faith in Germany. It will be a faith, religiously more profound than that of many of its critics; but it will have learned to overcome the one fateful error of German Protestantism, the complete dichotomy between faith and political life.[2]

In the past half-century this prediction has become true not only within the boundaries of Bonhoeffer's native Germany, but also far beyond.

Bonhoeffer's life is a story of family solidarity, of faith and faithfulness, of courage and compassion and of true patriotism. Moreover, Bonhoeffer's life is a necessary key to understanding his theology. The numerous writings which flowed from his creative pen can most effectively be interpreted when seen in the unfolding context of his life and times. In sum, biography inevitably sheds light on the foundational themes of his theology and is an interpretative key in reaching the depths of meaning in his writing.[3]

The *magnum opus* of the life of Bonhoeffer for several decades has been the classic biography by his closest friend, Eberhard Bethge, *Dietrich Bonhoeffer: Theologian, Christian, Contemporary*.[4] Indisputably, this account of Bonhoeffer's life and context will reign supreme among the various lives that will continue to be available to a contemporary reader, and to readers in the twenty-first century.[5]

THE BONHOEFFER FAMILY

It is impossible to imagine what Dietrich Bonhoeffer's life might have been like if his family context had not been what it was. His early years in the midst of a cultured, privileged and prestigious family shaped his value and belief system beyond measure. Bethge puts it succinctly:

> He grew up in a family that derived its real education not from school, but from a deeply-rooted sense of being guardians of a great historical heritage and intellectual tradition. To Dietrich Bonhoeffer this meant learning to understand and respect the ideas and actions of earlier generations.[6]

The family trees on both sides speak of this 'great historical heritage'. The father's, Karl Bonhoeffer's, line is readily traced back to the early sixteenth century (1513), when his ancestors moved to Schwäbisch-Hall in Germany from Holland. An evolving procession of goldsmiths, doctors, clergy, lawyers and burgomasters evidence the solid middle-class character of the seventeenth- and eighteenth-century generations.[7] Dietrich's paternal grandfather, Friedrich von Bonhoeffer (1828–1907), served as president of the provincial court in Ulm. His grandmother, Julie Tafel Bonhoeffer, who outlived her husband by almost thirty years (1842–1936), left an indelible impression on both Dietrich and all his siblings.

Dietrich's mother's family heritage is likewise notable. His maternal great-grandfather was Karl August von Hase (1800–1890), who earned a widespread reputation as a church historian at the University of Jena. His grandfather was Karl Alfred von Hase (1842–1914), who, for several years, served as Court Preacher to William II, the last of the Hohenzollern emperors in Germany. He was also a distinguished professor of practical theology in Breslau. He was married to Countess Clara von Kalckreuth (1851–1903). Their daughter, Paula von Hase, was to become Dietrich's mother.[8]

Dietrich Bonhoeffer was born in Breslau on 4 February 1906, and a few moments later, his twin sister, Sabine, entered the world.[9] Prior to their birth, three brothers were born: Karl-Friedrich (1899); Walter (1899); and Klaus (1901). Two sisters also preceded the twins: Ursula (1902); and Christel (1903). The birth of Susanne (1909) completed the family circle.[10]

Dr Karl Bonhoeffer, Dietrich's father, was a distinguished university professor and physician. From 1904 to 1912 he was Professor of Psychiatry and Neurology in Breslau and also served as director of the University Hospital for Nervous Diseases. In 1912, he was appointed as Professor of

Psychiatry and Nervous Diseases at the University of Berlin and director of the psychiatric and neurological clinic at the Charité Hospital Complex. At home he exercised his parental authority and discipline in a manner charac-terised by 'empiricism, rationality, and liberalism'.[11] Sabine Bonhoeffer offers a word picture:

> He was rather distant and reserved, yet his eyes regarded the person in front of him with intense understanding. He would stress a point by preciseness, not loudness, of speech. He educated us by his example, by the way he lived his life. He spoke little, and we felt his judgement in a look of surprise, a teasing word and sometimes a slightly ironical smile . . . His great tolerance excluded narrow-mindedness from our lives and widened our horizons.[12]

Karl Bonhoeffer held high expectations for each child of the family, almost as if it were their inherent duty to fulfil the potential they had been given. It is little wonder that two of the older brothers, Karl-Friedrich and Klaus, exemplified in their life experience many of their father's traits.

Paula von Hase Bonhoeffer, Dietrich's mother, was completely devoted to her large family. A teacher by training, once she married in 1898, and especially as the family circle began to enlarge, she immersed herself in her family responsibilities. As the years passed, it was clear that she 'was the soul and spirit of the house'.[13] After the family had moved to Berlin-Grunewald, in 1912, she presided over a servant staff of seven – teacher, governess, housemaid, parlour maid, cook, receptionist and chauffeur. She also taught the older children at home, which included a 'big repertoire of poems, songs, and games'.[14]

The Bonhoeffers did not attend weekly worship in the neighbourhood church. Nevertheless, one could not grow up in such a household without being exposed to the basic rudiments of the Christian faith. To a limited extent, the children, especially the three youngest – Dietrich, Sabine and Susanne – were influenced by their nannies, Maria and Käthe Horn, who had come to the Bonhoeffer household from the Moravian Brethren. Paula Bonhoeffer also encouraged a formative religious climate for the family. In her youthful years, she herself had resided several months at Herrnhut, the life centre of the Moravian Church. While her piety was by no means worn on her sleeve, in subsequent years she was consistently concerned that her children encounter stories of the Bible, learn the great hymns of the Chris-tian tradition, offer grace before meals, participate in evening prayers, and be baptised and confirmed in the faith. Grandfather von Hase often served as a kind of family pastor, and following his death in 1914, Hans von Hase, the maternal uncle, was often the spiritual leader. After the formation of the Confessing Church in 1934, Dietrich's mother resumed her participation in church worship, and the Berlin-Dahlem parish of Martin Niemöller became the 'church home'.

Family life was also shaped by holidays spent at a second home in Friedrichsbrunn in the eastern Harz Mountains. This provided occasions for experiencing the natural joys of hills and forests, of swimming, of hiking and gathering mushrooms and berries, of playing ball in the evenings, singing folk songs, and reading. In these serene surroundings, Dietrich first read such classics as *Pinocchio, Heroes of Everyday* and *Uncle Tom's Cabin*, as well as many great poets.[15] That this segment of family life made its indelible impression on Dietrich's own life is evidenced in the fact that no fewer than six times in his prison letters, he calls Friedrichsbrunn to memory.[16]

The serenity of the family was demonstrably shaken in the closing weeks of the First World War. Dietrich's brother, Walter, serving in the German army, was wounded on 23 April 1918, and died five days later. The effect on the parents was devastating. Paula Bonhoeffer withdrew from family life for weeks on end, and Karl Bonhoeffer discontinued his practice of writing entries in his New Year notebook.[17] Dietrich, only twelve years old at the time, was distraught:

> The death of his brother Walter and his mother's desperate grief left an indelible mark on the child Dietrich Bonhoeffer. This grief and the way in which his brother died came vividly to mind years later, when Dietrich talked to his students about the reverent conduct of services of national sorrow.[18]

The parents then gave Dietrich Walter's confirmation bible, which he kept by him for the rest of his life.

Two years later, at the age of fourteen and, much to the disappointment of his father and his remaining brothers, he made the decision to become a minister and a theologian. They even sought to dissuade him, claiming that the church was not really worthy of his commitment; it was, they insisted, 'a poor, feeble, boring, petty bourgeois institution'. To which Dietrich replied: 'In that case I shall reform it!'[19]

The entire family regarded Hitler's coming to power in January 1933 as a bad omen. Grandmother Julie Bonhoeffer symbolised this unflinching opposition. Renate Bethge depicts the scenario:

> With the rest of the family, from the very beginning, she was an out-spoken enemy of the Nazis. On April 1, 1933, Hitler ordered that

nobody was to buy anything in a Jewish shop, and storm troopers stood guard before such shops and stores. She just walked through the row of these watchmen, did her shopping, and came out through the row of the perplexed men, saying, 'I do my shopping where I always do my shopping.'[20]

Julie Bonhoeffer died three years later at the age of ninty-three. Dietrich preached at the funeral, and one can sense the impact that she had had on his own evolving views about the plight of Jews in Germany:

> She could not bear to see the rights of a person violated . . . Thus her last years were darkened by the grief that she bore about the fate of the Jews in our country, which she suffered with them. She came out of a different time, out of a different spiritual world, and this world will not shrink into the grave with her. This heritage, for which we are grateful to her, puts us under obligation.[21]

The shaping influence of the Bonhoeffer family persisted all through the years, even to Dietrich's lonely months in Tegel Prison. His prison writings are permeated by references to family life, just as his drama and fiction pictured what life was like growing up in Berlin in the early twentieth century. Ruth Zerner's observation is apt: 'in his prison play and novel, Bonhoeffer – in addition to the recreation of deeply felt life experiences and human relationships – recreated this family setting from which he drew strength and confidence'.[22] One commentator extends the ideational link between Dietrich's family experience and his later views of the church: 'The picture he draws in his doctoral dissertation of the structure of the church is a functional description of this family.'[23]

In recent years, new glimpses have appeared of the impact of Dietrich's family on his life and theology, enriching our understanding and insight. One resource is Eberhard Bethge's 'Marienburger Allee 43: The House, its Family, and Guests'.[24] Another is a volume produced by the Board of the Bonhoeffer House in Berlin, *Dietrich Bonhoeffer, Pfarrer*. The book centres around an exhibition in Marienburger Allee 43, stressing 'the special significance of the Bonhoeffer family and its influence upon the shaping of his life'.[25] Enormously helpful also is an essay by Renate Bethge, 'Bonhoeffer's Family and its Significance for his Theology'.[26] Connecting links are discerned between life in the family circle and some of Bonhoeffer's key theological motifs. This essay, together with others by both Renate and Eberhard Bethge, notably his discussion of the influence on Dietrich of his older brother, Karl-Friedrich,[27] and still others by family members and those close to the family, point us to new, engaging vistas of Bonhoeffer studies.

STUDENT YEARS

Bonhoeffer's older brothers and sisters were initially taught by their mother, but following the family move to Berlin, the twins were taught by Käthe, the resident sister of their governess, Maria Horn. At the age of seven, Dietrich continued his studies at the Friedrich Werner grammar school. While his older brothers were orientated towards the sciences, following the model of their empirically minded father, Dietrich's leaning lay elsewhere. During his adolescent years, Dietrich read philosophy and religion, including such notables as Euripides, Schleiermacher, Goethe, Schiller, Tönnies and Max Weber. At the same time, he cultivated his musical talents. At age ten, he was playing Mozart sonatas. Bethge reports that

> on Saturday evenings he skilfully accompanied *Lieder* by Schubert, Schumann, Brahms, and Hugo Wolf sung by his mother and his sister, Ursula, who had a good voice. After this, no amount of irregularity by any singer could dismay him. He got used at an early age to playing in company without shyness or embarrassment . . . Thus in his boyhood and youth it was music that gave him a special position at school and among his fellow-students.[28]

At the age of seventeen, Dietrich entered Tübingen University, where his father and older brothers had also studied. Inflation during the 1920s rendered the day-to-day economic life of a student unsettling and precarious. He wrote home to his parents in June 1923: 'Müller's *History of the Church* now costs 70,000 marks instead of 55,000.' In October he reported that every meal costs 1,000 million marks. Students at that time had contracted for fifty meals in advance for 2,500 million marks.[29]

Dietrich's more informal education continued with a three months' visit to Rome, accompanied by his brother, Klaus. His diary offers a kaleidoscope of those sites that have moulded the city – St Peter's, the Colosseum, the Pantheon, the Roman Forum, the Pincio, Trinità dei Monti, the Trevi Fountain, Santa Maria Maggiore, the Catacombs, the Vatican Museum, St John Lateran.[30] As his diary indicates, Holy Week 1924 in St Peter's made a powerful impact on him: 'Palm Sunday . . . the first day on which something of the reality of Catholicism began to dawn on me: nothing romantic or the like. I think I'm beginning to understand the concept of the church.'[31] In

Bethge's words, 'Bonhoeffer's trip to Rome played a vital part in the formation of his attitude to the subject of the church. The idea of concreteness, i.e.,
of not getting lost in metaphysical speculation, was one of the real roots of
this approach.'[32] Following their sojourn in Rome, Dietrich and Klaus
continued their travels across the Mediterranean, spending several days in
Sicily, Tripoli and the Libyan desert.

Later in 1924 Dietrich returned to his formal education at the University
of Berlin where he was to concentrate on studies in theology for the next
three years. His encounter there with such renowned scholars as church
historian Adolf von Harnack, Luther interpreter Karl Holl, church historian
Hans Lietzmann, and systematic theologian Reinhold Seeberg was strategic
in shaping his own theological journey. Under Seeberg's tutelage, he wrote
his doctoral dissertation, *Sanctorum Communio*, which was published in
1927. His description of the church as 'Christ existing as community' proved
to be formative for his subsequent theological perspectives. In 1928 Dietrich
served his initial pastoral ministry as a curate in a German-language Lutheran congregation in Barcelona. Returning to Berlin in 1929, he continued
his formal educational pilgrimage by writing his *habilitation*, entitled *Act
and Being*, to pave the way for an appointment as a university lecturer.

In the autumn of 1930 Dietrich arrived at New York's Union Theological Seminary for a year of post-doctoral studies as a Sloane Fellow. It was to
be a pivotal year for the young theologian. He found the state of theology in
this prestigious Manhattan school to be unbearably thin and disappointing-
ly shallow. In fact, he wrote that,

> the theological atmosphere of the Union Theological Seminary is
> accelerating the process of the secularisation of Christianity in
> America . . . A seminary in which it can come about that a large
> number of students laugh out loud in a public lecture at the quoting of
> a passage from Luther's *De Servo Arbitrio* on sin and forgiveness
> because it seems to them to be comic has evidently completely
> forgotten what Christian theology by its very nature stands for.[33]

In spite of these negative notes Dietrich found much to celebrate during his
Union days. Reinhold Niebuhr was one of his mentors who challenged him
to think deeply about the church's involvement in the aches and pains of
society. Niebuhr remained a friend for the following decade, exchanging
correspondence with consistent frequency.[34]

Beyond the classroom, Dietrich's close circle of friends had a life-long
influence. Erwin Sutz, a Swiss Sloane Fellow, joined him in fulfilling a role
as an interpreter of European theology in the seminary community. Having

studied under Karl Barth and Emil Brunner, he significantly enlarged Bonhoeffer's own appreciation for the emerging 'crisis theology'. Moreover, Sutz played a key role in enabling Bonhoeffer to spend two weeks in Bonn later in 1931 with Barth.[35] Another European to become a close companion was a Frenchman, Jean Lasserre. The two friends did not speak each other's language so practised their English on each other, sharing hour after hour of theological conversation. It was Lasserre who challenged his German colleague to a new and profound encounter with the Sermon on the Mount, especially grappling with the claims of Jesus' peace commands. On a trip to Mexico in June 1931, together with Erwin Sutz and Paul Lehmann, both Lasserre and Bonhoeffer spoke passionately about their peace concerns at a public meeting in Victoria, arranged by a Quaker friend. Bonhoeffer never forgot his friendship with Lasserre.[36]

Two American students were also among the coterie of Bonhoeffer's good friends. One was Paul Lehmann, whose apartment at Union was perennially available for conversation. 'Lehmann helped Bonhoeffer deepen his appreciation for the church to become involved in civil rights and the cause of economic justice.'[37] A second was a black student from Alabama, Frank Fisher, who was assigned to the Abyssinian Baptist Church in Harlem for his field education. Bonhoeffer accompanied him to church, and, during the spring of 1931, assisted in teaching a Sunday-school class. Bethge concludes that through his friendship with Fisher, Dietrich gained 'a detailed and intimate knowledge of the realities of Harlem life'.[38] Later when back in Berlin at the university, Bonhoeffer shared his Harlem-based experiences with his theological students, playing records of black spirituals. One of his students, Wolf-Dieter Zimmermann, reported him saying at the conclusion of an evening gathering: 'When I took leave of my black friend, he said to me: "Make our sufferings known in Germany, tell them what is happening to us and show them what we are like." I wanted to fulfil this obligation tonight.'[39]

TEACHER, PASTOR AND PREACHER

At the age of twenty-four, Bonhoeffer was invited to join the faculty of the University of Berlin as a lecturer in systematic theology. For the following two years he offered courses which included 'The History of Systematic Theology in the Twentieth Century', 'The Idea of Philosophy in Protestant Theology', 'The Nature of the Church', 'Creation and Sin' and 'Christology'. Wolf-Dieter Zimmermann has left us this description:

When I entered the lecture room, there were about ten to fifteen students, a disheartening sight. For a moment I wondered whether I should retreat, but I stayed out of curiosity. A young lecturer stepped to the rostrum with a light, quick step, a man with very fair, rather thin hair, a broad face, rimless glasses with a golden bridge. After a few words of welcome, he explained the meaning and structure of the lecture, in a firm, slightly throaty way of speaking.[40]

'Bonhoeffer', Zimmermann recalled, 'was very concentrated, quite unsentimental, almost dispassionate, clear as crystal, with a certain rational coldness, like a reporter.'[41]

Bonhoeffer's lectures and seminars began to gather student interest and, beyond that, loyalty. It was at a time when many of the thousand students of theology at the university were being attracted to National Socialism. Bethge even describes the young lecturer as 'a minor sensation', a teacher who 'was talked about'. 'His regular followers were self-selected by the intellectual and personal standards required. There were none of the German Christians among them, except perhaps some who believed that politically they could line up with the Nazi party without their theology being affected.'[42]

Bonhoeffer was aware that effective teaching goes beyond the four walls of a classroom. A number of his theological students frequently spent evenings and weekends with him. A hut at Biesenthal on the outskirts of Berlin served as a gathering point. It is not surprising that several eventually formed part of the core opposition to Hitler and Nazism. Their names also became familiar to those later influenced by the Bonhoeffer legacy.[43]

The last lectures that Bonhoeffer gave at the university were offered in the summer of 1933. Hitler's grip on Germany had formally begun in January that year when he was appointed Chancellor. It was in this context that the Christology theme gathered potency and definition. Bethge refers to these lectures as 'the high point of Bonhoeffer's academic career'. In formulating his Christology, Bonhoeffer 'was finally trying to bring together all the disparate threads of his new understanding of both himself and of his commitment to Jesus Christ. In these lectures his life and his theology appeared to converge.'[44] The teacher was also becoming a disciple.

As previously noted, Bonhoeffer began his life-long pastoral ministry at the age of twenty-two in 1928 as a curate in the German Lutheran Church in Barcelona. The congregation consisted largely of expatriate businessmen. Bonhoeffer's vitality was poured into the lifeblood of the congregation. Over the course of the year he delivered nineteen sermons, started a children's service, taught a boys' class, lectured, and became involved in dealing with social problems in the community. In the middle of the year he wrote to his good friend, Helmut Rössler:

> I'm getting to know new people every day; here one meets people as they are, away from the masquerade of the 'Christian world', people with passions, criminal types, little people with little ambitions, little desires, and little sins, all in all people who feel homeless in both senses of the word, who loosen up if one talks to them in a friendly way, real people.[45]

It is clear that Bonhoeffer's relationships with the people were marked by caring and concern. As Bethge puts it:

> Even though the sermons that Bonhoeffer preached so passionately to the Barcelona congregation to a great extent passed far over their heads, he nevertheless spoke to them as one who, during the week, visited them, and filled them with a warmth and pastoral concern to which they were unaccustomed.[46]

Bonhoeffer's own world was expanding in this new geographical zone. Beyond the boundaries of the congregation he witnessed the plight of the poor and the dispossessed. The devastation of the Depression had penetrated the community, prodding Bonhoeffer to stir the conscience and the concern of the people.

The report of his Supervisor, Pastor Fritz Olbricht, to the church authorities in Germany spoke of the sensitivities which Bonhoeffer appeared to possess for ministry: 'He has proved most capable in every respect and has been a great help in my many-sided work. He has been able in particular to attract children who are very fond of him. Recently an average of forty children have been coming to his Sunday School. He has been very popular throughout the colony.'[47] Bonhoeffer was invited to stay for a second year in Barcelona, but he chose to study the following year at Union Theological Seminary in New York.

In America's largest metropolis, it was important to Dietrich that he establish a vital link with a local, thriving congregation. Not satisfied with the preaching and ministry at the adjacent Riverside Church, he found a spiritual home at the large Abyssinian Baptist Church in Harlem. He wrote about the experience: 'For more than six months I've been almost every Sunday lunchtime, about twenty to three, to one of the great Negro Baptist churches in Harlem . . . I have heard the gospel preached in the Negro churches.'[48] In this congregation Bonhoeffer taught a Sunday-school class of junior boys, occasionally helped in a weekday religious school, and led a group of women in Bible studies.

Back in Berlin in 1931, Bonhoeffer's pastoral ministries were multiple. Newly ordained, he served for a time as chaplain to the Technical University at Charlottenburg, and then became the teacher of a confirmation class of fifty boys in the squalid and poverty-stricken Zion parish of Prenzlauer Berg, Berlin. An insight into his pastoral relationships in this setting is given us in a letter he wrote to his friend Erwin Sutz:

> At the beginning the young lads behaved crazily, so that for the first time I had real problems of discipline . . . Now there is absolute quiet, the young men see to that themselves, so I need no longer fear the fate of my predecessor, whom they literally worried to death. Recently I was out with some of them for two days; another group is coming tomorrow. We've all enjoyed this being together. As I am keeping them until confirmation, I have to visit the parents of all fifty of them and will be living in the neighbourhood for two months in order to get it done.[49]

Preaching also served as a conduit for Bonhoeffer's pastoral orientation. On a number of occasions he preached at the prestigious Kaiser Wilhelm Memorial Church in Berlin and in other congregations. For him the preparation of a sermon and its subsequent delivery was unique in its privilege and responsibility. 'Preaching was the great event in his life; the hard theologising and all the critical love of his church were all for its sake, for in it the message of Christ, the bringer of peace, was proclaimed. To Bonhoeffer, nothing in his calling competed in importance with preaching.'[50]

Bonhoeffer was involved in the early stages of the church opposition to Nazism, notably in drafting the Bethel Confession.[51] But he was unhappy about the lack of decisiveness even in these circles and decided to leave Germany in October 1933, when he became pastor of two small German-speaking congregations in London – one in Sydenham, the other in the East End.[52] His decision was roundly chided in a letter from Karl Barth: 'You are a German . . . the house of your church is on fire . . . you must return to your post by the next ship. As things are, shall we say the ship after next?'[53] But Bonhoeffer remained, serving his London congregations for the next eighteen months. This meant, amongst other things, that he was absent from the founding of the Synod of the Confessing Church in Barmen in 1934. But he helped, on behalf of the Confessing Church, to mobilise the German pastors in London against Nazism, as well as assisting German refugees who were then arriving in England. 'It was undoubtedly due to Bonhoeffer's presence in London', Bethge later wrote, 'that, of all the German congregations abroad, only those in England made any real or effective attempt to intervene in the church struggle at home.'[54]

A most significant outgrowth of Bonhoeffer's pastoral months in London was his friendship with the Bishop of Chichester, George K. A. Bell. The two had met in 1932 at an ecumenical conference in Geneva. Even though they were separated from each other in age by over twenty years, they were united in their discernment of the ominous happenings in Bonhoeffer's Germany. The role that Bell was to play in the saga of Bonhoeffer's life was to continue until the very day of Bonhoeffer's martyrdom in April 1945.

The call from the Confessing Church to serve as director of a newly formed illegal seminary in his homeland brought the curtain down on Bonhoeffer's pastoral ministry in London. It did not, however, conclude his continuing role as pastor. He was a pastor to the very end. [55]

THE ECUMENICAL MOVEMENT

During the mid 1930s, Bonhoeffer participated in numerous ecumenical conferences in his capacity as a regional secretary of the Joint Youth commissions of two bodies – the World Alliance for Promoting International Friendship through the Churches, and the Universal Christian Council for Life and Work. His overwhelming concern was that the churches of the world would discern their God-given mandate to be in the vanguard for peace. Equally urgent was his desire that the oikoumene would develop a solidarity with the Confessing Church in Germany. In his letters to George Bell, he articulated his belief that the churches were engaged in a life-and-death struggle in his native Germany. He wrote to his friend:

> The question at stake in the German Church is no longer an internal issue but is the question of the existence of Christianity in Europe; therefore a definite attitude of the ecumenical movement has nothing to do with 'intervention', but it is just a demonstration to the whole world that Church and Christianity as such are at stake.[56]

Subsequently, Bonhoeffer assisted Bishop Bell in drafting a pastoral Ascensiontide letter which conveyed the seriousness of the church struggle in Germany:

> The situation is, beyond doubt, full of anxiety. To estimate it aright we have to remember the fact that a revolution has taken place in the German state, and that as a necessary result the German Evangelical

Church was bound to be faced with new tasks and many new problems requiring time for their full solution . . . The chief cause of anxiety is the assumption by the Reichbishop in the name of the principle of autocratic powers unqualified by constitutional or traditional restraints which are without precedent in the history of the Church.[57]

Fanö, a small island off the western coast of Denmark, was the scene in August 1934 for the meetings of three ecumenical bodies – the Management Committee of the World Alliance, the Universal Christian Council for Life and Work, and the International Youth Conference (planned and executed by the joint Youth Commission of the World Alliance and the Universal Christian Council). By his public presentations at Fanö, by his personal linkage with Bishop Bell, who presided as president, and by his daily dialogue with many of the delegates, Bonhoeffer managed to make an indelible impression on the fledgling ecumenical movement.[58] Especially notable was his sermon, 'The Church and the Peoples of the World', in which he exhorted the churches to accept their responsibility as peace-makers. 'The hour is late', he declared. 'The world is choked with weapons, and dreadful is the distrust which looks out of every human being's eyes. The trumpets of war may blow tomorrow. For what are we waiting? Do we want to become involved in this guilt as never before?'[59] One eyewitness described the sermon as 'possibly the most decisive, certainly the most exciting moment of the Conference'.[60] Another eyewitness reported that Bonhoeffer's words had the 'effect of a bomb at Fanö'.[61]

But as the 1930s moved on, Bonhoeffer grew disenchanted with the failure of the ecumenical bodies to live in solidarity with the Confessing Church. He steadfastly refused to participate in any meeting to which both the Reich Church and the Confessing Church were invited. In 1935 he had written an essay which was published in *Evangelische Theologie*, 'The Confessing Church and the Ecumenical Movement'. The church struggle, he insisted, 'puts demands both on the ecumenical movement, to live up to the spirit of Fanö and so live up to its promise to be the church of Jesus Christ, and on the Confessing Church, to see the struggle as one for the very life of Christianity'.[62] In short, the struggle that was being waged for justice and truth by the Confessing Church was a vicarious struggle for the whole church of Jesus Christ. When Bonhoeffer realised by 1937 that the ecumenical leaders were not about to follow the clear counsel of the Fanö Conference, he requested that he be relieved of his task as a regional youth secretary. That decision, however, has not diminished his ongoing impact on the continuing ecumenical movement throughout the twentieth century.[63]

The church struggle in Germany was a struggle to be obedient and faithful to the Lord of the church. At its centre was the challenge to Christians to identify with the plight of the Jews in German society. Shortly after the passing of anti-Jewish legislation in April 1933, Bonhoeffer gave a controversial address on 'The Church and the Jewish Question'. Originally presented to a group of clergy who were meeting in the home of Pastor Gerhard Jacobi in Berlin, it was soon published in a journal. Its primary thrust was to help determine a Christian response to the evolving anti-Semitic policies of the Nazi government, including the insistence that pastors of Jewish ancestry must immediately be dismissed from their posts. Bonhoeffer challenged this immoral legislation, called the churches to come to the aid of the victims of injustice – whether they were baptised or not – and, further, 'not just to bandage the victims under the wheel, but to jam a spoke in the wheel itself'.[64] In other words, there may be times when it becomes necessary for the church, in the advance of justice, to resort to direct action against the state. Bonhoeffer, as Heinz Eduard Tödt reminds us, 'was almost alone in his opinions; he was the only one who considered solidarity with the Jews, especially with the non-Christian Jews, to be a matter of such importance as to obligate the Christian churches to risk a massive conflict with that state – a risk which could threaten their very existence'.[65]

Bonhoeffer's life story constantly intersected with the tragic unfolding of the Nazis' persecution of the Jews: his insistence at ecumenical conferences that serious attention be given to their plight; his assistance to refugee Jews in England; his unforgettable exclamation in 1935 after the propagation of the infamous Nuremberg Laws ('Only he who shouts for the Jews is permitted to sing Gregorian chants!'); his calling the students at the Finkenwalde Seminary in 1935–7 to intercede for the Jews; his insistence that there could be no compromise with the 'German Christians' or the Reich Church; his participation in rescue efforts on behalf of Jews, notably 'Operation 7'; his eventual entry into the resistance movement. All of these facets of Bonhoeffer's own personal involvement in the church struggle exemplify his conviction that Christianity and Nazism were absolutely and perennially incompatible.

FINKENWALDE: LIFE IN COMMUNITY

To assist in the preparation of parish pastors, the Confessing Church established five seminaries in Germany to be supported by free-will offerings and to maintain independence as far as possible from state government. As I have intimated, Bonhoeffer was invited to return to Germany from England in the spring of 1935 to direct one of these illegal seminaries. Before leaving England he visited several Anglican monasteries and a Quaker centre (in order to prepare his own spirit and mind for this new and challenging assignment). 'The approaching task acted as a catalyst for everything that had been preoccupying Bonhoeffer during the past few years: a theology of the Sermon on the Mount, a community in service and spiritual exercises, a witness to passive resistance and ecumenical openness.'[66] During the following three years, 1935–7, all of these motifs were amply and unforgettably demonstrated.

In 1935, twenty-three pastoral candidates convened at Zingst on the beautiful coast of the Baltic Sea. A few weeks later in June they moved to an old manor house near a small rural town, Finkenwalde, just east of the Oder River and about two hundred-fifty kilometres from Berlin. Most of those who came to the seminary had already received a university education and were well on their way to ordination. During the six months that they shared life together under the tutelage of 'Brother Bonhoeffer', as most referred to him, their lives were indelibly influenced by him. When the first course was completed, a 'Brothers' House' was approved by the Council of Brethren of the Old Prussian Union. Most of the original group – Eberhard Bethge, Winfried Maechler and Albrecht Schönherr – would later embody the legacy of Bonhoeffer in significant ways.

Bonhoeffer's classic book *Life Together* reflects the spiritual and corporate atmosphere of the Finkenwalde community. Written in 1938 at his sister Sabine's home in Göttingen in only four weeks, it brought together the basic components of the seminarians' experience – personal and corporate meditation, prayer, solitude, Bible study, fellowship, singing, recreation, ministry, worship, the eucharist, confession and spiritual care.[67]

The Finkenwalde years provided the opportunity for Bonhoeffer and the seminarians to intermingle with a number of Confessing congregations, on whom they substantially depended, and families of the Pomeranian nobility. Significant among these were the von Kleist estates in Kieckow and Klein-Krossin. Ruth von Kleist-Retzow of Klein-Krossin began to attend the Sunday services in Finkenwalde with several of her school-age grandchildren. One of these granddaughters was Maria von Wedemeyer. Eighteen years younger than Bonhoeffer, Maria became his fiancée shortly before his imprisonment.

Finkenwalde was also the context for Bonhoeffer's lectures on discipleship, which were later published as *The Cost of Discipleship*. In them, Bonhoeffer addressed the question, 'How can we live the Christian life in the modern world?'[68] This was not only a general question for the followers of Christ but also a very autobiographical question for Bonhoeffer himself. At the same time as he was writing this foundational work, his brother-in-law, Hans von Dohnanyi, was assembling his 'Chronicle of Shame', a day-by-day account of Nazi policies and actions. As a member of the Ministry of Justice staff under Franz Guertner, von Dohnanyi was privy to information on the injustices and persecutions perpetrated by the Nazi regime.[69] Bonhoeffer consequently knew far more than the average German citizen about Nazi criminality. Against this background, discipleship was indeed costly, even to the point of martyrdom.

In September 1937 the seminary was closed by order of the Gestapo. By the end of that year twenty-seven of the students had been arrested and imprisoned. Nevertheless the teaching and the learning continued, albeit in a new form. For the next three years, 1938–40, the backwoods of Pomerania housed 'the collective pastorate'. Co-operating superintendents in two districts, Schlawe and Gross-Schlönwitz, appointed the seminarians as assistant clergy. In 1939 the site of the Schlawe group was moved to Sigurdshof, taking over an empty farmhouse. Bonhoeffer divided his time between the two sites.

> Work and meditation, prayer, instruction in preaching and examination of the ideas underlying the New Testament – all this was carried on in the small undistracted circle of the collective pastorates, almost more intensively than in the spacious house at Finkenwalde so close to the big town of Stettin.[70]

But the Gestapo continued their relentless pursuit of the illegal seminary and its participants. Eventually, they moved to close down the Schlawe-Sigurdshof collective pastorate. When they arrived to carry out the deed, they found only an empty farmstead. By March 1940, all of the seminarians had been summoned to military service. There was no exemption for servants of the church, nor was there any provision for conscientious objection.[71]

Meanwhile, family matters were also of concern. Bonhoeffer's twin sister and her husband, Gerhard Leibholz, and their two daughters, Marianne and Christiane, were compelled to leave their home in Göttingen. Professor Leibholz's Jewish ancestry placed their existence in jeopardy, and so the painful decision was made to leave Germany. Eberhard Bethge and Dietrich drove them to the Swiss border in September 1938; they successfully crossed and ultimately made their home in England (primarily Oxford) until their return to Germany in 1947, following the end of the war.[72]

As the 1930s drew to a close, Bonhoeffer became increasingly disappointed and disillusioned about the Confessing Church's lack of forthrightness and assertiveness in the struggle against Nazism. Bethge refers to 1938 as 'the year when the Confessing Church reached its lowest point', the 'darkest moment of the Church Struggle'.[73] This coincided with the infamous 'Crystal Night' on 9 November, when Nazi depravity destroyed more than seven thousand Jewish shops, burnt synagogues, desecrated Torah scrolls, murdered over ninety Jews and sent more than 20,000 to concentration camps. In Bonhoeffer's Bible, Psalm 74:8 was deeply underlined: 'they say to themselves: Let us plunder them! They burn all the houses of God in the land.' In the margin Bonhoeffer wrote the date, 9 Nov. 1938. Scarcely any pastors or church leaders spoke out against these acts of blatant anti-Semitism. Bonhoeffer was outraged.

His mood of disillusionment deepened the following year on the occasion of Hitler's fiftieth birthday. The Minister for Church Affairs, Herr Werner, called on all pastors of the Reich to swear an oath of loyalty to Hitler, 'I swear that I will be loyal and obedient to Adolf Hitler, the Leader of the German Reich, and people.' Neither from the leadership of the Confessing Church, nor from any other church in Germany, was there any significant resistance. Sadly, most of the Confessing Church pastors complied.

Bonhoeffer's distress was sharpened by the possibility of being drafted for military service in Hitler's army. He needed to take action for his own conscience' sake and peace of mind. Hence his acceptance of an invitation to go to America for a second time. He travelled by way of England, visiting the Leibholz family, then crossing the Atlantic by boat with his brother, Karl-Friedrich, who had been offered a professorship at the University of Chicago. Dietrich was to travel on a lecture tour himself, plans having been enthusiastically laid by Reinhold Niebuhr, his friend and teacher from Union Seminary days, and his closest American friend, Paul Lehmann. He was also to teach a summer course at Union, and undertake pastoral services to German refugees. None of these plans were to be fulfilled. Bonhoeffer was restless, aware not only of the continuing fight against Hitler and his minions, but also of the possibility of war breaking out in Europe. After wrestling with his situation for several days, he came to a monumental decision: he must reverse his course and re-enter the fray. In a deeply moving farewell letter to Reinhold Niebuhr, he etched his thoughts:

> I have made a mistake in coming to America. I must live through this
> difficult period of our national history with the Christian people of
> Germany. I will have no right to participate in the reconstruction of

Christian life in Germany after the war if I do not share the trials of this time with my people ... Christians in Germany will face the terrible alternative of either willing the defeat of their nation in order that Christian civilisation may survive, or willing the victory of their nation and thereby destroying our civilisation. I know which of these alternatives I must choose; but I cannot make that choice in security.[74]

Bonhoeffer left New York in July 1939, stopping off in London to see the Leibholz family. His sister's conclusion was surely on target. In America, 'he could perfectly well be replaced, whereas he was needed in Germany. He could not leave his young theologians, his brethren, in the lurch in this difficult crisis of conscience to which the war would now expose them. He must return.'[75] Further words from Dietrich's sister reveal the pathos and the wrenching caused by family partings: 'We all accompanied Dietrich to the station. It was a grave parting. In his own way, optimistic and self-controlled as ever, Dietrich helped us through it. But we had all seen the storm signals ahead, and we had not much hope of seeing each other again very soon. I never saw Dietrich again.'[76]

CONSPIRATOR AND LOVER

At the end of the 1930s, Dietrich Bonhoeffer's life turned a corner that has intrigued and challenged all those who have followed his biography. Just before leaving for America on his second visit, his disillusionment about the churches of Germany, including the Confessing Church, had plumbed new depths. His beloved country was completely captivated by a political regime which clearly ranked with the most tyrannical governments in all of human history. Its crimes seemed to be without parallel. Church leaders, university professors, the press, doctors, lawyers, industrialists and enlightened generals all seemed helpless in the face of this juggernaut of power and authority. Yet there were also those who had embarked on a risky, underground resistance movement to topple Hitler from power, through assassination if necessary.

When Bonhoeffer returned to Germany after his aborted visit to America, the door opened for him to participate in the resistance. Dietrich's brother-in-law, Hans von Dohnanyi, was a leading member of the *Abwehr*, the counterintelligence agency of the armed forces in Nazi Germany, and as such held the key to Bonhoeffer's direct involvement. The *Abwehr*, one of the primary centres of the resistance movement against the Nazis, was headed by Admiral Wilhelm Canaris. Together with General Hans Oster as chief of staff, they were responsible for providing cover-ups for the war-time activities of the resistance, including various assassination attempts on Hitler. Convinced that 'true patriotism'[77] called for a concerted attempt to remove Hitler and his entourage from national leadership, Bonhoeffer became a civilian member of the *Abwehr* until his arrest on 9 April 1943.

Dohnanyi and Oster managed to secure Bonhoeffer's exemption from the military draft, insisting that his efforts were indispensable for espionage activities. The argument which finally persuaded a sceptical Gestapo was that Bonhoeffer's ecumenical contacts could be exceedingly useful for gathering intelligence information. Ostensibly, he could provide background for assessing the political situation in Allied as well as neutral countries. In short, the ecumenical friendships that Bonhoeffer had established during previous years could now be manipulated in the service of Nazi Germany's war effort. Of course, in his guise as a 'double agent', Bonhoeffer used his travels abroad as occasions to cultivate a closer communication between the resistance and the Allies.

Bonhoeffer was instrumental in the implementation of a top-secret plan to assist in the smuggling of Jews out of Germany, referred to as 'Operation 7'. Three times he crossed the border to Switzerland, connecting with key ecumenical figures, including Karl Barth and W. A. Visser't Hooft, the General Secretary designate of the World Council of Churches. Together with Helmut Count von Moltke, he also travelled to Norway making contacts for the resistance. Their encouragement strengthened the Norwegian Lutheran Church, its clergy and its leaders (for example Bishop Eivind Bergraav) in their struggle against the Nazi occupiers of their country.

The capstone of Bonhoeffer's dangerous journeys came in the spring of 1942, when he met his British ecumenical friend, Bishop George Bell, in Sigtuna, Sweden. The crucial importance of this mission can scarcely be exaggerated. In a secret rendezvous, Bonhoeffer relayed to the bishop precise information about the resistance, including names of key members of the underground. He also asked Bell to pass on an urgent message to British Foreign Secretary Anthony Eden, thence to Winston Churchill as well as President Franklin Roosevelt, requesting support for the resistance and especially for negotiating a compromise peace after Hitler had been overthrown. There was no return message from the Allied leaders.[78]

It was during these years that Dietrich Bonhoeffer worked on the manuscript that he hoped would be his *magnum opus*, the *Ethics*. As is the case with Bonhoeffer's other writings since 1933, this fragmentary collection also needs to be read against the background of his life story, especially from 1939 to 1943. The themes of Christ and reality, concreteness, the natural, the penultimate and the ultimate, the four mandates, deputyship, responsibility, state and church and 'telling the truth' all profoundly reflect the endeavour by Bonhoeffer 'to address the great moral dilemmas posed by the war and the need to resist a blatantly evil government'.[79]

During these difficult years not only was Dietrich Bonhoeffer a double agent whose life was full of risks and dangers, but he also unexpectedly fell in love. Bonhoeffer had been in love before, with a woman described in Bethge's biography simply as 'a girl-friend', but later identified as Elizabeth Zinn. Years later, sitting in his Tegel prison cell, he wrote about this relationship:

> I was once in love with a girl; she became a theologian, and our paths ran parallel for many years; she was almost my age. I was 21 when it began. We didn't realise we loved each other. More than eight years went by . . . I sensed at the time that if I ever did get married, it could only be to a much younger girl, but I thought that impossible, both then and thereafter. Being totally committed to my work for the Church in the ensuing years, I thought it not only inevitable but right that I should forgo marriage altogether.[80]

An important side-benefit of Dietrich's relationship with Elizabeth is the survival of several of his sermon manuscripts from the months of his London pastorate, in 1933–5. He had sent copies to her and, fortunately, she had kept them. He also sent a number of letters to her, almost all of which she eventually discarded. One, however, from Finkenwalde dated 1 January 1936, which she did retain, offers us a glimpse of a significant milestone in Bonhoeffer's life story:

> I plunged into work in a very unChristian way. An . . . ambition that many noticed in me made my life difficult . . . Then something happened, something that has changed and transformed my life to the present day. For the first time I discovered the Bible . . . I had often preached, I had seen a great deal of the Church, and talked and preached about it – but I had not yet become a Christian . . . Since then everything has changed.[81]

It was in Finkenwalde, however, that Dietrich first met his future fiancée, Maria von Wedemeyer, the granddaughter of Ruth von Kleist-Retzow. The latter was a strong supporter of the Confessing Church and seminary, and an informed conversation-partner of Dietrich's, indeed a 'matriarch of conspiracy'.[82] Numerous times in the late 1930s Dietrich visited the von Kleist home, primarily at holiday times. It was there that he completed his manuscript of *The Cost of Discipleship* in 1937, and later, worked on his *Ethics*. It was there, too, that he filled a pastoral role, particularly after Maria's father had been killed at Stalingrad, and, a few months later, her brother, Max von Wedemeyer. Right up to 1942, Dietrich was addressed as 'Pastor Bonhoeffer'.

Love blossomed that same year, even though Maria was just eighteen and Dietrich was already over thirty, and despite the fact that Maria's mother had firm reservations about the wisdom of travelling further on the road to matrimony. However, 13 January 1943 was the day of their engagement, as Maria's warm-hearted letter carried her answer: 'With all my happy heart, I can now say yes.' [83] The salutation of this monumental letter was still 'Dear Pastor Bonhoeffer'.

Just a few weeks later on 5 April, Dietrich was arrested and imprisoned at Tegel; Maria and he were never to consummate their marriage, but in spite of that, their mutual correspondence and the several visits Maria made to the prison deepened and matured their loving relationship. Bonhoeffer's own letters from prison disclose more clearly than ever before the tender, intimate, caring and loving side of his person. His letter of 11 March 1944 from Tegel is illustrative:

> My dear, dear Maria, It's no use, I have to write to you at last and talk to you with no one else listening. I have to let you see into my heart without someone else, whom it doesn't concern, looking on. I have to talk to you about that which belongs to no one else in the world but us, and which becomes desecrated when exposed to the hearing of an outsider. I refuse to let anyone else share what belongs to you alone; I think that would be impermissible, unwholesome, uninhibited, and devoid of dignity, from your point of view. The thing that draws and binds me to you in my unspoken thoughts and dreams cannot be revealed, dearest Maria, until I'm able to fold you in my arms. That time will come, and it will be all the more blissful and genuine the less we seek to anticipate it and the more faithfully and genuinely we wait for each other.[84]

In October 1944 Dietrich was transferred to the Gestapo prison in Prinz-Albrecht-Strasse, Berlin, and, in February 1945, to the Buchenwald concentration camp. In spite of Maria's desperate, determined efforts to locate his whereabouts, they had no further contact with each other. She did not hear of his martyrdom until several months afterwards, during the summer of 1945.

PRISONER AND MARTYR

For the final two years of his life Bonhoeffer was a prisoner of the Third Reich, confined for the first eighteen months to Berlin's Tegel military prison. His 'home' during this time of incarceration was a cell room, six by nine feet, characterised by the simplest and humblest accommodation – a hard, narrow bed, a shelf, a stool, a bucket and a skylight window. This scarcely promised to be a setting in which some of the most creative theological thinking of the twentieth century could be born. It did, however, become precisely that as the months of confinement passed.

From April 1943 to August 1944 correspondence from cell 92 managed to reach the hands of Dietrich's parents, as well as Maria, and Eberhard Bethge. Most of these letters were addressed to Bethge, and are among 'the most inspiring of the Bonhoeffer theological legacy'. [85] It is only recently that the dramatic story of how the prison letters, especially those written to Bethge, survived the maniacal Nazi era has finally come to light. Fortunately, one of the guards, Corporal Knobloch, proved to be willing to smuggle letters out of Tegel Prison. When Bethge, then in the German army, was able to return to Berlin, he took them with him, and buried most in gas-mask containers in the Schleichers' garden. 'We actually found them again after the war – not something to be taken for granted, for many similar caches were not found again, or if they were found, they had already been plundered by others.' [86]

Bonhoeffer's own intellectual life while he was in prison was steadily stimulated by books that were brought by his parents, many upon his request. A few examples illustrate the breadth of his selection: Karl August von Hase, *Ideals and Errors*; Martin Heidegger, *Phenomenology of Time-Consciousness*; Adalbert Stifter, *Thoughts and Reflections*; W. Dilthey, *Experience and Poetry*; N. Hartmann, *Systematic Philosophy*; Paul De Kruif, *The Microbe Hunters*; Delbrück, *World History*; R. Benz, *German Music*; Wolf Dietrich Rasch, *Lesebuch der Erzähler*; *Don Quixote*; Gotthelf, *Berner Geist*; W. H. Riehl, *Stories from Olden Times*; Karl Barth, *The Doctrine of God*. Not only were the daylight hours opportunities for reading diversely, but they were also the occasions for continuing reading of the Bible; for writing poems, a novel and a play; and for profound self-searching, deep reflection and productive theologising.

After eighteen months in Tegel Prison, Dietrich was transferred in October 1944 to the Gestapo prison at Prinz-Albrecht-Strasse. By then the Gestapo, after relentless pursuit, had discovered secret papers and documents of the *Abwehr* in Zossen. The evidence was damning enough to incriminate key figures in the resistance and conspiracy, including Bonhoeffer and Hans von Dohnanyi. Other members of the Bonhoeffer family circle were arrested and imprisoned, including Klaus Bonhoeffer, Rüdiger Schleicher and, eventually, Eberhard Bethge.

From February until April 1945, Bonhoeffer was an inmate of the concentration camp at Buchenwald. From that hellhole of Nazi brutality the major resource of reporting on Bonhoeffer is *The Venlo Incident*, written subsequently by Captain Payne Best, an officer of the British Secret Service who had been captured by the Gestapo in 1939. His thumbnail sketch of Prisoner Bonhoeffer was laudatory: He 'always seemed to diffuse an atmosphere of happiness, of joy in every smallest event in life, and a deep gratitude for the mere fact that he was alive . . . He was one of the very few men I have ever met to whom his God was real and ever close to him.' [87]

Payne Best and Dietrich Bonhoeffer, as 'special prisoners', were among those loaded on 3 April 1945 into a prison van, heading for still another destination, the extermination camp at Flossenbürg. Just outside the city of Regensburg the van broke down, and the prisoners were transferred to a bus at the little Bavarian village of Schönberg. In the schoolhouse where the small coterie of prisoners were detained, Bonhoeffer was asked to conduct a prayer service on their behalf. It was Low Sunday in the church calendar, 8 April 1945, and Bonhoeffer, pastor to the end, meditated briefly on two of the pericope texts for the day, Isaiah 33:5 ('By his wounds we are healed') and I Peter 2:3ff. ('Blessed be the God and Father of our Lord Jesus Christ! By his great mercy he has given us a new birth into a living hope through the resurrection of Jesus Christ from the dead . . . '). It was to his prison friend, Payne Best, that Bonhoeffer spoke his final recorded words, to be relayed eventually to his ecumenical friend, Bishop Bell of Chichester: 'Tell him . . . with him I believe in the principle of our universal Christian brotherhood which rises above all national interests, and that our victory is certain – tell him, too, that I have never forgotten his words at our last meeting.' [88]

The final destination on the road to martyrdom was another of the Nazis' infamous concentration camps, Flossenbürg. That night there was a brief trial in the camp laundry-house by an SS court. A verdict of high treason was pronounced on the co-partners of the resistance present: Wilhelm Canaris, Hans Oster, Karl Sack, Ludwig Gehre, Theodor Strunck, Friedrich von Rabenau and Dietrich Bonhoeffer. A stark sentence in Bethge's classic and authentic biography of Bonhoeffer encapsulates the final moment in the martyr's earthly pilgrimage: 'In Flossenbürg the execution took place in the grey dawn of Monday' (9 April 1945).[89]

Nearly thirteen years before this ignominious end to his life, Bonhoeffer had said in a sermon preached at the Kaiser Wilhelm Memorial Church in Berlin, 19 June 1932:

> We must not be surprised if once again times return for our Church when the blood of martyrs will be required. But even if we have the courage and faith to spill it, this blood will not be as innocent or as clear as that of the first martyrs. Much of our own guilt will lie in our blood. The guilt of the useless servant who is thrown into the darkness. [90]

The debate about whether or not Dietrich Bonhoeffer stands in the long procession of Christian martyrs since the Age of the Apostles or if he should be primarily counted among the political conspirators against tyranny will probably continue well into the next century. Pertinent in consideration of this issue are the words of Bonhoeffer's brother-in-law, Gerhard Leibholz, whose impact on his wife's twin brother is still being studied:

> Bonhoeffer's life and death belong to the annals of Christian martyrdom . . . His life and death have given us great hope for the future. He has set a model for a new type of true leadership inspired by the gospel, daily ready for martyrdom and death and imbued by a new spirit of Christian humanism and a creative sense of civic duty. The victory which he has won was a victory for us all, a conquest never to be undone, of love, light, and liberty. [91]

Notes

1 R. Niebuhr, 'The Death of a Martyr', *Christianity and Crisis*, 25 (June 1945), 6.

2 ibid., 7.

3 See C. Green, *The Sociality of Christ and Humanity: Dietrich Bonhoeffer's Early Theology, 1927–1933* (Missoula: Scholars Press, 1975) for a well-argued perspective on the interrelation of theology and autobiography in Bonhoeffer.

4 Out of print for several years, the title is being republished by Fortress Press in an unabridged edition. The detailed account of the family heritage which appeared in the original German edition, E. Bethge, *Dietrich Bonhoeffer: Theologe, Christ, Zeitgenosse* (Munich: Chr. Kaiser Verlag, 1967), is being restored, as well as other segments which were unfortunately excluded from the initial English-language edition.

5 For additional biographies of Dietrich Bonhoeffer see the bibliography.

6 E. Bethge, *Dietrich Bonhoeffer: Theologe, Christ, Zeitgenosse*, p. 4.

7 In the church of St Michael in Schwäbisch-Hall, one can still see a prominent plaque which indicates that Johann Friedrich Bonhoeffer was a pastor of the congregation (d. 1783).

8 A detailed account of Bonhoeffer's ancestral heritage can be found in the

original German Bethge biography, *Dietrich Bonhoeffer: Theologe, Christ, Zeitgenosse.*

9 Sabine Leibholz-Bonhoeffer is the only one of the eight siblings still living. Over ninety years of age, she resides with her older daughter, Marianne, in Göttingen, Germany.

10 A detailed description of each member of the family, including the parents, can be found in S. Leibholz-Bonhoeffer, *The Bonhoeffers: Portrait of a Family* (Chicago: Covenant Publications, 1994). The volume was originally published by Johannes Kiefel Verlag, Wuppertal-Barmen, Germany, 1968. The first English edition was published in 1971 by Sidgwick & Jackson, London.

11 A description given by Dietrich Bonhoeffer's niece, Renate Bethge, 'Bonhoeffer's Family and its Significance for his Theology', in L. Rasmussen, *Dietrich Bonhoeffer: His Significance for North Americans* (Minneapolis: Fortress Press, 1990), p. 16. Bethge uses the terms 'empiricism, rationality, and liberalism' to depict the spirit of the parents' home, but especially relates them to the father.

12 Sabine Leibholz-Bonhoeffer, 'Childhood and Home', in *I Knew Dietrich Bonhoeffer: Reminiscences by his Friends*, ed. W. Zimmermann and R. G. Smith (New York: Harper and Row, 1973), p. 21.

13 R. Bethge, 'Bonhoeffer and the Role of Women', *Church and Society* (July/August 1995), 35.

14 E. Bethge, *Dietrich Bonhoeffer: Theologe, Christ, Zeitgenosse*, p. 7.

15 Bonhoeffer's sister, Sabine, offers an idyllic description of the enjoyable days at Friedrichsbrunn the children shared, 'Childhood and Home', in Zimmermann and Smith, *I Knew Dietrich Bonhoeffer*, pp. 25–7.

16 D. Bonhoeffer, *Letters and Papers from Prison: The Enlarged Edition* (New York: Macmillan, 1972), pp. 40, 73, 88, 117, 206, 211.

17 E. Bethge, *Dietrich Bonhoeffer: Theologe, Christ, Zeitgenosse*, p. 16.

18 ibid.

19 ibid., p. 22.

20 R. Bethge, 'Bonhoeffer and the Role of Women', 36.

21 ibid., p. 36.

22 D. Bonhoeffer, *Fiction from Prison: Gathering up the Past*, ed. E. Bethge and R. Bethge (Philadelphia: Fortress Press, 1981), p. 141.

23 T. I. Day, *Dietrich Bonhoeffer on Christian Community and Common Sense*, Toronto Studies in Theology, vol. 11 (New York: Edwin Mellen Press, 1982), p. 2.

24 E. Bethge, *Friendship and Resistance: Essays on Dietrich Bonhoeffer* (Geneva: WCC, 1995), pp. 72–9.

25 (Berlin: Board of the Bonhoeffer House, 1996); English translation by James Patrick Kelley.

26 In L. Rasmussen, *Dietrich Bonhoeffer: His Significance for North Americans*, (Minneapolis: Fortress Press, 1990), pp. 1–30.

27 See Eberhard Bethge's essay, 'The Nonreligious Scientist and the Confessing Theologian: The Influence of Karl-Friedrich Bonhoeffer on his Younger Brother Dietrich', in *Bonhoeffer for a New Day: Theology in a Time of Transition*, ed. J. de Gruchy (Grand Rapids: Eerdmans, 1997).

28 E. Bethge, *Dietrich Bonhoeffer: Theologe, Christ, Zeitgenosse*, pp. 13–14.

29 ibid., p. 30.

30 D. Bonhoeffer, *Jugend und Studium. 1918–1927, Dietrich Bonhoeffer Werke*, vol. IX (Munich: Chr. Kaiser Verlag, 1986), pp. 81–112.

31 Quoted in E. Bethge, R. Bethge and C. Gremmels, *Dietrich Bonhoeffer: A Life in Pictures* (Philadelphia: Fortress Press, 1986), p. 55.

32 ibid., p. 44.

33 'Report on a Period of Study at the Union Theological Seminary in New York, 1930–31', in D. Bonhoeffer, *No Rusty Swords: Letters, Lectures and Notes, 1928–1936, Collected Works of Dietrich Bonhoeffer*, vol. I (New York: Harper & Row, 1965), p. 91.

34 Unfortunately, Niebuhr did not save most of the letters which had been written to him by Bonhoeffer in the 1930s. Personal conversation, Ursula Niebuhr and F. Burton Nelson, in March 1983.

35 E. Bethge, *Dietrich Bonhoeffer: Theologe, Christ, Zeitgenosse*, p. 112.

36 For a more detailed account of this singular friendship, see F. B. Nelson, 'The Relationship of Jean Lasserre to Dietrich Bonhoeffer's Peace Concerns in the Struggle of Church and Culture', *Union Seminary Quarterly Review*, 40 (1–2) (1986), 71–84.

37 G. Kelly and F. B. Nelson, *A Testament to Freedom: The Essential Writings of Dietrich Bonhoeffer* (New York: Harper Collins, 1990), p. 11.

38 E. Bethge, *Dietrich Bonhoeffer: Theologe, Christ, Zeitgenosse*, p. 109.

39 Zimmermann and Smith, *I Knew Dietrich Bonhoeffer*, pp. 64–5.

40 ibid., p. 60.

41 ibid., p. 62.

42 E. Bethge, *Dietrich Bonhoeffer: Theologe, Christ, Zeitgenosse*, p. 158.

43 ibid.

44 Kelly and Nelson, *A Testament to Freedom*, p. 111.

45 ibid., p. 380.

46 E. Bethge, *Dietrich Bonhoeffer: Theologe, Christ, Zeitgenosse*, p. 79.

47 Cited in E. Bethge, R. Bethge and C. Gremmels, *Dietrich Bonhoeffer: A Life in Pictures*, p. 69.

48 ibid., p. 76.

49 Kelly and Nelson, *A Testament to Freedom*, pp. 384–5.

50 E. Bethge, *Dietrich Bonhoeffer: Theologe, Christ, Zeitgenosse*, pp. 174–5.

51 E. Bethge, *Dietrich Bonhoeffer: Theologian, Christian, Contemporary* (London: Collins, 1970), pp. 231–4.

52 Both of the church buildings were struck in bombing raids during the Luftwaffe's attack on London during the war. Eventually, a new church edifice, the Dietrich Bonhoeffer Kirche, was rebuilt on the same location in Forest Hill. The congregation still meets for worship there, but only a few members from both churches still personally remember the pastoral ministry of Bonhoeffer.

53 D. Bonhoeffer, *No Rusty Swords: Letters, Lectures and Notes, 1928–1936, Collected Works of Dietrich Bonhoeffer, vol. I* (London: Collins, 1977), p. 235.

54 E. Bethge, *Dietrich Bonhoeffer: Theologe, Christ, Zeitgenosse*, p. 262.

55 For a more detailed account of this theme, see F. B. Nelson, 'Pastor Bonhoeffer', *Christian History*, 4 (32) (1992), 38–9.

56 D. Bonhoeffer, *Ökumene: Briefe Aufsätze Dokumente 1928–1942, Gesammelte Schriften*, vol. 1 (Munich: Chr. Kaiser Verlag, 1958), p. 184.

57 The full text of Bishop Bell's appeal appears in the official minutes of the Fanö, Denmark meeting, Universal Christian Council for Life and Work, Fanö, Denmark, 1934, pp. 65–6.

58 For a more precise account of Bonhoeffer's role at the Fanö ecumenical conference, see F. B. Nelson, 'The Holocaust and the Oikoumene: An Episode for Remembrance', in *Faith and Freedom*, ed. R. Libowitz (Oxford: Pergamon Press, 1987), pp. 71–81.

59 Kelly and Nelson, *A Testament to Freedom*, p. 229.

60 Otto Dudzus in Zimmerman and Smith, *I Knew Dietrich Bonhoeffer*, p. 85.

61 Correspondence from Jean Lasserre to F. Burton Nelson, 4 October 1976.

62 G. Kelly and F. B. Nelson, *A Testament to Freedom*, p. 140.

63 For assessment of this impact, see W. A. Visser't Hooft, 'Dietrich Bonhoeffer and the self-understanding of the Ecumenical Movement', *The Ecumenical Review*, 28(2), April (1976), 198–203. See also Konrad Raiser, in de Guchy, *Bonhoeffer for a New Day*, pp. 319–39.

64 Kelly and Nelson, *A Testament to Freedom*, p. 132.

65 Cited in Eberhard Bethge, in *Ethical Responsibility: Bonhoeffer's Legacy to the Churches*, ed. J. D. Godsey and G. B. Kelly (New York: Edwin Mellen Press, 1981), p. 63.

66 E. Bethge, *Dietrich Bonhoeffer: Theologe, Christ, Zeitgenosse* (Munich: Chr. Kaiser Verlag, 1967), p. 336.

67 Volume v of the *Dietrich Bonhoeffer Works, Life Together; The Prayerbook of the Bible* (Minneapolis: Fortress Press, 1996). 'The Editor's Introduction to the English Edition' by Geffrey B. Kelley gives a perceptive contextual setting for two of Bonhoeffer's most widely read writings, *Life Together* and *Prayerbook*.

68 D. Bonhoeffer, *The Cost of Discipleship* (New York: Macmillan, 1960), p. 60.

69 This 'Guertner Diary' kept over a five-year period by Hans von Dohnanyi is on microfilm in the Washington National Archives. The documents were used by the prosecution in the Nuremberg War Crimes Trials after the Second World War. See E. Bethge, *Dietrich Bonhoeffer: Theologian, Christian, Contemporary*, p. 528.

70 E. Bethge, *Dietrich Bonhoeffer: Theologe, Christ, Zeitgenosse*, p. 497.

71 A recent booklet describes Bonhoeffer's life story from Finkenwalde, eastwards to Köslin and Schlawe, then southwards to the landed estates of the von Kleists and the von Wedemeyers. See J. Pejsa, *To Pomerania in Search of Dietrich Bonhoeffer* (Minneapolis: Kenwood Publishing, 1995). For another recent 'snapshot' of the Finkenwalde community, see E. Gordon, *And I Will Walk at Liberty: An Eye-Witness Account of the Church Struggle in Germany* (Suffolk: Morrow & Co., 1997). Ernest Gordon, Jewish in ancestry, visited Bonhoeffer in Finkenwalde and committed him to the care of Bishop Bell in England. He served as a priest in the Church of England until his death in 1991.

72 The emotional and dramatic account of the Leibholz journey to freedom is told in detail in S. Leibholz-Bonhoeffer, *The Bonhoeffers: Portrait of a Family*, (Chicago: Covenant Publications, 1994).

73 E. Bethge, *Dietrich Bonhoeffer: Theologe, Christ, Zeitgenosse*, p. 501.

74 ibid., p. 559.

75 Leibholz-Bonhoeffer, *The Bonhoeffers*, p. 111.

76 ibid., p. 112.

77 Title of volume III of the letters, lectures and notes of Bonhoeffer, 1939–45. Ed. Edwin H. Robertson (New York: Harper & Row, 1973). The subtitle describes Bonhoeffer's persistent dilemma: 'One man's struggle between individual conscience and loyalty to his country'.

78 For a detailed account of Bonhoeffer's secret mission to meet Bishop Bell in Sweden, see F. Burton Nelson, 'Bonhoeffer at Sigtuna, 1942: A Case Study in the Ecumenical Church Struggle', in Godsey and Kelly, *Ethical Responsibility*, pp. 131–42.

79 Kelly and Nelson, *A Testament to Freedom*, p. 354.

80 D. Bonhoeffer and M. von Wedemeyer, *Love Letters from Cell 92: The Correspondence Between Dietrich Bonhoeffer and Maria von Wedemeyer*, ed. R. von Bismarck and U. Kabitz (Nashville: Abingdon Press, 1994), p. 246. The publication of this correspondence illumines the bond of love between Dietrich and Maria, but also, as Eberhard Bethge phrases it: 'We can now, step by step, trace the course of Dietrich's life in Tegel Prison far more completely and in much greater depth' (p. 365).

81 'Letter to a Woman to whom Bonhoeffer had been Engaged', in Kelly and Nelson, *A Testament to Freedom*, p. 424.

82 Title of a volume by Jane Pejsa (Minneapolis: Kenwood Publishing, 1991). The book is the most comprehensive coverage available of Ruth von Kleist, including details of the Dietrich–Maria connection.

83 Bonhoeffer and von Wedemeyer, *Love Letters from Cell 92*, p. 338.

84 ibid., p. 200.

85 Kelly and Nelson, *A Testament to Freedom*, p. 40.

86 'How the Prison Letters Survived', in E. Bethge, *Friendship and Resistance*, pp. 38–57.

87 P. S. Best, *The Venlo Incident* (London: Hutchinson, 1950), p. 200.

88 Kelly and Nelson, *A Testament to Freedom*, p. 44.

89 E. Bethge, *Dietrich Bonhoeffer: Theologe, Christ, Zeitgenosse*, p. 830.

90 Cited in E. Bethge, *Bonhoeffer: Exile and Martyr*, ed. John de Gruchy (London: Collins, 1975), p. 155.

91 'Memoir', in Bonhoeffer, *Cost of Discipleship*, p. 35.

3 The formation of Bonhoeffer's theology

MARTIN RUMSCHEIDT

Theology entered the Bonhoeffer household, embedded as it was in the culture of the German aristocracy, through Paula von Hase, Dietrich's mother. Her mother, a countess, had been a pupil of Franz Liszt and Klara Schumann. This undoubtedly found its way into the artistry Dietrich Bonhoeffer displayed in his piano playing. Paula von Hase's maternal grandfather, the painter Count von Kalckreuth, founded and directed the Academy of Fine Arts in Weimar. Her father, son of a professor of church history and historical theology, was a professor of practical theology. A distinctly political and somewhat 'anti-aristocratic' spirit entered into this tradition when Paula von Hase married Karl Bonhoeffer. The democratic republicanism, socialism and patriotism of the German Student Association, founded in 1815, were anticipated by the forebears of Dietrich's father. They had drawn the rulers' wrath and exacted the price of personal suffering of several of Dietrich's ancestors. Eberhard Bethge sums up this legacy and its significance for the young Bonhoeffer in these words:

> The rich world of his forebears gave Dietrich Bonhoeffer the standards
> for his own life. He owed it an assurance of judgement and bearing
> that cannot be acquired in a single generation. He grew up in a family
> that did not look to the school for what makes for real education but to
> the deeply rooted obligation to be guardian of a great historical legacy
> and intellectual tradition. To Dietrich Bonhoeffer this meant learning
> to understand and respect what others before him had thought and
> done. But it could also constrain him so to determine his actions that,
> in essence, they were in conflict with his forebears but precisely in
> that contradiction paid them respect.[1]

Bonhoeffer spent nearly all of his 'formative years' in Berlin, the city he genuinely loved. His family moved there from his native city Wrocław (Breslau) when he was six years old; four years later, they settled in a part of

Berlin that was home to many of the academic community. Among the neighbours were the families of the physicist Max Planck and the historians Adolf von Harnack and Hans Dellbrück. For many years, on Wednesday evenings, a number of intellectuals gathered in Dellbrück's home for discussion. 'Even though the Bonhoeffer children had no occasion as yet to attend the Wednesday-Circle, its atmosphere and outlook left their mark on them.'[2]

But Berlin made more than an intellectual impact on Bonhoeffer. Especially during the First World War, industry grew rapidly in the city, accompanied by the all too familiar social problems associated with such growth. This was the Berlin that changed from imperial to republican to National Socialist within fifteen years; it was the liberal and ecclesiastical, the conservative and cosmopolitan Berlin that experienced revolution and street fighting. In this Berlin Bonhoeffer experienced the First World War, the deaths of a brother and cousins at the front.

That Berlin's artistic life, its music, theatre and painting, surrounded Bonhoeffer cannot be overlooked. Its nineteenth-century literature also held a special place in his imagination. What seems not to have touched him until it came under attack by National-Socialist Germany was the vibrant Jewish life of Berlin and its illustrious tradition. 'He listened with surprise when his fellow-student Helmut Rössler recited to him poems by Franz Werfel; he had not heard them before. Like other theologians of those years, Bonhoeffer had no contact with the great Jewish thinkers, such as Rosenzweig, Buber, and Baeck.'[3]

Bonhoeffer's theological development was greatly influenced by forces and factors beyond the narrow confines of the theological academy. These have been dealt with in the previous chapter and need not be repeated here. Our focus in this chapter is more specifically on the academy and, more broadly, the intellectual milieu within which Bonhoeffer's theological development was shaped. Every important change (*Wende*) in Bonhoeffer's thought and career in this respect occurred in the milieu of Berlin, but that is not where his formal theological education began. So let us now turn to his first year (1923/4) of theological study at the University of Tübingen before returning to Berlin, where he completed his studies and obtained his doctorate.

BONHOEFFER'S THEOLOGICAL TEACHERS

Bonhoeffer began his study of theology without the experience of a church-focused practice of the Christian faith. He knew the Christianity of

German culture, the music, poetry, literature and hymnody of the upper classes. It had strong personal dimensions in his father's reading of specific passages of Scripture on festive occasions and his mother's singing hymns with the children and telling them Bible stories. When Bonhoeffer began to study theology, faith was a component of the historical legacy and intellectual tradition to be guarded; it was only later that faith became a matter of discipleship. His study of theology was motivated by his existential concern to meet the scepticism of the 'cultured despisers of Christianity'. The question of epistemology absorbed his energy; theology was to be studied as a science, for therein lay its meaning for the young student in 1924.

Enrolled in the University of Tübingen, Bonhoeffer was drawn to Adolf Schlatter (1852–1938), the seventy-one-year-old Swiss Reformed-Church professor of New Testament studies. Rather than writing lectures with a view to future publication, Schlatter wrote them as a direct address to his students; they and not his colleagues in the discipline were his primary conversation-partners. Rigorously applying scholarly methods to the biblical texts, he aimed to integrate what was then referred to as 'the natural' and what the New Testament speaks of as 'the good'. Schlatter provided a perspective on 'the world' which later sustained Bonhoeffer's theology of the world.[4] Schlatter also conveyed a sense of the 'authority' of Scripture which diverged significantly from the prevailing liberal-Protestant view of the Bible as a 'source-book for religious ideas' to be found not *in* but *behind* the text.

Many denigrated as 'naïve biblicism' Schlatter's firm sense that in all decisions in matters of faith and church he was accountable to the Bible alone. Yet if that is naïveté, one must recognise it also in Bonhoeffer's later life, where it appears at the heart of the faith that results from having been captivated and convinced by the word of Jesus. Although Bonhoeffer learnt this understanding of faith from Martin Luther, it was this Reformed professor of New Testament who implanted it in the young student to the extent that it became an essential part of Bonhoeffer's epistemology and, finally, of his whole theological existence. Indeed, it was Schlatter's approach to the Scriptures which helped Bonhoeffer understand Barth more readily than many of Barth's critics within liberal theology and which, in the end, shaped Bonhoeffer's critique of Bultmann's programme of 'demythologisation'[5] in his prison letters.

Karl Heim (1874–1958) taught systematic theology, Bonhoeffer's preferred subject. Heim had a growing reputation for engaging the natural sciences, not least the quantum physics of Max Planck, as a serious interlocutor of Christianity. The intent was apologetic: a Christian epistemology was needed that could meet the challenges of the sceptic and the dejection of the faint-hearted. In this endeavour Heim continued the work of nineteenth-century liberal Protestant theology and its three most prominent protagonists, Friedrich Schleiermacher, Albrecht Ritschl and Adolf von Harnack.

Heim had just published an important study on the certainty of faith, so it was no surprise that Bonhoeffer found his way to his lectures. A child of Swabian Pietism and erstwhile secretary of the German Student Christian Movement, Heim made it his goal to combine the proclamation of Jesus Christ as Lord of all reality and the necessity to confront modern thinking with the experience of God's grace. The hermeneutical foundation on which he built was the vision of an original oneness of believing and thinking beyond the modern distinction between reality and consciousness, matter and spirit.

After an intensive two-month sojourn in Rome, and still deeply preoccupied with epistemology, Bonhoeffer registered at the University of Berlin in June 1924. He continued there until July 1927, when he completed his doctoral dissertation. Bethge sums up those student years:

> what really attracted him was theological Berlin . . . When he first
> went to Berlin University his turbulent thirst for knowledge was still
> lacking in direction. The broad front of the Berlin liberal and
> 'positivist' school of theology, embodied in its great teachers, opened
> out before him.

It was also in Berlin, as Bethge goes on to say, that 'the decisive turning-point for his future direction came . . . when, by way of a literary detour, dialectical theology took hold of him'.[6] This comment refers, of course, to the decisive impact which Karl Barth's theological revolution had upon Bonhoeffer's theological development. But before we can consider the influence of Barth on the young Bonhoeffer, we must first give our attention to his Berlin teachers.

The most distinguished member of the Berlin faculty was undoubtedly Adolf von Harnack (1851–1930), and in the judgement of one of his interpreters, Bonhoeffer was Adolf von Harnack's 'most genuine pupil'.[7] The unique personal links between the two suggest that this may well be an appropriate assessment. Carl Jürgen Kaltenborn cites an entry from Harnack's diary which indicates that Bonhoeffer's parents were members of the von Harnacks' 'neighbourhood circle' just before their son entered the University of Berlin.[8] The younger Bonhoeffer children were also part of the group of youngsters to whom Harnack read stories.[9] At university, Bonhoeffer belonged to the group of students whom Harnack personally selected to work with him in his church history seminars after his retirement in 1923. Often the two walked together to the train-station on their way to the university. Bonhoeffer clearly had great respect for his teacher. At the close of their three semesters together, Bonhoeffer wrote to Harnack: 'What I have learned and come to understand in your seminar is too closely associated with my whole person for me to be able ever to forget it.'[10]

The work of Adolf von Harnack is characterised as 'liberal theology at its height'.[11] The term 'liberal' must not be read in its polemic sense, as used by critics, but as used by its defenders. It was a theology under the imperative of freedom: freedom of thought and the pursuit of truth on every path it took, freedom from interference by those to whom authority has been given. It was the imperative that conscience develop itself as freely and fully as possible while attaining to and maintaining full responsibility. The 'liberal' position exhibited confidence in the human spirit, reverence for the dignity, competence and authority of the power of thinking, and trust in the ability of human beings to transcend their subjectivity in the endeavour to reach true objectivity.

Liberal theology, as a scholarly discipline, and liberal faith, as a faith that knows, are modern in that they affirm an article of the Enlightenment's creed that the dignity of human beings resides in their ability to comprehend, that is to lay hold of reality. Such 'grasping' is methodical, so that the faith which knows not only knows God and the reality God created, but also knows *how* it knows them. The Enlightenment may, in one of its dimensions, be called 'the age of methodology'. It is the Cartesian heritage of Liberal Protestantism that the *noetic ratio* of the mind's comprehension is univocally expressive of the *ontic ratio* of what is being comprehended.

In theological terminology, liberal theology assumes the existence of a perfectly symmetrical relation between faith and what faith claims to be its subject or object. In the method of liberal theology, the distance between the knower and the known – it was axiomatic that faith was a matter of knowledge – is reduced to the extent that what is known cannot be a limit on the knower. Thus, the knower or believer is radically free from *and* for reality. The imperative of freedom establishes its own commandments, which constrain the knower to methodological objectivity and ethical responsibility and to placing everything before the judgement of reason, the final arbiter.

Harnack represented the laudable and critical aspects of this liberalism: an incorruptible reasonableness in the rigours of his methodical approach, an unflagging confidence in the authority and ability of thought. He also showed an unshakeable religious faith. Yet, the focus of his work is not the Christian faith *qua* faith, but as an expression of what has been hailed since the Enlightenment as a basic human 'faculty': religion. The *theologian* focused on the meaning of faith-expressions, the *historian* on how this meaning arose and developed. As a *historical theologian*, he studied the adequacy of diverse faith-expressions in relation to the 'essence' of the Christian religion. This combination expressed the character of late-nineteenth- and early-twentieth-century scholarship, namely the close tie between religion and culture, between Christianity and *Bildung*, the formation of the human character. The *relation* of the human being of modernity and her/his world predominates over faith itself; it is *method* that finally legitimates the theological endeavour rather than its subject. Liberal theology wanted to become a theology of the church, a church, however, which had also chosen to be a church in relation to modernity. The primary addressee was the cultured individual of modern times who sought, in freedom from any strictures which associating with the institutional church was believed to bring, to be religious and cultured, a person of reason *and* faith.[12]

Harnack was, in fact, the architect of a method that served the Liberal Protestant vision of the indissoluble synthesis of religion and cultural/intellectual/spiritual formation. As he had already stated in 1888:

> I am convinced that we shall not be led into a healthy progress and into an increasingly purer knowledge of what is original and valuable by exegesis and dogmatics alone but by a better comprehension of history. Not exegesis and dogmatics, but the results of church-historical research and their acceptance generally will break the chains of burdensome and confusing traditions . . . We are confident that with this method we shall not demolish but build up.[13]

Still, the switch from exegesis and dogmatics to the study of history 'did not signify a change in substance but in the manner in which it was approached'.[14] However Bonhoeffer viewed the epistemological concern of Harnack's work, what left a permanent mark on him was the positive character his teacher assigned to the world. In this, as well as in the rigours of scholarship, Harnack was Dietrich Bonhoeffer's eminent teacher, even though the latter went his own way in both method and interpretation.

The year 1917 was the beginning of the 'Luther Renaissance', a phenomenon that fascinated church and academy for years. It was the 400th anniversary of Martin Luther nailing his ninety-five theses to the Castle Church door in Wittenburg, an event that symbolically inaugurated the Protestant Reformation. What set this interest in motion, however, was not the anniversary itself but the commemorative lecture by the Berlin church historian Karl Holl (1866–1926) on 'What Did Luther Understand by Religion?'[15] A few years later, in 1921, Holl published a collection of his essays on the German Reformer. This established him as one of the foremost interpreters of Luther at the time. His work helped displace the current nationalistic-liberal and bourgeois image of Luther and prepared for a more genuine understanding of the Reformer. At the same time, it had an important cultural-political effect. Because it gave the interpretation of Luther a different basis, the Reformation itself came to be seen from a perspective that, because it was more contextual, highlighted its German aspects. Luther's theology regained a dimension that was not derived solely from the intellectual and spiritual development of the West. Regarding Luther's work as an aspect of that development, Holl argued, prevents an engagement with the paradoxes of faith with which the young Luther had wrestled, and within which had grown the startling insights of faith that mark his work.

Holl had joined the faculty in Berlin and became Harnack's colleague in 1906. During the First World War he strongly supported the greatest possible expansion of German territory into the Baltic region, while Harnack opposed it as a provocation and an enormous threat to peace. Next to ancient church history, Holl was drawn to English and Russian church history, questions confronting German church-life at the time, and the Reformation. At the heart of his *theological* reflection was the understanding of God that he approached, in radical distinction from the idealistic-Liberal understanding, from the doctrine of justification. Luther's teaching of *simul iustus et peccator* (humans are at one and the same time justified and sinners) was interpreted by Holl as a paradoxical integration of the justice and love of God. This is experienced only in conscience by those who take the claim of the Law seriously, but who are also broken by it and find inner transformation through the promise of divine forgiveness.

Holl was among the first to rely extensively on Luther's early writings as sources of Reformation theology. His claim that Luther's doctrine of justification was already fully developed in his 1515/16 lectures on Romans[16] drew the attention of the scholarly world to the young Luther for several decades. Holl also persuasively opposed the psychologically framed image of Luther in Roman Catholicism (for example by Denifle and Grisar), as well as Troeltsch's interpretation of him as a phenomenon of the late Middle Ages. Holl presented Luther as someone relevant for today. Luther's famous slogan, *sola gratia, sola fide* (by grace and by faith alone), provides as viable a road to Christian existence today as it did in the sixteenth century. Holl combined this conviction with Luther's insistence that justification is God's gift and promise through the church, the visible, incomplete and broken community that lives in the here and now, awaiting and praying for its fulfilment. Holl thereby contributed to a growing perception of theology as a function of the church.

In his resistance to modern individualism Holl emphasised the dimensions of sociality in both dogmatics and ethics. Stressing that what Luther taught was a 'religion of conscience' rooted in the uniqueness of Jesus, Holl found a language which, defending the dignity of every human being, offered solace to a generation that had to live with defeat. Indeed, both in tone and in substance, Holl's Luther-essays spoke strongly to the generation shaken by the ravages of the First World War. And because he held firmly to the interlinking of religion and 'the moral' or 'conscience', Holl was also seen as representing continuity with the nineteenth century.

A number of scholars, including Dietrich Bonhoeffer, attacked Holl's position. Indeed, Luther's Christology and his claim that the assurance of faith rests solely on God's gracious act *extra nos sed pro nobis* (independently of but for us) gave Bonhoeffer a basis for repudiating the notion of 'religion of conscience'. To Bonhoeffer, Holl appeared to derive the assurance of faith from some aspect of conscience itself. This critique notwithstanding, Holl had posed a most challenging question, namely how is the question of the church that exists today to be raised on the basis of the truth taught by the Reformation? A theological movement which drew its strength from the language of the past could no more help here and now than in the sixteenth century. Luther had to turn deliberately to God's revelation alone, and one would need to do so again in order to address the question of the church today. Whatever Bonhoeffer's reservations, the influence of Holl on his theology is clear. In Bethge's words:

> So firmly did Holl implant the doctrine of the *sola gratia* as the *articulus stantis et cadentis ecclesiae* [the place on which the church stands or falls], that [Bonhoeffer] never lost it again. He convinced him that even the devout are not able really to love God. Henceforward, Luther's dictum of the *cor curvum in se* [the heart turned inward on itself] became a key word to him. He applied it again and again also to the domain of epistemology in order to refute the noetic optimism of Idealism and the localisation of God in the individual's consciousness.[17]

In Berlin, systematic theology was taught by Reinhold Seeberg (1859–1935), a theologian also associated with the 'rediscovery' of the young

Luther. Bonhoeffer participated in every seminar Seeberg offered between 1925 and 1927, and he also wrote his dissertation under his direction. From Seeberg he obtained an even deeper insight into nineteenth-century Protestant theology than he had in Tübingen; he also came to know Seeberg's third 'great model',[18] namely Hegel.

Hegel had spoken of the Lutheran Reformation and its approach to the world as an all-transforming light that had shown more clearly the nature of God's reconciliation with the world. The history of the world is the history of God and of God's reconciliation. The Absolute Spirit, Eternal Reason, unfolds itself in the world as the will of God. Religion is the penultimate stage of ultimate knowledge, the possibility fully to know God. Hegel therefore spoke of the history of the development of religious consciousness as an ascending and progressing series of divine revelations, the highest and ultimate of which is Christianity in its radiant manifestation in the Reformation. He and his followers could identify God's revelation concretely, in the world; one need no longer discern the reality of the Divine solely in the domain of consciousness.[19]

There was one concept in particular that Bonhoeffer took from Hegel's vocabulary: 'Christ existing in community'. In this term he brought together the Lutheran *extra nos*, the positive valuation of the world that he found in Harnack and Seeberg and, perhaps most importantly, the impact of the 'discovery of the church' during his visit to Rome. The concept of the church he was 'beginning to understand' was that of the church as *Gemeinde*, community or congregation. Still moved by epistemological concerns, he now asked how the church is to be located theologically in the search for knowledge of God and the self.

Studying Hegel's *Introduction to the History of Philosophy*, Bonhoeffer read that to deny Christ's presence in his community in a real, genuine manner was *the* sin against the Holy Spirit. Seeberg had commented on that assertion in his 1924 *Dogmatics*: as the *logos* became flesh in Jesus, so the Holy Spirit becomes flesh in the community of Jesus Christ.[20] Seeberg spoke of Jesus as the inaugurator of a new humanity, the identification of Jesus and the community of the church. Here is Hegel's dialectic of the unfolding of the Holy Spirit, the *logos* in the world. Christ, the incarnate *logos*, is truly present and in a real manner in his community and, therefore, in the world, hence 'Christ existing as community'. This insight permitted Bonhoeffer to integrate sociality into epistemology. From an initially epistemological category, sociality eventually developed into a central theological one for Bonhoeffer.

As he began to work in Seeberg's seminars with Luther's doctrine of justification by faith alone and the conviction it expressed, that even the most devout cannot find God, Bonhoeffer recognised that seeking to establish one's identity on one's own inevitably leads to an exaggeration of the self and to a concomitant prison-like solitude. This led Bonhoeffer to Christology. Luther's emphasis on the crucially important dimension of the *extra nos et pro nobis* meant that reconciliation is for us, but also outside or beyond us, in the person and work of Christ. Reconciliation, Bonhoeffer claimed, frees us from the solipsistic solitude of the exaggerated self that results from the attempt to derive identity through focusing on the consciousness of the self. With Luther, Bonhoeffer spoke here of the *cor curvum in se*, discovered in Seeberg's seminars. The *extra nos et pro nobis* came to be integrated into the concept of sociality within a dialectic of 'the other'.[21]

Clearly Bonhoeffer's theological development was decisively shaped by the Luther he encountered during his Berlin years. This lasted right through to the end of his life. Indeed, the contribution of Bonhoeffer's teachers to the modern development of an autonomous culture, science, art and philosophy, is precisely what Bonhoeffer later referred to in prison as 'the world come of age'. So let us explore how he appropriated this legacy from his teachers further in relation to the debates of the day, and the challenge presented by Karl Barth and dialectical theology.

THE LEGACY OF MARTIN LUTHER

To appropriate the legacy of Luther means to take upon oneself an unfinished and unfinishable task with the same conscientiousness as Luther did. It also means to address what he gave his followers in his partial solutions. Albeit from diverse perspectives, his teachers at the University of Berlin hailed Luther in their work. The critical question about how the legacy associated with Luther's name was to be properly received was very much in the air, especially with regard to the widely held perception of Luther as the 'essential German' who helped 'the metaphysical essence of Germans attain to self awareness'. This had made Luther more than a figure of history. He was 'a symbol', as the historian Gerhard Ritter put it in his book on Luther in 1925.[22]

One of the liabilities of focusing on the theology of Luther rather than on its objectification in the changing historical forms of church-practice and polity and their results in civil life was that it became connected with other systems of thought and their epistemologies. Consequently, Luther's theology came into the hands of left-wing and right-wing epigones: the orthodox scholastics and the humanists, both of whom developed the anthropocentrism which led to what modernity came to call 'religion'. Whether we look at Pietism, the Enlightenment or Idealism, the system of thought prevailed over the legacy. Through the study of the early Luther and his theology, the 'Luther Renaissance' sought to overcome a *Luther Orthodoxy* that was becoming vacuous, and a *Luther Pietism* that turned faith into a matter of pious, individual conscience.

The synthesis of the Enlightenment and the newly found Luther, who was said to represent the 'real' Reformation, becomes most apparent in the ethics of the experience of justification developed by the tradition of German Idealism. Holl and Seeberg, drawing more extensively than even Harnack on the early Luther, broke with the commonplace notion that the Protestant Reformation began in the indulgence controversy of late 1517. It was from the heart of Luther's theological development that they began to interpret the Reformation. The issue was not so much controversy with papacy and Emperor as the quest for the true church and the understanding of the gospel as the judgement of all religion. In Luther's view, religion was the apex of the spiritual achievements of human beings and the accolades they generate. Religion was works-righteousness.

Reinhold Seeberg's theological image of Luther was richer in material substance than that of his predecessors, placing the accent on a quite different aspect of the Reformer's work. In Bonhoeffer's words: 'Harnack had been interested in the intellectual-history context while Seeberg focused on matters internal to theology.'[23] Yet Seeberg's interpretation of Luther's concept of faith in terms of transcendentalism provoked criticism from Bonhoeffer. For him it was a speculative construction, as a passage from the first volume of Seeberg's 1924 *Dogmatics* signals in terms of both the 'religious a priori' and Hegel's influence.

> The 'a priori' in religion is a purely formal primary disposition of the created spirit or self which enables and constrains the latter to become directly aware of the Absolute Spirit. This implies two things, first that the created will is so disposed that it becomes aware by an act of volition of the primary will and, second, that thereby reason is at the same time given the capacity to acquire an intuition of it.[24]

Luther's doctrine of justification by faith alone was the crucial element that caused Bonhoeffer and dialectical theology to oppose any synthesis of Luther and the systems of Idealism. Such syntheses represented a false assurance, devoid of what Luther often faced and spoke about: *Anfechtung*, the attack on the soul. The assurance offered by them transformed the deeply perturbing biblical message into a Christian world view and morality. What Luther meant by reconciliation turned into the realisation of a human ideal – life that is in the best sense 'rational', life that mirrors dutifulness towards the regulations of work and virtue, therein fulfilling the example of Christ. Justification enabled the attainment of this ideal.

Bonhoeffer's reception and interpretation of Luther were clearly influenced by how dialectical theology appropriated the Reformer. It can even be said that it was Karl Barth's thinking that extricated Bonhoeffer from the synthesis of Luther and the system of German Idealism. Thus, even while Holl and Seeberg drew him fully into the exploration of Luther's theology, particularly the earlier expressions of it, Bonhoeffer maintained a critical distance from their interpretations.[25] From Bonhoeffer's perspective, when Holl turned Luther's faith into a 'religion of conscience', conscience being human receptiveness to duty, faith itself became possible for humans again. So too, Seeberg's religious 'a priori' posited certain preconditions in the human spirit for God's revelation and spoke of 'points of contact' in human receptiveness and activity, even though the former is defined as 'faith' and the latter as 'love'. Thus, faith was portrayed as corresponding to the needs of the human spirit.[26] In this way Seeberg failed to do justice to Luther's view of the gospel as the judgement of all religion.

According to Luther, faith is an utterly new creature that comes to be through God's creative word of revelation. A church that has 'rediscovered' Luther's legacy and wishes to appropriate it has to ask how it can frame the necessary questions of its time in the light of the insights of the Reformation. For a number of theologians, Bonhoeffer among them, that meant working out, but in a thoroughly different manner, a theology that turned towards the word of God revealed in Jesus Christ. As already intimated, Barth's dialectical theology offered Dietrich Bonhoeffer the necessary perspective.

THE INFLUENCE OF KARL BARTH

Eberhard Bethge has detailed Bonhoeffer's preoccupation with dialectical theology and his personal encounters with Karl Barth (1886–1968).[27] In addition to the highly significant theological issues involved, there was a personal dimension. In 1923, Harnack and Barth engaged in public debate in a respected, popular journal. It showed the encounter of two fundamentally different worlds, and that they were not just different theological worlds.[28] Barth radically challenged every one of Bonhoeffer's Berlin teachers. But, as Bethge reports, 'It was only now that he found genuine joy in theology; it was like a real liberation. The mere fact that the new theology took its start from a task as unmistakable as preaching . . . tore him away from the games of speculation.'[29] Bethge continues:

> Bonhoeffer was arrested by the fact that Barth pulled attention away from the facts of humanity that had been laid bare so disastrously in that generation. The religious experience that Bonhoeffer also had long searched for with youthful seriousness, which had caused him no little embarrassment, Barth laid aside as of no consequence. The certainty that was the issue of much discussion was anchored not in the human being but in the majesty of God so that it could no longer be a separate concern in itself next to God. In contrast to many who thought Barth to be ever so gloomy, Bonhoeffer ascribed to him true *hilaritas*.[30]

As we have noted, Protestant theological thinking in Germany at that time was permeated by the Hegelian notion of Universal Reason unfolding itself in nature and history, reaching its fulfilment in Christianity. But this, according to Barth, eroded the very foundation of Christian theology. Indeed,

> the history of the church had become the history of the Christian religion; the history of doctrine the history of the formation of religious ideas; the study of the Bible the history of literature and biblical theology the history of Israelite-Jewish or Christian religion. It was an enormous movement, interwoven with the general history of culture and the mind, subject to the unending, relativizing flow of becoming and ending, with no absolute value.[31]

The aim of 'dialectical theology' or the 'theology of crisis', as outsiders named it, was to make the message of the Holy God revealed in Jesus Christ the sole centre of Christian proclamation, in contrast to contemporary historical-relativistic, conservative-orthodox and pietistic-romantic understandings of the Bible.

In the first edition of his *The Epistle to the Romans*,[32] and again in the wholly revised second edition of 1922, Karl Barth stated that the Bible was not about the cultivation of a religious existence enriched by tradition, but solely about listening to God's voice. Barth's move was not one of correlating human questions with biblical answers – assuming there are such answers – but of hearing what questions the Bible raises in its answers. What had to be taken seriously is that God is God, and the reality of Christ. This meant a decisive *no*! to all the forms of secular or sacral deification of the created that had spread like a corrosive poison in empirical Christianity and its theological eudaemonism of culture and experience.

The personal relation between Barth and Bonhoeffer calls for a few comments on the person of Karl Barth. Clifford Green's perceptive juxtaposition of observations by two different people, Dietrich Bonhoeffer and the novelist John Updike, is helpful in this regard. First, Bonhoeffer:

> Barth is even better than his books. There is an openness, a willingness to listen to relevant criticism, and at the same time such an intensity of concentration on and impetus pressing for the subject which can be discussed proudly or with modesty, dogmatically or with tentativeness, and it is certainly not meant primarily to serve his own theology.[33]

John Updike, who was personally indebted to Barth, was, to quote from Green, 'somewhat surprised that a theologian, of all people, could so obviously enjoy living in the world'.

> Karl Barth's insistence on the otherness of God seemed to free him to be exceptionally . . . appreciative and indulgent of this world, the world at hand. His humour and love of combat, his capacity for friendship even with his ideological opponents, his fondness for his tobacco and other physical comforts, his tastes in art and entertainment were heartily worldly, worldly not in the fashion of those who accept this life as a way-station and testing ground but of those who embrace it as a piece of Creation.[34]

At the time when Bonhoeffer was a student at university, no other discipline in the humanities explored the source of its existence as radically as did theology. It was there that the decisive engagements of the spirit took place. The unity of religion and culture, built on the foundation of Christianity, that German Idealism and Liberal Protestantism had made their goal broke apart at every crucial point under the weight of the historical crises of the time. None the less, Harnack confidently predicted that 'should Barth's way of "teaching the gospel" come to prevail, it will not be taught any more, it will rather be given over into the hands of devotional preachers who freely create their own understanding of the Bible and who set up their own dominion'.[35] Harnack's prediction failed to materialise. Instead, partly under the influence of Barth, Luther and Calvin were read again or anew. It is noteworthy and perhaps ironical that it was this new theological movement that led to the republication of the theology of Martin Luther by Theodosius Harnack, the father of Adolf von Harnack.[36]

Karl Barth described his new departure in theology with these words:

In [those] years I had to rid myself of the last remnants of a philosophical, i.e. anthropological (in America one says 'humanistic' ...) foundation and exposition of Christian doctrine ... I had to learn that Christian doctrine, if it is to merit its name and if it is to build up the Christian church in the world as she must needs be built up, has to be exclusively and conclusively the doctrine of Jesus Christ – of Jesus Christ as the living Word of God spoken to us [human beings] ... My new task was to take all that has been said before and to think it through once more and freshly and to articulate it anew as a theology of the grace of God in Jesus Christ.[37]

As Barth unlearned, relearned and learned anew, he said things – integral to his learning – that, according to Bethge, were of decisive importance for Bonhoeffer:

indeed astonishingly close in their language to [assertions in] *Letters and Papers from Prison*: 'Those who felt the whole importance and gravity of the question about God have often been decidedly unreligious people (73; 56) – Biblical piety is not really pious; one must rather characterise it as well-considered, qualified worldliness (80; 66). – Its thought and speech spring from what is original, issuing from and moving toward the whole ... this is what I call the Bible's other-worldliness (84; 73) – [God] does not want to be an above and beyond over against a here and now ... [God] does not wish to form history of religion, but be the Lord of our life (85; 74) – Biblical history is ... first and foremost the history of humankind (97; 94).'[38]

Bethge concludes: 'These are themes which were perhaps still sounding in Bonhoeffer's ears with which, so it appeared to him, Barth had indeed "begun" but "not carried to their completion".'[39]

Barth's radical critique of the concept of religion and the place it held in theological hermeneutics clearly captured Bonhoeffer's imagination. It allowed him to set what Luther had called 'faith' free from religion, and to recognise that its claim to being a dimension of human self-transcendence was in actuality a means of self-justification. Religion was the *cor curvum in se* (the heart turned in upon itself). Bonhoeffer's critique of Barth was that he appeared to make God's revelation his point of departure rather than the community to which God's revelation is addressed, the church. In terms of the dissertation Bonhoeffer was writing at that time, *Sanctorum Communio*, if revelation is to be spoken of Christologically, then the aspect of Christ existing as community needs to be the point of departure and proceed with the concreteness of that factor.[40] But Bonhoeffer's critique never diminished the significance of and the need for a theology like Barth's. In his lectures on twentieth-century systematic theology, delivered in Berlin in 1931/2, he declared 'We cannot go back behind this beginning.'[41] None the less, Bonhoeffer's theology developed also in other directions, not least through his own encounter with secular thought.

ENGAGEMENT WITH SECULAR THOUGHT

When Bonhoeffer came to write his *Habilitationsschrift*, his director Wilhelm Lütgert considered him a Heideggerian.[42] Heidegger's seminal *Sein und Zeit* had appeared two years before Bonhoeffer wrote *Act and Being*,[43] where he makes extensive reference to Heidegger and uses his understanding of intersubjectivity. Seeking to speak of the concreteness of God's revelation within the context of current theological discussion, Bonhoeffer had to address Heidegger's fundamental ontology and German Idealism. What was useful to Bonhoeffer's insistence on the *extra nos* of God's revelation was Heidegger's repudiation of the view that reality is constituted only through the concept, as Idealism maintained. Reality is given before, *vorgegeben,* as Bonhoeffer put it in his 1931/2 seminar on 'The Idea of Philosophy and Protestant Theology'.[44] But how is this prior givenness to be interpreted, especially when the issue is God's revelation? Bonhoeffer criticised Heidegger because his ontology of human existence suspends that prior givenness in the understanding of *Dasein* (Heidegger's term in *Being and Time* for human existence), depriving it of its priority or, in theological terms, of its *extra nos* character. But Heidegger's critique of the ontology of Idealism provided the tools for Bonhoeffer's *theological* critique of the *cor curvum in se*; it was 'a philosophical affirmation of the . . . insight of the Reformers, which they expressed in terms of the *cor curvum in se, corruptio mentis.* Human beings *in statu corruptionis* are indeed alone',[45] an aloneness the gospel addresses in terms of the revelation and reconciliation of God in Christ.

The question of the human being's 'aloneness' in that *status corruptionis* arose in Bonhoeffer's thinking not only in connection with God's revelation but also with regard to the neighbour. 'Sociality' was part of his family tradition and, subsequently, of his pastoral work in an industrial quarter of Berlin. The social passion of Friedrich Naumann and Ernst Troeltsch, and the way in which Karl Marx had influenced them, had a strong impact on Bonhoeffer. Indeed, those men were 'the two great names of [his] pre-Barthian years'.[46] The Bonhoeffers had come to know Karl Marx's thought through their acquaintance with socialism rather than vice versa. Dietrich's older brother Klaus, executed by the Nazis two weeks after Dietrich for his part in the conspiracy against Hitler, had studied *Das Kapital* with care at the time when Dietrich began to manifest interest in the political events in Berlin following the defeat in 1918.[47] Bonhoeffer depicts that legacy in a fascinating passage in his *Christology* lectures of 1933:

> What does it mean when proletarians say, in their world of distrust, 'Jesus was a good man'? It means that nobody needs to mistrust him. Proletarians do not say, 'Jesus is God.' But in saying 'Jesus was a good man' they definitely say more than the bourgeois when they repeat, 'Jesus is God.' God is something for the proletarians that belongs to the church. But, Jesus can be present on the factory floor as a socialist; in political engagement, as an idealist; in the proletarians' world, as a good man. He fights with them in their ranks against the enemy, Capitalism.[48]

The excursus on the church and the proletariat in *Sanctorum Communio* also indicates how Bonhoeffer had been engaged by Marxist-socialist reflection on the problem of capitalist economies.[49]

There were two other prominent scholars who strongly influenced the intellectual milieu in which Bonhoeffer matured but who had little impact on his thinking. They are Sigmund Freud (1856–1939) and Max Weber (1864–1920). Their work cannot be described here; it must suffice to comment briefly on why they left no mark on him.

Bonhoeffer did not allow psychoanalysis to enter his reflection; he actually regarded it with contempt. This was largely due to his father, a distinguished psychiatrist and neurologist, who rejected psychoanalysis for what he regarded as its failure to remain empirical. This view held Dietrich Bonhoeffer back from exploring Freud's work and its possible value in his own pastoral care.[50]

Weber's sociology of religion and his exploration of the question of church and sect appear to be no more than a foil against which Bonhoeffer developed his theological interpretation of the church as community. *Sanctorum Communio* is subtitled *A Dogmatic Study on the Sociology of the Church*. Bonhoeffer expresses his critique there of Weber's (and Troeltsch's) understanding of 'sect' and finds Tönnies' distinction between *Gemeinschaft* and *Gesellschaft* far more useful in seeking to provide a theological understanding of the church. In his lectures on the theology of the twentieth century, Bonhoeffer hints at the reason why he cannot make much of Weber: in his sociology one talks about religion – as understood by modernity – but not of God as the one who in self-revelation establishes the community that bears the name of Christ.[51]

Two philosophers remain to be named: the American William James (1842–1910) and the German Wilhelm Dilthey (1813–1911). Of particular relevance in regard to James is Bonhoeffer's letter of 12 April 1931, written while at Union Seminary in New York, to Karl-Friedrich and Grete Bonhoeffer: 'I have come to know American philosophy fairly thoroughly . . . Even though I do not believe in it all much more than previously, I have learned a great deal from it. James is especially interesting to read.'[52] Later that year Bonhoeffer lectured on the history of theology at the University of Berlin and dealt with James as well as Dilthey. James' understanding of 'religion', coupled with Barth's critique of the interpretation of Christianity as 'religion', initiated the thought-process which would eventually result in the concept of 'religionless interpretation of biblical concepts' found in the Tegel letters.[53] James had stressed individuality and privacy or inwardness as positive dimensions of religion. The element of 'feeling' is also highlighted, as is the 'usefulness' or 'efficacy' of truth. All of this reflects James' pragmatism. In a seminar at Union Theological Seminary in 1931, Bonhoeffer, drawing on Barth's critique, had rejected the notion that the 'efficacy' of God takes precedence in the believer's mind over God's 'reality'.[54] To speak of God demonstrating the divine reality through 'usefulness' (in James' terminology), or to say that God is humankind's highest good, in that God enables us to transcend the merely natural and attain to spirit and culture (as Harnack had put it), is to lose God's reality. In developing this critique of religion, Bonhoeffer encountered Dilthey. He also lectured on both in the course on the history of systematic theology at Berlin.

Dilthey's philosophical historicism, a part of his 'philosophy of life', provided Bonhoeffer with terms which the reader familiar with the prison letters will recognise instantly as most significant for the theology Bonhoeffer developed at that time. 'World come of age', 'autonomy', 'worldliness', 'metaphysics' and 'inwardness' among others signal Dilthey's presence to Bonhoeffer's mind. But instead of working on a new understanding of religion in the light of Dilthey, Bonhoeffer turned Dilthey's own concept of religion against him, as he had done with James, and developed the notion of 'religionless'. He does not share the two thinkers' separation of institutionalised and private religion, or their view that the former has had its day, whereas the latter needs to be fostered. But Bonhoeffer applied the distinction in his critique of the concept of religion, overcoming both the distinction as well as the liberal construct of 'religion' in the notion of 'religionless'. It may, therefore, be said that Bonhoeffer moved from a positive view of religion to a critical one and, in the end, to a position of non-religion.[55]

When Bonhoeffer lectured on the history of Protestant theology in the twentieth century, he entitled an important section 'Die Wende'.[56] It is the same word that described the event of November 1989 when the Wall came down in Berlin, ushering in a new period in history. Bonhoeffer's theology moved from its inception towards an irreversibly different world of faith and thought. His theology was always in the process of relating faith and historical context. It would have meant a betrayal of faith if he had remained bound to the theological formulae of the past before each critical 'Wende' in his journey.

Notes

1 E. Bethge, *Dietrich Bonhoeffer: Theologian, Christian, Contemporary* (London: Collins, 1970), p. 4.
2 ibid., p. 52.
3 E. Bethge, *Bonhoeffer: An Illustrated Introduction* (London: Collins, 1979), p. 36.
4 E. Bethge, *Dietrich Bonhoeffer: Theologian, Christian, Contemporary*, p. 34.
5 D. Bonhoeffer, *Letters and Papers from Prison: The Enlarged Edition* (New York: Macmillan, 1972), p. 285.
6 E. Bethge, *Dietrich Bonhoeffer: Theologian, Christian, Contemporary*, p. 44.
7 *A Bonhoeffer Legacy: Essays in Understanding*, ed. A. J. Klassen (Grand Rapids: Eerdmans, 1981), p. 48.
8 C. J. Kaltenborn, *Adolf von Harnack als Lehrer Dietrich Bonhoeffers* (Berlin: Evangelische Verlagsanstalt, 1973), p. 106.
9 Private conversation between the contributor and Margarete von Zahn, the granddaughter of Adolf von Harnack.
10 E. Bethge, *Dietrich Bonhoeffer: Theologian, Christian, Contemporary*, p. 46.
11 *Adolf von Harnack: Liberal Theology at its Height*, ed. M. Rumscheidt (London: Collins, 1989).
12 See ibid., pp. 33–41, for a full discussion of this point.
13 M. Rumscheidt, *Revelation and Theology: An Analysis of the Barth–Harnack Correspondence of 1923* (Cambridge: Cambridge University Press, 1972), p. 71.
14 T. Rendtorff, 'Adolf von Harnack', in *Tendenzen der Theologie im 20. Jahrhundert: Eine Geschichte in Porträts*, ed. H. J. Schultz (Stuttgart: Kreuz Verlag, 1966), p. 47.
15 K. Holl, *What Did Luther Understand by Religion?* (Philadelphia: Fortress Press, 1977).
16 *Luther: Lectures on Romans*, ed. W. Pauck (Philadelphia: Westminster Press, 1961). Holl's lectures were published for the first time in 1908.
17 E. Bethge, *Dietrich Bonhoeffer: Theologian, Christian, Contemporary*, p. 46.
18 ibid., p. 48.
19 *G. W. F. Hegel: Theologian of the Spirit*, ed. Peter C. Hodgson (Minneapolis: Fortress Press, 1997), pp. 92ff.

20 C. Gremmels and H. Pfeiffer, *Theologie und Biographie: Zum Beispiel Dietrich Bonhoeffers* (Munich: Chr. Kaiser Verlag, 1983), p. 32.
21 W. W. Floyd, Jr, *Theology and the Dialectics of Otherness: On Reading Bonhoeffer and Adorno* (Baltimore: University Press of America, 1988), pp. 1–90.
22 G. Ritter, *Luther, Gestalt und Symbol* (Munich: F. Buckmann Verlag, 1925).
23 ibid., p. 171.
24 E. Bethge, *Dietrich Bonhoeffer: Theologian, Christian, Contemporary*, p. 48.
25 D. Bonhoeffer, *Ökumene, Universität, Pfarramt: 1931–1932. Dietrich Bonhoeffer Werke*, vol. XI (Gütersloh: Chr. Kaiser/ Gütersloher Verlagshaus, 1994), pp. 184–5.
26 ibid., pp. 171–2.
27 E. Bethge, *Dietrich Bonhoeffer: Theologian, Christian, Contemporary*, pp. 50–5, 131–42.
28 This is examined in detail in the work cited in note 8 above.
29 E. Bethge, *Dietrich Bonhoeffer: Theologian, Christian, Contemporary*, p. 52.
30 ibid.
31 K. Kupisch, *Zwischen Idealismus und Massendemokratie* (Berlin: Lettner Verlag, 1959), p. 47.
32 K. Barth, *Der Römerbrief* (Bern: G. A. Bäschlin, 1919).
33 *Karl Barth: Theologian of Freedom*, ed. Clifford Green (London: Collins, 1989), pp. 12–13.
34 ibid.
35 Rumscheidt, *Adolf von Harnack*, p. 94, n. 6.
36 Theodosius Harnack published his influential book *Luthers Theologie mit besonderer Beziehung auf seine Versoehnung – und Erloesungslehre* in 1862 (Erlangen: T. Blaesing Verlag). The work lost its status with the coming of the Luther Renaissance associated with Karl Holl and others. The circle of theologians who composed what outsiders called 'dialectical theology' republished the work in 1927. For Adolf von Harnack, this republication signalled yet again how his own work, itself in fundamental disagreement with that of his predecessors, was being despised by a new generation (see note 8 above).
37 K. Barth, *How I Changed my Mind*, ed. J. D. Godsey (Richmond, Va.: John Knox Press, 1966), pp. 42–3.
38 The page numbers cited in parentheses refer first to K. Barth, *Das Wort Gottes und die Theologie* (Munich: Chr. Kaiser Verlag, 1924) and secondly to K. Barth, *The Word of God and the Word of Man* (New York: Harper & Row, 1957).
39 E. Bethge, *Dietrich Bonhoeffer: Theologian, Christian, Contemporary*, pp. 54–5.
40 P. Lehmann, 'The Concreteness of Theology: Reflections on the Conversation between Barth and Bonhoeffer', in *Footnotes to a Theology: The Karl Barth Colloquium of 1972*, ed. M. Rumscheidt (Waterloo: Canadian Corporation for Studies on Religion, 1974), pp. 53–76.
41 A. Pangritz, *Karl Barth in der Theologie Dietrich Bonhoeffers* (Berlin: Alektor Verlag, 1989), p. 44.
42 E. Bethge, *Dietrich Bonhoeffer: Theologian, Christian, Contemporary*, p. 94.
43 D. Bonhoeffer, *Act and Being: Transcendental Philosophy and Ontology in Systematic Theology, Dietrich Bonhoeffer Works*, vol. II, trans. M. Rumscheidt (Minneapolis: Fortress Press, 1996).
44 D. Bonhoeffer, *Theologie Gemeinde: Vorlesungen Briefe Gespräche 1927–1944*,

Gesammelte Schriften, vol. *iii* (Munich: Chr. Kaiser Verlag, 1960), pp. 160–1.

45 D. Bonhoeffer, *Act and Being*, p. 16.

46 E. Bethge, *Dietrich Bonhoeffer: Theologe, Christ, Zeitgenosse* (Munich: Chr. Kaiser Verlag, 1967), p. 257.

47 ibid., p. 54.

48 Bonhoeffer, *Theologie Gemeinde*, p. 174; D. Bonhoeffer, *Christ the Centre*, trans. E. H. Robertson (New York: Harper & Row, 1978), p. 35. Trans. altered.

49 D. Bonhoeffer, *Sanctorum Communio: Eine dogmatische Untersuchung zur Soziologie der Kirche* (Munich: Chr. Kaiser Verlag, 1986), pp. 290–3.

50 E. Bethge, *Dietrich Bonhoeffer: Theologian, Christian, Contemporary*, pp. 11–12.

51 E. Bethge, *Dietrich Bonhoeffer: Theologe, Christ, Zeitgenosse*, pp. 1052–3.

52 D. Bonhoeffer, *Barcelona, Berlin, Amerika: 1928–1931, Dietrich Bonhoeffer Werke*, vol. x (Munich: Chr. Kaiser Verlag, 1992), p. 250. See also Eberhard Bethge, 'The Non-religious Scientist and the Confessing Theologian: The Influence of Karl-Friedrich on his Younger Brother Dietrich', in *Bonhoeffer for a New Day: Theology in a Time of Transition* ed. J. de Gruchy (Grand Rapids: Eerdmans, 1997), p. 45.

53 This view is brilliantly presented and documented in a dissertation presented in 1994 to Humboldt University in Berlin by Ralf K. Wüstenberg and now published in English translation as R. K. Wüstenberg, *To Live as to Believe: Dietrich Bonhoeffer and the Non-Religious Interpretation of the Biblical Message* (Grand Rapids: Eerdmans, 1998).

54 D. Bonhoeffer, *Barcelona, Berlin, Amerika: 1928–1931*, p. 410.

55 Ralf K. Wüstenberg, 'Religionless Christianity: Dietrich Bonhoeffer's Tegel Theology', in de Gruchy *Bonhoeffer for a New Day*, p. 59.

56 E. Bethge, *Dietrich Bonhoeffer: Theologe, Christ, Zeitgenosse*, p. 1052.

4 Bonhoeffer's literary legacy

WAYNE WHITSON FLOYD, JR

Perhaps because they provide us with no self-evident hermeneutical key by which to understand them, Bonhoeffer's writings have served as 'a veritable Rorschach test' for late-modern theology.[1] Yet they do not comprise a systematic theology, and even his longer writings did not appear according to any overall plan. One might conclude then that it is his remarkable life, not the substance of his thought and writing, that provides Bonhoeffer's legacy with its coherence, its integrity. But until now, despite the plethora of works that have been and still are being written about him,[2] no one could judge the relative significance of the life and the work, lacking as we have the written legacy in its entirety.

At last, with the emergence of the *Dietrich Bonhoeffer Werke* (*DBW*) – and with the English translation of this critical edition (*DBWE*) well under-way – we can view the entire written legacy, resisting all temptations to reduce Bonhoeffer's enduring significance to his remarkable biography alone.[3] This literary estate now stands before us, virtually complete, de-manding of students at least as much attention as they would grant the life, to which Bonhoeffer's works lend their testimony. His writings provide not only an example of intellectual and theological preparation for the recon-struction of German culture after the war but also a rare insight into the vanishing world of the old social and academic elites. His thought resonates with a prescience, subtlety and maturity that continually belies the youth of the thinker.

Indeed, the more one delves into Bonhoeffer's complete *Werke*, the more one begins to suspect that the process of writing itself has been no insignificant factor in rendering coherent his otherwise unfinished life.[4] The writings *both* connect the parts, making sense where history left it lacking, *and* hold onto and hallow the fleeting particularities of his human journey. His was a life well written, celebrated in literary fragments – letters, poems, essays, sermons, each of which becomes a note played against 'a kind of *cantus firmus* to which the other melodies of life provide the counterpoint' (*Letters and Papers from Prison* (*LPP*) 303) – a moving but enduring ground that subsists, undergirds, raises up the entirety into a meaningful unity.

The sixteen volumes of the *DBW*, itself the textual basis for the English translation of the *DBWE*, are organised in two main sections. The first eight volumes contain works that either were published as independent books during Bonhoeffer's own lifetime (*DBW* i–*DBW* v) or have achieved an independent life of their own after being published posthumously after the Second World War (*DBW* vi–viii). *Sanctorum Communio* (*DBW* i) (title untranslated into English) and *Akt und Sein* (*DBW* ii) (*Act and Being*, *DBWE* ii) were Bonhoeffer's two academic theses at the University of Berlin. *Schöpfung und Fall* (*DBW* iii) (*Creation and Fall*, *DBWE* iii) was originally a lecture series in 1932–3. *Nachfolge* (*DBW* iv) (formerly translated as *The Cost of Discipleship* but in the new English edition to be named simply *Discipleship*, *DBWE* iv), and *Gemeinsames Leben* (*DBW* v, published together with *Das Gebetbuch der Bibel* (*Life Together*, published together with *The Prayerbook of the Bible*, *DBWE* v) emerged out of Bonhoeffer's leadership of the Confessing Church's seminary at Finkenwalde. The *Ethik* (*DBW* vi) (*Ethics*, *DBWE* vi), the *Fragmente aus Tegel* (*DBW* vii) (*Fiction from Tegel Prison*, *DBWE* vii) and *Widerstand und Ergebung* (*DBW* viii) (*Letters and Papers from Prison*, *DBWE* viii) all are reconstructions, originally by Eberhard Bethge, of writings left in fragmentary and unpublished form at Bonhoeffer's death.

Volumes viii through xvi are arranged largely chronologically, beginning with *Jugend und Studium: 1918–1927* (*DBW* ix) (*The Young Bonhoeffer: 1918–1927*, *DBWE* ix). This is followed by *Barcelona, Berlin, Amerika: 1928–1931* (*DBW* x) (*Barcelona, Berlin, New York: 1928–1931*, *DBWE* x), *Ökumene, Universität, Pfarramt: 1931–1932* (*DBW* xi) (*Ecumenical, Academic and Pastoral Works: 1931–1932*, *DBWE* xi), *Berlin: 1933* (*DBW* xii) (title same in English, *DBWE* xii) and *London: 1933–1935* (*DBW* xiii) (title same in English, *DBWE* xiii), by which we follow Bonhoeffer from his student days, through his brief time teaching at the University of Berlin, and to his pastorates at two German-speaking parishes in London. *Illegale Theologenausbildung: 1935–1937* (*DBW* xiv) (*Theological Education at Finkenwalde: 1935–1937*, *DBWE* xiv) follows him from London, to Zingst, then to Finkenwalde up to the time of its closing by the Gestapo. *Illegale Theologenausbildung: 1937–1940* (*DBW* xv) (*Theological Education Underground: 1937–40*, *DBWE* xv) traces Bonhoeffer's continued participation in theological education through the collective pastorates. And *Konspiration und Haft: 1940–1945* (*DBW* xvi) (*Conspiracy and Imprisonment: 1940–1945*, *DBWE* xvi) tells the tale of the political conspiracy in which Bonhoeffer was involved up through his death at Flossenbürg. A final volume will contain a synoptic index (*DBW* xvii).

THE FORMATION OF THE THEOLOGIAN

Bonhoeffer's earliest and latest surviving writings are letters to family and friends. *Jugend und Studium: 1918–1927*⁵ (*DBW* ix) contains more than a hundred examples of these, through which we observe Bonhoeffer's formative years – as a student at Tübingen in 1923–4 (*DBW* ix:49–81), on a study trip to Italy in 1924 (*DBW* ix: 81–136) and as a student at Berlin from 1924 to 1927 (*DBW* ix:137–89).

The role of Berlin in Bonhoeffer's life was central. There he lived, attended university, and began his professional life. His earliest surviving academic writings are those of a nineteen-year-old student of Harnack writing 'Das jüdische Element im ersten Clemensbrief' (*DBW* ix:220–71) ('The Jewish Element in First Clement'). In Karl Holl's seminars he writes on 'Luthers Stimmungen gegenüber seinem Werk in seinen letzten Lebensjahren' (*DBW* ix: 271–305) ('Luther's Feelings toward his Work at the End of his Life'). Reinhold Seeberg's seminar in systematic theology sees Bonhoeffer writing 'Läßt sich eine historische und pneumatische Auslegung der Schrift unterscheiden . . .?' (*DBW* ix:305–23) ('Can one distinguish a historical from a spiritual interpretation of Scripture?'), puzzling already over the manner in which he – like Karl Barth, whom Bonhoeffer had discovered just before enrolling at Berlin – as a theologian will approach biblical texts. And presaging the theme of *Act and Being* (*DBWE* ii), Bonhoeffer is writing on 'Vernunft und Offenbarung in der altlutherischen Dogmatik' (*DBW* ix:325–35) ('Reason and Revelation in the Old Lutheran Theology').

Leading towards his first dissertation, *Sanctorum Communio*, Bonhoeffer in Seeberg's seminar in 1926 writes on 'Kirche und Eschatologie (oder: Kirche und Reich Gottes)' (*DBW* ix:336–54) ('Church and Eschatology (or: Church and the Kingdom of God)') and 'Die Lehre der altprotestantischen Dogmatik vom Leben nach dem Tode und den letzten Dingen' (*DBW* ix:430–40) ('The Teaching of the Old Protestant Dogmatics about Life after Death and the Last Things'). Karl Holl's seminar has Bonhoeffer writing about 'Luthers Anschauungen vom Heiligen Geist' (*DBW* ix:355–410) ('Luther's Views on the Holy Spirit'). And for the celebration of Harnack's seventy-fifth birthday on 7 May 1926, Bonhoeffer writes on '"Freude" im Urchristentum [bei Johannes]' (*DBW* ix:412–30) ('"Joy" in Early Christianity [according to John]'). Bonhoeffer's interest in biblical studies is evident not only in his paper 'Das 15. Kapitel des Johannesevangeliums und Paulus'

(*DBW* IX:441–52) ('The fifteenth Chapter of the Gospel of John and Paul'),
where his conversation with Barth continues on issues of biblical interpretation, but also in an essay on 'Die verschiedenen Lösungen des Leidensprob-
lems bei Hiob' (*DBW* IX:452–73) ('The Various Solutions to the Problem of
Suffering in Job'), which reveals Bonhoeffer's developing understanding of
the relationship between the Jewish Bible and the Christian New Testament.

Bonhoeffer the *theologian*, however, is also the *pastor*-in-formation,
learning how to preach and teach in the church, as evidenced by the
sermons and addresses written in the winter semester 1925/6 for a seminar
in practical theology (*DBW* IX:485–516) and for a homiletics and catechesis
seminar in the summer of 1926 (*DBW* IX: 517–49). In 1926 and 1927 he was
writing for children's services on Luke and the Psalms, Jeremiah and John
(*DBW* IX: 550–77). These practical concerns, however, were about to yield to
– or perhaps better, be joined by – Bonhoeffer's first sustained attempt at
systematic theology.

Sanctorum Communio: the sociality of Christ and humanity

For Bonhoeffer's doctoral thesis for his licentiate in theology he chose 'a
theme . . . that is half historical and half systematic . . . the theme of religious
community' (*DBW* IX:156). *Sanctorum Communio: Eine dogmatische Untersuchung zur Soziologie der Kirche*[6] (*DBW* I) was completed in 1927, but not
published until September 1930. Here Bonhoeffer distances himself from
his liberal theological mentors such as Harnack, orientating himself more by
the Luther scholar Holl, as well as the systematician Seeberg. Here we first
encounter a leitmotif of Bonhoeffer's theology as a whole, 'the sociality of
Christ and humanity'.[7] For Bonhoeffer both human beings themselves –
particularly in the church – and the divine-human being Jesus the Christ
must be understood as essentially social beings, intelligible only in the
matrix of their relationships, their 'sociality'.

Bonhoeffer's dissertation treats not just the social philosophy of Plato,
Aristotle, Thomas Hobbes, Hegel and Max Scheler, but also the social-
theoretical writings of Max Weber, Emile Durkheim, Theodor Litt, Georg
Simmel, Alfred Vierkandt and Ferdinand Tönnies, among others. Clearly
influenced by personalist philosophy's social model of self and other, Bonhoeffer is attracted by its explicit rejection of German Idealism's implicit
claim to have unleashed the power of reason to overcome all such supposed
dichotomies.

Yet *Sanctorum Communio* remains a profoundly theological work. For
the sociality of the church is defined by what Bonhoeffer calls the *Stellvertretung* or 'vicarious representative action' of the incarnate and crucified

Christ (*DBW* I: 75, 91ff., 99f., 121ff., 125, 166, 260, 262).[8] Many readers encounter *Stellvertretung* first in his *Ethik* (*DBW* VI:234, 256–8, 289, 392–3, 408) and assume this to be an expression of his late, rather than his early, theology. It is here, rather, that Bonhoeffer begins a life-long preoccupation with his conviction that the church 'is' its sociality – that community which, as he will later put it from prison, 'exists for others' (*LPP* 382). Christ, the collective-person (*DBW* I: 48, 65ff., 71, 74ff., 91, 93, 128, 146, 179, 194ff., 210, 229, 244, 260, 298) of redeemed humanity, is the reality that founds the church in its existence; in this sense, Bonhoeffer can say, echoing Hegel, that the church is 'Christ existing as *Gemeinde*', church-community (*DBW* I: 76, 87, 126ff., 133f., 139, 142, 144f., 159, 180, 198, 258f., 295; cf. *DBW* XI: 269, 271f.).

A first interlude: Barcelona

Bonhoeffer spent February 1928 to February 1929 as vicar, or assistant pastor, to the German-speaking Lutheran congregation in Barcelona. The first section of *Barcelona, Berlin, Amerika: 1928–1931*[9] (*DBW* X) chronicles this formative year, in which he undoubtedly faced the gulf between the grand vision of *Sanctorum Communio* and the empirical bourgeois Protestant community in Barcelona.

From Barcelona he writes letters to his family, Harnack, Seeberg. Three addresses and lectures survive from his stay: 'Die Tragödie des Prophetentums und ihr bleibender Sinn' ('The Tragedy of the Prophetic Movement and its Enduring Meaning'), 'Jesus Christus und vom Wesen des Christentums' ('Jesus Christ and the Essence of Christianity') and 'Grundfragen einer christlichen Ethik' ('Basic Issues in Christian Ethics') (*DBW* X: 285–302, 302–22 and 323–45). Increasingly aware of the international financial crisis of the late 1920s and the resulting social chaos in Europe, he commented that 'All at once and without warning, the ground from under our feet, or rather the bourgeois rug from under our feet, has been pulled away and now it is a question of seeking the solid ground on which we stand' (*DBW* X:285–6).[10]

Most of all in Barcelona Bonhoeffer was learning to be a pastor. Almost a score of examples show us Bonhoeffer the preacher (*DBW* X: 453–548). Powerfully incarnational passages hearken back to *Sanctorum Communio* and point forward to his 'Christologie' lectures, as well as the themes of call and response in *Nachfolge*: 'God wanders among us in human form', he preaches, 'speaking to us in those who cross our paths, be they stranger, beggar, sick, or even in those nearest to us in everyday life' (*DBW* X: 472–3).[11] It was this theme of encounter with God, the theological category of revelation, that was to captivate Bonhoeffer's attention on his return to Berlin the following year.

Act and Being: a philosophical theology of revelation

In 1929 Bonhoeffer returned to Berlin from Barcelona to begin his work on his *Habilitationsschrift, Akt und Sein: Transzendentalphilosophie und Ontologie in der systematischen Theologie*[12] (*DBW* II). His progress is chronicled in *Barcelona, Berlin, Amerika* (*DBW* x), including Bonhoeffer's last letter from Harnack, discussions of his preparations for a post-doctoral year in America, and correspondence and records concerning his second theological examinations (*DBW* x: 138–96, 340–57). Included, too, is his eulogy at Harnack's memorial service in June 1930 (*DBW* x: 346–9).

Act and Being, however, dominated the eighteen months between Barcelona and New York. This work is 'a theology of consciousness, from within the perspective of the Reformation tradition's insights about the origin of human sinfulness in the *cor curvum in se* – the heart turned in upon itself and thus open neither to the revelation of God, nor to the encounter with the neighbour' (*DBWE* II:7).[13] Drawing upon resources as diverse as Luther's commentary on *Galatians* and Heidegger's *Being and Time*, Bonhoeffer was exploring the moral nature of the process of knowledge itself, a matter of power and control over the possibility of authentic otherness. For this reason, 'the concept of revelation', Bonhoeffer wrote in *Act and Being*, 'must . . . yield an epistemology of its own' (*DBWE* II:31). In this process, concepts from *Sanctorum Communio* such as *Stellvertretung* are provided with a more solid philosophical and theological foundation (*DBWE* II:87, 120); and phrases such as 'Christ existing as community' are employed to demonstrate the integral connection in his theology of revelation between Bonhoeffer's commitments to sociality and those to critical rationality (*DBWE* II: 111, 112, 115).

Bonhoeffer left us with three opportunities to watch as he interpreted *Act and Being* for a variety of audiences. The first is his inaugural lecture at Berlin on 31 July 1930, 'Die Frage nach dem Menschen in der gegenwärtigen Philosophie und Theologie' (*DBW* x: 357–78) ('The Question of Humanity in Contemporary Philosophy and Theology'). The second is a lecture prepared in English at Union Theological Seminary in 1931, 'The Theology of Crisis and its Attitude toward Philosophy and Science' (*DBW* x: 434–49), in which Bonhoeffer presents his own ideas in close concert with the dialectical theology of Karl Barth. The third, also written in English in 1931, is 'Concerning the Christian Idea of God' (*DBW* x: 423–33).

A second interlude: Union Theological Seminary, New York

Only a year into the Great Depression, Bonhoeffer travelled in 1930 to

New York as a Sloane Fellow at Union Theological Seminary. *Barcelona, Berlin, Amerika: 1928–1931* (*DBW* x) reveals Bonhoeffer's awkwardness at being a German studying in America so soon after Germany's defeat in the First World War (*DBW* x: 381–8), yet his determination to help avoid future conflict (*DBW* x: 389–90). However, he was not always so diplomatic. Encountering American Liberal Protestantism for the first time, he concluded in a letter from December 1930: 'There is no theology here' (*DBW* x: 220). But others among the letters he wrote while at Union (*DBW* x: 197–262), as well as two reports presented upon his return (*DBW* x: 262–82), made clear that whatever his original negative evaluation of Union Seminary, studying theology in New York City turned out to be quite an education in itself.

The elite, *wissenschaftlich* scholar finds himself writing on war literature, 'negro literature', Ibsen, Bernard Shaw, Sinclair Lewis, Theodor Dreiser, Ludwig Lewisohn, and others (*DBW* x: 390–8). Harry Ward has him reporting on his reading about 'The Wickersham Report on Prohibition', on 'Black Friday' and the bank situation in America, and on the Muscle Shoals power project for his ethics course (*DBW* x: 390–403). Also included are a short paper on William James' *Varieties of Religious Experience*, and two essays for Reinhold Niebuhr, on the 'Character and Ethical Consequences of Religious Determinism' and 'The Religious Experience of Grace and the Ethical Life' (*DBW* x:408–23).

Bonhoeffer returned to Germany in July 1931 facing a very different academic – and a dramatically changed political, social and economic – environment with its own demands for active ethical responsibility by the church. Perhaps these were the 'first impressions abroad' to which Bonhoeffer referred later in a letter of 22 April 1944 to Bethge – the point at which Bonhoeffer said: 'I turned from phraseology to reality' (*LPP* 275).

BERLIN – ECUMENIST, ACADEMIC, PASTOR

Ökumene, Universität, Pfarramt: 1931–1932[14] (*DBW* xi) contains Bonhoeffer's writings during a time of impending societal and cultural crisis in Germany. Fourteen sermons and devotional writings are collected here (*DBW* xi:377–466), along with almost one hundred letters (*DBW* xi: 13–122).

Full of enthusiasm from his first meeting with Karl Barth in Bonn in July 1931, Bonhoeffer the next month joined the theological faculty at Berlin and saw the publication of *Act and Being* two months later. Also he began formal participation in the ecumenical movement, which would provide the personal connections upon which he drew in his participation in the conspiracies against Hitler. Bonhoeffer went to England to attend a meeting of the World Alliance for Promoting International Friendship through the Churches – which he later came to see as rendered ineffectual by the nationalism of some of its influential members – followed by a meeting of the Mittelstelle für ökumenische Jugendarbeit in Berlin-Charlottenburg (see *DBW* xi: 125–38).

That winter semester of 1931/2 Bonhoeffer delivered his first set of university lectures, 'Die Geschichte der systematischen Theologie des 20. Jahrhunderts' (*DBW* xi: 139–214) ('The History of Systematic Theology in the Twentieth Century'). On 15 November 1931, he was ordained and began duties at the Technical College at Charlottenburg, where he served until 1933 (*DBW* xi: 215–28). Also there is a copy of the 'Versuch eines lutherischen Katechismus' (*DBW* xi: 228–37) ('Attempt at a Lutheran Catechism') that he co-authored with his friend Franz Hildebrandt, who was later forced to emigrate because his mother was of Jewish descent.

In the summer of 1932 Bonhoeffer taught a seminar, 'Gibt es eine christliche Ethik?' (*DBW* xi:303–13) ('Is There a Christian Ethics?') as well as 'Das Wesen der Kirche' (*DBW* xi:239–303) ('The Essence of the Church'), which continued the theme of *Sanctorum Communio* and *Act and Being*: the community of the church as the locus of revelation. But now it is not enough to speak of Christ 'in' the world or 'in' the church; one must also be able to speak of the church itself as at the centre of worldly reality, not at its periphery (*DBW* xi:250). This metaphor of 'centre' would remain with Bonhoeffer from the 'Schöpfung und Sünde' ('Creation and Sin') and 'Christologie' ('Christology') lectures that he delivered the following year all the way to his recognition in prison of the church's need 'to speak of God not on the boundaries but at the centre . . . not at the boundaries . . . but in the middle of the village' (*LPP* 282; cf. 312, 318, 337). For the church is called to be 'Christ existing as the church-community' (*DBW* xi: 271), the community of Christ 'the *Stellvertreter* of humanity' (*DBW* xi:266) whose 'first form of confession of faith . . . before the world is the deed' (*DBW* xi: 285; cf. *LPP* 300).

A number of reports from 1932 detail Bonhoeffer's activities in the World Alliance for Promoting International Friendship through the Churches and the Mittelstelle für ökumenische Jugendarbeit (*DBW* xi: 314–27, 344–66). In the report from an April meeting Bonhoeffer objects to any appeal to 'orders of creation', proposing instead to speak only of 'orders of preservation' of a fallen world, refusing to make idols of historically changeable realities (*DBW* xi: 317–27).[15] In his essay 'Zur theologischen Begründung der Weltbundarbeit' (*DBW* xi: 327–44) ('The Theological Basis of the World Alliance') Bonhoeffer succinctly argues that any talk of 'orders' must be talk of God's 'orders of preservation', for none of them – neither *Volk*, blood, soil nor even peace – can be understood as fixed for all time. For each can and must be broken when it becomes not a vehicle for, but an obstacle to, the revelation of God's preserving activity in the world (*DBW* xi:337).

Berlin: 1933[16] (*DBW* xii) begins with Bonhoeffer's letters from the end of 1932, most of which arise from ecumenical activities. But there are letters to friends such as Anneliese Schnurmann, who early in 1933 was forced to leave Germany because of her Jewish background. And there is Bonhoeffer's earliest surviving letter to Karl Barth, dated Christmas Eve 1932, and one to Reinhold Niebuhr the week after Hitler became Chancellor of Germany.

During the 1932/3 winter semester he was holding 'Besprechung und Diskussion systematisch-theologischer Neuerscheinungen' ('Meetings and discussions on new works in systematic theology') and 'Dogmatische Übungen "Theologische Psychologie"' ('Doctrinal exercises on "theological psychology"'). He wrote a review of Robert Jelke's *Vernunft und Offenbarung* and a short article on Karl Heim's *Glauben und Denken*. He preached powerful sermons, such as 'Dein Reich komme! Das Gebet der Gemeinde um Gottes Reich auf Erden' ('Thy Kingdom Come: The Prayer of the Church for God's Kingdom on Earth'), plus six others between November 1932 and July 1933.

The centre of his attention, however, was clearly his lecture course 'Schöpfung und Sünde: Theologische Auslegung von Genesis 1–3' ('Creation and Sin: Theological Interpretation of Genesis 1–3'), from which came his third book, *Schöpfung und Fall*[17] (*DBW* iii), so named to avoid confusion with Emmanuel Hirsch's 1931 book, *Schöpfung und Sünde*. *Creation and Fall* was the only one of his Berlin lecture courses to survive in its entirety in Bonhoeffer's words.[18] The implication is profound: just at the moment that the Deutsche Christen increasingly urged a Marcionite rejection of the Old Testament, Bonhoeffer in *Creation and Fall* is showing the way for Christianity's return to its Jewish wellspring.

The imagery of limit and centre becomes the guiding metaphor for his interpretation. God comes in the middle of time and the world (*DBWE* iii: 31), creating humanity in its creaturely freedom (*DBWE* iii:62ff.): a freedom-in-relation of one creature to another and both to God (*DBWE* iii:64). The *imago dei* 'is' this relationality – this sociality of creatureliness. It is an *analogia relationis*, an analogy of relationship (*DBWE* iii:65f.). As God is freely in relationship with God's creation, so is the creature created to be free-for the other (*DBWE* iii:66). This is the basis of all authentic community; it is the basis of the church itself (*DBWE* iii:99). To stay centred in relationship is to have life (*DBWE* iii:83); to transgress the limits of relation-

ship – to transgress the other as a limit or boundary to one's own pretensions of power – is to desire to be God, not a creature (*DBWE* iii:112). God's
way of ordering this fracture of relationships, this loss of created sociality, is
through the 'orders of preservation', protecting a broken world from itself
(*DBWE* iii:139–40).

Berlin: 1933 (*DBW* xii) reminds us that two days after Hitler became
Chancellor, Bonhoeffer is presenting his radio address 'Der Führer und der
Einzelne in der jungen Generation' ('The Leader and the Individual in the
Younger Generation'). He is writing 'Die Kirche vor der Judenfrage' ('On the
Church and the Jewish Question'),[19] proposing for the first time that the
church may be called upon to undertake direct political action. In 'Der
Arier-Paragraph in der Kirche' ('The Aryan Paragraph and the Church') he is
wrestling with what the church must do about Hitler's repudiation of its
members of Jewish descent. With Martin Niemöller he forms the *Pfarrernot-
bund* (the Pastors' Emergency League) and drafts the Bethel Confession (see
DBW xii, 'Betheler Bekenntnis [Entwurf und Augustfassung]' 'Bethel Confession[Draft and August Version]'). He is wrestling with questions such as
'Was ist Kirche?' ('What is the Church?') and 'Was soll der Student der
Theologie heute tun?' ('What Should the Student of Theology Do Today?').

The complexity of this thinker is nowhere better seen than in the fact
that during Bonhoeffer's final term at Berlin, the summer of 1933 – when
the Deutsche Christen had made such shocking inroads that Bonhoeffer is
driven to see the church as having reached its first *status confessionis* since
the Protestant Reformation – he taught two courses: a lecture series on
'Christologie' and a seminar on G. W. F. Hegel![20] Notes of only two-thirds of
those 'Christologie' lectures survived.[21] In *Berlin: 1933* (*DBW* xii) these
lectures have been placed alongside Bonhoeffer's concurrent writings on the
Jewish question and the Aryan paragraph. Bonhoeffer's incarnational
'Christologie' appeals again to the metaphor of limit and centre-who-is-
Christ. Here the notion of *Stellvertretung* – of vicarious representative
suffering, or 'humiliation' – challenges the triumphalism of the Deutsche
Christen, with their swastikas placed on the altar beside the cross. A decade
later he concludes the same: 'only the suffering God can help' (*LPP* 361).

A third interlude: London

It was an undoubtedly exhausted and dispirited twenty-seven-year-old
who arrived in London on 17 October 1933, the new pastor of two German
congregations. *London: 1933–1935*[22] (*DBW* xiii), reflects his sudden change
in circumstances. Gone entirely are academic lectures and seminars, replaced by more than twenty sermons and devotional writings (*DBW*

xiii:313–421). And his letter-writing expands exponentially, more than two hundred letters surviving from the London period alone (*DBW* xiii:11–288). Surprisingly, these include fewer than ten to his family, although several of their letters to Dietrich are included. Among them is Dietrich's letter to his brother Karl-Friedrich, where he speaks of the pathos of the visits to him of the first German immigrants arriving in London, 'mostly Jews, who know me from somewhere and want something' (*DBW* xiii: 75). Since he was a German pastor, his country and the Church Struggle are much on his mind, as represented by the half-dozen letters to Niemöller, as well as colleagues in the ecumenical movement such as Henriod and Félice.

One conversation in particular takes on a new prominence, that with George Bell, Anglican Bishop of Chichester – whom Bonhoeffer had met in 1932 in Geneva. They shared the same birthday. More importantly, they shared an appreciation of the significance of the German Church Struggle for the church's ecumenical integrity, as is evidenced in the twenty letters from Bonhoeffer to Bell and the latter's numerous letters in return. The immediate issue for Bonhoeffer, however, was the impact on the church of the threat to peace, as we see in his paper for the World Alliance for Promoting International Friendship through the Churches at Fanö, Denmark, 'Die Kirche und die Welt der Nationen' (*DBW* xiii:295–7) ('The Church and the World of Nations') and his address delivered there in English, 'The Church and the Peoples of the World' (*DBW* xiii:302–5), where he wrote: 'The hour is late. The world is choked with weapons, and dreadful is the distrust which looks out of all men's eyes. The trumpets of war may blow tomorrow. For what are we waiting?' (*DBW* xiii: 304).

Bonhoeffer was searching for answers. Bell wrote to Gandhi on Bonhoeffer's behalf (*DBW* xiii:210) informing him of Bonhoeffer's intention to spend the first few months of 1935 in India; included is Gandhi's reply (*DBW* xiii:213–14) inviting Bonhoeffer to lodge with him if Gandhi was out of prison at that time. But there are also three letters to Barth, and Barth's sharp reply from November 1933 rebuking Bonhoeffer for fleeing Germany: 'the building of your church is burning . . . come home on the next ship!' (*DBW* xiii: 33). In the end, Barth's position, not Gandhi's invitation, won out; Bonhoeffer never got to India.

FORMATION FOR RESISTANCE: FINKENWALDE AND BEYOND

An invitation to lead the Confessing Church's seminary at Zingst, soon relocated at Finkenwalde, brought Bonhoeffer home in the spring of 1935.

From this period come two of the best-known texts by Bonhoeffer: *Nachfolge*[23] (*DBW* IV) and *Gemeinsames Leben* (*DBW* V). Originally lectures to Bonhoeffer's students at Finkenwalde, *Nachfolge* is presented in the new German critical edition in its original form, as a two-part construction that looks at the themes of discipleship and the theology of the church, as these twin concerns have been presented in the synoptic gospels and then in Paul. 'Bonhoeffer clearly wanted to show that following Jesus the suffering Messiah (the Synoptics) is an integral part of believing in and obeying Christ as Lord (Paul). In this way he sought to counter the Lutheran tendency to separate justification by faith from costly discipleship both in theology and practice.'[24]

Discipleship must be read in concert with Bonhoeffer's classic of spirituality-in-community, *Gemeinsames Leben*[25] (published together with *Das Gebetbuch der Bibel*) (*Life Together, DBWE* V). *Gemeinsames Leben* was written a year after the 1937 publication of *Nachfolge*. Between the two books, however, came not only the closing of Finkenwalde, but Bonhoeffer's own initial contacts with the leaders of the military and political resistance to Nazism. During this same year came the infamous 'oath of allegiance' by German pastors to Hitler as a fiftieth birthday present. As Germany slid slowly towards war, Bonhoeffer's twin sister and her family were forced to escape to England. And it was in their abandoned home in Göttingen that Bonhoeffer, accompanied by his Finkenwalde student and now trusted friend, Eberhard Bethge, wrote *Life Together*.

This is without a doubt the most easily misunderstood and egregiously misused of Bonhoeffer's writings.[26] It is not about monastic retreat from the world; it implies no turn away from the costliness of grace demanded by *Nachfolge*. It is rather about an experiment unprecedented in German Lutheran church life, an experiment in intentional community. *Life Together* is about the implications of understanding the church as the context out of which individual faith and life are to be lived and understood. It recounts the rhythm of the day at Finkenwalde, the discovery of the manifold gifts of service in which community members were engaged, and the ways in which they were nurtured by the tender mercies of personal confession and sustained by the paschal memory of sacramental celebration.

Illegale Theologenausbildung: Finkenwalde 1935–1937[27] (*DBW* XIV) collects all the other surviving materials documenting life at Finkenwalde. It is divided into three sections by literary genre; each section is then divided into five subsections representing the most decisive events for each of the five 'courses' or 'classes' of students: (1) the seminary's founding at Zingst and its relocation to Finkenwalde; (2) the foundation of the Brothers' House and the Preachers' Seminary visit to Sweden; (3) the Evangelical Missions and the 'Life and Work' meeting at Chamby; (4) the Confessing Church's break with the Ecumenical Movement and Bonhoeffer's work on 'Discipleship'; and (5) the completion of *Nachfolge*, the closing of the Finkenwalde seminary, and the end of the Brothers' House.

There are more than one hundred and fifty letters exchanged with family and friends, professional colleagues such as Niemöller and Barth, and students (including almost a dozen letters to Bethge). We get to see Bonhoeffer's approach to homiletics in the 'Vorlesung über Homiletik' (*DBW* xiv: 478–527) ('Lectures on Homiletics'), including many examples of sermons, meditations and Bible studies (*DBW* xiv: 849–988). The 'Vorlesung über Katechetik' (*DBW* xiv:530–4) ('Lectures on Catechesis') continue to show us how he approached the catechetical task. And in his July 1935 'Vortrag über Christus in den Psalmen' (*DBW* xiv: 369–77) ('Presentation on Christ in the Psalms'), we see the formation of the perspective that eventually issued in his 1940 *Das Gebetbuch der Bibel* (*DBW* v).[28] Also included are Bonhoeffer's 'Vorlesung über Seelsorge' (*DBW* xiv:554–91) ('Lectures on Pastoral Care, or the "Care of Souls"') – as well as reflections on confession and the Lord's Supper, to which he returns in *Gemeinsames Leben*. Throughout, Bonhoeffer is exploring the nature of the church and its responsibilities, as his lecture on 'Sichtbare Kirche im Neuen Testament' (*DBW* xiv:422–35) ('The Visible Church in the New Testament') and 'Gemeindeaufbau und Gemeindezucht im Neuen Testament' (*DBW* xiv:820–9) ('The Building and Care of the Church Community in the New Testament') make clear.

The Confessing Church and the ecumenical movement each, Bonhoeffer hoped, had something important to teach the other during this crucial time. At first he was more hopeful, as seen in the 'Aufsatz über Bekennende Kirche und Ökumene' (*DBW* xiv:378–99) ('Essay on the Confessing Church and the Ecumenical Movement') from August 1935. But by the spring of 1936 his controversial article 'Zur Frage nach der Kirchengemeinschaft' (*DBW* xiv:655–80) ('The Question about the Community of the Church') expresses Bonhoeffer's exasperation with the Confessing Church. *Extra ecclesiam nulla salus* now means for Bonhoeffer that all who knowingly cut themselves off from the community of the Confessing Church have, in the situation of Nazi Germany, cut the themselves off from salvation.

Illegale Theologenausbildung: Sammelvikariate 1937–1940[29] (*DBW* xv), covers the time immediately following the closing of Finkenwalde. This includes the so-called 'collective pastorates' through which Bonhoeffer and his former Finkenwalde students continued their work in Köslin, Schlawe (later moved to Sigurdshof) and Gross-Schlönwitz. A few of these documents have appeared previously in English in the anthologies *The Way to Freedom: Letters, Lectures and Notes, 1935–1939* and *True Patriotism: Letters, Lectures and Notes, 1939–1945*;[30] but no complete collection of Bonhoeffer's writings from this important period of the church struggle has ever before been available.

This volume covers the time of the infamous 'birthday present to Hitler' – the oath of allegiance to *der Führer* signed by many in the Confessing Church – which Bethge has called the 'darkest moment of the church struggle' (*Dietrich Bonhoeffer: Theologian, Christian, Contemporary*, pp. 501–12). It includes the Bible study *Versuchung* (*Temptation*), from the summer 1938 reunion of Finkenwalde seminarians (*DBW* xv: 371–406). It covers the time of *Kristallnacht*. It includes the time of Bonhoeffer's trip in 1939 to London and Oxford for consultations with George Bell, Willem Visser't Hooft and others. It documents Bonhoeffer's final brief trip to America (*DBW* xv: 217–40) in 1939, including the poignant account of his letter to Reinhold Niebuhr explaining his reasons for returning to Germany, as well as his perceptive critique of American theology published just after his return, 'Protestantismus ohne Reformation' ('Protestantism without Reformation') (*DBW* xv: 431–60).

Also included are examples of the circular letters Bonhoeffer wrote to the collective pastorates, such as 'Unser Weg nach dem Zeugnis der Schrift' ('Our Way according to the Testimony of Scripture') (*DBW* xv: 407–30) from 1938, whose words, Bonhoeffer wrote, 'are meant to provoke you to serious reflection and renewed joy over the way of the church of Jesus Christ'.[31] It encompasses some of the most powerful examples of Bonhoeffer's own preaching, for example the 1938 sermon on the theme of Christ's love and our enemies (*DBW* xv: 463–70), where Bonhoeffer spoke of 'giving up our desire to take revenge', which he called 'a hard sacrifice, perhaps the hardest, which Christ requires of us'.[32] Take heed of the fact, he concluded, that 'The first person born on this earth to humankind murdered his brother . . . "Never be conceited" – lest you become murderers of your brothers.'[33]

A dream unfinished: the theological *Ethics*

Ethik[34] (*DBW* vi) presents a new reconstruction of the text that Bonhoeffer considered 'the culmination of his life work',[35] his unfinished book, left lying on his desk at the time of his arrest in 1943. Not least among the challenges in piecing together the *Ethik* manuscripts has been the thorny hermeneutical issue 'that the chronological order of composition might differ significantly . . . from the order in which Bonhoeffer intended they be presented and read'.[36] The critical edition's reconstruction of the *Ethik* (*DBW* VI) has followed the assumed chronological order of composition, arranged in five 'work periods'. This order thus differs from both the original German edition edited by Bethge in 1949 and the sixth edition's alternative reconstruction published in German in 1963 (which became the basis of the 1964/5 editions in English).

In the critical edition the theme of 'worldliness' takes centre stage: 'The reality of God discloses itself only by setting me entirely in the reality of the world, and when I encounter the reality of the world it is always already sustained, accepted and reconciled in the reality of God' (*DBW* VI:40).[37] A number of previously appearing themes reappear, each transformed into a more mature theological statement. 'Christ existing as church-community' becomes the church as that 'section of humanity in which Christ has really taken form' (*DBW* VI:83). The theme of creation, about which Bonhoeffer had maintained a 'qualified silence' for almost a decade, now re-emerges under the heading of 'Das natürliche Leben', 'Natural Life' (*DBW* VI: 163–217). The 'concrete command' of God according to the *Ethik* comes in the form of the 'divine mandates' (*DBW* VI: 392ff.), the heir to Bonhoeffer's concept of the 'orders of preservation'. And the concept of *Stellvertretung*, vicarious representative action, reappears as the heart of 'the structure of responsible life' (*DBW* VI: 234, 256–8, 289) for the world as a whole.

CONSPIRACY AND IMPRISONMENT: A LIFE IN FRAGMENTS

Konspiration und Haft: 1940–1945[38] (*DBW* XVI) traces the life of Bonhoeffer between the beginning of the *Ethik* project and the events surrounding his death. It should be read in concert with two other volumes, *Fragmente aus Tegel* (*DBW* VII) and *Widerstand und Ergebung* (*DBW* VIII), augmented by the only group of Bonhoeffer's letters not included in the *DBW* critical edition, the *Brautbriefe Zelle 92*, the correspondence between Bonhoeffer and Maria von Wedemeyer between 1943 and 1945.[39] Taken together, these remarkable four volumes provide a detailed picture of a complex man in the midst of the chaos of a world at war.

Konspiration und Haft: 1940–1945 (Part 1) (*DBW* XVI: 13–468) contains a wealth of letters and documents spanning the end of the collective pastorates in 1940 to the reports of Bonhoeffer's death in 1945. We follow Bonhoeffer's life from the closing of the collective pastorates, through his subsequent travels in east Prussia, to his being banned from speaking in public in September 1940. We see him living at the Benedictine Abbey in

Ettal, near Munich, in 1940–1, then travelling to Switzerland for the first time for the conspiracy. In May 1941 he is banned from further publications, but nevertheless makes a second trip to Switzerland in August 1941; that October he is at work on 'Operation 7', helping Jews escape Germany into Switzerland disguised as agents of the *Abwehr*. We see him travel to Norway and Sweden for the *Abwehr* in April 1942, then to Switzerland again in May 1942. Now he is on a crucial trip to Sigtuna, Sweden, in June 1942, and then he is travelling to Italy in June and July 1942. We get to overhear family correspondence from the von Kleist estate Klein-Krössin, and the von Wedemeyer estate at Pätzig between July 1942 and March 1943. A penultimate section covers Bonhoeffer's arrest on 5 April 1943 and his interrogation at Tegel military prison; and a final second-hand set of accounts 'documents' Bonhoeffer's death, including Payne Best's letter to George Bell containing Bonhoeffer's final recorded words (*DBW* xvi: 468). The remainder of this volume (Parts 2 and 3) contains various outlines, sketches, reflections and fragments, including 'Was heißt die Wahrheit sagen?' ('What Does it Mean to Tell the Truth?') (*DBW* xvi: 619–29), written after six months of interrogation in Tegel Prison, as well as a meagre five sermons and meditations that in their very sparseness bear witness to a once powerful public voice now silenced.

Widerstand und Ergebung[40] (*DBW* viii), although containing what are by far the best known of Bonhoeffer's letters,[41] remains among the most difficult of his works to assess. The critical edition as a whole is the necessary backdrop for these fragmentary reflections – largely in the form of letters, but also including poetry and sketches for unwritten works; because of it, readers of the prison writings will have before them as never before the continuity of themes throughout the development of Bonhoeffer's thought. However, the same reader must now avoid the temptation thereby to 'domesticate' the letters, to make Bonhoeffer's proposals – especially in the 'theological' letters following 30 April 1944 – merely an extension of the theology that had preceded them. On the contrary, there is a sharpness to these reflections that seems to get lost the more 'systematically' Bonhoeffer's theology gets read. They must be allowed to remain 'radical' in the truest sense, for they go directly to the root of issues, saying things that perhaps *should* have been obvious to Christians even in the 1940s, but certainly still haven't been entertained by much of the church even a half-century later. Unlike so many of his contemporaries, Bonhoeffer could hear the freshness and the prophetic challenge of the language of biblical texts, and the theological tradition of Paul and Luther, within a world that had taken humanity to the very brink of its annihilation.

Interspersed among all the personal letters in the first half of the *Letters and Papers from Prison* are various shorter writings, such as the eloquent 'After Ten Years', from Christmas 1942, containing the famous section on 'the view from below' (*LPP* 17). Also included are poignant pieces such as the wedding sermon Bonhoeffer wrote in May 1943 for Eberhard and Renate Bethge, as well as his 'Thoughts on the Day of the Baptism of Dietrich Wilhelm Rüdiger Bethge' from May 1944 (*LPP* 294–300). There are also the letters he wrote both in his own defence and to cover up the participation in conspiracy by others. And there is the enigmatic 'Outline for a Book', leading towards a church understood as a servant community which 'must share in the secular problems of ordinary human life, not dominating, but helping and serving . . . [and telling persons] of every calling what it means to live in Christ, to exist for others' (*LPP* 282–3).

During this time Bonhoeffer was also writing a drama and a novel, sizeable fragments of which are published as *Fragmente aus Tegel*[42] (*DBW* VII). These thinly veiled biographical fictions give us insight into the Bonhoeffer family and its friends, their world and outlook, or as Bonhoeffer put it in a contemporary letter to Bethge, 'middle-class life as we know it in our own families, and especially in the light of Christianity' (*LPP* 129–30).

There are also a number of pieces of poetry in the *Letters and Papers from Prison*, such as 'Who Am I?' and 'Night Voices in Tegel', reflecting on prison life. Others, such as 'Christians and Pagans', 'Jonah' and 'Powers of Good', are overtly theological, extensions of the reflections in the later letters themselves. Still others, such as 'Stations on the Road to Freedom', convey the development of Bonhoeffer's theological interpretation of his own plight. And 'The Friend' is a deeply personal meditation on his relationship with Bethge (*DBW* VIII: 513f., 515–23, 570ff., 585ff., 606, 607f.).

Once the letters to Bethge began in late 1943, their intensity and seriousness of purpose immediately dominated Bonhoeffer's correspondence. These letters themselves then took an unexpected turn, when on 30 April 1944, Bonhoeffer began those evocative questions and proposals in the 'theological letters' to Bethge (*LPP* 279). During the time of the theological letters to Bethge, which lasted through the failed plot of 20 July 1944, against Hitler, there are only four surviving letters from Dietrich to Maria. 'The intervals between the couple's extant letters were steadily lengthening, whereas Bonhoeffer's correspondence with Eberhard Bethge . . . was entering its most frequent phase' (*Love Letters from Cell 92*, p. 253). The surviving letters to Bethge end in the fall of 1944; and Dietrich's last letter to Maria is dated 19 December of that year.

DIETRICH BONHOEFFER WORKS: THE CRITICAL EDITION

Eberhard Bethge himself edited the first chronological anthology of Bonhoeffer's works, the *Gesammelte Schriften*, published in six volumes between 1965 and 1974.[43] After years of planning by Bethge and colleagues to address the incompleteness of this collection and the flaws in the methodology according to which it had originally been arranged, in 1986 the Christian Kaiser Verlag marked the eightieth anniversary of Bonhoeffer's birth by issuing the first volumes of the *Dietrich Bonhoeffer Werke* (*DBW*). Preliminary discussions about an English edition, the *Dietrich Bonhoeffer Works* (*DBWE*), had begun even before Chr. Kaiser Verlag, now a part of Gütersloher Verlagshaus, began their new series. With the authorisation of the German publisher, the International Bonhoeffer Society, English Language Section, undertook the organisational work for the project. Since September 1993 the *DBWE* translation project has been located in the newly established Dietrich Bonhoeffer Centre located on the campus of the Lutheran Theological Seminary at Philadelphia.

The *DBWE* provides the English-speaking world with an entirely new, complete and unabridged translation of Bonhoeffer's writings. Volumes include introductions written by the editors of the English edition (incorporating each German editor's Foreword), footnotes provided by Bonhoeffer, editorial notes by the German and English editors, and translations of each German editor's Afterword. Volumes provide lists of abbreviations used in the editorial apparatus, as well as bibliographies which list sources used by Bonhoeffer, literature consulted by the editors, and other works related to each particular volume. Finally, volumes contain pertinent chronologies, charts, and indexes of scriptural references, names and subjects. Biograms in most volumes give details of all persons mentioned in the texts.

The *DBWE* strives, above all, to be true to the language, style and – most importantly – the theology of Bonhoeffer's writings.[44] Translators have sought, none the less, to present Bonhoeffer's words in a manner that is sensitive to issues of language and gender. Consequently, accurate translation has removed sexist formulations that had been introduced inadvertently or unnecessarily into earlier English versions of his works. In addition, translators and editors have generally employed gender-inclusive formulations in their work, so far as this was possible without distorting Bonhoeffer's meaning or dissociating him from his own time. As a result, these translations often sound fresh and modern, not because the translators have made them so, but because Bonhoeffer's language still speaks with a hardy contemporaneity even after more than half a century. In other instances, Bonhoeffer sounds more remote, not through any lack of facility by the translators and editors, but because Bonhoeffer's concerns and his rhetoric are indeed, in certain ways, bound to a time that is past. Bonhoeffer left us the legacy of a life well written; the *Dietrich Bonhoeffer Werke / Works* seeks above all to keep that legacy alive for coming generations.[45]

Notes

1 H. G. Cox, 'Using and Misusing Bonhoeffer', *Christianity and Crisis,* 24 (October 1964), 199.

2 W. W. Floyd, Jr, 'Recent Bonhoeffer Scholarship in Europe and America', *Religious Studies Review,* 23/3 (July 1997), 219–30. Also W. W. Floyd, Jr and C. Green, *Bonhoeffer Bibliography: Primary Sources and Secondary Literature in English* (Evanston: ATLA, 1992).

3 The *DBWE* translation project is also helping to fund a new English edition of Eberhard Bethge's classic biography, *Dietrich Bonhoeffer: Theologian, Christian, Man for his Time,* ed. Victoria Barnett (Minneapolis: Fortress Press, forthcoming).

4 W. W. Floyd, Jr, 'Style and the Critique of Metaphysics: The Letter as Form in Bonhoeffer and Adorno', in *Theology and the Practice of Responsibility,* ed. W. W. Floyd, Jr and C. Marsh (Valley Forge: Trinity Press International, 1994).

5 Ed. Hans Pfeifer, with Clifford Green and Carl-Jürgen Kaltenborn (Munich: Chr. Kaiser Verlag, 1986). *DBWE* IX: *The Young Bonhoeffer: 1918–1927,* ed. Paul Matheny, trans. Mary Nebelsick (Minneapolis: Fortress Press, forthcoming, 2000).

6 Ed. Joachim von Soosten (Munich: Chr. Kaiser Verlag, 1986); *DBWE* I: *Sanctorum Communio: A Theological Study of the Sociology of the Church,* ed. Clifford J. Green, trans. Reinhard Krauss and Nancy Lukens (Minneapolis: Fortress Press, forthcoming, 1998).

7 See C. Green, *The Sociality of Christ and Humanity: Dietrich Bonhoeffer's Early Theology, 1927–1933* (Missoula: Scholars Press, 1975).

8 See also 'Das Wesen der Kirche' (*DBW* XI: 239–303) ('The Essence of the Church').

9 Ed. Reinhart Staats and Hans Christoph von Hase, together with Holger Roggelin and Matthias Wünsche (Munich: Chr. Kaiser Verlag, 1991). *DBWE* X: *Barcelona, Berlin, New York: 1928–1931* (Minneapolis: Fortress Press, forthcoming).

10 He returns to this metaphor of 'ground' and 'groundlessness' in 'Grundfragen einer christlichen Ethik' (*DBW* X: 344–5) and again fifteen years later in 'After Ten Years' from *Widerstand und Ergebung* in *Letters and Papers from Prison* (New York: Macmillan, 1970), p.3.

11 Translation from G. B. Kelly and F. B. Nelson, *A Testament to Freedom: The Essential Writings of Dietrich Bonhoeffer,* revised edition (San Francisco: Harper-Collins, 1990), p. 8.

12 Ed. Hans-Richard Reuter (Munich: Chr. Kaiser Verlag, 1988); *DBWE* II: ed. Wayne Whitson Floyd, Jr, trans. H. Martin Rumscheidt, *Act and Being: Transcen-*

dental Philosophy and Ontology in Systematic Theology (Minneapolis: Fortress Press, 1996).

13 See *DBWE* ii, 'Editor's Introduction to the English Edition' (pp. 1–24) and 'Editor's Afterword to the German Edition' (pp. 162–83). Also see W. W. Floyd, Jr, *Theology and the Dialectics of Otherness: On Reading Bonhoeffer and Adorno* (Baltimore: University Press of America, 1988).

14 Ed. Eberhard Amelung and Christoph Strohm (Gütersloh: Chr. Kaiser/Gütersloher Verlagshaus, 1994). *DBWE* xi: *Ecumenical, Academic and Pastoral Works: 1931–1932,* ed. Michael Lukens, trans. Nicolas Humphrey (Minneapolis: Fortress Press, forthcoming, 2003).

15 See W. W. Floyd, Jr, 'The Search for an Ethical Sacrament: From Bonhoeffer to Critical Social Theory', *Modern Theology,* 7, 2 (January 1991), 175–93.

16 Ed. Carsten Nicolaisen and Ernst-Albert Scharffenorth (Gütersloh: Chr. Kaiser/Gütersloher Verlagshaus, 1997). *DBWE* x: *Berlin: 1933,* ed. Philip D. W. Krey, trans. Peter D. S. Krey (Minneapolis: Fortress Press, forthcoming, 2002). *Berlin: 1933* (*DBW* x) is not yet published; the unpublished manuscript was provided for this chapter by Dr Hans Pfeifer.

17 Ed. Martin Rüter and Ilse Tödt (Munich: Chr. Kaiser Verlag, 1989); *DBWE* iii: *Creation and Fall,* ed. John de Gruchy, trans. Douglas Bax (Minneapolis: Fortress Press, 1997).

18 See *DBWE* iii, 'Editor's Introduction to the English Edition' (pp. 1–17) and 'Editors' Afterword to the German Edition' (pp. 147–73).

19 See Eberhard Bethge, 'Dietrich Bonhoeffer and the Jews', in *Ethical Responsibility: Bonhoeffer's Legacy to the Churches,* ed. John Godsey and Geffrey B. Kelly (New York: Edwin Mellen Press, 1981), pp. 46–96.

20 *Dietrich Bonhoeffers Hegel-Seminar 1933: Nach den Aufzeichnungen von Ferenc Lehel. International Bonhoeffer Forum* 8, ed. Ilse Tödt (Munich: Chr. Kaiser Verlag, 1988).

21 First published as *Christology* (London: Collins, 1966, these lectures appeared under the title *Christ the Centre* in the USA. (New York: Harper & Row, 1966); a revised translation by Edwin H. Robertson (London: Collins, 1978, appeared as *Christ the Centre* (San Francisco: Harper & Row, 1978).

22 Ed. Hans Goedeking, Martin Heimbucher and Hans-Walter Schleicher (Gütersloh: Chr. Kaiser/Gütersloher Verlagshaus, 1994). *DBWE* xiii: *London: 1933–1935,* ed. Keith Clements, trans. Honor Alleyne, Sheila Brain and Kenneth Walker (Minneapolis: Fortress Press, forthcoming, 2001).

23 Ed. Martin Kuske and Ilse Tödt (2nd edn, Gütersloh: Chr. Kaiser/Gütersloher Verlagshaus, 1989, 1994); *DBWE* iv: *Discipleship,* ed. Geffrey Kelly and John Godsey, trans. Reinhard Krauss and Barbara Green (Minneapolis: Fortress Press, forthcoming, 2000).

24 J. de Gruchy, *Dietrich Bonhoeffer: Witness to Jesus Christ* (London: Collins, 1987), p. 25.

25 Ed. Gerhard Ludwig Müller and Albrecht Schönherr (Munich: Chr. Kaiser Verlag, 1987); *DBWE* v: *Life Together* and *The Prayerbook of the Bible,* ed. Geffrey B. Kelly, trans. Daniel Bloesch and James Burtness (Minneapolis: Fortress Press, 1996).

26 See *DBWE* v, 'Editor's Introduction to the English Edition' and 'Editors' After-

word to the German Edition'.

27 Ed. Otto Dudzus and Jürgen Henkys, together with Sabine Bobert-Stützel, Dirk Schulz and Ilse Tödt (Gütersloh: Chr. Kaiser/Gütersloher Verlagshaus, 1996). *DBWE* xiv: *Theological Education at Finkenwalde: 1935–1937*, ed. Gaylon Barker, trans. Fritz Wendt (Minneapolis: Fortress Press, forthcoming, 2003).

28 Previous translations have appeared by James H. Burtness (Minneapolis: Augsburg, 1970); and Sister Isabel Mary, SLG (Oxford: SLG Press, 1982).

29 Ed. Dirk Schulz (Gütersloh: Chr. Kaiser/Gütersloher Verlagshaus, forthcoming). *DBWE* xv: *Theological Education Underground: 1937–40*, ed. and trans. TBA (Minneapolis: Fortress Press, forthcoming, 2004).

30 Ed. Edwin H. Robertson, trans. Edwin H. Robertson and John Bowden (London: Collins, 1966, 1973).

31 Translated in Kelly and Nelson, *A Testament to Freedom*, p. 168.

32 ibid., p. 287.

33 ibid., p. 285.

34 Ed. Ilse Tödt, Heinz Eduard Tödt, Ernst Feil and Clifford Green (Munich: Chr. Kaiser Verlag, 1992; 2nd edn, 1998); *DBWE* vi: *Ethics*, ed. Clifford Green, trans. Reinhard Krauss and Charles West (Minneapolis: Fortress Press, forthcoming, 2001).

35 See *Bonhoeffer's Ethics: Old Europe and New Frontiers*, ed. Guy Carter et al. (Kampen: Kok Pharo, 1991), p. 32.

36 ibid., p. 33.

37 Translated ibid., p. 36.

38 Ed. Jørgen Glenthøj (†), Ulrich Kabitz and Wolf Krötke (Gütersloh: Chr. Kaiser/Gütersloher Verlagshaus, 1996). *DBWE* xvi: *Conspiracy and Imprisonment: 1940–1945*, ed. Mark Brocker, trans. Lisa Dahill (Minneapolis: Fortress Press, forthcoming, 2001).

39 (C. H. Beck'sche Verlagsbuchhandlung, 1992); *Love Letters from Cell 92*, ed. Ruth-Alice von Bismarck and Ulrich Kabitz, trans. John Brownjohn (Nashville: Abingdon, 1995).

40 Ed. Eberhard Bethge, Renate Bethge and Christian Gremmels (Gütersloh: Chr. Kaiser/Gütersloher Verlagshaus, 1998); *DBWE* viii: *Letters and Papers from Prison*, ed. Wayne Whitson Floyd, Jr, trans. by H. Martin Rumscheidt (Minneapolis: Fortress Press, forthcoming, 2002).

41 See Eberhard Bethge, 'How the Prison Letters Survived', *Newsletter* of the International Bonhoeffer Society, English Language Section, 48 (October 1991), 49 (February 1992) and 50 (May 1992), 9–12, 24–7, 6–10.

42 Ed. Renate Bethge and Ilse Tödt (Gütersloh: Chr. Kaiser/Gütersloher Verlagshaus, 1994); *DBWE* vii: *Fragments from Tegel Prison*, ed. Clifford Green, trans. Nancy Lukens (Minneapolis: Fortress Press, forthcoming, 1999).

43 *Gesammelte Schriften*, vol. i, 1965; vol. ii, 1965; vol. iii, 1966; vol. iv, 1965; vol. v: 1972; vol. vi, 1974, ed. E. Bethge (Munich: Chr. Kaiser Verlag).

44 See John Godsey, 'Reading Bonhoeffer in English Translation: Some Difficulties', in *Bonhoeffer in a World Come of Age*, ed. P. Vorkink (Philadelphia: Fortress Press, 1986); and W. W. Floyd, Jr, 'Re-visioning Bonhoeffer for the Coming Generation: Challenges in Translating the *Dietrich Bonhoeffer Works*', *Dialog*, 34 (Winter 1995), 32–8.

45 Visit the 'Dietrich Bonhoeffer Home Page' on the world wide web, at http://www.cyberword.com/bonhoef/, for full details about the *DBW* English edition.

5 The reception of Bonhoeffer's theology

JOHN W. DE GRUCHY

Prior to 1963 Dietrich Bonhoeffer was largely known in the English-speaking world as a martyr of the Confessing Church struggle (*Kirchenkampf*) in Germany, and the author of *The Cost of Discipleship*.[1] The publication of *Honest to God* in 1963,[2] in which Bishop John Robinson interpreted Bonhoeffer on the basis of his fragmentary theological reflections in prison,[3] significantly changed this perception. Bonhoeffer became the radical theologian of secular Christianity and was even held responsible for the 'theology of the death of God' which became the rage in some circles at the time.[4] This confusion about the significance of Bonhoeffer's life and thought was compounded by the apparent contradiction between his pacifism during the mid 1930s and his later involvement in the attempt to assassinate Adolf Hitler. Bonhoeffer was a riddle.[5]

The controversy surrounding *Honest to God* none the less sparked off renewed interest in Bonhoeffer, especially in the English-speaking world. As his friend and biographer Eberhard Bethge later put it, Robinson's 'fascinatingly one-sided' interpretation of Bonhoeffer 'introduced the most fruitful period for the study, translation and publication of all of Bonhoeffer's works in the Protestant, Roman Catholic and secular spheres'.[6] Bonhoeffer, however understood and interpreted, soon became one of the most widely known theologians of the twentieth century both within and beyond the boundaries of the church. Even today, more than fifty years after his death in 1945, his life and thought continue to inspire and challenge Christians of many different denominations, as well as secular people with no religious commitment, throughout the world.[7]

DIVERSITY OF RECEPTION AND INTERPRETATION

The considerable range of Bonhoeffer's interests, grounded in careful theological and philosophical reflection yet sharply focused on the urgent issues of the day, has ensured a remarkable breadth as well as depth in his writings. This accounts in large part for Bonhoeffer's widespread appeal. His life was of such a quality that it continually attracts biographers,[8] novelists,[9] dramatists[10] and film-makers,[11] just as his poetry has inspired composers.[12] Although there is much consensus on his significance, the range and character of Bonhoeffer's legacy, coupled with the diverse nature of those attracted by him, has led to different responses and interpretations. This has been as true amongst scholars as amongst those for whom Bonhoeffer has become an icon of twentieth-century Christian faith and witness.

There are several further reasons for the diverse ways in which Bonhoeffer has been received and interpreted. One is the piecemeal way in which his writings have become known.[13] Those who initially encountered Bonhoeffer in *The Cost of Discipleship* or his widely read *Life Together* and only then came across the *Ethics* or the *Letters and Papers from Prison* can be forgiven for not knowing how to reconcile much of what they read. Another illustration of the problem is that Bonhoeffer's first two books, his doctoral dissertation *Sanctorum Communio* (1930) and his habilitation thesis *Act and Being* (1931), were neither well received by theologians in Germany when they were originally published nor widely known until the sixties. Only then was it recognised that these early academic treatises are seminal sources for understanding Bonhoeffer's theological development as a whole. This led to considerable revision in scholarly interpretation.[14]

Another reason for the diverse way in which Bonhoeffer's legacy has been received is the varied and often fragmentary nature of his written work. This was due to the historical context within which his writing was embedded. The circumstances in which he lived for the rest of his life after his return from his year of study in New York (1931) were not conducive to careful, systematic theological research and reflection. Much of his written legacy of these years is contained in essays, papers and lectures prepared for specific occasions, as well as in his sermons and wide-ranging correspondence.[15] Even the book which he regarded as his major project during the mid thirties, namely his *Ethics*, was never completed, and there has been much debate about its intended content and structure.[16] And, of course, his theological reflections in the *Letters and Papers from Prison* were not intended for publication, at least in their present exploratory form.

All this does make interpretation problematic, yet by the same token the open-ended character of Bonhoeffer's legacy also means that we are not constricted by a closed system but are, rather, invited to become participants in a continuing quest which borders on our own horizons. This leads us to a further factor which accounts for the diversity in the reception of Bonhoeffer, namely the interests of his interlocutors within the changing contours of their own situations.

Bonhoeffer has been read and studied, discussed and written about in many different countries throughout the world by academic theologians as well as pastors and lay people. The way in which he has been understood in the United States,[17] where there has been a mixture of considerable scholarly and popular interest, has differed from his reception, for example, in Britain,[18] the Netherlands,[19] Poland,[20] Japan,[21] Latin America,[22] or South Africa.[23] But even within Germany itself his reception within some academic circles has differed from the influence he has had on the lay academies or the annual *Kirchentag*.[24] Moreover, his influence in East Germany, where the Protestant Church sought to be a 'church within socialism',[25] differed significantly from the way in which he was interpreted in West Germany. Diversity of interpretation has been reinforced in some measure by the way in which Bonhoeffer has also been understood along confessional lines, primarily as a Lutheran theologian, but also by those who have read him, for example, through Catholic,[26] conservative Evangelical[27] or Anabaptist[28] eyes. Hence the kaleidoscope of Bonhoeffer interpretation.

The international reception of Bonhoeffer has led to another complication in the interpretation of his theology. Bonhoeffer has often been read in translation rather than in the original German. The problems in this regard are self-evident, but they have been exacerbated by the piecemeal way in which the translations have appeared; by the fact that they have sometimes only been published in shortened editions; by the mistranslation of certain key concepts; and by the inevitable interpretation that accompanies translation.[29] These are some of the reasons why the new critical edition of Bonhoeffer's works in German is being translated in its entirety into English.[30]

Although some awareness of the way in which Bonhoeffer has been received and interpreted is helpful in appropriating his legacy for today, nothing can take the place of reading his own writings. Nevertheless, the diversity in Bonhoeffer interpretation reminds us that the way in which we read texts and appropriate their meaning is a complex matter. As much as we might seek objectivity, we inevitably bring to the task our own perspectives, pre-understandings and agendas. Hence the danger that we might 'creatively misuse' Bonhoeffer's life and thought to support our own cause. A cavalier treatment of the sources is of little value if we are seriously interested in understanding Bonhoeffer's legacy. At the same time we must avoid boxing Bonhoeffer within the constrictive framework of religious or academic 'orthodoxy'. Part of Bonhoeffer's lasting relevance is that he refuses to be reduced to such sterility. If we are truly receptive to his legacy then it is not a matter of merely repeating his words but of responding to the challenge of what it means to follow Jesus Christ within our own historical context. For this reason we need to learn from those who have studied his thought in depth, as well as from those who, inspired by his witness, have sought to be faithful in their witness to the gospel.

Given this diversity of Bonhoeffer reception and interpretation, there are several possible ways in which we could proceed in our discussion. In the interests of simplicity, however, we shall do so under two broad headings: first, the scholarly debate about key issues in Bonhoeffer interpretation, and secondly, the more popular contextual reading of Bonhoeffer within the life of Christian communities, especially those engaged in the struggle for justice and peace. Of course, all readings of Bonhoeffer are contextual in the sense that those who study Bonhoeffer are part of a specific context and read his writings through spectacles shaped by that context. It may also be said that all who read Bonhoeffer are, in some sense, scholars, for even reading Bonhoeffer's more 'popular' writings requires a certain degree of theological literacy.

Before we turn to our consideration of scholarly debates about and popular appropriations of Bonhoeffer's theology, it is both appropriate and necessary to reflect on the remarkable role and influence of Eberhard Bethge in the transmission of that legacy. Bethge has not only helped to define the contours of the scholarly debate, but also been instrumental in enabling many to discover the relevance of Bonhoeffer's theology to the life and witness of the church in many different contexts around the world. Virtually the whole of Bethge's life since the end of the Second World War has been dedicated to making Bonhoeffer better known so that his challenge to faithful Christian witness might be more clearly understood.

THE ROLE OF EBERHARD BETHGE

Our understanding of Bonhoeffer has been immeasurably enriched by the contribution of those within his own family circle,[31] as well as that of his former students and colleagues.[32] Pre-eminent amongst these as both a member of the family and a former student has been Eberhard Bethge, Bonhoeffer's close friend from the time he joined Bonhoeffer's seminary in Finkenwalde until his mentor's death.[33] Many of Bonhoeffer's celebrated letters from prison were sent to Bethge who hid them until he was able to edit and seek their publication after the Second World War. Indeed, his editing and publishing of so much of Bonhoeffer's corpus,[34] which has now culminated in the publication of the *Dietrich Bonhoeffer Werke*, has been a life-long and dedicated task. Of course, Bethge has done far more than hand on Bonhoeffer's legacy: he has also been Bonhoeffer's most significant interpreter through his numerous writings, his extensive lecture tours, his gracious counsel to students and, perhaps above all, his monumental biography *Dietrich Bonhoeffer: Theologian, Christian, Contemporary*.[35] As Konrad Raiser, General Secretary of the World Council of Churches, has put it, 'most of what we know about Bonhoeffer has come to us through Eberhard Bethge'.[36]

Our focus here is not, however, on Bethge's role in the transmission of Bonhoeffer's literary legacy, but on the influence of his biographical or narrative approach to that legacy for our understanding of Bonhoeffer's theology. For Bethge it is virtually impossible to understand Bonhoeffer's thought without constant reference to his life and fate. This does not mean that his ideas cannot be critically examined and evaluated on their own merits; nor does it mean that his martyrdom provides them with an imprimatur which we dare not challenge. At the same time, the development of Bonhoeffer's theology was so related to his historical context and the way in which his life unfolded that the separation of his thought from his life inevitably becomes artificial and problematic. In some respects this could be said of all theologians, especially if we take as seriously as we must the extent to which all thought is embedded in social location. However, in Bonhoeffer's case the reason is not just his social location, but the extent to which so much of his theology was consciously related to his historical context.

Bethge's narrative approach to Bonhoeffer's theology was initially set out in his three Alden-Tuthill Lectures given at Chicago Theological Seminary in 1961.[37] Bethge divided Bonhoeffer's theological development into three periods. The first, 1927–33, which he labelled 'Foundation: The Quest for the Concrete Nature of the Message', began with *Sanctorum Communio* and ended with Bonhoeffer's lectures on 'Christology' at Berlin University in 1933; the second period, 1933–9, labelled 'Concentration: The Narrow Pass for Christianity' covered the period of the *Kirchenkampf*, and included the publication of *Cost of Discipleship* and *Life Together* as well as many other papers related to the confession of Christ in relation to world peace, ecumenism, the 'Jewish question', and the struggle against Nazi ideology. The third period, 1940–5, which Bethge labelled 'Liberation: Christianity without Religion', covered the years from the disbanding of the Finkenwalde seminary, through his underground work for the conspiracy, his arrest and imprisonment by the Gestapo, to his untimely death. It was during this final stage that Bonhoeffer worked on his unfinished *Ethics* and wrote the letters, poems and theological reflections which were posthumously published in *Letters and Papers from Prison*. Bethge's periodisation, with various modifications, has been widely accepted, and it goes a long way in helping to structure Bonhoeffer's legacy and so enabling us to understand better the development of his theology.

Central to Bethge's interpretation has been a recognition of both continuity and discontinuity in Bonhoeffer's theological development. This approach stands in direct contrast to that of the first major study on Bonhoeffer's theology to appear in German, namely Hanfried Müller's *Von der Kirche zur Welt*, published in 1961.[38] For Müller, a professor at the Humboldt University in East Berlin who was committed to a socialist interpretation of Christianity, the key to understanding Bonhoeffer lay in recognising a radical discontinuity which separated all of Bonhoeffer's theology from its beginnings in *Sanctorum Communio* to the way in which it was formulated in his *Ethics* from that which was expressed in the prison letters starting with that of 30 April 1944. From Müller's perspective, to understand Bonhoeffer correctly today we must turn away from the church and embrace the world in all its secularity; we must reject bourgeois religion and affirm socialism. The gospel set people free to be mature and responsible in the world. The question is not, Müller insisted, what Bonhoeffer meant, but where he would stand now.

Müller was by no means wrong in some of his insights. The letter of 30 April 1944 does indicate a significant shift in Bonhoeffer's development, and it is, as Müller stressed, essential that we do not simply ask what Bonhoeffer meant, but where he would now stand in relation to contemporary issues. But in so stressing the discontinuity Müller failed to discern the deep connections within Bonhoeffer's theology from the earliest of his writings to his final fragments.[39] His radical thoughts in prison are built on foundations laid in *Sanctorum Communio* and *Act and Being*; they also reflect the deep biblical spirituality and commitment to the church which characterised his witness to Christ during the church struggle against Nazism. Indeed, Bonhoeffer's theological development was not worked out in logical steps, but was, as Bethge points out, 'an auspicious synthesis brought out of [his] sensitive perceptiveness as he faced the challenges of his day'.[40] 'Let us remember', Bethge writes, 'Bonhoeffer says explicitly, there is nothing new invented; the basic concepts were laid out before, yet something is round the corner. There are more dimensions to the foundations which will stand the test than were first thought.'[41] Bonhoeffer was engaged in a relentless attempt to discover the significance of Jesus Christ in relation to an ever-changing world.

Bethge's contribution to Bonhoeffer studies has not been confined to the process of transmission of the legacy, or in helping us understand Bonhoeffer's theology in its context. Over the years he has increasingly sought to relate Bonhoeffer's insights – and develop many of his own – in relation to contemporary issues. This has been particularly the case with regard to the church's relationship to Judaism, and therefore its responsibility and guilt for the Holocaust. In this respect, Bonhoeffer's own witness, ambiguous as it was at times, has provided Bethge with a way into the problem. At the same time, Bethge has obviously gone beyond Bonhoeffer through his own research, through his dialogue with Jewish scholars, and in his attempt to change the thinking and attitudes of the Protestant Church in Germany. In this, and in similar ways, Bethge has demonstrated not only that an authentic interpretation of Bonhoeffer requires us to go back to the text and examine it within its own context, but that any attempt to do theology in dialogue with Bonhoeffer must go beyond him and seek to relate the gospel to our own time and place.[42]

SCHOLARLY DEBATES AND ISSUES

Bonhoeffer studies has gone through several phases since the 1950s. In his survey of the literature, Ralf Wüstenberg speaks of four epochs, the first three of which had clear profiles.[43] During the first decade the focus was on biographical studies; during the 1960s the major issue was the question of secularisation; during the 1970s the dominant concern centred around Bonhoeffer's philosophical roots. No clear focus yet characterises the 1980s and early 1990s. Wüstenberg's organisation of the material is helpful and to the point, yet, as he himself indicates, the range of themes and issues discussed in each epoch has been considerable, leading to a variety of approaches. Indeed, in a comprehensive examination of the history of Bonhoeffer interpretation in German scholarship Ernst Feil notes four major characteristics in German Bonhoeffer research which reflect these different approaches.[44] Although Feil does not deal with English-language studies, similar characteristics are to be found there as well, and I have also included other topics in the English literature which relate to Feil's schema.[45]

The first characteristic is that of comprehensive studies of Bonhoeffer's theology, to which we shall turn in a moment. The second characteristic concerns the different phases in Bonhoeffer's theological development, beginning with ecclesiology,[46] then focusing on Christology,[47] and finally grappling with the reality of the world 'come of age'.[48] The third characteristic Feil notes is that of studies on special topics in Bonhoeffer's theology. Major studies published in English include his use of the Old Testament;[49] his anthropology;[50] the philosophical foundations of his theology;[51] and the development of his ethics.[52] But as the bibliographies indicate, there are many other specialised monographs on topics ranging from Bonhoeffer's understanding of the sacraments, to his treatment of guilt and conscience, the doctrine of providence, and his use of the 'discipline of the secret' (*disciplina arcanum*). The fourth characteristic has to do with practical theology, for example with Bonhoeffer's approach to preaching,[53] or pastoral care.

Many of the initial studies on Bonhoeffer, mostly German, were published in the collected volumes entitled *Die mündige Welt*, which set the direction for subsequent debates.[54] The earliest collection of essays in English, *The Place of Bonhoeffer*, was published in 1962.[55] Since the establishment of the International Bonhoeffer Society in 1971, and the subsequent formation of its various language and regional sections, many collections of the papers presented at conferences and symposia have been published.[56] These provide an indispensable source for tracing the way in which the scholarly study of Bonhoeffer has developed. The more comprehensive studies of Bonhoeffer's theology have varied in approach and emphasis, leading to differences of interpretation. I shall not attempt to deal with all of these major studies, but briefly introduce a few of the most important in order to highlight some of the problems in Bonhoeffer interpretation.

The first major study of Bonhoeffer's theology, *Von der Kirche zur Welt* (*From the Church to the World*), by the East German theologian Hanfried Müller, to whom I referred earlier, was published in 1956.[57] It was, it may be recalled, Müller's contention that the only interpretation of Bonhoeffer for our time is that which builds on his radical prison reflections. Since Müller lived in a communist state, it is not surprising that his interpretation was distinctly Marxist. The first major English exposition of Bonhoeffer's theology was John Godsey's *Theology of Dietrich Bonhoeffer*, published in 1960,[58] which he wrote as a doctoral dissertation under the supervision of Karl Barth. Godsey's treatment stood in marked contrast to Müller's. By discussing all of Bonhoeffer's works in their historical sequence he emphasised the continuities in Bonhoeffer's theological development, and the extent to which Bonhoeffer was influenced by Barth. If Müller overstated the case for radical discontinuity in Bonhoeffer's theology, Godsey erred in not taking that sufficiently into account; if Müller tried to fit Bonhoeffer into a Marxist mould, Godsey probably overstated the Barthian character of his theology.[59]

A major French exposition of Bonhoeffer's theology was that of André Dumas, translated into English and published in 1971 as *Dietrich Bonhoeffer: Theologian of Reality*.[60] Dumas affirmed both the continuity in Bonhoeffer's theological development and the considerable influence of Karl Barth. But his discussion is noteworthy for the way in which he sought to show the extent to which Bonhoeffer was influenced by the great German philosopher G. W. F. Hegel. Although this, too, should not be over-stressed, the relationship of Bonhoeffer to Hegel has been a feature of some more recent Bonhoeffer studies in English. Both Charles Marsh's *Reclaiming Dietrich Bonhoeffer*[61] and Wayne Whitson Floyd's *Theology and the Dialectics of Otherness*[62] are noteworthy in this respect, though they demonstrate too the extent to which Bonhoeffer was also influenced by and engaged in the philosophical debates of his time, notably those associated with the work of Martin Heidegger.[63] Yet it is equally clear from such studies that while Bonhoeffer incorporated much from Barth, Hegel and Heidegger into his theology, he was never captive to any of them. His theology was not an amalgam of the insights of others but uniquely his own attempt to discern the significance of God's revelation in Jesus Christ in and for the world.

This latter point was already stressed by Ernst Feil, a Catholic theologian, whose important *Die Theologie Dietrich Bonhoeffers*, published in German in 1971 and in an abridged English version in 1985, was a response to the attempts in the sixties to reduce Bonhoeffer's theology to fit into prevailing ideological parameters or categories. 'We cannot learn from Bonhoeffer', Feil wrote in his Preface to the English edition,

> when we see our own presuppositions confirmed by him nor can we repudiate what he said approaching him from our own presuppositions. The more significant he and his work become in countries whose political situations challenge Christian faith in a special way, the more serious must be the effort to discern Bonhoeffer's real intention.[64]

Although Feil does not refer a great deal to the narrative of Bonhoeffer's life, his work builds on and complements that of Eberhard Bethge. Affirming the continuity in Bonhoeffer's theological development, Feil argues that the decisive change in Bonhoeffer's journey was in his turn to radical action, a turn which was intrinsically related to the way in which his theology developed. 'The claim of Jesus Christ on the "world come of age" was the theme of Bonhoeffer's life, and to that claim he gave his service.'[65]

In his comprehensive discussion of the history of Bonhoeffer interpretation, Feil points out that German scholarship has generally been divided into two main schools: that influenced by Rudolf Bultmann and the hermeneutical discussion, and that involving those scholars who located Bonhoeffer far more in terms of Barth and dialectical theology.[66] With regard to the former, Gerhard Ebeling's programmatic essay on 'The Non-Religious Interpretation of Biblical Concepts'[67] has been particularly important, and with regard to the latter, along with works to which I have already referred, those of Jürgen Moltmann,[68] and especially the more recent works of Andreas Pangritz[69] and Ralf Wüstenberg, are relevant.

This division of Bonhoeffer interpretation into two main schools of German theology also relates to how we are to understand the question of continuity and discontinuity in Bonhoeffer's theological development. Ralf Wüstenberg has argued that while Bonhoeffer's theology throughout is informed by his Christology, nevertheless within that continuity there is also significant discontinuity. This view, which is a restatement of Bethge's position, would probably receive the widest support amongst Bonhoeffer scholars today. So too would Wüstenberg's related contention that Bonhoeffer's prison theology has to be understood not so much in terms of Barth's theology as against the background of the 'philosophy of life' (*Lebensphilosophie*) of the late nineteenth and early twentieth century associated with Wilhelm Dilthey and the Spanish philosopher Ortega y Gasset. As Wüstenberg argues, the 'non-religious interpretation of biblical concepts' has to do with the relationship between Jesus Christ and life in all its maturity.

Enough has been said to help readers understand some of the strands in the scholarly debate about Bonhoeffer interpretation. But the debate about Bonhoeffer, certainly in the English-speaking world, while not disengaged from such themes, has also gone in other directions, and often focused more on contextual issues.

THE 'POPULAR' AND POLITICAL RECEPTION OF BONHOEFFER

Since the 1960s, when Bonhoeffer's name became a household word in progressive Christian communities and congregations, numerous seminars and workshops have been held around the world which have sought to explore his legacy for their particular contexts. There is even a programme of tours or, better, pilgrimages to the various Bonhoeffer sites in Germany. It is impossible to document all this here, but it would be a major oversight if we did not acknowledge the importance of such events in the reception of Bonhoeffer, and for the appropriation of his legacy today.

Most of those who have been influenced by Bonhoeffer's legacy in ways such as these have not been acquainted with the scholarly debates and issues which we have discussed. But they have found in Bonhoeffer's life and work a witness which has challenged them to greater Christian commitment and faithfulness. Those familiar with the problems of hermeneutics will appreciate that it is always difficult to interpret the thought of those who lived in different historical epochs and contexts so that it relates in a meaningful way to other contexts without undue distortion. Several Bonhoeffer scholars, not least Eberhard Bethge himself, have given much time and energy to assisting in this task of interpretation.[70]

A perusal of this more 'popular' (in quotation marks in order to avoid the danger of reducing Bonhoeffer's theology to the level of 'cheap grace') treatment of Bonhoeffer's life and work suggests that there are three major themes, related to the threefold structure of his legacy as proposed by Bethge, which continue to attract attention. These may be broadly stated as, firstly, discipleship and community, then involvement in the struggle for justice and peace, and finally faith in a secular age. The first theme clearly relates to Bonhoeffer's *Cost of Discipleship* and his *Life Together*; the second theme relates to his political involvement both during the *Kirchenkampf* and as a member of the conspiracy, a theme which finds expression in many of his lectures of the period, notably that on the 'Jewish question' and in his *Ethics*; the third theme obviously has to do with his theological reflections in prison as published in the *Letters and Papers from Prison*.

Undoubtedly, it is the contemporary relevance of these themes which accounts for the wide and lasting interest in Bonhoeffer's legacy, and which has ensured that the particular volumes mentioned here have not only remained in print but also been translated into different languages and in several cases been revised. This also accounts for several compendiums of Bonhoeffer's writings which have been published for the use of students and study groups.[71] Indeed, without this interest it is unlikely that the more scholarly editions of the *Dietrich Bonhoeffer Werke* would have been translated and published in English.

The 'popular' reception of Bonhoeffer has invariably been related in some way to the burning issues facing Christians in various parts of the world not just by scholars (often he is neglected by them), but even more by those who have sought to be faithful in their Christian witness within the political arena.[72] In many respects, the political appropriation of Bonhoeffer's theology relates well to the popular appropriation because it is primarily concerned to discover resources within Bonhoeffer's legacy which are of help in the struggle for justice and liberation. By 'political appropriation' here I am not referring to the attempt, as by Hanfried Müller, to fit Bonhoeffer's theology into a somewhat closed ideological framework.[73] This is usually what 'political theology' refers to within the European context, whether of the right or the left. Bonhoeffer simply does not fit into such a schema. But that is different from discovering trajectories in his legacy which help Christians to engage in the struggle for justice and liberation more faithfully in terms of the gospel. This was certainly the case for those Christians who found dialogue with Bonhoeffer to be of considerable help and inspiration in the struggle against apartheid and now in the struggle to construct a just democratic society.[74]

The extent of the appropriation of Bonhoeffer within the political arena in many contexts, as well as his use in reflecting on a variety of contemporary issues, may be discerned from a perusal of the papers which were given at the Seventh International Bonhoeffer Congress held in Cape Town in 1996. These included, inter alia, presentations on Bonhoeffer's relevance for ethics and human rights in Africa; for the relationship between church and state, race relations and civil rights in the United States; for the struggle against apartheid and the reconstruction of a just society in South Africa; for global peace and environmental issues.[75] Many other contexts and issues were dealt with in other presentations. Indeed, Bonhoeffer would surely have been amazed by the range of the papers and the fact that all of them claimed, in one way or another, to be related to his life and thought.

The theme of the Cape Town Congress was Bonhoeffer's own question to his fellow conspirators, 'Are we still of any use?' But this was turned around and asked of Bonhoeffer himself. One of the sharpest of his 'interrogators' was the Korean feminist theologian Chung Hyun Kyung, whose paper took the form of a letter addressed to Bonhoeffer. It was noteworthy that while some Bonhoeffer scholars reacted somewhat negatively to Chung's presentation, others discerned in it something of Bonhoeffer's own 'popular' appeal. All, however, could identify with her recollection of Bonhoeffer's significance for the Korean Student Christian Movement. 'You were', Chung 'wrote' to Bonhoeffer, 'the major theological mentor of our movement, not because we understood the details and nuances of your theology but because we were inspired by your life story.'[76]

Notes

1 The first English edition of *The Cost of Discipleship* was translated by Reginald Fuller and published by SCM Press, London, in 1949.
2 John A. T. Robinson, *Honest to God* (London: SCM, 1963).
3 Edited by Eberhard Bethge and published posthumously in 1951. The first

English edition of *Letters and Papers from Prison* was translated by Reginald Fuller and published in 1953 (London: SCM). A revised and enlarged edition was published in 1967.

4 See W. Hamilton, 'A Secular Theology for a World Come of Age', *Theology Today*, 18 (1962); P. Van Buren, *The Secular Meaning of the Gospel* (New York: Macmillan, 1963); T. J. Altizer, *The Gospel of Christian Atheism* (Philadelphia: Westminster Press, 1966); R. G. Smith, *Secular Christianity* (New York: Harper & Row, 1967).

5 M. Thornton, *The Rock and the River* (London: Hodder & Stoughton, 1965), pp. 49–64.

6 E. Bethge, *Bonhoeffer: Exile and Martyr*, ed. J. W. de Gruchy (London: Collins, 1975), p. 15.

7 John W. de Gruchy, 'Bonhoeffer, Apartheid, and Beyond: The Reception of Bonhoeffer in South Africa', in *Bonhoeffer for a New Day: Theology in a Time of Transition*, ed. J. W. de Gruchy (Grand Rapids: Eerdmans, 1997).

8 M. Bosanquet, *The Life and Death of Dietrich Bonhoeffer* (London: Hodder & Stoughton, 1968); E. Bethge, *Dietrich Bonhoeffer: Theologian, Christian, Contemporary* (London: Collins, 1970); E. H. Robertson, *The Shame and the Sacrifice: The Life and Teaching of Dietrich Bonhoeffer* (London: Hodder & Stoughton, 1987); R. Wind, *Dietrich Bonhoeffer: A Spoke in the Wheel* (Michigan: Eerdmans, 1991).

9 M. Glazener, *The Cup of Wrath: The Story of Dietrich Bonhoeffer's Resistance to Hitler* (Macon, Ga.: Smyth & Helwys, 1992).

10 W. Harrison, *Coming of Age* (Petersfield: Fernhurst Press, 1973).

11 For example 'Hitler and the Pastor – the Dietrich Bonhoeffer Story', the Dietrich Bonhoeffer Film Project, New York.

12 Herman Berlinski, Heinz Werner Zimmermann and Robert M. Helmschrott, *Bonhoeffer Triptychon*. This work was commissioned by Union Theological Seminary in New York and premiered there with the Dresden Chamber Choir under the direction of Hans-Christoph Rademann on 16 August 1992. VMM 3027.

13 Eberhard Bethge, 'The Response to Bonhoeffer', in E. Bethge, *Bonhoeffer: Exile and Martyr*.

14 C. Green, *The Sociality of Christ and Humanity: Dietrich Bonhoeffer's Early Theology, 1927–1933* (Missoula: Scholars Press, 1975).

15 These are all published in the *Dietrich Bonhoeffer Werke*. For a well-chosen selection in English translation, see B. G. Kelly and F. B. Nelson, *A Testament to Freedom: The Essential Writings of Dietrich Bonhoeffer* (San Francisco: Harper & Row, 1990).

16 W. J. Peck, *New Studies in Bonhoeffer's Ethics*, Toronto Studies in Theology, vol. 30 (New York: Edwin Mellen Press, 1987).

17 L. Rasmussen, *Dietrich Bonhoeffer: His Significance for North Americans* (Minneapolis: Fortress Press, 1990).

18 K. Clements, *A Patriotism for Today: Love of Country in Dialogue with the Witness of Dietrich Bonhoeffer* (London: Collins, 1986).

19 G. T. Rothuizen, *Aristokratisch Christendom* (Kampen: J. H. Kok, 1969).

20 Dietrich Bonhoeffer was born in Breslau, East Prussia, which is now Wrocław,

Poland. Much of his illegal work of theological education on behalf of the Confessing Church also took place in modern-day Poland (Finkenwalde, Schlawe, Köslin). In June 1996 a Polish Section of the International Bonhoeffer Society was established. See *Bonhoeffer Rundbrief*, no. 50.

21 H. Murakami, 'What has the Japanese Church Learned from Dietrich Bonhoeffer?', in *Bonhoeffer's Ethics: Old Europe and New Frontiers*, ed. G. Carter, R. Van Eyden, H. Van Hoogstraten and J. Wiersma (Kampen, Netherlands: Kok Pharos, 1991), pp. 217–21.

22 J. de Santo Ana, 'The Influence of Bonhoeffer on the Theology of Liberation', *The Ecumenical Review*, 28 (2) (April 1976); Carl-Jürgen Kaltenborn, 'Nicht-religiöses Credo in Latinamerika: zur Bonhoeffer-Rezeption in Latinamerika', in *Bonhoeffer-Studien: Beiträge zur Theologie und Wirkungsgeschichte Dietrich Bonhoeffers* (Berlin: Evangelische Verlagsanstalt, 1985).

23 J. W. de Gruchy, *Bonhoeffer and South Africa: Theology in Dialogue* (Grand Rapids: Eerdmans, 1984); de Gruchy, 'Bonhoeffer, Apartheid, and Beyond', pp. 353–72.

24 The *Deutsche Evangelische Kirchentag* has been held annually since the Second World War. Attended by thousands of Protestant Christians, it seeks to relate Bible study to the urgent tasks and issues facing the church and the nation.

25 H. Müller, 'Zur Problematik der Rezeption und Interpretation Dietrich Bonhoeffers', in *Die mündige Welt IV* (Munich: Chr. Kaiser Verlag, 1996); E. Bethge, *Bonhoeffer: Exile and Martyr*, pp. 11–13; G. Baum, *The Church for Others: Protestant Theology in Communist East Germany* (Grand Rapids: Eerdmans, 1996), pp. 83–102; J. Moses, 'Bonhoeffer's Reception in East Germany', in de Gruchy, *Bonhoeffer for a New Day*.

26 The first Catholic study on Bonhoeffer in English was William Kuhns, *In Pursuit of Dietrich Bonhoeffer* (London: Burns & Oates, 1967).

27 G. Huntemann, *The Other Bonhoeffer: An Evangelical Reassessment of Dietrich Bonhoeffer* (Grand Rapids: Baker Books, 1993).

28 Abram J. Klassen, 'Discipleship in Anabaptism and Bonhoeffer', Ph.D. dissertation, Claremont Graduate School, Berkeley, Calif., 1971.

29 See John Godsey, 'Reading Bonhoeffer in English Translation: Some Difficulties', in *Bonhoeffer in a World Come of Age*, ed. Peter Vorvink (Philadelphia: Fortress Press, 1968).

30 The new volumes of the *Dietrich Bonhoeffer Works* in English will, when complete, become the standard, critical edition. See Wayne Floyd's chapter in this volume. There are also some collections of Bonhoeffer's writings which are useful introductions to his writings as a whole. See J. de Gruchy, *Dietrich Bonhoeffer: Witness to Jesus Christ* (London: Collins, 1988); Kelly and Nelson, *A Testament to Freedom*.

31 S. Leibholz-Bonhoeffer, *The Bonhoeffers: Portrait of a Family* (London: Sidgwick & Jackson, 1971).

32 *I Knew Bonhoeffer: Reminiscences by his Friends*, ed. W. Zimmermann and R. G. Smith (London: Collins, 1966).

33 See especially E. Bethge, *Friendship and Resistance: Essays on Dietrich Bonhoeffer* (Geneva: WCC, 1995). Bethge's wife and Bonhoeffer's niece, Renate née Schleicher, has also contributed greatly to our understanding of Bonhoeffer's life

and times. See Renate Bethge, 'Bonhoeffer's Family and its Significance for his Theology', in Rasmussen, *Dietrich Bonhoeffer*, pp. 1–30.

34 See Bethge's own account of the way in which Bonhoeffer's legacy was received, and his role in that process. E. Bethge, *Bonhoeffer: Exile and Martyr*, pp. 11–25.

35 E. Bethge, *Dietrich Bonhoeffer: Theologian, Christian, Contemporary*.

36 Preface to E. Bethge, *Friendship and Resistance*.

37 Eberhard Bethge, 'The Challenge of Dietrich Bonhoeffer's Life and Theology', *The Chicago Theological Seminary Register*, 51 (2) (February 1961). Also published as Eberhard Bethge, 'The Challenge of Dietrich Bonhoeffer's Life and Theology', in *A World Come of Age: A Symposium on Dietrich Bonhoeffer*, ed. Ronald Gregor Smith (London: Collins, 1967).

38 H. Müller, *Von der Kirche zur Welt* (Hamberg-Bergstedt: Herbert Reich Evang. Verlag, 1966).

39 For Bethge's earliest response to Müller, see Eberhard Bethge, 'Besprechung: Hanfried Müller, Von der Kirche zur Welt', in *Gesammelte Schriften I*, ed. E. Bethge (Munich: Chr. Kaiser Verlag, 1963), pp. 169–74.

40 E. Bethge, 'The Challenge of Dietrich Bonhoeffer's Life and Theology', 19.

41 ibid., 29.

42 Eberhard Bethge, *Ohnmacht und Mündigkeit* (Munich: Chr. Kaiser Verlag, 1969); Eberhard Bethge, *Am gegebenen Ort* (Munich: Chr. Kaiser Verlag, 1979); Eberhard Bethge, *Bekennen und Widerstehen* (Munich: Chr. Kaiser Verlag, 1984).

43 R. K. Wüstenberg, *Glauben als Leben: Dietrich Bonhoeffer und die nichtreligiöse Interpretation biblischer Begriffe* (Frankfurt-on-Main: Peter Lang, 1995), pp. 255–341; R. K. Wüstenberg, *To Live as to Believe: Dietrich Bonhoeffer and the Non-Religious Interpretation of the Biblical Message* (Grand Rapids: Eerdmans, 1998).

44 See the detailed discussion of Bonhoeffer interpretation by Ernst Feil, 'Aspekte der Bonhoefferinterpretation', *Theologische Literaturzeitung*, 117 (1–2) (January–February 1992). (This is published in English as *Bonhoeffer Studies in Germany: An Overview of Recent Literature* (Philadelphia: International Bonhoeffer Society, English Language Section, 1997).) Earlier discussions include Rudolf Schulze, 'Hauptlinien der Bonhoeffer-Interpretation', *Evangelische Theologie*, 25 (1965); Jørgen Glenthøj, *Dokumente zur Bonhoeffer-Forschung* (Munich: Chr. Kaiser Verlag, 1969); James H. Burtness, 'Reading Bonhoeffer: A Map to the Literature', *Word and World*, (3) (Summer 1982).

45 Readers should consult Feil's discussion for the information on the German studies. The notes which follow are largely related to English-language studies or to those German studies which have been translated into English.

46 T. I. Day, *Dietrich Bonhoeffer on Christian Community and Common Sense*, Toronto Studies in Theology, vol. 11 (New York: Edwin Mellen Press, 1982).

47 J. A. Phillips, *Christ for Us in the Theology of Dietrich Bonhoeffer* (New York: Harper & Row, 1967).

48 J. Woelfel, *Bonhoeffer's Theology: Classical and Revolutionary* (New York: Abingdon, 1970).

49 M. Kuske, *The Old Testament as the Book of Christ: An Appraisal of Bonhoeffer's Interpretation* (Philadelphia: Westminster, 1976).

50 Green, *The Sociality of Christ and Humanity*.

51 W. W. Floyd, Jr, *Theology and the Dialectics of Otherness: On Reading Bonhoeffer and Adorno* (Baltimore: University Press of America, 1988).

52 L. Rasmussen, *Dietrich Bonhoeffer: Reality and Resistance* (Nashville: Abingdon, 1972); J. H. Burtness, *Shaping the Future: The Ethics of Dietrich Bonhoeffer* (Philadelphia: Fortress Press, 1985); R. W. Lovin, *Christian Faith and Public Choices: The Social Ethics of Barth, Brunner and Bonhoeffer* (Philadelphia: Fortress Press, 1984); and Peck, *New Studies in Bonhoeffer's Ethics.*

53 C. E. Fant, *Bonhoeffer: Worldly Preaching* (New York: Crossroad, 1990).

54 *Die mündige Welt*, ed. E. Bethge, vols. i–iv (Munich: Chr. Kaiser Verlag, 1956–63).

55 *The Place of Bonhoeffer: Problems and Possibilities in his Thought*, ed. M. E. Marty (New York: Association Press, 1962).

56 Notably the volumes published in the series Internationales Bonhoeffer Forum and the East German collection *Bonhoeffer-Studien*, ed. A. Schönherr and W. Krötke (Berlin: Evangelische Verlagsanstalt, 1985).

57 Müller, *Von der Kirche zur Welt.*

58 J. Godsey, *The Theology of Dietrich Bonhoeffer* (London: SCM, 1960).

59 On Barth's own thoughts on his relationship with Bonhoeffer see K. Barth, *Fragments Grave and Gay* (London: Collins, 1971). See also E. Bethge, *Dietrich Bonhoeffer: Theologian, Christian, Contemporary*, pp. 131–42 and J. Godsey, 'Barth and Bonhoeffer: The Basic Difference', *Quarterly Review*, 7 (1) (Spring 1987).

60 A. Dumas, *Dietrich Bonhoeffer: Theologian of Reality* (New York: Macmillan, 1971).

61 C. Marsh, *Reclaiming Dietrich Bonhoeffer: The Promise of his Theology* (New York: Oxford University Press, 1994).

62 Floyd, *Theology and the Dialectics of Otherness.*

63 See Chapter 3 above.

64 E. Feil, *The Theology of Dietrich Bonhoeffer*, trans. M. Rumscheidt (Philadelphia: Fortress Press, 1985), p. xvi.

65 ibid., p. 204.

66 See the detailed discussion of Bonhoeffer interpretation by Feil, 'Aspekte der Bonhoefferinterpretation'. Earlier discussions include Schulze, 'Hauptlinien der Bonhoeffer-Interpretation'; Glenthøj, *Dokumente zur Bonhoeffer-Forschung*; Burtness, 'Reading Bonhoeffer'.

67 G. Ebeling, 'The Non-Religious Interpretation of Biblical Concepts', in *Word and Faith* (Philadelphia: Fortress Press, 1963); see also H. Ott, *Reality and Faith: The Theological Legacy of Dietrich Bonhoeffer* (London: Lutterworth, 1971).

68 J. Moltmann and A. Weissbach, *Two Studies in the Theology of Dietrich Bonhoeffer*, trans. R. Fuller (New York: Charles Scribner's Sons, 1967).

69 A. Pangritz, *Karl Barth in the Theology of Dietrich Bonhoeffer* (Grand Rapids: Eerdmans, 1988).

70 For example G. B. Kelly, *Liberating Faith: Bonhoeffer's Message for Today* (Minneapolis: Augsburg Publishing House,, 1984).

71 de Gruchy, *Dietrich Bonhoeffer: Witness to Jesus Christ*; Kelly and Nelson, *A Testament to Freedom.*

72 de Gruchy, *Bonhoeffer and South Africa*; Clements, *A Patriotism for Today*; Rasmussen, *Dietrich Bonhoeffer: His Significance for North Americans.*

73 For a comprehensive study of Bonhoeffer's theology as a 'political theology' see T. R. Peters, *Die Präsenz des Politischen in der Theologie Dietrich Bonhoeffers* (Munich: Chr. Kaiser Verlag, 1976).

74 See H. Russel Botman, 'Afterword: Is Bonhoeffer Still of Any Use?', in de Gruchy *Bonhoeffer for a New Day.*

75 de Gruchy, 'Bonhoeffer, Apartheid, and Beyond'.

76 Chung Hyun Kyung, 'Dear Dietrich Bonhoeffer: A Letter', in de Gruchy, *Bonhoeffer for a New Day*, p. 10.

Part two

Major themes in Bonhoeffer's theology

6 Human sociality and Christian community

CLIFFORD GREEN

Bonhoeffer provided the title of this chapter in his doctoral dissertation, *Sanctorum Communio*, when he said that theological doctrines such as creation, sin and revelation can only be fully understood in terms of sociality. If the venerable English word 'sociality' does not spring to our lips in everyday speech, that reflects the degree to which practical and philosophical individualism pervades modern Anglo-Saxon culture. But to use 'sociality' as a fundamental category to describe Dietrich Bonhoeffer's theology is not simply to distinguish German from American and British culture. The reason is essentially theological: 'the concepts of person, community and God are inseparably and essentially interrelated'.[1]

This means that articulating a Christian understanding of human sociality is an inner-theological task. What 'person' and 'community' mean is a question of theological anthropology. It is not as if one could take an already developed interpretation of human social existence and then simply pour Christian content into it. For there are many different systems embedding competing world views: in the modern world, theories of social contract, civil rights, utilitarianism and Marxism have powerfully shaped economic and political systems, and the mentality and mores of whole populations. Similarly, philosophy from Aristotle to the Stoics and up to Idealist epistemology and Hegelianism have all developed views of human persons and social life.[2] The challenge for theology, Bonhoeffer recognised, is to articulate 'a specifically Christian social philosophy'.[3] This he set out in a theology of sociality which is particularly evident in his first two dissertations (*Sanctorum Communio – The Communion of Saints* – and *Act and Being*), in writings deriving from Berlin lecture courses (*Creation and Fall* and *Christology*), and later in his theological interpretation of the common life at Finkenwalde (*Life Together*). Indeed, its central ideas and basic conceptual structure are so fundamental for his *Ethics* and *Letters and Papers from Prison* that we have to regard it as formative for his whole theology.[4] Sociality is a complex category, and what Bonhoeffer specifically means by it must be built up from its component concepts.

A theological focus on human sociality naturally entails attention to the Christian community, the church. Or perhaps a reverse formulation is better: because being-Christian is life-in-church-community, so this communal–social paradigm informs Bonhoeffer's thinking about human sociality generally. What 'church' means, however, cannot be taken for granted, especially in Germany in the 1930s. There the dispute over the meaning of 'church' was not confined to books and journals; it was a political church struggle (*Kirchenkampf*) between the Confessing Church and the majority 'church' (Reichskirche) which tolerated or, worse, enthusiastically supported National Socialism.

THEOLOGY OF PERSON

While Bonhoeffer himself laid out his understanding of sociality by beginning with a Christian concept of person, his statement that this is inseparable from Christian beliefs about community and God allows another starting point. *Act and Being*, the work of philosophical theology which qualified him to be a lecturer at the University of Berlin, is a description of the freedom of God seen in Jesus Christ. Contending that the early Barth in his *Epistle to the Romans* reacted against human idolatry by speaking of a formal freedom of God *from* the world, Bonhoeffer spoke vividly of God's freedom *for* humanity in Jesus Christ.

> In revelation it is not so much a question of the freedom of God –
> eternally remaining within the divine self, aseity – on the other side of
> revelation, as it is of God's coming out of God's own self in revelation.
> It is a matter of God's given Word, the covenant in which God is
> bound by God's own action. It is a question of the freedom of God,
> which finds its strongest evidence in that God freely chose to be bound
> to historical human beings and to be placed at the disposal of human
> beings. God is free not from human beings but for them. Christ is the
> word of God's freedom. God is present, that is, not in eternal
> nonobjectivity but . . . 'haveable', graspable in the Word within the
> church.[5]

God's being is not in transcendent isolation and absence. God is free for humanity in our history; that is, in the light of Jesus Christ, God is revealed as present to us in the world – God's being is being-in-relation-to-us. This is the meaning of the incarnation: God with us, and God for us.

If this is so, it follows that human existence is also fundamentally relational. To be human is to be a person before God, and in relation to God. The relation of individual persons to each other, and relations between human communities of persons, has this theological understanding of God and human existence at its core. If the mature Barth ultimately grounds his understanding of human community in the inner-trinitarian life of God, Bonhoeffer grounds it in God's incarnation in Jesus Christ. The focus is Christocentric – the trinitarian articulation is present in Bonhoeffer, but Christology is in the foreground.

Charles Marsh has argued persuasively that Bonhoeffer presents a 'christological description of life with others [which] offers a compelling and unexpectedly rich alternative to post-Kantian models of selfhood – to conceptions of the self as the centre of all relations to others'.[6] Marsh builds on Bonhoeffer, who criticised the subject–object model of epistemology as incapable of describing the social and ethical relations of human persons. While the subject–object model may be useful for thinking about how we know scientifically (it may be an adequate model of a scientist looking through a microscope or a telescope at an object), it is no help for understanding relations between human persons – particularly ethical relations – and relations between human communities.

Central to the complex conceptuality of sociality is Bonhoeffer's understanding of person – though always in the context of a community, as discussed below. If the premise of theological anthropology is that the human person exists in relation to God, then the human counterpart of this is person in relation to person. This is the I–You relation: persons are independent, willing subjects who exist in relation to others. They encounter each other by making ethical claims upon one another; and the independent will of one constitutes a limit for the other. The person is a socio-ethical, historical being whose identity is formed in such ethical encounters with others. Long before post-modernists discovered 'otherness', the You as other was crucial in Bonhoeffer's theological anthropology. 'The individual exists only in relation to an "other"; individual does not mean solitary. On the contrary, for the individual to exist, "others" must necessarily be there.'[7] But the other is not merely alien or unreachable; the other is the You whom I meet in ethical encounter.

Critical here is Bonhoeffer's assertion that the You, the other person, constitutes a barrier or boundary to the self. When I encounter the will of another who resists my own will, I am obliged to respond: I am accountable, responsible, I must answer (the German word for responsibility, *Verant-wortlichkeit*, literally means 'answerability'). This image of conflicting wills is not only the result of sin; in the world of creation there can be natural and constructive conflict. Nevertheless, in the situation of sin the challenging will of the other counters the pretensions of the self – its propensity to dominate, manipulate or use the other person.

Bonhoeffer's stress on the I–You relation has reminded many of Martin Buber, whose well-known book, *I and Thou,*[8] appeared in 1923, four years before Bonhoeffer completed his doctoral dissertation. But Buber, whose distinction between I–It and I–You relations was rooted in Marburg neo-Kantianism, had a quite different understanding of the I–You relation from Bonhoeffer. The Buber scholar Walter Kaufmann has rightly described 'the sense of intimacy that pervades Buber's book';[9] the aim is to create a realm of intimacy between persons, overcoming the objectified I–It world. But Bonhoeffer, who objects to objectifying persons as much as Buber does, stresses the other as boundary and barrier to the self – he emphasises ethical encounter rather than intimacy; the other transcends the self in this ethical encounter – indeed, the human You is a form and analogy of the divine You. This personal-ethical model of transcendence is found throughout all Bonhoeffer's theology.[10] While Bonhoeffer knew of Buber, he does not cite *I and Thou* but draws on other philosophers of the I–You relation such as Griesebach and Hirsch.

This understanding of persons in a web of ethical relations is the basis of Bonhoeffer's fresh and far-reaching interpretation of the image of God (*imago Dei*). He developed it in a 1932 Berlin University lecture course which was then published as *Creation and Fall: A Theological Interpretation of Genesis 1–3*. Bonhoeffer's innovation is apparent in contrast to the view of previous theologians, all of whom have said that the human image of God consisted in some quality or property of the individual. This has been identified variously as free-will, as reason, as a quality of the soul such as immortality or, in Augustine, as a similarity to the trinitarian God seen in the unity of human memory, intellect and will.

In contrast to all individualistic interpretations of the image of God, Bonhoeffer insists that this image or likeness must be understood as a particular relationship between persons. He takes his cue from Genesis 1:26f. (see also 5:1–2), which tells of God creating humanity in God's image by creating two people in relation, male and female. Then, arguing that God wants to be seen or imaged in creatures who freely worship their Creator, Bonhoeffer writes, 'No one can think of freedom as a substance or as something individualistic. Freedom . . . is simply something that . . . happens to me through the other.'

For in the language of the Bible freedom is not something that people have for themselves but something they have for others. No one is free 'in herself' or 'in himself' [*an sich*] – free as it were in a vacuum, or free in the same way that a person may be musical, intelligent or blind in herself or in himself. Freedom is not a quality a human being has, it is not an ability, a capacity . . . Because freedom . . . is not a possession, something to hand, an object; nor is it a form of something to hand; instead it is a relationship and nothing else. To be more precise, freedom is a relationship between two persons. Being free means 'being-free-for-the-other', because I am bound to the other. Only by being in relationship with the other am I free.[11]

Being-free-for-the-other-in-love images God's loving freedom for humanity. The theological warrant for this account of the image of God among human beings must be found in the nature of God's freedom. Here Bonhoeffer restates a familiar axiom: 'Because God in Christ is free for humankind, because God does not keep God's freedom to God's self, we can think of freedom only as a being-free-for . . .'[12] So the likeness, image or analogy of creaturely being to the Creator must be an *analogia relationis*, analogy of relationship. 'God . . . must be thought of as one who is not alone, inasmuch as God is the one who in Christ attests to God's "being for humankind".' It is important to note that Bonhoeffer is not expounding some speculative ontology of the Creator here; it is a Christological interpretation focused on the incarnation and resurrection of Jesus Christ. To summarise in this light, since God's being is being-for-humanity, so human relationships image this in one person 'being-free-for-the-other' in love.[13]

THEOLOGY OF COMMUNITY

We have focused thus far on Bonhoeffer's theological understanding of persons and their relationships. But his theology of sociality cannot be reduced to an interpersonal 'personalism'.[14] Sociality concerns human communities just as much as individual persons. In fact, there is a reciprocal relationship between person and community, which can be stated this way: just as persons are created for community, communities consist of persons; each is irreducibly real and requires the other. One of the interesting commentaries on recent history and social philosophy which Bonhoeffer's approach suggests is this: if the modern West exalted the individual at the expense of community and society, the Soviet East exalted the social and collective at the expense of the individual. In other words, both in their different ways are caricatures of the Christian understanding which sees a reciprocal relation, a mutuality, between community and individual person. It is also pertinent to observe here that 'person' is Bonhoeffer's term of choice, rather than 'individual'. Bonhoeffer uses the term 'community' to include a comprehensive range of social forms. Forms as small as a marriage, family or friendship, and as large as a people, a nation or a whole church, are all communities – indeed, he regards the whole of humanity (standing before God as one person, so to speak, represented by Adam or Christ) to be the 'community of the whole'. Communities are not utilitarian, as are business corporations or political organisations, which are organised to serve purposes other than the organisations themselves. Communities, and the individual persons who comprise them, are willed as ends in themselves; they are structures of meaning, life-communities.[15]

At this point the term 'person' is used in a new way. Bonhoeffer uses his model of the person in ethical relationships and accountability to interpret the relations of communities to each other; he also uses it to interpret the way individuals take responsibility for their communities. Some examples illustrate his meaning. In the Civil Rights movement in the United States led by Dr Martin Luther King, Jr, the community of African-Americans encountered the white community with an urgent ethical claim for justice and freedom. Just as in ethical encounters between individual people, the black community resisted the injustices perpetuated by the white community, and challenged the white community to make a responsible answer in legislation, economic policy and social behaviour and customs. Other examples come quickly to mind: a similar encounter between opponents and proponents of apartheid in South Africa; or between Vietnamese nationalists and French colonialists and American Cold War strategists; or between British colonialists and the Indian independence movement led by Gandhi; or between the Western and Eastern blocs in the Cold War.

In all of these conflicts and encounters, communities constituted by ethnic, religious and political principles encounter each other and press their ethical claims upon one another. But how exactly does this ethical encounter actually take place? Bonhoeffer answers: in people who represent their communities and act responsibly on their behalf. Here one of Bonhoeffer's key theological-ethical terms comes into play: *Stellvertretung*. Literally it means standing in the place of another, but it means much more than words like 'proxy', 'deputy' and 'representative' convey. Bonhoeffer's meaning is best expressed by speaking of people who personify their communities, and act vicariously on their behalf. People like Martin Luther King, Jr, Nelson Mandela and Mahatma Gandhi illustrate what Bonhoeffer means. He himself pointed to the example of the biblical prophets who both spoke the word of God's justice and judgement to the people as a whole and in themselves repent on behalf of the whole community. We can now add the name of Dietrich Bonhoeffer himself, who acted in responsibility for his communities – first for the Protestant Church, in the church struggle, and then for the German nation, in the resistance movement.

In highly individualistic cultures people often assume that God is only interested in individuals. Bonhoeffer asserts that God has a word and will for communities as such, as well as for individuals. Through persons who act in the name of and for the sake of the corporate body, the community as an 'I' can be addressed by God as a 'You'; human communities, like individual persons, can be called into ethical responsibility.

> God does not desire a history of individual human beings, but the
> history of the human community. Nor does God want a community
> which absorbs the individual into itself, but a community of human
> beings. In God's sight community and individual are present in the
> same moment and rest upon one another.[16]

Having developed this conceptuality of sociality, Bonhoeffer employs it in his theological argument to portray the biblical drama of creation, sin and revelation. Adam and Christ are the two primal figures who personify humanity as a whole – Adam personifying created and sinful humanity, Christ personifying redeemed humanity. This leads to the Christian community and its story.

CHRISTIAN COMMUNITY

If Christian community is normally discussed in terms of the church, Bonhoeffer's experience in Germany immediately requires this disclaimer: not everything that calls itself church is church – theology has no place for sociological fundamentalism. The problem of a church which betrays Christ and the gospel is not confined to Germany under National Socialism, of course, but that example is vividly instructive. Everything that follows presupposes that the reader is familiar with the German church struggle (*Kirchenkampf*) between those who, actively or passively, made the church a tool of National Socialist ideology, and that minority like Dietrich Bonhoeffer who belonged to the Confessing Church (Bekennende Kirche). When they issued their confession of faith in the Barmen Declaration in May 1934, and then organised ecclesially in the Synod of Dahlem in October that year, they were not forming another denomination. Rather, they boldly claimed that they were faithful to the church of the Reformation, and that the Reich Church and the German Christian Movement had betrayed the gospel by substituting for Christ a creed of blood, soil and the Thousand-Year Reich. As a theological teacher of the Confessing Church, Bonhoeffer stated the challenge forcefully: those who knowingly separate themselves from the Confessing Church separate themselves from salvation.[17]

When he first wrote in 1927 about the Christian community in his doctoral dissertation, Bonhoeffer hardly anticipated the church crisis which would occur when Hitler became Chancellor in January 1933. However, he laid down the foundation which was to be invulnerable to all Nazi co-opting of the church. That was the simple theological axiom: the church is *Christus als Gemeinde existierend*, Christ existing as community. This phrase was an adaptation of Hegel's statement, 'God existing as community',[18] with the alteration of only one word. But given the ease with which people project all manner of self-serving ideas into the word 'God', and the difficulty of doing it so easily with the name of Christ, the Christological concentration of Bonhoeffer's axiom was liberating. Single-minded adherence to Christ was all it took to resist the whole worldly panoply of National Socialism.

With this perspective, Bonhoeffer's understanding of Christian community can now be explored. In his *Ethics* he pithily stated the view which he had held from the beginning: 'The church is nothing but the part of humanity in which Christ has really taken form.'[19] Two points are involved here: the church results from divine initiative (Christ taking form); this initiative is for humanity as a whole and produces a 'new humanity'. *Sanctorum Communio* lays out the argument in three steps. Creation, sin and revelation are all interpreted in terms of sociality. Adam personifies created and fallen humanity, Christ the new humanity.

In describing creation as the original, unbroken community, Bonhoeffer argues that to be human is to live in community with God and with others. Of course we have no access, in the midst of sinful history, to such a primal community of mutual love. It can only be reconstructed theologically from the revelation in Christ. This discloses (for example in Mark 10:35ff.) that God's rule is a rule of loving service, which creates a community in which human beings serve God and one another by mutual love. Community with God is not an individualistic possibility, but is actual and real in the community of God's creatures with each other; to serve and love God is simultaneously to serve and love God's creatures, one's fellow human beings. Community with God is simultaneously the community of co-humanity.[20]

Sin brings us into a familiar world; expounded in the light of sociality, sin is the world of broken community. If sin is self-will, not as an appropriate self-affirmation, but the assertion of self by denying the other, then community is impossible; created sociality is contradicted, and becomes the solidarity of self-isolation. Self-seeking rather than love of other, demanding rather than giving, isolated self-love rather than mutual love – these are the dynamics which destroy the primal community. At the root of Bonhoeffer's picture of sin is that Promethean assertion of the autonomous ego so typical of modernity. In the language of Genesis 3:5, he calls it the effort to become *sicut deus*, like God.[21] This throws retrospective light on his account of the I–You relationship, in which the You was described frequently as 'barrier' and 'boundary'. In large part this is because he understands sin as the assertion of self-serving power which must be resisted and called to account by the resisting will of another independent subject.[22]

Since sociality for Bonhoeffer is as much concerned with corporate life as with interpersonal relations, the effect of sin on societal organisation should equally be noted. The purposes of instrumental associations – economic, political, labour, military, academic – become distorted so that through the evil will operating in them they become 'institutions of systematic exploitation of one person by another'.[23] Communities of meaning (the *Gemeinschaft* type) do not escape corruption: because of sin the community is not willed as an end in itself, but as a means for the ends of the self; so families, marriages, friendships, ethnic groups, nations all suffer. The world of the lost primal community and the broken community of sin is nevertheless the world God created and loves and the world which Christ reconciles. In a profound departure from Patristic soteriology, which held that God became human in order that human beings might be deified, Bonhoeffer states: God became human in order that we might become human.[24] The incarnation is about the humanisation of the human race, not its divinisation; it is about restoring and redeeming humanity to its true but lost nature in community with God and fellow human beings.

Bonhoeffer's approach to the Christian church-community reminds one of Athanasius, the champion of Nicene Christianity. In his *On the Incarnation of the Word*,[25] Athanasius presented the biblical narrative as the story of God's creatures, who were created out of nothing and were entirely dependent on their Creator, and who slid into corruption and non-being as a result of sin. In the incarnation, cross and resurrection, the same Logos through whom the world was created comes to save the world by what is, in effect, an act of re-creation. In short, the church-community is humanity being remade and redeemed as a result of God's creative grace.

This is what Bonhoeffer means when he says that the church is 'the part of humanity in which Christ has really taken form'. It is not the creation of a religious organisation, not the setting up of another religion alongside or over against other religions; it is the renewal, the humanisation, of humanity per se. 'The church is God's new will and purpose with humanity.'[26]

Now, Bonhoeffer was by no means alone in addressing the theme of community in the Germany of the 1920s. The theme was in the air – not only in theology, but in the youth movement and in politics. Indeed, the issue for Christian theology would quickly become: what distinguishes *Christian* community from a community grounded in principles such as blood and soil, or, to be quite specific, Aryan anti-Semitism and the Thousand-Year Reich of National Socialism? In other words, how is Christian community distinguished from community rooted in the natural vitalities of a people, a *Volksgemeinschaft*? For Bonhoeffer the answer was clear: the Christian church-community does not emerge from the *Volksgemeinschaft* – it is a *Christusgemeinschaft*. It is not a community of blood, but a community of water; it is constituted by baptism, not by race.

Bonhoeffer's first affirmation about the Christian community is that the church is established and real in Christ; it is a divine reality, the social form of revelation. This means that the first thought about the church must be to realise that it comes from God's action and presence. It is not an organisation to fulfil religious needs. It is not an institution with local manifestations and impressive centres in London, Rome, Moscow, Athens, Geneva or New York. It is not the partner of governments to provide moral legitimation or to support law and order. It is God's creation in Christ. Here Bonhoeffer's ecclesiology was quite consistent with Karl Barth's theology of revelation and, because this approach was so unusual in Berlin when Bonhoeffer wrote *Sanctorum Communio*, Barth called the work a theological miracle.[27] If the church grows by the Holy Spirit, this too is God's initiative and means that people are brought into a divine reality already created by God.

Bonhoeffer was a Chalcedonian theologian, as is evident in his lectures on Christology as well as in spontaneous, passing remarks.[28] Related to his understanding of the church, this meant that he not only said 'the church is a divine reality'; he also said 'the church is a human reality'. The second statement does not cancel the first. So Bonhoeffer explored the 'sociological marks' of the church which were characteristic of a specific community rooted in God's revelation in Christ.[29]

In addition to affirming the traditional marks of the church as the community where the gospel word is proclaimed and the sacraments celebrated, Bonhoeffer also paints a distinctive picture of life in the Christian community. The 'life principle' of the new humanity is that free, loving, self-giving of Christ which Bonhoeffer calls *Stellvertretung*, vicarious action on behalf of others. Concretely this takes two forms among the members of the community: 'being-with-each-other' and 'being-for-each-other'. The Christian life is a shared life, not a private spirituality; it is a life of bearing each other's burdens, being 'Christ to one another', as Luther put it. Being-for-each-other takes very practical forms, which Bonhoeffer puts in italics: '*self-renouncing, active work for the neighbour; intercessory prayer; and finally the mutual forgiveness of sins in the name of God*'.[30] In *Life Together* we see how powerfully this understanding of Christian community shaped Bonhoeffer's leadership of the Finkenwalde theological college.

How did this brilliant young theologian, finishing his first book at the age of twenty-one, view the actual church in Germany at the time? It was, of course, a *Volkskirche*, embracing everyone in the nation, and had close ties to the state which collected church taxes and paid clergy and professors of theology. Bonhoeffer thought that such a national church could be a sign that the gospel is for all people, and that its deep historical roots were a strength which did not necessarily prevent change. At the same time, a national church should always strive, like the voluntary churches, to be a community of people who freely confess their faith. If this does not happen, Bonhoeffer warned, a national church 'is in the gravest internal danger'. Prophetically he added: 'There is a moment when the church may no longer be a church-of-the-people (*Volkskirche*); this moment has come when the church can no longer recognise its all-inclusive form as the means for becoming a voluntary church.'[31] He wrote these words afraid that the national church might become fossilised, an empty shell. Seven years later Bonhoeffer found the national church all too alive and full of spirits – strange spirits, false gods, the seductive idols of nationalism, anti-Semitism and militarism.

Bonhoeffer's theological and ethical work after Hitler's ascent in 1933 had two foci: first, the struggle for the church to be faithful, the *Kirchen-kampf*; secondly, beginning in the late 1930s, working for peace and Germany's future in the resistance movement.

SOCIALITY AND CHRISTIAN COMMUNITY AFTER 1933

In his 1933 lectures on *Christology* Bonhoeffer expanded on two themes from his earlier theology. First, Christology concerns the Christ who is personally present; it is not a speculative inquiry into divine and human natures as reified entities. Christ is present in the personal community of proclaimed word and enacted sacrament. Christian community is not some vague feeling of 'togetherness' or indeterminate 'spirituality'. The community is given quite definite form, content and meaning by the gospel. In the sermon the gospel is heard as personal address from Christ; in the celebration of baptism and eucharist the gospel message is enacted in all its sensuous immediacy, for human beings are body as well as spirit (not one without the other), and Christ cannot be sublimated into a doctrine, idea or general truth. Christ is present in the threefold form of word, sacrament and community. This does not mean that community is a third element distinct from the other two; rather it means that word and sacrament are intrinsically communal. As in *Sanctorum Communio*, community is understood in terms of ethical personalism. God's transcendence is not remote otherness or absence; God's otherness is embodied precisely in the other person who is real and present, encountering me in the heart of my existence with the judgement and grace of the gospel. In this way Christ is present *pro me*, for me. Bonhoeffer's Christology is simultaneously incarnational and communal.

The second theme developed in the Christology lectures is Christ as Mediator.[32] Taken out of context, Bonhoeffer's formula 'Christ existing as community' might be misunderstood in a sectarian or privatised sense. But the same Christ who is present in the most personal way in the Christian community is also the universal Mediator of existence, history and nature.[33] To describe Christ as Mediator Bonhoeffer uses as a key Christological metaphor the word 'centre', which recurs in the *Ethics* and prison *Letters* in his discussions of 'reality' and 'Christ as the centre of life'. If the previous paragraph in effect focused on Christ as the Mediator of personal existence, what does it mean to call Christ the Mediator of history made by the state?

Following Luther, Bonhoeffer holds that Christ is present in the twofold form of church and state. But Christ is not revealed in the state as he is in the church. Political history is replete with efforts to achieve human well-being, peace, happiness and even glory – the Pax Romana, the British Empire, modern democracy, communism, even National Socialism in its perverse way; in this sense, political history has a 'messianic' character. Christ, the crucified Messiah, exposes the self-glorifying corruption of all these efforts, as the illustrations confirm in their different ways. History is not God's eschatological realm of justice, peace and love. The crucified Christ is not only judge of history, however; as the Incarnate and Resurrected One he is God's promise of fulfilment. The church, where Christ is revealed, reads the state, politics and history in the light of God's eschatological purpose for the whole creation. The Christian community knows that the state and politics, have a provisional legitimacy in God's purpose, namely to create a just order through law. It is an order of preservation to protect life and human communities, and to restrain evil.[34]

These are not academic musings. They disclose much of the basis of Bonhoeffer's own political responsibility and action. For example, in a radio address around the time of these Christology lectures, Bonhoeffer attacked the idolatry of the Nazi Führer concept.[35] In his 1933 essay on 'The Church and the Jewish Question'[36] he argued that the church had three forms of responsibility to the state: (1) to remind it of its God-given vocation to preserve life through just law; (2) to aid all the victims of state action, not only Christians; (3) to resist the state by direct political action when the state was failing its responsibility, for example by depriving citizens of their rights, or by imposing anti-Semitic laws on church membership.[37]

During the second half of the 1930s Bonhoeffer was the director of the Confessing Church's theological college at Finkenwalde. When the Gestapo closed it down, he quickly wrote a book summarising its theology and practice. In *Life Together* we see many ways in which Bonhoeffer's theology of sociality and his understanding of Christian community in *Sanctorum Communio* shaped the actual daily life of the college. First, Bonhoeffer's model was a community, not an academy. The German title of the book, *Gemeinsames Leben*, could well be translated *Life in Community*; indeed, as courses of students came and went, Bonhoeffer organised a 'House of Brothers', six graduates of the course who, with himself, formed a continuing community to work with new students and neighbouring churches.

The pattern of daily life for the college included worship, study of the Bible, meditation, prayer, lectures, sermon practice, meals and recreation. Some of these belonged to 'the day together', others to 'the day alone'. Here we see the counterpoint of community and individual person noted above, which Bonhoeffer now formulated as follows: 'Whoever cannot be alone should beware of community. Whoever cannot stand being in community should beware of being alone.'[38] Other themes of Finkenwalde life also come straight out of *Sanctorum Communio*. Being-with-each-other and being-for-each-other are spelt out in relation to intercessory prayer by the community members for each other; 'active helpfulness'; bearing the burdens of others; and mutual admonition.[39] Being-for-each-other also involves personal confession and mutual forgiveness of sins.[40]

Bonhoeffer practised oral confession himself at Finkenwalde, and strongly encouraged his students to do so. This pastoral encounter of persons, of self and other, is an excellent example of his understanding of sociality as the form of transcendence. By confessing to another we are delivered from the self imprisoned in itself, with its self-deception, self-justification and self-forgiveness – which is no forgiveness at all. More, by hearing the word of God's forgiveness pronounced by another, I receive an assurance which is truly for me because it is beyond me; I 'experience the presence of God in the reality of the other'.[41]

Fundamental to the theology and practice of Finkenwalde was the affirmation 'Christ existing as community'. This means that all relationships are mediated by Christ. To understand what Bonhoeffer means by Christ as Mediator in this context, consider how mediation functions in everyday life. I am not thinking here of a mediator in a dispute, but rather of the way that our beliefs, images, stereotypes mediate our experience – how they profoundly shape the way we perceive and relate to other people and groups. This is quite evident in people with strong racial or anti-Semitic prejudices. But it also holds, perhaps more subtly, for people in a market economy, saturated by advertising, who regard themselves and others as consumers. To generalise briefly, all experience is culturally mediated. Bonhoeffer argues that in Christian community it is Christ who is the Mediator of all experience and relationships. 'Christian community means community through Jesus Christ and in Jesus Christ.'[42] As the one eternal Mediator, Christ stands between me and the other person; there are no unmediated relationships in true Christian community.[43] That one sees others – and oneself – through the eyes of Christ has very practical effects. These include, among others: refraining from judging people, resisting our desire to impose our will and ideals on others, praying for one another, forgiving enemies, regarding ourselves and others as sinners forgiven by the grace of God, and helping one another with deeds of love and mercy.

The practice of Christian community described in *Life Together* was the context in which Bonhoeffer wrote most of *The Cost of Discipleship*, and they should be regarded as companion books, each illuminating the other. Further, all the basic concepts of his theology of sociality are presupposed in his discussion of discipleship.[44] The message of single-minded obedience to Christ, whose word is equally heard in the Sermon on the Mount and in the sermon in the church, is its controlling theme, and can be explored further in Chapter 9 below.

During most of the 1930s, Bonhoeffer was acting in responsibility on behalf of his church community in the church struggle and in his theological teaching. By the end of the decade he is acting in responsibility on behalf of the national community of Germany as a member of the resistance movement. The latter, as much as the former, is a Christian and theological task. As we have seen above, from the outset Bonhoeffer understood ethics as involved both in individual relationships between persons and also in responsible action on behalf of the communities to which those persons belong. How else can responsibility for a community be exercised, if not through persons who act as its representatives? Now Germany was controlled by a fascist dictatorship, and waging war in Europe under the aegis of a pagan ideology. Bonhoeffer joined his brother Klaus and his brother-in-law Hans von Dohnanyi and their colleagues in the movement to overthrow Hitler, bring peace to Europe, and reconstruct a new future for the coming generation. This is the context for his work on *Ethics*.

At Christmas 1942, Bonhoeffer gave several friends a piece he called 'After Ten Years'; most of it is also incorporated in his *Ethics*.[45] He first profiles several ethical postures based, respectively, on reason, moral fanaticism, conscience, duty, freedom, and private virtuousness, arguing that they have all failed the test in the previous decade's struggle against National Socialism. He then states that the only ethical stance for a Christian is 'obedient and responsible action in faith and in exclusive allegiance to God'.[46] This leads to some striking polemics. The first task of a Christian ethic is to reject the definition that ethics is about knowledge of good and evil. Instead of the questions 'How can I be good?' and 'How can I do good?' a Christian ethic must begin by asking 'What is the will of God?'[47] In approaching ethics this way, asking about the will of God for responsible human action, Bonhoeffer is clearly reflecting on his driving ethical concern as he participates in planning a *coup* which includes killing Hitler.[48] This critical concern is the special focus of the section 'The Structure of Responsible Life'.[49] (He is also using 'responsibility' as a key term in his ethic, just as he had early defined the Christian concept of person in terms of ethical responsibility in the I–You encounter.)

The question of the will of God is a Christological question, as it was when Bonhoeffer was dealing with discipleship and the Sermon on the Mount. So it was originally when he was dealing with the church as the social form of God's revelation in *Sanctorum Communio*. There Christ embodies and creates God's new reality for the world: the Christian community is the new humanity – part of the world reconciled and being made new.[50] In *Ethics* Bonhoeffer pursues this Christological understanding of reality. In his first book the question was: how is the Christian community the revelation of God in and for the world? Now the question is: how does the Christian enact God's will in the world of history?

A Christological understanding of reality means seeing history, society and politics in the light of God's being and purposes. A Christological understanding of reality is therefore different from what typically goes by the name of 'realism'; such 'realistic' thinking usually consists of a calculus based on 'history' and 'experience' – apart from God! Bonhoeffer links God and the world Christologically in this way:

> In Christ we are offered the possibility of partaking in the reality of God and in the reality of the world, but not in the one without the other. The reality of God discloses itself only by setting me entirely in the reality of the world, and when I encounter the reality of the world it is always already sustained, accepted, and reconciled in the reality of God.[51]

In several passages Bonhoeffer begins to spell out what it means to see the world 'sustained, accepted, and reconciled' in Christ, and does so with unmistakable allusions to the contemporary situation in Germany. His discussions of Christ under the themes of incarnation, cross and resurrection are not abstract ruminations but loaded with ethical freight.[52]

Two more themes of Bonhoeffer's theology of sociality need to be noted in *Ethics*. One, rendered in the current translation 'deputyship', is in fact the word *Stellvertretung*, which Bonhoeffer has used all along to mean responsible action on behalf of others, particularly action which takes responsibility for the communities to which we belong. It is no accident that a major treatment of this idea is the first topic in his discussion of responsible life, for here Bonhoeffer is reflecting about his own activity in the resistance movement on behalf of Germany.[53] At the deepest theological level, the paradigm of such vicarious responsible action for others is the incarnation, cross and resurrection of Christ, in whom God acts in freedom and love for the sake of all humanity.[54] In its ethical form in human life this paradigm emphasises the fact that persons are not isolated individuals, responsible only for themselves, but are also responsible for the communities to which they belong.

Another theme of the theology of sociality is found in Bonhoeffer's discussion of 'mandates',[55] by which he refers to labour, marriage and family, government, and church.[56] A 'mandate' is a concrete form of life commissioned by God for all people. Calling it a 'mandate' points to its origin and purpose in God, who appoints these forms of life as tasks for humanity. Bonhoeffer refuses to regard these forms of life as 'orders of creation', since Nazi sympathisers claimed to read the will of God, apart from revelation in Christ, off 'orders' such as government or marriage; instead they read their own ideology into these orders. To counteract this, Bonhoeffer initially spoke of 'orders of preservation toward Christ', where the name of Christ served as the criterion which resisted Nazi co-option.[57]

The 'mandates' in *Ethics* are a new and more developed version of the 'orders of preservation'. They also develop the idea from *Christology* of Christ as centre and Mediator, especially Christ as the centre of history and the state. Further, when Bonhoeffer writes that the mandates are '"with", "for", and "against" each other', that they mutually support and limit each other,[58] he is employing the model of persons and communities in ethical encounter first articulated in *Sanctorum Communio*.

The telegraphic theological formulations in the *Letters and Papers from Prison* presuppose all that has gone before. The one new idea, intellectually appropriated from Wilhelm Dilthey, is that of the 'coming of age', or adulthood, of humanity. The existential *sitz im leben* of this insight is Bonhoeffer's experience in the resistance movement with responsible, autonomous and often secular people – including his own brother and brothers-in-law. They are not 'religious' in the specific sense in which Bonhoeffer uses the term, but they are risking their lives for the sake of humanity, peace and future generations. In the chapter of *Ethics* on 'The Church and the World', particularly the section on 'Christ and Good People', Bonhoeffer reveals the human and historical context which stimulated his reflections on 'religionless christianity'.[59]

To understand the theology informing Bonhoeffer's 'religionless christianity' project, the following familiar themes of his theology of sociality should be noted.[60] Central to a 'non-religious interpretation of biblical and theological concepts' is Bonhoeffer's Christology. First we hear the familiar affirmation of Christ as the centre of life, which goes back to the Christology lectures and the presentation of Christ in *Sanctorum Communio* as the reality of the new humanity. Then the deceptively simple phrase 'Jesus, the man for others', pregnant with meaning, recurs like a litany. This recalls, of course, the Christological interpretation of God's freedom in *Act and Being*, where Bonhoeffer insisted that 'God is free not from human beings but for them. Christ is the word of God's freedom.' This is the governing paradigm: freedom is freedom for. In the *Letters* the *theologia crucis* (theology of the cross) expresses this Christology perhaps more intensely than ever before.

This Christological understanding of God's freedom in love for humanity is the basis for the anthropological corollary which is likewise found in the theology of religionless christianity. The *analogia relationis* developed in *Creation and Fall* goes as follows: as God's being in Christ is a being in love and freedom for humanity, so human being in the image of God is being in a like relation of freedom and love for others. Freedom is a relationship of being free for the other. This leads to Bonhoeffer's statement 'our relation to

God is a new life in "existence for others", through participation in the being of Jesus'.[61]

In the same place, in the book outline for his new project, Bonhoeffer also restates his socio-ethical understanding of transcendence in terms of the I–You relation of persons. Jesus' freedom for others is 'the experience of transcendence' and faith is participating in his incarnation, cross and resurrection. So relation to the transcendent God is not a relation to an imagined most powerful Supreme Being – 'that is not authentic transcendence . . . The transcendent is . . . the neighbour who is within reach in any given situation.'[62] As *Sanctorum Communio* puts it, encounter with the human You is the form in which we encounter the divine You.

In an infatuation with secularism, some early readers of Bonhoeffer's *Letters* misinterpreted 'religionless christianity' as churchless christianity. While he certainly hoped for transformation of the church – indeed, radical changes – the Christian church community remains central to Bonhoeffer's theology. At the beginning of his theological discussion about the real Christ and authentic Christianity, he asked the question: 'What do a church, a community, a sermon, a liturgy, a Christian life mean in a religionless world?'[63] He answered: 'the church is the church only when it exists for others . . . It must tell people of every calling what it means to live in Christ, to exist for others.'[64] By interpreting the church with his Christological paradigm Bonhoeffer not only demonstrated that the Christian community remained central to his religionless christianity; he also provided a model of transformation which included radical changes – for a start, the church 'should give away all its property to those in need'![65]

Bonhoeffer's was not a static theology. The work on discipleship in the 1930s had deep personal meaning for Bonhoeffer, as well as calling the Confessing Church to faithfulness in the *Kirchenkampf*. The resistance movement provided profound stimulus for creative new ethical thinking. And the insight of human adulthood and autonomy led to the important new project on christianity without religion. Through all these developments the basic conceptuality of Bonhoeffer's theology of sociality provided the foundation and framework for his reflection.

Notes

1 D. Bonhoeffer, *Sanctorum Communio: A Dogmatic Enquiry into the Sociology of the Church* (London: Collins, 1963). In this chapter, quotations from *Sanctorum Communio* will be given in the translation of the new *Dietrich Bonhoeffer Works* edition (Minneapolis: Fortress Press, 1998), but cited according to the 1963 translation.

2 ibid., see chapter 2.

3 ibid., Foreword to original dissertation typescript.

4 See C. Green, *Bonhoeffer: A Theology of Sociality* (Grand Rapids: Eerdmans, 1999), previously published as *The Sociality of Christ and Humanity: Dietrich Bonhoeffer's Early Theology, 1927–1933* (Missoula: Scholars Press, 1975).

5 D. Bonhoeffer, *Act and Being: Transcendental Philosophy and Ontology in Systematic Theology, Dietrich Bonhoeffer Works*, vol. II, trans. M. Rumscheidt (Minneapolis: Fortress Press, 1996), p. 90.

6 C. Marsh, *Reclaiming Dietrich Bonhoeffer: The Promise of his Theology* (New York: Oxford University Press, 1994), p. vii.

7 D. Bonhoeffer, *Sanctorum Communio*, p. 32.

8 M. Buber, *I and Thou* (New York: Charles Scribner, 1970).

9 ibid., p. 37.

10 See, for example, D. Bonhoeffer, *Letters and Papers from Prison: The Enlarged Edition* (New York: Macmillan, 1972), p. 381: 'The transcendent is . . . the neighbour who is within reach in any given situation. God in human form . . . "the man for others", and therefore the Crucified.'

11 D. Bonhoeffer, *Creation and Fall: A Theological Exposition of Genesis 1–3, Dietrich Bonhoeffer Works*, vol. III, trans. Douglas Bax (Minneapolis: Fortress Press, 1997), pp. 62–3.

12 ibid., pp. 63, 65.

13 *Creation and Fall* was the first of Bonhoeffer's books read by Karl Barth. In *Church Dogmatics* (especially III/I, 194ff.) he appropriated Bonhoeffer's understanding of *analogia relationis* in his own doctrine of creation.

14 This is a fault of Charles Marsh's otherwise excellent book, *Reclaiming Dietrich Bonhoeffer.*

15 Here Bonhoeffer is adapting Ferdinand Tönnies' well-known distinction between community (*Gemeinschaft*) and association (*Gesellschaft*); the latter is a structure of purpose such as a business corporation or a political organisation, and is not willed as an end in itself but as a means to an end.

16 D. Bonhoeffer, *Sanctorum Communio*, p. 52.

17 G. Kelly and F. B. Nelson, *A Testament to Freedom: The Essential Writings of Dietrich Bonhoeffer* (San Francisco: Harper & Row, 1990), p. 173.

18 G. W. F. Hegel, *Lectures on the Philosophy of Religion*, vol. III, ed. P. C. Hodgson (Berkeley: University of California Press, 1985), p. 331.

19 D. Bonhoeffer, *Ethics* (New York: Macmillan, 1965), p. 83, trans. altered.

20 'God's New Action', in Bonhoeffer, *Creation and Fall*, p. 139.

21 ibid., p. 111.

22 For a detailed analysis of Bonhoeffer's understanding of sin in a characteristically modern form, and on 'power as a soteriological problem', see chapter 4 in Green, *Bonhoeffer: A Theology of Sociality.*

23 D. Bonhoeffer, *Sanctorum Communio*, p. 82.

24 D. Bonhoeffer, *Ethics*, pp. 82ff.

25 Athanasius, *The Nicene and Post-Nicene Fathers*, Second Series, vol. 4 (Grand Rapids: Eerdmans, 1980), pp. 36–67.

26 D. Bonhoeffer, *Sanctorum Communio*, p. 103.

27 E. Bethge, *Dietrich Bonhoeffer: Theologian, Christian, Contemporary* (London:

Collins, 1970), p. 60.

28 D. Bonhoeffer, *Christ the Centre*, trans. E. H. Robertson (New York: Harper & Row, 1978), p. 87; Bonhoeffer, *Letters and Papers from Prison*, p. 303.

29 Using sociological categories of his time, he argued that the church was a distinctive sociological form. It had dimensions of the community type (*Gemeinschaft*) in that it is an end in itself, a community of love created by the Holy Spirit; of the society type (*Gesellschaft*) in that it is an instrument of God's purpose in the world; and of the 'association of authentic rule' (*Herrschaftsverband*), in that it was constituted by the rule of God's love in Christ.

30 D. Bonhoeffer, *Sanctorum Communio*, p. 130.

31 ibid., pp. 189f.

32 D. Bonhoeffer, *Christ the Centre*, pp. 59–65.

33 ibid., pp. 59ff.

34 On Christ as Mediator between God and nature see Bonhoeffer, *Christ the Centre*, p. 64; on Bonhoeffer's theology of nature see L. Rasmussen, *Earth Community, Earth Ethics* (Maryknoll: Orbis, 1996).

35 D. Bonhoeffer, *No Rusty Swords: Letters, Lectures and Notes, 1928–1936, Collected Works of Dietrich Bonhoeffer*, vol. 1 (New York: Harper & Row, 1965), p. 190.

36 See Eberhard Bethge, 'Dietrich Bonhoeffer and the Jews', in *Ethical Responsibility: Bonhoeffer's Legacy to the Churches*, ed. J. D. Godsey and G. B. Kelly (New York: Edwin Mellen Press, 1981).

37 D. Bonhoeffer, *No Rusty Swords*, p. 225.

38 D. Bonhoeffer, *Life Together; Prayerbook of the Bible, Dietrich Bonhoeffer Works*, trans. D. W. Bloesch and J. H. Burtness (Minneapolis: Fortress Press, 1996), p. 83.

39 ibid., pp. 90f., 98ff.

40 D. Bonhoeffer, *Sanctorum Communio*, pp. 173, 240; Bonhoeffer, *Ethics*, pp. 292f.

41 D. Bonhoeffer, *Life Together; Prayerbook of the Bible*, p. 113.

42 ibid., p. 31.

43 ibid., pp. 33, 43f.

44 See chapter 4 in Green, *Bonhoeffer: A Theology of Sociality*.

45 D. Bonhoeffer, *Letters and Papers from Prison*, pp. 3ff.; Bonhoeffer, *Ethics*, pp. 65ff.

46 Bonhoeffer, *Letters and Papers from Prison*, p. 5.

47 Bonhoeffer, *Ethics*, pp. 17, 188.

48 Killing Hitler would not be simply assassination, and not murder, but tyrannicide. There is a tradition in Christian ethics dealing with this, analogous to the 'just war' analysis, but Bonhoeffer of course could not write about this in his *Ethics*.

49 Bonhoeffer, *Ethics*, pp. 224ff.

50 Cf. ibid., p. 83.

51 ibid., p. 195.

52 ibid., pp. 75–82, 296–9.

53 ibid., pp. 224ff.

54 ibid., pp. 225f.; Bonhoeffer, *Sanctorum Communio*, p. 223, n.36.

55 Bonhoeffer, *Ethics*, pp. 207ff., 286ff.

56 Sometimes Bonhoeffer spoke of 'culture' rather than 'labour' (ibid., p. 291); see

also the interesting discussion of friendship as a realm of freedom apart from the mandates (p. 286).

57 Bonhoeffer, *Creation and Fall*, pp. 139f., *Ethics*, pp. 282f.

58 ibid., pp. 291–2.

59 D. Bonhoeffer, *Fiction from Prison: Gathering up the Past*, ed. E. Bethge and R. Bethge (Philadelphia: Fortress Press, 1981). This was written during Bonhoeffer's first year at Tegel. The novel fragment especially contains a number of striking formulations and scenes which express the theology of sociality.

60 See chapter 6 in Green, *Bonhoeffer: A Theology of Sociality*. This also contains an analysis of what Bonhoeffer means by 'religion' and his critique of it.

61 Bonhoeffer, *Letters and Papers from Prison*, p. 381.

62 ibid.

63 ibid., p. 282.

64 ibid.

65 ibid., p. 382.

7 'Who is Jesus Christ, for us, today?'

ANDREAS PANGRITZ

'God revealed in the flesh', the God-man Jesus Christ, is the holy mystery which theology is appointed to guard. What a mistake to think that it is the task of theology to unravel God's mystery, to bring it down to the flat, ordinary human wisdom of experience and reason! It is the task of theology solely to preserve God's wonder as wonder, to understand, to defend, to glorify God's mystery as mystery.[1]

With these nearly mystical words, Dietrich Bonhoeffer, in a 'Circular Letter' of Christmas 1939 to the brethren of the Finkenwalde seminary and the pastors of the Confessing Church, describes the task of Christian theology in general and of Christology in particular: to praise the glory of God in the wonder of his incarnation.

It has become customary to regard Christology as the centre of Bonhoeffer's thought. And indeed, the question 'Who is Jesus Christ?' forms the *cantus firmus* of Bonhoeffer's theological development from the beginning to the end. This question, originally latent in *Sanctorum Communio*, becomes explicit in Bonhoeffer's academic *Christology* lectures of 1933, that crucial year of German history in the twentieth century when Hitler came to power. And still in 1944, in his *Letters and Papers from Prison*, the programmatic question 'who Christ really is, for us today' forms the starting point of Bonhoeffer's new theological reflections.

CHRISTOLOGICAL CONCENTRATION

Throughout his life Bonhoeffer participated in the movement towards Christological concentration inaugurated by Karl Barth and dialectical theology after the First World War. However, in Bonhoeffer's thought this concentration does not lead to isolation from other theological and non-theological themes. Rather the centrality of Christ serves as the decisive motive for opening the horizons of the church towards the world in its concrete reality. Sometimes the tasks of this secular reality almost seem to be identified with Christ. Bonhoeffer wrote to his brother in 1935: 'At present there are still some things for which an uncompromising stand is worthwhile. And it seems to me that peace and social justice or Christ himself are such.'[2] In any case, the Christological *cantus firmus* is continuously accompanied by 'worldly' counterpoints, as Bonhoeffer phrases it in a draft for his *Ethics*, which he intended to become his main work: 'The greater the exclusiveness, the greater the freedom . . . The more exclusively we acknowledge and confess Christ as our Lord, the more fully the wide range of His dominion will be disclosed to us.'[3]

It is not difficult to demonstrate that the Christological question is present, albeit sometimes only in a latent form, in much of Bonhoeffer's writings. Some examples may suffice. Already in his dissertation *Sanctorum Communio* in 1927, Bonhoeffer cannot speak of the church without reflecting on Christ. The close relationship between Christ and the church has as a consequence the often problematised formula of 'Christ existing as community'. Again in his 1932 lectures at Berlin University on *Creation and Fall* Bonhoeffer rejects the concept of 'order of creation', which was then widespread in conservative Lutheranism, and proposes instead the Christologically qualified concept of 'order of preservation', i.e. an order which remains open for the revolutionary acts of Christ himself.

Bonhoeffer's famous book *The Cost of Discipleship*, written in 1937, ends with a chapter on 'The Image of Christ'. Following Christ as a disciple is described here as being 'conformed to the image of Christ . . . We must be assimilated to the form of Christ in its entirety, the form of Christ incarnate, crucified and glorified . . . He has become like a man, so that people should be like him.'[4] Again, in a draft for his *Ethics*, Bonhoeffer refers to the notion of 'conformation to Christ'. Whenever the Holy Scriptures speak of 'forming' they are – according to Bonhoeffer –

> concerned only with the one form which has overcome the world, the form of Jesus Christ . . . Formation comes only by being drawn into the form of Jesus Christ. It comes only as formation in His likeness, as *conformation* with the unique form of Him who was made man, was crucified, and rose again.[5]

Later drafts for his *Ethics* bring the world as 'the penultimate' under justification by Christ as the 'ultimate', emphasise 'the amplitude of Christ's lordship', or reason 'from incarnation to historical responsibility'. There can be no doubt that in Bonhoeffer's theological thought Christology and ethics are closely interrelated. Each new approach for his *Ethics* combines 'a more resolute Christ-centredness' with 'a more realistic openness to the world'.[6]

In spite of the Christocentric conception of Bonhoeffer's theology, only a few of his texts deal with Christology explicitly. One exception is the 'Circular Letter' of Christmas 1939 mentioned above. The most detailed reflection on Christology, however, has been expounded by Bonhoeffer in his *Christology* lectures at Berlin University, which have been handed down to us by notes from his students.[7] According to Eberhard Bethge these lectures form 'the high point of Bonhoeffer's academic career'. At the same time, they can be read as a commentary on the socio-political context in Germany: Hitler had been Chancellor for three months when Bonhoeffer began his *Christology* lectures in summer 1933. As an academic teacher he attempted to speak strictly theologically, yet indirect reflections on the political context can be discovered in the text.

THE 'CHRISTOLOGY' LECTURES

A superficial reading of the *Christology* lectures might give the impression that Bonhoeffer is simply defending Christian tradition. In contrast to his liberal teacher Adolf von Harnack he even seems to find reason to applaud the doctrine of the early church on the 'two natures' of Christ. At a time when the 'German Christians' (the Deutsche Christen or the Nazi party of the church) attempted to construct an 'Aryan' Christ, such a merely apologetic conception of Christology would have had indirect political implications. And indeed, one year later (in May 1934) the majority of the participants at the founding assembly of the Confessing Church in Barmen simply attempted to defend the traditional creed concerning Jesus Christ when they adopted the Barmen Confession with its opening statement: 'Jesus Christ as He has been witnessed by the Holy Scriptures is the only word of God that we have to hear, to trust in life and death, and to obey.'

But Bonhoeffer does not restrict himself to apologetics. His Christocentrism is at the same time the precondition for an unprecedented opening of the horizons of the church. By no means does he try to define Jesus Christ. On the contrary: his purpose is to liberate Christ from every Christian and non-Christian definition of the time. His question is the 'question of encounter' between Christ, the church and the world, in other words the question 'Who are you? Speak for yourself!'[8]

There is a run-up to Bonhoeffer's approach to this crucial question of Christology. He starts his lectures by emphasising the 'doxological' structure of the Christian dogma. The meaning of 'dogma' is not so much 'doctrine', but rather praise of the 'doxa', the glory of the Lord. In Bonhoeffer's introductory words:

> Teaching about Christ begins in silence ... That has nothing to do with the silence of the mystics, who in their dumbness chatter away secretly in their soul by themselves. The silence of the Church is the silence before the Word. In so far as the Church proclaims the Word, it essentially falls down silently before the inexpressible ... The 'study of this proclamation' is possible only on condition of the humble silence of the worshipping congregation ... To pray is to be silent and at the same time to cry out, before God and in the presence of his Word.[9]

According to Bonhoeffer, the invocation of God's love is the precondition of every theological inquiry. Therefore, the Christological question is legitimately asked 'in the setting of the Church' only, where the answer is already given. It can only be put

> where the basic presupposition, that Christ claims to be the Logos of God, is accepted ... In the Church, where Christ has revealed himself as the Word of God, the human logos puts the question: 'Who are you, Jesus Christ, Word of God, Logos of God?' The answer is given, the Church receives it new every day.[10]

Christology can do nothing but unfold this question 'Who?'. This question is, in fact, the question of encounter. The thought form of Christology itself will be determined by this question. In this way Christology should be acknowledged – according to Bonhoeffer – as 'the unknown and hidden centre of the *universitas litterarum*' – a definition which certainly can be accepted 'within the sphere of the Church' only.[11]

By situating the Christological question within the church Bonhoeffer intends to exclude two philosophical questions (as applied, for example, by Hegel) from Christological thinking: 'The question of whether the answer already given and the Church's corresponding question, "Who?", can be justified or not'. And: 'The question of how the "truth" of the revelation can be conceived'. This second question 'would mean going behind Christ's claim and finding an independent reason for it'.[12]

With these two questions excluded from Christological thought, only one question remains: the decisive question of encounter, the question about the person of Christ, 'the question, "Who?". According to Bonhoeffer 'the question: Who are you? is the question of the dethroned and distraught reason; but it is also the question of faith: "Who are you? Are you God himself?" This is the question with which Christology is concerned. Christ is the Counter-Logos.'[13]

THE HUMILIATION OF GOD IN CHRIST

We have already seen that the centrality of Christology is realised in a 'hidden' way only, 'unknown' to the secular academy. The reason for this seclusion lies in the fact that the presence of Christ himself is concealed: his 'presence is a hidden presence . . . This God-Man, Jesus Christ, is present and contemporary in the form of the *homoioma sarkos* (likeness of the flesh), i.e. in veiled form, in the form of a stumbling block.' According to Bonhoeffer 'that is the central problem of Christology'.[14]

But what is the essence of the offence caused by Jesus Christ, what is the essence of the *scandalon*? Bonhoeffer typically points out that 'the offence in Jesus Christ is not his incarnation – that indeed is revelation! – but his humiliation'.[15] In the phrase of the Swabian Pietist Oetinger, which was dear to Bonhoeffer, the incarnation of Christ implies his 'corporeality' as 'the end of the ways of God'.[16] This 'corporeality' is a cause of joy, not of offence. Offensive is the 'humiliation' of Christ, his 'concealment within history',[17] in the history of the cross: 'The meaning of history is tied up with an event which takes place in the depth and hiddenness of a man who ended on the cross. The meaning of history is found in the humiliated Christ.'[18] In this way Christ becomes the 'centre of history', but his centrality is concealed in the offence of his humiliation to death on the cross.

It is important to see that for Bonhoeffer the presence of Christ attains its social concreteness in the Christian community. Therefore the offence of the humiliation of Christ finds its counterpart in the corresponding existence of the church, an equivalent with political consequences in the context of the situation of 1933: 'The community is the body of Christ . . . His being as community, like his being as Word and sacrament, has the form of a stumbling block.'[19]

As the body of Christ the church cannot wish to be exalted above her Lord: 'Because Christ, since the cross and resurrection, is present in the Church, the Church also must be understood as the centre of history. It is the centre of a history which is being made by the state. Again this is a hidden and not an evident centre of the realm of the state.' That means that the church may never 'show itself to be the centre by visibly standing at the centre of the state or by letting itself be put at the centre, as when it is made a state Church'.[20] In 1933 this rejection of the concept of a state church would be perceived as a protest against the attempts of the 'German

Christians', but also of the conservative Lutherans, to establish a German national church with a *Reichsbischof* as its 'Führer' – according to the slogan: 'One nation, one Reich, one church'. And precisely the fact that the centrality of the church is 'hidden' enables the church at the same time to become the 'boundary' of the state: 'It is the boundary of the state in proclaiming with the cross the breaking-through of all human order.'[21]

In this concept of the relation of church and state we can recognise Bonhoeffer's critical adoption of the Lutheran doctrine of the 'two king-doms', as it has been worked out by him especially in his essay 'The Church and the Jewish Question' (April 1933). Here he emphasises the 'boundaries' of state legislation by considering the extreme 'possibility' that the church would 'not just . . . bandage the victims under the wheel, but jam a stick between the spokes of the wheel'.[22]

The offence caused by the humiliation of Christ, his obedience implying his death on the cross, destroys any abstract idea of God: 'If we speak of Jesus Christ as God, we may not say of him that he is the representative of an idea of God, which possesses the characteristics of omniscience and omnip-otence (there is no such thing as this abstract divine nature!); rather, we must speak of his weakness, his manger, his cross. This man is no abstract God.'[23] Nevertheless, we have to say of this 'humiliated one . . . "This is God."' He makes none of his divine properties manifest in his death. On the contrary, we see a man doubting God as he dies. But of this man we say, "This is God."'[24]

And again Bonhoeffer emphasises an equivalent in the Christian com-munity: as Christ 'goes incognito, as a beggar among beggars, as an outcast among outcasts, as despairing among the despairing, as dying among the dying',[25] in the same way 'it is with this humiliated one that the Church goes its own way of humiliation'. In the 'encounter' with the humiliated one the church 'cannot strive after visible confirmation of its way while he renoun-ces it with every step'.[26]

Already one year earlier Bonhoeffer had been even more concrete, when in his lectures on 'The Nature of the Church' (1932) he reflected on the way of the church: here, it is 'the secularity of the church' which 'follows from the incarnation of Christ. The church, like Christ, has become world . . . For the sake of real people, the church must be thoroughly worldly.' This means that the church, too, 'is subjected to all the weakness and suffering of the world. The church can at times, like Christ himself, become homeless.' And 'real secularity' of the church implies 'its being able to renounce all privi-leges and all its property . . . With Christ and the forgiveness of sins to fall back on, the church is free to give up everything else.'[27]

Once we accept that Christ is 'the Counter-Logos' it becomes clear that Bonhoeffer's approval of the dogma of the 'two natures' of Christ, which is so central in his conception, does not simply mean apologetics. In Bonhoeffer's interpretation, the creed of the fathers of the early church, according to which Christ is confessed as true God and true human being at the same time (Chalcedon 451), should be explained in a critical way. Whereas liberal theology had regretted the introduction of the concept of '*ousia*, nature, being' into Christology, because it had 'Hellenized and thereby corrupted the evangelical understanding of Jesus Christ', Bonhoeffer claims that 'in its own way there is no more "un-Greek" product of thought than the Chalcedonian Definition'.[28]

In Chalcedonian Christology the 'Counter-Logos' has superseded any 'objectifying thought-forms'.[29] Speaking of the nature of God and human nature 'in a theoretical and objectifying way' is a theological 'mistake'. 'The two natures' should not be 'treated like two distinguishable entities, separated from each other, until they come together in Jesus Christ. The relationship between God and man cannot be thought of as relationship of entities'; it can only be thought of as a relationship 'between persons'.[30]

According to Bonhoeffer the doctrine of the God-Man, Jesus Christ, has found its 'classical formulation' in the Chalcedonian Definition. The person of Jesus Christ is perceived 'in two natures, without confusion and without change . . . without separation and without division'. Bonhoeffer interprets:

> What remains are simple negations. No positive form of thought
> remains to say what happens in the God-Man Jesus Christ. The
> mystery is left as a mystery and must be understood as such. The
> approach is reserved for faith only. All forms of thought are broken
> off . . . Since the Chalcedonian Definition, the theologian who is
> concerned with Christology must keep within the boundaries drawn
> by the conceptual tension of this negative formula and preserve it . . .
> In its characteristic form the Definition cancels itself out . . . It speaks
> about 'natures', but expresses the facts in such a way as to show that
> the concept of 'natures' is quite inappropriate for this use. It works
> with concepts which it declares to be heretical formulas unless they
> are used in contradiction and paradox.[31]

The Chalcedonian formula 'that Christ is one person in two natures' continued to provoke further discussions 'within the Protestant tradition'. Lutheranism developed 'the doctrine of the communication of properties', which according to Bonhoeffer is 'the most acute speculation that theology has brought to the Christological question'.[32] The 'heart' of this Lutheran doctrine is the *genus majestaticum* saying: 'Those things which are predicated of the eternal deity may and must be ascribed to the human nature . . . We have here the *Est* of the Eucharistic Doctrine.'[33] However, the consciously Lutheran theologian Bonhoeffer admits that at this point Lutheran Christology comes 'into conflict with what the Bible states' and with the Chalcedonian Definition: 'There is . . . danger of the return of monophysitism, because the humanity becomes deity.'[34] No wonder therefore that the theologians of the Reformed Church 'protested against this Lutheran Christology'. Their main objection was that 'Lutheran Christology is not basically speaking of the real humanity of Christ any more'. Their answer to the *genus majestaticum* was *extra Calvinisticum*: 'The Logos continues in his trinitarian relationship and therefore also *extra carnem* (outside the flesh).' There is no 'divinising of human nature . . . *Finitum incapax infiniti* (the finite *cannot contain* the infinite).'[35]

Bonhoeffer applauds the emphasis laid down by Calvinistic Christology, 'upon preserving clearly what God is and what man is; salvation depends upon retaining the true humanity of Jesus'. On the other hand, he tries to preserve the Lutheran concern by proposing a mediating formula: 'The finite can hold the infinite, not by itself, but by the aid of the infinite!'[36] This attempt to reconcile Lutheran and Calvinistic Christology can be regarded as taking place one year later, when Lutherans and Reformed theologians adopted the Barmen Declaration together.

According to Bonhoeffer 'the abstract duality of the natures and the abstract unity of the person are alike unbiblical'.[37] It is a mistake of both Lutheran and Calvinist Christology that they run the risk of 'rejecting the "two nature" teaching of the Chalcedonian Definition', in so far as they do not accept its 'negativity'. But, as Bonhoeffer states, it is just in 'its negative formulations' that the Chalcedonian Definition is 'the ideal conciliar theological statement'.[38] It entails a 'prohibition against using objectifying categories for the solution of the question of the God–Man relationship' in Jesus Christ. 'By its insistence on the negative in contradictory opposites' the Chalcedonian Definition has, indeed, 'superseded the doctrine of the two natures . . . This critical significance of the Chalcedonian Definition is to be taken further.'[39]

Bonhoeffer claims that in its negativity this definition provides a free space for the mystery of Christ. The question 'How?' has been 'eliminated' by the 'two contradictory, opposing statements'. In its own way 'the Chalcedonian Definition is itself ultimately the question, "Who?"'.[40]

CHALLENGING CHRISTOLOGICAL TRADITION

We have already seen that doxology is the starting point for Bonhoeffer's inquiry into Christological dogma. This does not mean that he distrusts human reason, but rather that he seeks to preserve the social concreteness of Christology in its relation to the Christian community. For this reason theological thinking should be 'humble'. Such theological 'humility' has nothing to do with submission to clerical demands. Rather it is an expression of partisanship with humiliated humanity. Theology, according to Bonhoeffer, stands on the side of the concrete human being, i.e. the 'humiliated' one, Christ. Thus, theological reason is humbled and at the same time exalted as an 'instrument of the praise of God's revelation'.[41] Such an understanding of the task of theology challenges the systematised and petrified forms of Christology in the dogmatic tradition.

One of these challenges is presented by the poor. As Bonhoeffer notes: 'For the proletariat, it is easy to depict Christ as allied with the Church of the bourgeois society. Then the worker sees no reason any more to give Jesus a qualified place or status.' The identification of Christ with the bourgeois society has as a consequence that the church is unmasked as a 'stupefying institution and sanctioning of the capitalist system'.[42] Any 'encounter with Jesus' becomes impossible. The decisive question 'Who?' seems to have received its negative answer already by means of the existence of the church.

Yet, there is another possibility: 'At this very point the working class may distinguish between Jesus and his Church; he is not the guilty party. Jesus, yes; Church, no! Jesus can then become the idealist, the socialist.'[43] For the sake of the humiliation of Jesus and for the sake of the humiliation and exploitation of the proletariat in the capitalist system Bonhoeffer risks theological correctness:

> The proletarian does not say, 'Jesus is God.' But when he says, 'Jesus is a good man', he is saying more than the bourgeois says when he repeats, 'Jesus is God.' God is for him something belonging to the Church. But, Jesus can be present on the factory floor as the socialist; at a political meeting, as an idealist; in the worker's world, as a good man. He fights in their ranks against the enemy, Capitalism.[44]

This challenges dogmatic tradition at its core. For the proletarian interest in Jesus does not refer to him as God, but as 'brother and master'. The question is whether in this way the decisive Christological question 'Who are you?' is put seriously or 'evaded'. It seems that Bonhoeffer leaves this issue open.[45]

Obviously 'proletarian' Christology can be traced back to the heresy of 'adoptionism' (the Jewish Christian heresy) or 'Ebionitism' (the heresy of the *ebionim*, i.e. the humiliated, the poor) in the early church. On the one hand, Bonhoeffer clearly expresses his disagreement with the ebionitic concept: 'The Church must condemn it',[46] as it 'must reject docetism' (the 'pagan-idealistic' heresy) 'in all its forms'.[47] On the other hand, it is remarkable that he does not really succeed in his attempt to find a middle course between the extreme solutions of 'docetism' and 'Ebionitism': 'Ebionitism is superior to docetic liberalism in that it fixes its eyes upon the particular person Jesus, the real man. Salvation is not associated with an ideal picture, but with the servant.' Jesus, the particular man, is a rejection of Docetism by the Ebionite heresy, which thereby holds fast to the God of the Old Testament.[48]

The observation is disturbing: on the one hand, Bonhoeffer attempts to defend the dogmatic tradition against modern heresies. Hegel's Idealistic philosophy is rejected, as well as nineteenth-century liberal theology from Schleiermacher to Harnack, and particularly the heresy of the German Christians, all of which are traced back by Bonhoeffer to the docetic model. On the other hand, he cannot avoid expressing his sympathies at least for the questions asked by 'Ebionitism' and by the proletariat. The assertion that Bonhoeffer's Christology contains a secret Ebionite tendency seems hardly to be exaggerated.

The disturbance of Christological dogmas by the proletariat was recognised by Bonhoeffer during his stay at Union Theological Seminary in New York (1930/1). There it was the 'black Christ' proclaimed in the African-American churches which made a strong impression on him. He referred to this experience later in his report, in a section with the subheading 'The Church of the Outcasts of America: The Negro Church'. Of most importance for Bonhoeffer was the fact that in the black churches he heard 'the gospel preached'. In contrast to the lecture style of 'white' sermons, 'the "black Christ" was proclaimed with thrilling passion and visual power'. And, he noted, 'The Negro churches are proletarian churches, perhaps the only ones in all America.'[49]

Again, in his lectures on 'Recent Theology' (winter 1932/3), Bonhoeffer referred to the 'Negro church' in America, now even identifying the Russian Revolution and the 'black Christ': Christ stands in opposition to the religion of 'Mammon'. Therefore the Russian Revolution could be understood as 'a protest against the capitalist Christ, not against Christ himself'. The only way in which the West knows Christ is as the capitalist Christ. Protest against *this* perverted understanding of Christ is more than legitimate. The same can be said of the demand for a 'black Christ' and the boycott of the white Christ by African-Americans. This boycott is directed against the Christ, who has become a camouflage of white domination.[50]

In his essay 'Protestantism without Reformation', written after his second stay in the United States in summer 1939, Bonhoeffer still refers to the problem of 'race' in a chapter on the 'Negro Church (*Negerkirche*)'. Now he seems to express a much more pessimistic view than at the beginning of the thirties: American Protestantism presents 'the image of a church torn by race'. The severe 'destruction' of the church is demonstrated by the fact that the 'white Christ' is confronted by a 'black Christ'. It is the 'guilt of the Church' that the 'ambitious young generation' of African-Americans turns away in general from 'the faith of the older ones' with its 'strong eschatological tendencies'.[51] The future may bring the same sort of development as in Europe: forced secularisation and the emigration of the proletariat from the church on a massive scale.

This disturbance of dogmatic tradition by the proletariat is also expressed in *Letters and Papers from Prison*.[52] In his 'Outline for a Book' Bonhoeffer first criticised the Confessing Church theologically: 'Generally in the Confessing Church: standing up for the church's "cause", but little personal faith in Christ. "Jesus" is disappearing from sight.' But typically, this criticism was combined with a 'sociological' argument: 'no effect on the masses – interest confined to the upper and lower middle classes. A heavy incubus of difficult traditional ideas. The decisive factor: the church on the defensive. No taking risks for others'.[53] But Bonhoeffer insisted: 'The church is the church only when it exists for others',[54] because Jesus Christ himself is the man who 'is there only for others'.[55]

Another challenge to Christological tradition is represented by the people of Israel. In the *Christology* lectures of 1933 this finds its expression primarily in some linguistic peculiarities: in some paragraphs of the chapter on 'Christ as the Centre of History' Bonhoeffer employs the title 'Messiah' instead of 'Christ', and finally he even speaks of 'this Messiah Christ'.[56] This did not happen by chance: the purpose of this chapter was to demonstrate the interrelation between Jesus the Jew and his primary context: the people of Israel. Bonhoeffer attacks the political ideology of the Third Reich when he notes: 'History is tormented by the impossibility of fulfilling corrupt messianic promises. It knows of its messianic determination and it comes to grief on it.' Opposed to Nazi ideology, according to which the German 'Führer' is the 'visible and demonstrated centre of history', Bonhoeffer emphasises that the Messiah 'must be the hidden centre appointed by God'.

This thought breaks through in history 'only at one point . . . This is the point at which there is a stream against the popular movement of corrupted messianism – it is in Israel. With its prophetic hope, it stands alone among the nations. And Israel becomes the place at which God fulfils his promise.'[57]

In view of the anti-Semitic legislation in the spring of 1933 in Nazi Germany, and the adoption of the 'Aryan clause' by the Reichskirche during that year, the introduction of Israel into the Christological understanding of history acted as a signal. Already in April 1933 Bonhoeffer had protested against the legal discrimination against the Jews with his address on 'The Church and the Jewish Question'.[58] Later in a draft section of his *Ethics* entitled 'Inheritance and Decay', Bonhoeffer noted that 'western history is, by God's will, indissolubly linked with the people of Israel'. And in 1941, when the mass deportations of the Jews began, he emphasised the Christological consequences of this insight, inserting into his manuscript a prophetic clause, according to which Western history is linked with Israel 'not only genetically but also in a genuine uninterrupted encounter. The Jew keeps open the question of Christ . . . An expulsion of the Jews from the west must necessarily bring with it the expulsion of Christ. For Jesus Christ was a Jew.'[59] After the Shoah this clause should be a source of permanent embarrassment to Western Christianity. Yet, strangely enough, the teaching of the Christological tradition goes on in the West as if nothing had happened.

'KING DAVID'

A new stage in the development of Bonhoeffer's Christological thinking after the *Christology* lectures of 1933 was reached in the mid thirties with his exegetical work during the Finkenwalde period. Well known are the Christological implications of the book *The Cost of Discipleship*, with its strong accent on the Lutheran understanding of Christ's condescension in incarnation and deputyship, suffering and cross. Well known also is the radicalisation of the ecclesiological implications of the slogan 'Christ existing as community' in the small volume *Life Together*.

Even more characteristic than these works, which draw their exegetical material nearly exclusively from the New Testament, is the way in which Bonhoeffer during this period interpreted the Hebrew Scriptures in the light of Christology. Here Bonhoeffer is obviously engaged in a 'Christological interpretation of the Old Testament', as elaborated by Wilhelm Vischer in his two-volume magisterial work *Das Christuszeugnis des Alten Testaments* (1934). In August 1933 Bonhoeffer had co-operated with Vischer in an attempt to insert a paragraph on the church and Israel into the 'Bethel

Confession'. In the historical context of the German church struggle the purpose of such a 'Christological interpretation' was an attempt to defend the Old Testament as part of the Christian Bible against the attacks of the 'German Christians' who despised the Hebrew Bible as 'oriental stories of pimps and wogs' and invented an 'Aryan' Christ devoid of his Jewish context.

As an example of Bonhoeffer's 'Christological interpretation' of the Old Testament we will examine his Bible study on 'King David' (1935).[60] The purpose of this Bible study was to make a 'contribution to the problem: Christ in the Old Testament'. [61] The relationship between King David and Jesus Christ is strongly emphasised by Bonhoeffer. Sometimes it seems that both persons are completely identified with each other. Christ is (pre-) existing in David:

> David is a witness of Christ and of his resurrection – in fact he is a
> qualified witness among all the prophets, because he bears Christ in
> his loins and because he lives by the promise, i.e. out of Christ existing
> in him. Thus, Christ really was in David, as flesh and as promise in
> David – and David was his witness.[62]

According to Bonhoeffer the relationship between David and Christ could not be reduced to the prophetic model of promise and fulfilment, as its theological meaning could only be realised in the context of the incarnation: 'David is the shadow of the Messiah incarnate. From the incarnation falls a shadow onto David.' The incarnation is the origin of David. In this sense we not only have to say that (historically) David precedes Christ, but also that (theologically) 'Christ precedes David.'[63] David is a 'personal type (*Personaltypus*) of Christ', and the exegetical task is, according to Bonhoeffer, to read the stories about David in a way that 'David can be understood in his person, in his office, in his word and in his history as the one *in whom according to the testimony of the New Testament Christ himself existed.*' The historical figure of David himself is not important; David is important only as a 'witness of Christ'.[64]

Bonhoeffer found the material for his identification of David and Christ in the biblical stories about King David, which he related to the stories of Jesus in the gospels. In the anointment of David he sees the foreshadowing of the baptism of Jesus: 'The spirit of the anointment is the spirit of the *messianic* kingdom. It is the one spirit of God, by which David is anointed, *and Christ* . . . It is the spirit which on the occasion of the baptism descends onto Jesus and seals him as the messianic king.'[65] David's struggle with Goliath, too, parallels the destiny of Jesus:

It is true humility towards God and his word which makes David defenceless. David says what he has to say in the certainty of his anointment: 'You have come against me with sword and spear and dagger . . . ' – Jesus says: 'You have come out with swords and cudgels to arrest me' – and he was defenceless, and they dropped on their knees in front of him.[66]

Another parallel between David and Christ also stresses the 'humility' of the anointed one. When David enters Jerusalem for the first time, he is dancing, because he wants to 'lower' himself, hoping that 'those girls . . . will honour' him (II Samuel 6:22). Bonhoeffer comments: 'A triumphal procession *in humility* and *meekness* – that is the way in which king David . . . enters Jerusalem, the king as a servant to his people.' And Bonhoeffer emphasises the parallel with Jesus entering Jerusalem in humility.[67] In 1935 this common feature of King David and Jesus Christ stood in a clear contrast to the German 'Führer' and his perverted messianic pretensions.

Bonhoeffer does not hesitate to find a parallel in the German church struggle in God's promise to David to build 'a house for him': 'It was David's misunderstanding to think that he himself could build a church for the Lord . . . God himself builds the church.'[68] And again the promise to David includes Jesus Christ: 'The house which God will build for himself is the seed of David, it is the body of Christ, his son – and this body is Christ and in him his community.'[69] David's prayer of thanksgiving answering God's promises (II Samuel 7:23ff.) is interpreted by Bonhoeffer in a way which in Nazi Germany inevitably would be heard as politically provocative: 'The people of Israel will remain God's people eternally, the only people that will not disappear, because God has become its Lord, God has settled in it and built his house.'[70]

Finally, even in his sins King David is an image of Christ, who bears our sins: 'As the *justified sinner*, David is the anointed king, an "example and shadow" of the crucified Christ.'[71]

The original purpose of Christological interpretation of the Old Testament was to defend the Hebrew Bible against 'German Christian' attacks. Christ is interpreted inclusively. He is not simply the man Jesus, but as a Jew he represents the whole history of God with his people Israel and its messianic aspirations. On the other hand, there can be no doubt that Bonhoeffer's Christological interpretation of King David makes Christian demands on the Hebrew Bible. These demands may imply a theological expropriation of the Jewish Bible. As Bonhoeffer notes: 'The Old Testament should be read proceeding from the incarnation and crucifixion, i.e. from the revelation given to us. Otherwise we remain within a Judaic (*judaistisch*) or pagan understanding of the Old Testament.'[72] Thus, the inclusiveness of Christ tends to exclude not only 'pagan' (Germanic) misinterpretations, but a Jewish understanding of the Hebrew Bible as well. This one-sidedness in the relationship between Christ and the Hebrew Bible is corrected and even reversed in Bonhoeffer's *Letters and Papers from Prison*.

PRISON CHRISTOLOGY

The main theological question of Bonhoeffer's *Letters and Papers from Prison* is a new formulation of the Christological problem. As he wrote in his famous letter to Bethge on 30 April 1944: 'What is bothering me incessantly is the question what Christianity really is, or indeed who Christ really is, for us today.'[73] Just as in his *Christology* lectures of 1933, Bonhoeffer obviously 'does not consider from a distance how much of tradition can be retained, but . . . enquires into the person of Christ and into the way in which he encounters and defines us today'. To put it more precisely, 'Bonhoeffer is enquiring into the way in which Christ is Lord' in a world come of age.[74] Or, in Bonhoeffer's own words (30 June 1944): 'Let me just summarise briefly what I am concerned about – the claim of a world that has come of age by Jesus Christ.'[75]

The lordship of Christ remains – according to this phrasing – undoubted. But, as Bethge puts it, 'this lordship . . . is saved' by Bonhoeffer 'from clericalization and hierarchic tendencies because this Lord exercises his lordship always and solely through powerlessness, service and the Cross'. Bonhoeffer's elaborations on his theme are 'entirely removed from the sphere of apologetics'. His aim is 'to discover the presence of Christ in the world of today: not a discovery of the modern world, not the discovery of him outside this modern world, but discovering HIM in this world'. Without taking into account the thematical question 'Who are YOU today?', the 'explosive formulae' of Bonhoeffer's *Letters and Papers* – 'world come of age, non-religious interpretation, arcane discipline, etc.' – could easily provoke misunderstanding. Only 'in the Christological perspective of his main theme [do] they achieve their full and independent justification'.[76]

Only some aspects of Bonhoeffer's formulation of the Christological problem in *Letters and Papers from Prison*, which are new compared with earlier formulations, will be examined more closely in what follows. Already in the first smuggled letter to Bethge (18–21 November 1943) Bonhoeffer notes that he now understands better than before 'the fact that the Israelites *never* uttered the name of God'.[77] One consequence of this observation is an important reservation with respect to all too direct Christological thinking, as he himself had employed, for example, in *The Cost of Discipleship*. Now, in his letter of Advent 2 (5 December) 1943, Bonhoeffer is convinced that 'it is only when one knows the unutterability of the name of God that one can utter the name of Jesus Christ'. In Bonhoeffer's opinion 'it is not Christian to want to take our thoughts and feelings too quickly and too directly from the New Testament . . . One cannot and must not speak the ultimate word before the penultimate.'[78] Again, at the end of the letter of 30 April 1944, Bonhoeffer emphasises that the New Testament has to be read 'in the light of the Old'.[79]

Accordingly, he did not want to speak any longer of 'salvation' in terms of 'redemption'. He was convinced that 'unlike the other oriental religions, the faith of the Old Testament isn't a religion of redemption. It is true that Christianity has always been regarded as a religion of redemption.' But Bonhoeffer asks, 'isn't this a cardinal error, which separates Christ from the Old Testament and interprets him on the lines of the myths about redemption?' The 'redemptions' referred to in the Old Testament are, according to Bonhoeffer, '*historical*, i.e. on *this* side of death . . . Israel is delivered out of Egypt so that it may live before God as God's people on earth' (27 June 1944). Thus Bonhoeffer claimed that it is a 'mistake' and 'danger' to contend that, in contrast to the religion of the Old Testament, Christianity is 'a genuine religion of redemption', where redemption means 'redemption from cares, distress, fears, and longings, from sin and death, in a better world beyond the grave'. So, Bonhoeffer asks: 'Is this really the essential character of the proclamation of Christ in the gospels and by Paul?' His answer is:

> I should say it is not. The difference between the Christian hope of resurrection and the mythological hope is that the former sends a man back to his life on earth in a wholly new way . . . The Christian . . . like Christ himself . . . must drink the earthly cup to the dregs, and only in his doing so is the crucified and risen Lord with him, and he is crucified and risen with Christ. This world must not be prematurely written off; in this the Old and New Testaments are at one.[80]

In these and some other places of *Letters and Papers from Prison* it becomes clear that Bonhoeffer's discovery of what Kornelis H. Miskotte[81] has described as the theological 'surplus' of the Old Testament compared with the New results in a complete reversal of 'Christological interpretation' of the Old Testament. The close relationship between Jesus Christ and the Hebrew Bible no longer leads to an interpretation of the Old Testament in the light of the New; conversely, the Christological and soteriological statements of the New Testament are interpreted in the light of the 'worldly', i.e. political, carnal, materialistic perspective of the Hebrew Bible: 'I'm thinking about how we can reinterpret in a "worldly" sense – in the sense of the Old Testament and of John 1.14 – the concepts of repentance, faith, justification, rebirth, and sanctification.'[82]

The fragmentary 'Outline for a Book' (August 1944) presents Bonhoeffer's later Christological reflections in a very condensed form. Once more the question 'Who?' is the starting point. Bonhoeffer asks: 'Who is God?' And he answers:

> Encounter with Jesus Christ. The experience that a transformation of all human life is given in the fact that 'Jesus is there only for others.' His 'being there for others' is the experience of transcendence. It is only this 'being there for others', maintained till death, that is the ground of his omnipotence, omniscience, and omnipresence.[83]

According to these insights the exaltation of Christ can be described in terms of humiliation only: 'God in human form . . . "the man for others", and therefore the Crucified . . .'[84]

The social concreteness of this Christological insight would be actualised in a Christian life described by Bonhoeffer in this context as 'participation in the being of Jesus'. Such 'new life in "existence for others"' would be 'faith'.[85] In other words, as Bonhoeffer wrote in his letter to Bethge the day after the failed *coup d'état*: 'It is only by living completely in this world that one learns to have faith.'[86] Such 'this-worldliness' would consist in 'participation in the sufferings of God in the secular life', and in allowing oneself to be 'caught up into the messianic sufferings of God in Jesus Christ'. And typically Bonhoeffer describes this participation in the 'messianic sufferings' as the fulfilment of Isaiah 53, the prophetic song on the sufferings of the 'servant of God',[87] who in Jewish tradition has always been identified with Israel. Christian participation in the sufferings of Christ is thus realised in solidarity with the people of Israel, and with those who are 'led like a lamb to the slaughter' (Isaiah 53:7).

Interestingly enough, Bonhoeffer's new awareness of the 'worldly' perspective of the Hebrew Bible leads him to a deeper understanding of the Chalcedonian Definition as well. Impressed by the erotic power of the Song of Songs, he attempts to liberate the doctrine of the 'two natures' in Christ from its dogmatic petrification by employing the musical imagery of polyphony:

> Even in the Bible we have the Song of Songs; and really one can

imagine no more ardent, passionate, sensual love than is portrayed there . . . It's a good thing that the book is in the Bible, in face of all those who believe that the restraint of passion is Christian (where is such a restraint in the Old Testament?). Where the *cantus firmus* is clear and plain, the counterpoint can be developed to its limits. The two are 'undivided and yet distinct', in the words of the Chalcedonian Definition, like Christ in his divine and human natures. May not the attraction and importance of polyphony in music consist in its being a musical reflection of this Christological fact and therefore of our *vita christiana*?[88]

Bonhoeffer's quest for social concreteness of Christology endures in this simile of *cantus firmus* and counterpoint in musical polyphony. Yet the earlier, sometimes almost compulsive identifications of Christ and community, Christ and peace, Christ and David, are relaxed and finally liquefied by a new conception, in which 'divine and human nature', love of 'God and his eternity' and 'earthly, erotic love' can communicate with consummate ease in a Christological interplay.

Notes

1 G. Kelly and F. B. Nelson, *A Testament to Freedom: The Essential Writings of Dietrich Bonhoeffer* (San Francisco: Harper & Row, 1990), p. 472.
2 ibid., p. 447.
3 D. Bonhoeffer, *Ethics* (New York: Macmillan, 1965), p. 58.
4 Kelly and Nelson, *A Testament to Freedom*, p. 339.
5 Bonhoeffer, *Ethics*, p. 80.
6 E. Bethge, *Dietrich Bonhoeffer: Theologian, Christian, Contemporary* (London: Collins, 1970), p. 625.
7 D. Bonhoeffer, *Christ the Centre*, trans. E. H. Robertson (New York: Harper & Row, 1978).
8 ibid., p. 30.
9 ibid., p. 27 (trans. altered).
10 ibid., p. 32.
11 ibid., p. 28 (trans. altered).
12 ibid., p. 32.
13 ibid., p. 30.
14 ibid., p. 46 (trans. altered).
15 ibid.
16 D. Bonhoeffer, *Illegale Theologenausbildung: Sammelvikariate 1937–1940, Dietrich Bonhoeffer Werke*, vol. xv (Gütersloh: Chr. Kaiser/Gütersloher Verlagshaus, 1998), p. 543.
17 Bonhoeffer, *Christ the Centre*, p. 74.
18 ibid., p. 62.

19 ibid., p. 59 (trans. altered).
20 ibid., p. 63.
21 ibid.
22 Kelly and Nelson, *A Testament to Freedom*, p. 139 (trans. altered).
23 Bonhoeffer, *Christ the Centre*, p. 104.
24 ibid., p. 106.
25 ibid., p. 107.
26 ibid., p. 113.
27 Kelly and Nelson, *A Testament to Freedom*, p. 92.
28 Bonhoeffer, *Christ the Centre*, p. 101 (trans. altered).
29 ibid., p. 102.
30 ibid., p. 101 (trans. altered).
31 ibid., pp. 87f. (trans. altered).
32 ibid., p. 89.
33 ibid., p. 91.
34 ibid.
35 ibid., p. 92.
36 ibid., p. 93.
37 ibid.
38 ibid., p. 88.
39 ibid., pp. 97f.
40 ibid., p. 102.
41 Bonhoeffer, *Illegale Theologenausbildung: Sammelvikariate*, p. 542: 'Werkzeug der Verherrlichung der göttlichen Offenbarung'.
42 Bonhoeffer, *Christ the Centre*, p. 34 (trans. altered).
43 ibid., pp. 34f.
44 ibid., p. 35.
45 ibid.
46 ibid., p. 84.
47 ibid., p. 82.
48 ibid., pp. 84, 82 (trans. altered).
49 D. Bonhoeffer, *Barcelona, Berlin, Amerika: 1928–1931, Dietrich Bonhoeffer Werke*, vol. x (Munich: Chr. Kaiser Verlag, 1992), p. 274.
50 D. Bonhoeffer, *Berlin 1932–1933, Dietrich Bonhoeffer Werke*, vol. xii (Gütersloh: Chr. Kaiser/Gütersloher Verlagshaus, 1997), p. 159.
51 Bonhoeffer, *Illegale Theologenausbildung*, p. 453.
52 D. Bonhoeffer, *Letters and Papers from Prison: The Enlarged Edition* (New York: Macmillan, 1972).
53 ibid., p. 381.
54 ibid., p. 382.
55 ibid., p. 381.
56 Bonhoeffer, *Christ the Centre*, p. 62 (trans. altered).
57 ibid.
58 Bonhoeffer, *Berlin 1932–1933*, pp. 349ff.
59 Bonhoeffer, *Ethics*, pp. 89f.
60 D. Bonhoeffer, *Illegale Theologenausbildung: Finkenwalde 1935–1937, Dietrich Bonhoeffer Werke*, vol. xiv (Gütersloh: Chr. Kaiser/Gütersloher Verlagshaus,

1996), pp. 878ff. Other examples of 'Christological interpretation' of the Old Testament in this period are: 'Christus in den Psalmen', in Bonhoeffer, *Illegale Theologenausbildung: Finkenwalde*, pp. 360ff., 'Der Wiederaufbau Jerusalems nach Esra und Nehemia', in Bonhoeffer, *Illegale Theologenausbildung: Finkenwalde*, pp. 930ff., and also *Das Gebetbuch der Bibel*, in D. Bonhoeffer, *Gemeinsames Leben; Das Gebetbuch der Bibel, Dietrich Bonhoeffer Werke*, vol. v (Munich: Chr. Kaiser Verlag, 1987), pp. 105ff.

61 Bonhoeffer, *Illegale Theologenausbildung: Finkenwalde*, p. 878.
62 ibid., p. 879.
63 ibid., p. 881.
64 ibid., p. 882.
65 ibid., p. 883.
66 ibid., p. 884.
67 ibid., p. 890.
68 ibid., p. 892.
69 ibid., p. 893.
70 ibid., p. 894.
71 ibid., p. 902.
72 ibid., p. 878, n. 2.
73 Bonhoeffer, *Letters and Papers from Prison*, p. 279.
74 Bethge, *Dietrich Bonhoeffer: Theologian, Christian, Contemporary*, p. 767.
75 Bonhoeffer, *Letters and Papers from Prison*, p. 342.
76 Bethge, *Dietrich Bonhoeffer: Theologian, Christian, Contemporary*, p. 769.
77 Bonhoeffer, *Letters and Papers from Prison*, p. 135.
78 ibid., p. 157 (trans. altered).
79 ibid., p. 282.
80 ibid., pp. 336f.
81 K. H. Miskotte, *Wenn die Götter schweigen: Vom Sinn des Alten Testaments* (Munich: Chr. Kaiser Verlag, 1966), p. 179.
82 Bonhoeffer, *Letters and Papers from Prison*, pp. 286.
83 ibid., p. 381.
84 ibid., pp. 381f.
85 ibid.
86 ibid., p. 369.
87 ibid., pp. 361f.
88 ibid., p. 303.

8 Ecumenical witness for peace

KEITH CLEMENTS

From the early 1930s, the Christian witness for peace was one of Dietrich Bonhoeffer's most consuming preoccupations, both intellectually and in action. In this, far from being a lone voice, he was but one of numerous Christians in many countries for whom the cause of peace, set against the tragic experience of 1914–18 and the resurgence of nationalism and militarism in the 1930s, was paramount. To isolate Bonhoeffer from the wider movement in which he took part, casting him in the role of sole prophet or hero, would not only be historically unreal; it would also obstruct the view of his distinctive contribution. It was in his sharp theological interaction with his partners in ecumenical peace-work, no less than in his opposition to the menacing political demons of his time, that his critical – and continuing – significance is to be seen. This chapter will concentrate on Bonhoeffer's theological contribution during the critical years 1932–4.

PEACE AND THE CHURCHES

Throughout most of his student years, until about 1930, Bonhoeffer showed relatively little concern with international peace issues. Not that he was indifferent to war and its consequences: he could never forget the loss of his brother Walter on the western front in 1918 or, especially, the permanent scar of grief this left on his mother. But the notion of the church as having a particular calling to work for international peace, and of there being a specifically Christian basis for such world order, was as yet quite foreign to him. Both as a Lutheran, bred to make a sharp distinction between the respective roles of the church and the state, and as a fervent new convert to Karl Barth's rigorous separation between the kingdom of God and all human causes, however noble, he was highly suspicious of what he had heard about the post-war movements to 'build a better world'.

His year at Union Seminary in New York (1930–1) shook these assumptions decisively. For one thing, whatever the theological limitations of the 'social gospel' he learnt that certain social issues, above all the racism experienced by black people, could be ignored by the churches only by forfeiting the gospel itself. At least as crucially, he was deeply challenged by the pacifism of Jean Lasserre, a French Protestant student also at Union, with whom he developed a close friendship. Hitherto, pacifism was an almost unheard-of attitude among German Lutherans. It was virtually an anathema, an ethical disorder of misguided 'enthusiasts' and 'liberals', mainly in the English-speaking world, who did not see that Christianity involved giving Caesar his due and that bearing arms for the Fatherland when required was a natural and a Christian duty. The challenge presented to Bonhoeffer by Lasserre was not, however, primarily in terms of general ethical principles but centred on how to receive Jesus' teaching in the Sermon on the Mount. Jesus quite clearly enjoins non-violence on his disciples: turn the other cheek, return ill-treatment with blessing, pray for your enemies. The traditional Lutheran response to these words had been to see them as ideals for an ideal world, not the tragically sinful and disordered world in which we are actually living; and not as commands to be followed literally, but, by their very unrealisability, as showing just how sinful and morally bankrupt we are and therefore in need of repentance and grace.

Bonhoeffer now began to ask himself whether all such theological explanations were an attempt to escape from the *concreteness* of Jesus' command. Might not the 'otherness' of God's word, to which Karl Barth had pointed him, in fact be encountered precisely in this concreteness, and in the costly 'otherness' of the life, in contrast to the world, to which the individual disciple and the community of faith alike are thereby called?

Soon after his return to Berlin in the summer of 1931, Bonhoeffer accepted an invitation to be a German youth delegate to the conference of the World Alliance for Promoting International Friendship through the Churches, in Cambridge. This marked his entry into the ecumenical move-ment, and in some respects it was an incongruous entry-point for one so theologically rigorous and sophisticated. For the World Alliance epitomised liberal, idealistic internationalism – some would say utopianism. It had been founded on the very eve of war in 1914, the product of a number of European and American peace-movements. Far from being demolished by the experience of 1914–18, it was resurrected under the leadership of figures like Friedrich Siegmund-Schultze in Germany, Lord Willoughby Dickinson in England, Wilfred Monod in France and Henry Atkinson in the United States (from where a good deal of its funding, supplied by Andrew Carnegie, also came). It was held together by the belief that the nightmare of the First

World War would itself now prove to be a powerful impulse towards international peace. Never a large organisation, it aimed to foster international understanding through personal encounter, conferences and publications, and discussions of the issues which still divided peoples of the world. It saw a special calling for the churches to supply the moral impulses without which the newly founded League of Nations would surely founder. Peace, it believed, could and should be demonstrated to be in the best interests of rational people.

Bonhoeffer, however much he felt that the World Alliance lacked theological undergirding in its pragmatism and appeal to rationality, nevertheless threw himself energetically into its activities. Not only did he attend the Cambridge conference, but he was willingly appointed one of the two youth secretaries for Europe. Much of his time for the next two years, in addition to his academic duties at Berlin University, was spent organising and attending conferences in Germany and elsewhere in Europe on behalf of the ecumenical peace-movement. The theological input he himself gave to these meetings will be described later. Suffice it to say that he believed strongly that the World Alliance should take itself more seriously as an expression of the church of Christ, and not simply as an *ad hoc* gathering of like-minded Christians trying to make an impact on the world.

There was indeed a problem here about the ecclesial status of the World Alliance, its membership comprising voluntary enthusiasts for the cause rather than officially mandated representatives of the churches. This was not the case with the larger parallel body, the Universal Christian Council for Life and Work, set up to continue the concerns of the 1925 'Life and Work' Conference at Stockholm, and by now one of the main streams of the ecumenical movement. But the concerns of the World Alliance and Life and Work were closely parallel and indeed overlapping at a number of points, and co-operation between the two bodies grew. The high point came with their joint conference at Fanö in Denmark in 1934, an occasion when Bonhoeffer, in a paper and a sermon, made his most outspoken and uncompromising call for the churches to declare together to the world God's concrete command of peace. It was while relaxing on the beach at Fanö that Bonhoeffer was asked what he would do if war broke out, and replied, 'I pray that God will give me the strength not to take up arms.'[1]

By now Hitler had been in power for over a year. Bonhoeffer had moved to London in the autumn of 1933 to take charge of the two German congregations there. While there he had begun his close and crucial friendship with George Bell, the Anglican Bishop of Chichester, who was also chairman of the Council for Life and Work. Personal friendships across lines of confession and nationality have proved as important for the ecumenical movement as formal meetings and official bodies, and this was to prove outstandingly so with Bonhoeffer and Bell. At Fanö Bonhoeffer was co-opted onto the Council and was thus now linked directly into this main channel of the ecumenical movement. But the challenge he brought to Life and Work was no less rigorous than that which he presented to the World Alliance.

Moreover, regardless of whatever he actually said in these ecumenical gatherings, within his native German context Bonhoeffer's involvement – and that of other Germans who took part – was seen as highly provocative. Even before Hitler's advent to power, the tide of nationalism in German Protestant circles was rising fast, and there was widespread opposition to anything savouring of 'internationalism'. Church involvement on the wider ecumenical scene was viewed as no less unpatriotic and un-German. Meanwhile, Bonhoeffer himself was considering a still more radical venture down the route of non-violence. He was increasingly intrigued by the Mahatma Gandhi's methods of non-violent resistance in India, and was asking whether the East might have spiritual resources from which the ethically impoverished West could learn. His plans to visit India were well advanced when, in the spring of 1935, he was summoned back to Germany from England to lead the illegal seminary of the Confessing Church at Finkenwalde. It is tempting to speculate what might have resulted if he had managed to get to India.

Bonhoeffer's work now centred on the Confessing Church and its theological leadership. In any case, in Germany the work of the World Alliance crumbled under the Nazi state, and internationally much of its activity was now subsumed under Life and Work. Nevertheless at Finkenwalde the peace witness remained vital to Bonhoeffer's teaching. When in May 1935 his students heard the news that Hitler was reintroducing conscription, many of them rejoiced at this opportunity to prove that service in the Confessing Church did not signify any lack of patriotism. They were taken aback when he calmly suggested that the pacifist position should be considered seriously, even by Lutherans. Passages in *The Cost of Discipleship*, based on his seminary lectures, certainly read like a credo for non-violence.

From the relatively narrow base of his seminary, Bonhoeffer continued to be an international ecumenist. He still served on the Life and Work Council, which by now was preparing for the 1937 Conference on Church, Community and State to be held in Oxford. He and others from the Confessing Church were refused travel permission to attend the conference by the Nazi state. However, the fact that scarcely any other Germans were present at Oxford represented a kind of victory for the cause of the Confessing Church. Bonhoeffer and his colleagues, receiving the sympathetic ear of George Bell, had stoutly maintained that it was the Confessing Church alone, not the official Reich Church and still less the nazified 'Faith Movement of German Christians', which should be recognised by the ecumenical movement as the true Evangelical Church of Germany. Meanwhile, Bonhoeffer made great efforts to foster links between the Confessing Church and the churches abroad. In 1936, for example, he took his students on a visit to Sweden, much to the chagrin of the Reich Church authorities, who discovered that the Finkenwalde group had been publicly received by the Swedish church authorities, thus according the Confessing Church official status.

By 1939 Bonhoeffer's position on peace and non-violence was placing him in an acute personal dilemma, as his age-group was now liable to conscription. It was to try to help him escape this problem that his emigration to the United States was arranged in the summer of 1939; and it was his discovery that, come what may, he was a German and a Christian who had to remain in solidarity with his people – even as he prayed for its defeat for the sake of Christian civilisation – that led to his hasty return to Germany just before the outbreak of war in September 1939.

It will always be asked how Bonhoeffer the conspirator can be reconciled with Bonhoeffer the pacifist. The answer lies, first, in the fact that Bonhoeffer had never enjoined pacifism as an absolute requirement for all Christians. In refusing arms he was rejecting violence in an aggressive national cause, or in one's own individual interest. By the second year of the war the situation was quite different. He knew of the slaughter of countless Jews. The question was now, not that of preserving one's personal innocence in refusing to shed blood, but that of avoiding complicity in the greater guilt of allowing such genocide to continue. Secondly, the consistent thread in Bonhoeffer's pilgrimage from peace-worker to political resister lies in his ecumenism. In a time of peace threatened by war, he saw the ecumenical vocation as that of calling for peace among the nations. In a time of actual war when the nations were now in bloody conflict, he saw the ecumenical vocation as lying in the need to maintain the links between those in the churches, on all sides, who were working for a new, just order. Hence Bonhoeffer's repeated contacts with the wider ecumenical scene via the World Council of Churches in Geneva and above all, his visit to George Bell in Sweden in 1942 to inform him of the details of the resistance. His last known words, just before being taken away from his fellow prisoners for final court-martial at Flossenbürg, were a message to Bell: 'Tell him, that with him I believe in the principle of our universal Christian brotherhood which rises above all national interests and conflicts, and that our victory is certain.'[2]

WHY ECUMENISM? WHY PEACE?

For Bonhoeffer, ecumenical commitment and the witness to peace were inseparable aspects of the one calling of discipleship to Jesus Christ. This is a point of fundamental significance for an understanding of his theology and his particular contribution in the context of his time. By the early 1930s the 'ecumenical movement', largely a matter of the Protestant and Orthodox Churches, comprised three main streams. First to arise had been the efforts to secure greater missionary co-operation on a world scale, heralded by the World Missionary Conference at Edinburgh in 1910 and consolidated by the formation of the International Missionary Council in 1921. Close behind had come Life and Work, whose origins have already been outlined, and Faith and Order, the first international conference of which had been held at Lausanne in 1927.[3] While there was some overlap in the personnel participating in all three movements, there was also, especially between Life and Work and Faith and Order, not only a difference in emphasis but at times a distinct rivalry in claims to importance. Faith and Order was concerned with definitely 'ecclesiastical' concerns: the search for visible unity and therewith the means of overcoming the different understandings and practices relating to ecclesiology, ministry, sacraments. Life and Work, with its agenda of promoting justice in social and international relations, tended to attract those who were impatient with 'churchy' affairs and were more anxious to promote 'the kingdom of God on earth'. A popular slogan in the early days of Life and Work was 'doctrine divides, service unites'.[4]

It is striking that Bonhoeffer, while he threw his energies into Life and Work (or at least initially its smaller cousin, the World Alliance), never once gave voice to anything approaching this latter sentiment. It is true that he did feel increasingly uneasy with Faith and Order, and in 1939 had a very heated argument with its General Secretary, Leonard Hodgson of Oxford. This dispute, however, was not over the aims and purposes of Faith and Order, but over the stance it took on the church struggle in Germany. By contrast to Life and Work, which under the strong lead given by Bishop George Bell had essentially recognised the Confessing Church to be the true Evangelical Church of Germany, Faith and Order took a much more cautious line, insisting that it was in no position to be arbiter between the rival church groups. As a result, Faith and Order issued invitations both to the Confessing Church and to the Reich Church to participate in its meetings and in the 1937 Faith and Order Conference at Edinburgh. For Bonhoeffer and other radicals in the Confessing Church this was to miss the point about both the nature of the church struggle and the ecumenical movement. The Confessing Church was not just 'another' church in Germany. From the Barmen Confession of 1934 onwards, it was staking itself on nothing less than the actual gospel which the ecumenical movement itself claimed to be based upon. The Confessing Church was therefore representing the ecumenical cause itself inside Germany. Those who rejected Barmen were, *ipso facto*, rejecting the true basis of the ecumenical movement. They could have no claim upon the ecumenical movement, and the ecumenical movement in turn was undermining its own integrity whenever it tried to be inclusive of all groups irrespective of their confessional position. That Bonhoeffer felt so passionately about this issue indicates that he recognised the importance of the Faith and Order agenda, and all its ecclesiological concerns, no less than did any of the Faith and Order leadership themselves.[5]

As an ecumenist, therefore, Bonhoeffer is not to be ranged among the 'social activists' over against the 'ecclesiastics'. Rather, almost from his entry into the World Alliance, he expressed dissatisfaction with the self-proclaimed pragmatic, non-doctrinal approach of the peace movement, which would prefer to leave 'theology' to Faith and Order: an attitude both theologically unsound and in actual practice counter-productive. As he stated in his paper 'A Theological Basis for the World Alliance', given at a youth peace conference in Czechoslovakia in 1932:

> Because there is no theology of the ecumenical movement, ecumenical thought has become powerless and meaningless, especially among German youth, because of the political upsurge of nationalism. And the situation is scarcely different in other countries. There is no theological anchorage which holds while the waves dash in vain . . . *Anyone concerned in ecumenical work must suffer the charges of being unconcerned with the Fatherland and unconcerned with the truth*, and any attempt at an encounter is quickly cried down.[6]

Bonhoeffer was equally clear where that anchorage was to be found: in the doctrine of the church as the one body of Christ. Here he was bringing to bear all his earlier theological work, from *Sanctorum Communio* onwards, on the new human reality, 'Christ existing as community', which is the church. He is now transposing this communal emphasis into a transnational key. By its very nature the church transcends all human divisions and

challenges all human propensities to conflict. Bonhoeffer's ecumenical theology is a theology of peace because it is a theology of this one church drawn
from and found among all the nations. This is the bedrock of his challenge
to nationalism, as he states:

> There shall be peace because of the church of Christ, for the sake of
> which the world exists. And this church of Christ lives at one and the
> same time in all peoples, yet beyond all boundaries, whether national,
> political, social, or racial. And the brothers who make up this church
> are bound together, through the commandment of the one Lord
> Christ, whose Word they hear, more inseparably than men are bound
> by all the ties of common history, of blood, of class and of language.
> All these ties, which are part of our world, are valid ties, not
> indifferent; but in the presence of Christ they are not ultimate bonds.[7]

In effect, Bonhoeffer was saying that the first challenge facing the ecumenical peace movement was not how to make the League of Nations more
effective, but how to manifest the true, international unity of the one, holy,
catholic and apostolic church. Bonhoeffer's most forthright statement on
the church's witness for peace was made at the joint conference of the
World Alliance and Life and Work at Fanö, Denmark, in 1934. Again, his
premise was that peace is not first a human wish to be arrived at by human
technique and effort, but lies in God's own reconciling work in Christ, of
which the one church is sign and witness. It was on this basis that he uttered
the dramatic words:

> How does peace come about? Through a system of political treaties?
> Through the investment of international capital in different countries?
> Through the big banks, through money? Or through universal
> peaceful rearmament in order to guarantee peace? Through none of
> these, for the single reason that in all of them peace is confused with
> safety. There is no way to peace along the way of safety. For peace
> must be dared. It is the great venture. It can never be safe. Peace is the
> opposite of security. To demand guarantees is to mistrust and this
> mistrust in turn brings forth war. To look for guarantees is to want to
> protect oneself. Peace means to give oneself altogether to the law of
> God, wanting no security, but in faith and obedience laying the
> destiny of the nations in the hand of Almighty God, not trying to
> direct it for selfish purposes.[8]

It was at Fanö also that he made his startling call for nothing less than a
universal council – a truly ecumenical council – of all the churches to be

summoned, in order to reject war and to declare peace as God's will and promise to the whole world.

> Only the one great Ecumenical Council of the holy church of Christ over all the world can speak out so that the world, though it gnash its teeth, will have to hear, so that the peoples will rejoice because the church of Christ in the name of Christ has taken the weapons from the hands of their sons, forbidden war, proclaimed the peace of Christ against the raging world.[9]

Not until half a century later was there an attempt within the ecumenical movement to answer Bonhoeffer's call for a universal peace council of the churches.

THEOLOGY AND NATIONALISM

During the early 1930s, in his ecumenical witness for peace Bonhoeffer was engaging (if it is not an inappropriate metaphor) two fronts. As well as trying to inject theological rigour into the ecumenical peace movement, he was also in his immediate home context having to challenge theologically the rising tide of nationalism. The rise of Nazism leading to Hitler's political victory of 1933 had drawn upon the strong current of national feeling which had been running for over a century in Germany, and which was immeasurably deepened by the sense of grievance following the military collapse of 1918 and the terms of the Versailles Treaty. Hitler was able to exploit this sense of hurt national pride by promising a golden future for Germans if, like him, they would truly adopt as their credo that 'nothing in this wide world surpasses . . . this Germany, people and land'.[10] Patriotism is, of course, an almost universal human phenomenon in some form or other. The Nazi version of it, however, not only made the nation the highest and unsurpassable object of allegiance and loyalty, but saw the place of the nation in the world as relying, first, on its military strength and secondly, on its 'racial purity'. Again, neither militarism nor anti-Semitism originated in Nazism (nor, of course, in Europe have they been peculiar to Germany), but within the Nazi credo of 'blood, race and soil' they were taken to their most brutal extremes.

This extreme nationalist ideology, however, was aided and abetted not just by crude, populist political feeling but by sophisticated intellectual thought as well – including a good deal of theology. Indeed, there had been a German intellectual preoccupation with the concept of *das Volk*, the people or nation, as far back as some of the Romantic thinkers in the early nineteenth century, and some of the most influential Protestant theologians such as Friedrich Schleiermacher.

After the First World War, much effort was devoted in Germany to finding an explicit metaphysical basis for nationhood. For the more nationalistically minded Protestant theologians – who included erudite and sophisticated figures of international repute such as Paul Althaus and Emmanuel Hirsch – the key theological concept was that of 'orders of creation'. This is the doctrine that certain structures of human life are not just incidental biological or historical phenomena, but are deliberately ordained of God as essential and immutable conditions of human existence, without which humanity is not humanity as created by God.

The concept of orders of creation was not, as such, particularly exceptionable. Even Karl Barth, who was to lead the theological onslaught on nationalist religion in the church struggle, was not averse to using the term in his teaching on ethics during the 1920s. More generally, both Protestant and Catholic thought has traditionally maintained that certain features of human existence are especially significant for the way in which the 'image of God' is reflected in the human creature. The German nationalist theologians, however, made a much freer and quite arbitrary use of the idea of 'orders of creation', claiming above all that *the* supreme 'order of creation' is the people, race or nation to which one belongs and owes loyalty.

Such an understanding became the mould for recasting the meaning of the entire body of Christian belief. So, for example, when the creed confesses belief in God as maker of heaven and earth, this becomes the confession that God has created me with my particular nationality and its special characteristics. God has therewith bound me to submit myself to the forces working out the destiny of my nation, and to co-operate with its spirit, and it is in the flowering of a nation's life that we see what creation really is. As the 1932 manifesto of the Faith Movement of German Christians stated: 'In race, nation and cultural heritage we see the orders of existence which God has given us in trust; it is the law of God that we should be concerned to preserve them. Therefore racial admixture is to be opposed . . . faith in Christ does not destroy the race, it deepens and sanctifies it.'[11]

For Bonhoeffer, by contrast, and in line with Karl Barth's theology of revelation, all such attempts to talk about 'creation' in a general way were spurious. For him, as he made clear in his lectures on *Creation and Fall* given at about this time, it is Jesus Christ through whom we know both God and the world as God intends it to be. We cannot read God's will and purposes straight off from the world as it is, the fallen world of sin and division. Christian faith cannot be redefined in terms of nationhood. Rather, nationhood has to be understood in the light of the word of God, Jesus Christ.

Bonhoeffer therefore launched a full-scale attack on the 'orders of creation' theology, and he did so precisely in the ecumenical context of his work as youth secretary in the World Alliance. In April 1932 he organised a conference in Berlin. Bishop Wilhelm Stählin of Münster led off with an exposition of the nation as a God-given order of creation. Bonhoeffer followed with the criticism that it was impossible to single out some features of the world above others as orders of creation and base a course of Christian moral action upon them. 'It was just this presupposition, i.e. the orders of creation, which provided a justification of war between the nations.'[12] Bonhoeffer, however, was not against giving a due theological place to the nation. Instead of 'orders of creation' he proposed the concept of *orders of preservation*. The conference report ran:

> The difference was that in the light of the concept of orders of creation, certain ordinances and features of the world were regarded as valuable, original, 'very good' in themselves, whereas the concept of orders of preservation meant that each feature was only a feature preserved by God, in grace and anger, in view of the revelation in Christ. Any order under the preservation of God should be carried out by Christ and preserved for his sake. An order is only to be regarded as an order of preservation so long as it is still open for the proclamation of the Gospel. Where an order is basically closed to this proclamation, be it apparently the most original, marriage, nation, etc., it must be surrendered.[13]

Bonhoeffer is seeking to recognise the genuine reality of social structures such as the nation, and their normal sustaining and enriching roles in God's providential care of humans; while at the same time relativising them in face of what alone is ultimate, God's demand and promise in the gospel. Such a theology, affirming yet relativising, was necessary both to counteract the excessive – indeed obsessive – adulation of nationhood within Germany, and to provide a framework for international ecumenical encounter. The ecumenical context required a perspective which allowed for proper diversity of nations yet kept all the claims of nationhood open to revision in the light of Christ. It is no surprise, then, to find at the Youth Peace Conference of the World Alliance in Czechoslovakia, also in 1932, Bonhoeffer again critical of 'orders of creation' theology and advocating 'orders of preservation':

> Orders of preservation are forms of working against sin in the direction of the gospel. *Any order* – however ancient and sacred it may be – *can be dissolved*, and must be dissolved when it closes up in itself,

grows rigid and no longer permits the proclamation of revelation. From this standpoint the Church of Christ . . . haṣ to keep in mind only one thing: Which orders can best restrain this radical falling of the world into death and sin and hold the way open for the Gospel? The Church hears the commandment only from Christ, not from any fixed law or from any eternal order, and it hears it in the orders of preservation . . . It can demand the most radical destructions simply for the sake of the one who builds up.[14]

Bonhoeffer's theology of nationhood, it will be seen, differs sharply not only from the nationalism of his German context, but also from much of the rhetoric common to Christian and allied peace-movements. We do not find in Bonhoeffer universalist abstractions about the 'brotherhood of man' or even 'our common humanity'. We remain in the world of very concrete communities, the nation included. They are given their space – enough and no more. They are allowed to be – for the time being. But always over them hangs the question of whether they are providing a means for obedience to Christ, or an obstruction. '*Any order* – however ancient and sacred . . . *can be dissolved*': therein also lies one of the roots which eventually led Bonhoeffer into the most radical course of his life, political conspiracy to overthrow the regime. In 1932, several months before Hitler's coming to power, he himself could not have foreseen just what the momentous and fateful consequences of this kind of critical theology would be. For the time being his conscious efforts were directed at giving theological nerve and spine to the ecumenical peace-movement. Nor were his efforts wholly in vain. Life and Work's 1937 Oxford Conference on Church, Community and State took up the issue of the nation in Christian perspective. The section on the nation in the conference report clearly reflects the debates engendered in and around the German experience, and Bonhoeffer's part in them.[15]

As if Bonhoeffer had not already given his ecumenical contemporaries enough to think about in demanding a properly theological basis for their work, he also questioned their understanding of 'peace' itself. His concern centred on the looseness of 'Anglo-Saxon' (i.e. British and American) thought, which approached the peace question in an essentially pragmatic way. It saw peace as a 'problem' requiring for its solution some rational means – treaties, education, 'understanding' – of preventing the nations going to war again. At the 1932 youth conference in Czechoslovakia, having dealt with the falsities arising out of using 'orders of creation' theology for an understanding of nationhood, Bonhoeffer proceeded to detect a closely parallel error in much of the thinking of the peace-movement itself. This pragmatism views 'peace' as an absolute ideal, in effect an 'order of creation' identified with the gospel itself and as such to be preserved unconditionally. But peace, says Bonhoeffer, is not an end in itself. It is 'a command of the angry God, an order for the preservation of the world in the light of Christ'.[16] International peace may become an absolutely urgent necessity, but never for its own sake. It is for the sake of the lordship of Christ who requires some form of community for his word to be proclaimed and received. 'Peace' can therefore never be undefined as an entity in itself. It has certain clear boundaries:

> The broken character of the order of peace is expressed in the fact that the peace commanded by God has two limits, first the truth and secondly justice. There can only be a community of peace when it does not rest on *lies* and *injustice*. Where a community of peace endangers or chokes truth and justice, the community of peace must be broken and battle joined.[17]

We have already seen that for Bonhoeffer even the ecumenical movement itself could never simply be an all-embracing affair where the sharp differences of loyalty could be overlooked, or a neutral attitude be adopted to all rival positions. So too on the international level the search for peace could only have integrity if it meant acknowledging the painful and divisive realities. It should be noted that this was being said in 1932, when the Weimar Republic was still trying to survive. Bonhoeffer was writing as a representative of that defeated Germany, a Germany still feeling forced to act the role of under-dog. The ecumenical movement, in his eyes, needed to be a place where the actuality of such pain was brought to the surface, not smoothed over. This meant acknowledging the need for *struggle* if truth and justice are suppressed.[18] By 'struggle', however, Bonhoeffer does not mean war, which in the contemporary world is of a quite different nature. 'War in our day no longer falls under the concept of struggle because it is the certain self-annihilation of both combatants. It is in no way to be regarded as an order of preservation in the light of revelation, simply because it is so destructive.'[19]

A CONTINUING CHALLENGE TO ECUMENISM

In the more than fifty years since his death, Bonhoeffer has continued to challenge the ecumenical movement. Obviously a figure of such stature has more points of contact with the continuing and contemporary scene than can be adequately commented upon here. But four points at which his influence has been strongly manifest, or to which his challenge remains highly pertinent, can be emphasised.

First, Bonhoeffer has been cited repeatedly where the international ecumenical community has been called to stand with those churches and peoples facing oppression and struggling for justice and freedom in their own contexts. The challenge he laid upon the ecumenical movement of his time to takes sides with his Confessing Church was specifically called to mind many times during the years of struggle against apartheid in South Africa.[20] Still more to the point, the struggle for liberation in southern Africa as a whole produced perhaps the sharpest and most controversial debates which the World Council of Churches has ever experienced, surrounding the Programme to Combat Racism and the use of its Special Fund (set up in 1970) in support of the humanitarian work of the liberation movements. Bonhoeffer suddenly seemed very contemporary again, with his insistence that 'peace' is not a valid term if it means a refusal to confront the red-hot issues of truth and justice which are a matter of *struggle*.

Secondly, Bonhoeffer's call for a universal ecumenical council to call for peace was a powerful stimulus (half a century later!) in setting in motion the Conciliar Process on Justice, Peace and the Integrity of Creation (JPIC). This became part of the programmatic life of the World Council of Churches at its 6th Assembly in Vancouver, 1983. But it was in Europe, perhaps naturally, that the recollection of Bonhoeffer's vision was clearest and came to fruition in the (First) European Ecumenical Assembly at Basle in 1989. Significantly, such an assembly was first called for by the Protestant Churches of the then still-divided Germany, both East and West, and was sponsored by the Conference of European Churches and the Council of Catholic Episcopal Conferences in Europe. This made the gathering one of the most genuinely ecumenical of its size anywhere in the world, and its call for 'peace with justice' was deeply in line with Bonhoeffer's conviction that when the churches speak, they must do so concretely in a way that reaches to the heart of the human situation.[21] By contrast, it has to be said, the World Convocation on JPIC which met under WCC auspices in Korea in 1990 failed to reach the highest expectations – partly because Roman Catholic participation failed to materialise, and partly through the difficulty experienced in making statements on global issues which did not disappear into empty rhetoric and slogans.

Thirdly, Bonhoeffer continues to challenge nationalism. One of the most critical issues facing ecumenical witness today is, once again, the relation between Christian discipleship and membership of the universal church on the one hand, and national and ethnic loyalties on the other. The issue has resurfaced in Europe following the end of the Cold War, as seen most tragically in the conflicts in the former Yugoslavia, and continually simmering in many parts of the former Soviet Union. The issue is now especially clear-cut, precisely because the national or ethnic identities of many peoples in these regions are heavily defined by religion (Catholic Croatia, Orthodox Serbia or Bulgaria). Bonhoeffer's theology of nationhood, which recognises its reality as a means of God's providential care, but relativises it in the face of the gospel and of the universal church, has lost none of its cutting edge in this context. It is significant, for example, that this third point of Bonhoeffer's influence is now being taken seriously in some Orthodox circles.[22] Nor is the issue confined to Europe, as the ethnic conflicts in central Africa, Sri Lanka and elsewhere in the South have shown.

Fourthly, Bonhoeffer has been a major influence in bridging the gap between ecclesiology and ethics, between church unity and social witness. While both Life and Work and Faith and Order to a large extent became foundational to, and integrated into, the World Council of Churches, their different emphases have continued to be reflected within the World Council itself and the whole ecumenical movement. Socio-political activism on the one hand and concern for the visible unity of the churches on the other so often seem to be poles in marked tension if not mutual suspicion and outright rivalry. Bonhoeffer, we have seen, challenged his fellow peace-activists to discover a proper theological basis for their work, in ecclesiology: the one church of Christ transcending all national and racial barriers. At the same time he challenged Faith and Order to make a definite commitment to that church in Germany which represented resistance to nationalist and racist religion. In recent years, the World Council of Churches has attempted to face anew the need to relate concern for the integrity and unity of the church with commitment to justice and peace for the whole world. A particular example has been the programme on *Ecclesiology and Ethics* under the joint auspices of the Faith and Order Commission and Unit III (Justice, Peace and Creation). Bonhoeffer's role in the ecumenical movement of the 1930s has figured significantly as one of the pioneering attempts which only now are being followed up.[23]

HOW EFFECTIVE A WITNESS? A NECESSARY DISCUSSION

Any responsible assessment and contemporary use of Bonhoeffer's contribution to the ecumenical witness for peace must be prepared at least to eschew hero-worship and hagiography, and subject both his activities and thought to certain questions.

The first concerns his decision to identify with the World Alliance for Promoting International Friendship through the Churches. Bonhoeffer, we have seen, had doubts about the theological soundness of this organisation, and determined to do something about it. Was this effort justified, or was it rather attempting to fit a new, high-powered engine into a frail and leaking hull? Was the ecumenical peace-movement – including Life and Work up to 1937 – capable of renewal, or was it always fated to be the province of naïvety and utopianism? The historian John Conway summarises one line of criticism of the movement:

> These pacifists failed to recognise that the social function of the mainline churches, and of the educated bourgeoisie which upheld them, was largely, if often unconsciously, preservative of the existing social order, with an attendant attachment to the nation state and its apparatus of military defence forces, whose use could be justified in time of crisis.[24]

Or was it, Conway asks, that the chief weakness of the peace-movement 'lay exactly in its middle-class character, its ethical rationality and its lack of opening to the working classes or to the ranks of the oppressed peoples of the world'? One might indeed well ask why, in all the deliberations of the World Alliance during the 1930s, so little attention seems to have been paid to other peace-movements, one of the most powerful being the international labour movement. Did Bonhoeffer sufficiently challenge this bourgeois captivity of the peace-movement? Or, to ask the question in another way, if Bonhoeffer was right to challenge the untheological pragmatism of the World Alliance, did he himself sufficiently see that a theology unaided by some kind of political work would be dead? It has to be admitted that we do not find much attention overtly paid to this wider perspective in Bonhoeffer's peace teaching and preaching of the time. One important qualification has to be made, namely his growing interest in the non-violent resistance philosophy and techniques of Gandhi.

This brings us back to Bonhoeffer's statement of 1934 at the Fanö ecumenical conference, 'There is no way to peace along the way of safety. For peace must be dared. It is the great venture . . . Peace is the opposite of security.'[25] These words have been so often and so reverently quoted as to become a kind of sacred text for the peace commitment exemplified by Bonhoeffer. But it is not impious to ask just what Bonhoeffer was meaning here, in setting peace in contrast to all that financial, military and diplomatic concerns aim to achieve. (One person in Bonhoeffer's audience at Fanö was particularly critical: Richard Crossman, a young Oxford don and socialist, and a future Labour cabinet minister. He had been sent to Fanö by George Bell particularly to hear Bonhoeffer.) If peace is the opposite of security, precisely how then does faith in the peace which God commands engage with the world which, like it or not, *does* work in and through the big banks, government offices, media barons and – yes – the armed forces?

In setting peace and security so antithetically apart, can Bonhoeffer be saved from the charge of sheer rhetorical indulgence here? Perhaps he can, if some distinctions implicit in his approach can be made more explicit. It can be confirmed in many historical case-studies that the process of peace-making does often come about through representatives of the respective sides making ventures, often at great risk to their credibility among their followers, of trust, openness and determination to find a new way. The story of South Africa's transition from the apartheid regime to a non-racial democracy is a prime example in our age. Bonhoeffer's statement can be gladly accepted as highlighting this feature of peace. But such ventures also require preparation of a context, a particular time, a *kairos*, a set of circumstances and conditions which will at least give them the chance of some definite positive result. These are the *necessary* conditions for peace, though not the *sufficient* conditions, which – and here Bonhoeffer's point rings true – include ventures of trust.

But at least Bonhoeffer's own thought became more nuanced with time, as seen in his *Ethics*, where a new relationship between conformation to Christ and the 'natural' is sought. It was at the same time, during the Second World War, that Bonhoeffer made some highly perceptive comments on William Paton's paper 'The Church and the New Order', which he read while on one of his visits to the World Council of Churches in Geneva.[26] Paton, as a British church representative anxious for post-war reconciliation with a defeated, non-Nazi Germany, had spoken of the need for a charter of rights and liberties to provide the norm for actions by the state. This, argued Bonhoeffer in reply, was to ignore the conditions that would obtain in a Germany where in the chaos left by Nazism all order had been destroyed. There might well be need for a firm, indeed authoritarian, control for a time (as was indeed in effect provided by the Allied occupation).

It has been a long and still incomplete journey of discovery for the churches to realise that the search for world peace cannot be isolated from other, seemingly less glamorous, issues. As we approach the end of the century and of the millennium, Christian thought has barely begun to engage with the struggle for economic justice within and between communities. The dictum of Julius Nyerere when he was President of Tanzania that 'development is another word for peace' has only just begun to be heard. Peace may not come about through the big banks, as Bonhoeffer put it, but neither will it be possible if the role of financial institutions is ignored, and the search for a new economic order evaded.

If we admit that, irrespective of actual physical, armed violence, the contemporary world is nevertheless in real ways in conflict economically, then Bonhoeffer's war-time contacts with his British colleagues are perhaps the right point on which to conclude these reflections on his role as an ecumenical witness to peace on such issues. Involving as they did a careful listening to the others' concerns and in turn mediating his own perceptions of the reality of his home context, they were exemplary cases of ecumenical solidarity in the midst of conflict: signs of the peace to come. Bonhoeffer's own last message to Bishop Bell thus sums up so much of his life – and his significance for the ecumenical movement since.

Notes

1 E. Bethge, *Dietrich Bonhoeffer: Theologian, Christian, Contemporary* (London: Collins, 1970), p.314.

2 ibid., p. 830, n. 54.

3 *A History of the Ecumenical Movement, 1517–1948*, ed. R. Rouse and S. C. Neill (London: SPCK, 1953), pp. 420ff.

4 ibid., pp. 571f.

5 See Bonhoeffer's 1936 paper, 'The Confessing Church and the Ecumenical Movement', in D. Bonhoeffer, *No Rusty Swords: Letters, Lectures and Notes, 1928–1936, Collected Works of Dietrich Bonhoeffer*, vol. 1 (London: Collins, 1977), pp. 326–44.

6 Bonhoeffer, *No Rusty Swords*, vol. 1, p. 159.

7 ibid., p. 290.

8 ibid.

9 ibid., p. 291.

10 W. Shirer, *The Rise and Fall of the Third Reich* (Pan Books, 1964), p. 114.

11 Faith Movement of German Christians, 'Guiding Principles of the German Christians', in *The Third Reich and the Christian Churches*, ed. P. Matheson (Edinburgh: T. & T. Clark, 1981), p. 5.

12 Bonhoeffer, *No Rusty Swords*, p. 179.

13 ibid., p. 180.

14 ibid., p. 167.

15 'Volk', 'The Church and the National Community', in *The Churches Survey their Task: Report of the Oxford 1937 Conference on Church, Community and State* (London: Allen & Unwin, 1937), p. 71.

16 D. Bonhoeffer, *No Rusty Swords*, pp. 168f.

17 ibid.

18 ibid., pp. 169f.
19 ibid., p. 170. Also Bonhoeffer's remarks on modern war as annihilation in D. Bonhoeffer, *Ethics* (New York: Macmillan, 1965), p.73.
20 J. de Gruchy, *Bonhoeffer and South Africa: Theology in Dialogue* (Grand Rapids: Eerdmans, 1984).
21 *Peace with Justice*, Official Documentation of the European Ecumenical Assembly, Basle, 1989 (Geneva: Conference of European Churches, 1989).
22 V. Guroian, *Ethics After Christendom* (Grand Rapids: Eerdmans, 1994), especially chapter 5, 'Church and Armenian Nationhood: A Bonhoefferian Critique of the National Church'.
23 *Ecclesiology and Ethics: Costly Commitment*, ed. T. Best and M. Robra (Geneva: World Council of Churches, 1995), and D. Forrester, *The True Church and Morality: Reflections on Ecclesiology and Ethics* (Geneva: World Council of Churches, 1997).
24 J. Conway, 'The Struggle for Peace between the Wars: A Chapter from the History of Western Churches', *Ecumenical Review*, 35 (January 1983), 25–40.
25 Bonhoeffer, *No Rusty Swords*, p. 290–1.
26 E. Bethge, *Dietrich Bonhoeffer: Theologian, Christian, Contemporary*, pp. 643–9.

9 Costly discipleship

HADDON WILLMER

From 1935 to 1937 Bonhoeffer ran an illegal seminary for the Confessing Church, first in Zingst, then in Finkenwalde in east Prussia. When it was closed down by the Gestapo, he wrote three books reflecting the teaching, ethos and methods of the seminary, namely *The Cost of Discipleship, Life Together* and *The Prayerbook of the Bible: An Introduction to the Psalms*. These books take us to the heart of the theological and practical preparation Bonhoeffer gave to the five sets of ordinands who went through the six-month-long courses. *Life Together* conflates descriptions of the seminary's common ordered life, influenced by monastic models, with theological explanation and spiritual advice. This book and *The Cost of Discipleship* are probably Bonhoeffer's most famous and influential writings, apart from *Letters and Papers from Prison*. *The Prayerbook of the Bible* (1940) was the last of his writings published in his lifetime.

Though produced in the period when the Confessing Church, with Bonhoeffer on its most radical wing, came closest to institutional conflict with the Third Reich, these texts are not to be read essentially as political resistance literature. They are concerned with the *church* in a traditionally Christian society. Letters such as those to Elisabeth Zinn and Rüdiger Schleicher in 1936 show that his work then was rooted in his turn from being a self-willed theologian to being a Christian, which happened around 1930–1.[1] Bonhoeffer's becoming a Christian was not a superficial religious experience, after which life could go on much as before. He did not become Christian instead of being pagan or a 'scientific humanist', but from being already committed to the church and to theology as his profession. His becoming a Christian was a change of his whole being within the continuum of this social location and task. He thought that it saved him from being a godless church person – a danger far worse than being an honest unbeliever. Without God, he could be efficient and proud of his professionalism, but out of control, as his own lord – and therefore lonely and proud and lost. He became a Christian by submitting to God and becoming a disciple, a genuine believer because really obedient. His teaching in the seminary and the writing of these books depended on his being both a theologian and a Christian, in this sense.

Because he was already an activist pastor when he became a Christian, it is not surprising that he saw his conversion (as St Paul and others have done) as a commissioning to a task, not simply to being a certain sort of person. His *Beruf*, God's calling made concrete in a specific task, was to work for the renewing of the church and the pastors. Bonhoeffer understood office as the institutional definition of divine calling[2] – so his callings as a disciple and as a church professional reinforced each other. He worked within the understanding of the church and its mission which was articulated authoritatively in the Barmen Declaration (1934). There, Jesus Christ was acknowledged as the one Lord over all (Clause 1), whose word was not only God's gracious promise but his claim over the whole of life (Clause 2); thus the church was a Christian church of disciples in Bonhoeffer's sense. Further, the confession of the lordship of Jesus required a church where authority was by brotherly service, a life together (Clause 3), not a life subjected to leadership of a worldly sort. The church was free because in Christ's place, it communicated God's free grace (Clause 6) by word and sacrament. Both church and state were commissioned by God, and given particular tasks (Clause 5): in distinction from the state, the church must be obedient to its own call, which includes reminding the state of its duty, and denying any totalitarian claim; but because church and state complement each other under God, the Declaration does not contemplate the possibility that sometimes there might be a duty to resist and displace a particular state order. The key points of the Declaration corresponded to Bonhoeffer's agenda for life, as a disciple, and are reflected in his writings. Of course Bonhoeffer was not retreating into ecclesiastical seclusion from the world. His stance is clear in his letter to Rüdiger Schleicher written on 8 April 1936: 'how do I live a Christian life in this real world?'[3]

Bonhoeffer was to the end *a disciple*. Being a disciple included offering to God the unknown and unpredictable future; and conversely, it meant being ready to receive from his hand both suffering and joy. The future required openness not merely to growth, but also to loss and death. So in his letter to Zinn: 'The calling defines my future: what God will make out of it, I do not know.' This typical Bonhoeffer statement, expressed most powerfully at the end of his life in the poem 'Who Am I?',[4] points us to the foundations: trust in God and total yielding to God, without knowing what future will come out of it. Bonhoeffer, in himself, often felt weary, ready to give up, a prey to *accidie*. It was good, therefore, to be *called*: the call of God took away the freedom to be temperamental. The command gave strength for living.

These texts are not only rooted in a time before the Nazi Reich and *Kirchenkampf,* but they were also not discarded in prison. On 21 July 1944, he wrote that

> for a long time I didn't realise the depth of the contrast [between becoming a saint and learning to have faith]. I thought I could acquire faith by trying to live a holy life, or something like it. I suppose I wrote *The Cost of Discipleship* as the end of that path. Today I can see the dangers of that book, though I still stand by what I wrote.[5]

Every part of this statement is illuminating, not least the final, often minimised, affirmation: 'I still stand by what I wrote.' The prison letters cannot be understood except as the work of the author of *The Cost of Discipleship.* The letter of 21 August 1944 might be taken as the best possible résumé of his book of 1937. Bonhoeffer's thinking did not develop by linear progress through stages, so that what was earlier was left behind as redundant; rather his thinking circles round itself, playing variations on recurring motifs, concepts and concerns.[6] All through Bonhoeffer is asking 'How do I live a Christian life in this real world, and where are the final authorities for such a life which alone is worth living?' He was to live with this question, but not as though it were an unanswerable puzzle; rather he lived the answer of discipleship which never stifled the question as a real question.

THE COST

Bonhoeffer called this book *Nachfolge* (the German word, as Bonhoeffer says, means 'following', as in 'run along behind me!').[7] Some forms of discipleship (learning and serving relationships with a master) do not obviously involve following on a path. There are masters who ask us to *sit* at their feet and listen: they may do much good, but they do not literally lead us on a journey. The word *Nachfolge* comes to mean 'discipleship' only by its Christian location: Jesus summoned those who were to be his disciples 'to follow him'. The content of discipleship is defined by the way Jesus went to the cross and beyond. It is therefore tautologous to speak of the *cost* of discipleship, since denying self and taking up one's cross is integral to following *Jesus.*

Why, then, was the English translation called *The Cost of Discipleship?* Although he knew that Bonhoeffer had died and been a martyr many times before he died, Bishop George Bell began his Foreword to *The Cost of*

Discipleship (1958) by quoting Bonhoeffer's saying, 'When Christ calls a man, he bids him come and die', thus reading the book in the memory of his final martyrdom. Although Bonhoeffer was aware, when he wrote those words in 1937, that he might die a violent, shameful death, the prospect of achieving that kind of martyrdom did not inform or structure his book. The dying to self, and of self, intrinsic to discipleship, occurred in many ways in life: simply to hear the word of God where God chooses to speak it, at the cross, was to be exposed to that which does not comfortably fit our nature and so requires us to live with a contradiction akin to death.[8] Martyrdom and death as costly suffering within discipleship do not, therefore, explain the language of cost in *The Cost of Discipleship*. It is, however, essential to its first chapter, whose easily abused contrast of cheap and costly grace has become famous.[9]

Grace stands for the essence of the gospel, since it characterises the whole will, action and work of God for sinners. Luther's original sense of amazing, unexpected, undeserved and sufficient grace had excluded any reliance on human works for salvation and produced eventually a tradition in which God's grace was honoured in dishonourable ways. What Luther sensed as a miracle in God had been turned into what God was expected to do, because a gracious God could not be allowed to do otherwise.

Grace is cheap when the demands of God are silenced by trading on God's kindness. Amongst the examples Bonhoeffer draws upon in his pastoral polemic was Jesus' calling the rich young man to voluntary poverty (Matthew 19:16–22).[10] Knowing the grace of God, we argue ourselves out of obedience: Jesus does not mean his commands to be taken legalistically; he really wants us to have faith.[11] I can have faith, be rich and live with this story, so long as I have 'inner detachment'. Against such pious equivocation, Bonhoeffer calls for honest obedience – or disobedience. Yet simple literalism is not enough. Bonhoeffer argues that Jesus was calling the young man into a position where faith was possible, because in the last resort what matters is not what a man does, but only his faith in Jesus.[12] The call must not be dissolved by interpretation, yet it is possible to have wealth and to believe in Christ. This paradoxical response to the command might be appropriate in certain cases, but never as an evasion of concrete obedience. Anybody who does not feel that he would be much happier were he only permitted to understand and obey the commandments of Jesus in a straightforward literal way and, for example, surrender all his possessions at his bidding rather than cling to them has no right to this paradoxical interpretation of Jesus' words. Bonhoeffer's argumentation often skates on the edge of positions he elsewhere denounces. How is this position that Bonhoeffer permits different from the way of 'inner detachment' he earlier took as a sign of exploiting cheap grace? The formulation of this sentence reveals a mode of thought also found in his famous saying: 'Only he who cries out for the Jews may sing Gregorian chants'[13] and in his insistence in *Ethics* that considerations of the ultimate were only to be brought into play after the penultimate was taken seriously.[14]

It was not Bonhoeffer's method to eliminate cheap grace by giving up grace. There could be no switch from grace to law as the basic idiom of Christianity. Rather, the opposition of grace and law had to be resolved in such a way that grace determined and realised itself through the operations of law. Hence his formula: 'only he who believes is obedient and only he who is obedient believes',[15] which he surrounds with complex, even troubled argumentation to show that this is true Lutheran doctrine, as against degenerate Lutheran practice. His key to solving the problem is discipleship: obedience and faith, works and grace are harmonised in responding to the Lord whose claim upon us is both a total demand and the concrete fullness of grace.

Costly grace is necessary because cheap grace endangers salvation. The church too often (as with some German Christians) yielded to plausible pastoral and evangelistic temptations to make grace cheap in order to ease the way of outsiders into church while excusing them from discipleship. Cheap grace arises when grace is universalised as a principle, for if God does anything universally, it can be taken as given, existing reality and as automatically available to human beings. They do not need to seek it, or to get themselves into any place where they will receive what is in God's gift. When grace is not automatically available, when it has to be asked for, the person apprehends himself as one who is exposed to God's freedom to give or not to give. This is a true encounter with God, the essential element of a right relation with God.

There is only one discipleship, because discipleship is the immediate relation to the one and only Lord. There is not discipleship with, and without, the cross, but nor is it suffering as such which defines or exalts the disciple. The disciple is in the Lord's hands and receives without question whatever the Lord gives – whether it is ease or pain. Bonhoeffer's last poem from prison[16] expressed his readiness both to take the cup of suffering, if it is given by God's good and beloved hand, and to be released to 'life's enjoyment and its good sunshine'.

The upshot was that Bonhoeffer wanted costly grace – real grace which cost God the death of his Son and would be powerfully significant for human beings. And grace becomes costly to people as they respond to the call to discipleship. It is discipleship, as such, which is the cost of grace; and discipleship involves suffering because it means following Jesus, breaking with the world and therefore being vulnerable to rejection by the world. The disciple has no need to look for suffering; each disciple has a particular cross awaiting him. The sufferings of the Christian are defined by Christ – they involve, for example, bearing the sins of others in a ministry of forgiveness. It is not the suffering but the fellowship with Christ that is important; that is why the way of the disciples is seen as joyful and triumphant.[17]

THE LORD

Albert Schweitzer's final words in *The Quest of the Historical Jesus* set Bonhoeffer's doctrine of discipleship in a German perspective:

> The names in which men expressed their recognition of [Jesus] as such, Messiah, Son of Man, Son of God, have become for us historical parables. We can find no designation which expresses what he is for us . . . He comes to us as One unknown, without a name, as of old, by the lakeside, He came to those men who knew Him not. He speaks to us the same word: 'Follow thou me!' and sets us to the tasks which He has to fulfil for our time. He commands. And to those who obey Him, whether they be wise or simple, He will reveal Himself in the toils, the conflicts, the sufferings which they shall pass through in His fellowship, and, as an ineffable mystery, they shall learn in their own experience Who He is.[18]

In both writers discipleship is command and obedience to work at the Lord's tasks in our time. But for Bonhoeffer, the Lord was not the Unknown without a Name. When he asked who Jesus Christ was for us today, it was from within the dogmatic tradition of the church. Titles such as Son of God and Mediator were for him more than 'historical parables'. Discipleship was more than an open, indefinite and individualistic life-quest, because Jesus Christ who called was Lord of the world. Discipleship was not a humanist adventure but a theologically grounded obedience. These dimensions of discipleship are focused in Bonhoeffer's distinctive and varied use of the concepts of mediation, mediacy and immediacy. Discipleship for Bonhoeffer was an immediate (non-mediated) relation with Jesus. Nothing stands between disciple and Lord. He did not think that relations of openness and intimacy were merely rare in the world; despite their being frequently and frenetically sought, they were impossible – except in discipleship.

Bonhoeffer attacked as illusion the common-sense view that our relations with the world, and with other people, are direct and immediate. Bonhoeffer did not deny the goodness of the desire for intimacy and authenticity so that relations with others should not be blocked or filtered or controlled by alien intrusions. He denied, however, that immediacy could or should be realised anyway except in the relation to Christ. The disciple's relations go through Christ, depend upon and are determined by Christ. Bonhoeffer extends the traditional concept of Christ as Mediator: Christ not only mediates between God and sinners, but mediates all creatures to each other. True and good relationships are in Christ. Discipleship rests on acceptance of the immediacy of Jesus Christ as Lord and the consequent mediation of all other relationships, which have to be understood and lived in a disciplined way. The distinctiveness of the disciple's life, not least in community, arises from the consistency of its honouring and trusting and yielding to the mediation of Christ. The obedience of the disciple is not exhausted in doing particular actions, obeying specific commands; it cannot be defined moralistically. Rather, obedience means submitting to the Lord by taking only what comes through his mediation, by never seeking to by-pass it.

It is typical of Bonhoeffer to find complex theological ideas in apparently simple Bible reading. Do his theory and practice thereby find authoritative endorsement in the word of God, or does he do violence to the Bible by using it as the vehicle for provocative and precarious thinking? This general question is not yet laid to rest: it will be argued as long as Bonhoeffer is read. A mild example of the problem is found in the way he identifies immediacy to the Lord as the essence of discipleship in the gospel stories of the calling of the first disciples (Mark 2:41).[19] In those stories, no time elapses between call and response. By drawing attention to this feature, Bonhoeffer bans investigation into the natural question of how people made up their minds to follow Jesus. Bonhoeffer eschewed introspection and fascination with the self in the relationship to God; it was a self-indulgence, not the appropriate self-denial. If the decision to be a disciple was the result of weighing reasons for and against, then the call was not answered in a way that recognised the lordship of the one who called. The reasons, and with them the one who weighed the reasons, would in reality be the lord, the determining authority in the person's life. For Bonhoeffer, the point of discipleship is not primarily to achieve a certain kind of religious life, but rather that Jesus should be acknowledged as truly Lord of the world and the disciple's Lord. Jesus was not to be accepted as useful to people, helping them to be holy or fulfilled; rather people were called through holiness and obedient service to let Jesus be Lord. The lordship of Jesus was challenged not only by other powers, like

Hitler and atheistic secularity, but also by religious self-concern and fascination with psychological processes of the self. So for the theory and practice of discipleship, Bonhoeffer refused to deduce anything from conversion experiences. It may be asked, of course, whether that is a sensible pastoral or evangelistic approach and whether it is required by these gospel stories.

THE BREAK FROM THE WORLD

Disciples leave all to follow Jesus. They lose family and become individuals – but they do not remain so (Mark 10:28–31).[20] Beyond or around these concrete separations and sacrifices, Bonhoeffer, by means of his theology of mediation, sees that there is a breach with the world as such. The relation with the Lord is immediate in the strictest sense. Since the disciple is essentially open and directly answering to, and living from, the Lord, this unique immediate relation becomes the place from which, and the medium through which, all other relationships are made and carried on. Realising this way of being in relation to God and the world is what happens in discipleship. The immediate relation to the Lord is achieved simultaneously with the ending of all attempts at other immediate relations and their replacement with relations mediated by Christ. The disciple is separated off from everything but the Lord, in order to belong to him exclusively.

In the gospels, disciples had to leave homes to follow Jesus. For Christians after the time of Jesus, discipleship begins with baptism, which means dying in order to enter new life.[21] The call and baptism are significant initial moments, which symbolise the character of discipleship and get disciples started on the way. That way has then to be followed and discipleship has to be realised over the time, not merely of individual lives, but of the church until the end. Hence the need for training and encouragement within the community of disciples, which is what Bonhoeffer offered in the seminary and in these writings.

As true discipleship begins with a break from the world as a set of attempted direct relations, so it always realises and embodies the break within its primary direct response to the Lord. Giving up a direct relation with the world is a fundamental breach with normality and that breach is always present, though it may be concealed within the positive features of discipleship. The way of the disciple outlined in the Sermon on the Mount, which provides the central text for *The Cost of Discipleship*, points first to the 'extraordinariness' of the Christian life (Matthew 5), then to its 'hiddenness' (Matthew 6): both go to make up the 'separation' of the disciple community (Matthew 7).[22] Extraordinariness and hiddenness are two modes of participative response to the Lord as well as two ways in which, within the disciple's obedience, the breach with the world is worked out.

The demand for the extraordinary derives from Matthew 5:20, 47: Jesus requires a better righteousness of his disciples.[23] Disciples differ from others by virtue of the extraordinary, the unusual, that which is not a matter of course. 'It is "the more", the "beyond-all-that".'[24] It is extraordinary because it conflicts with ordinary human expectations and with what human beings can routinely accomplish. The Sermon on the Mount goes beyond the command not to murder, to rule out anger; beyond prohibiting adultery, to denying lust; and the 'extraordinary' climaxes in the command to be perfect, as the Father in heaven, by loving the enemy.[25] This command was urgent in the 'holy struggle which lies before us and in which we partly have already been engaged for years',[26] and it served as preparation for imminent widespread persecution and 'complete ostracism from "human society"'. Bonhoeffer's sense of the extraordinary demand to love enemies, centred on the love of enemies by Jesus on the cross, anticipates the prison poem 'Christians and Pagans'.[27] The breach with the world is incarnated in discipleship: but this breach is not realised in 'a surly contempt for the world'.

Bonhoeffer insists that the extraordinary is to be *done* in the world, not treated as an impracticable ideal; it is thus to be visible (Matthew 5:13–16).[28] 'Flight into the invisible is a denial of the call.'[29] Visibility must somehow be fitted with Matthew 6, which demands hiddenness from the disciple. The reality of righteousness is before God, rather than in public reputation. The disciple has broken with the world and does not use it to build himself up before God, thus denying the immediacy of the relation with God. Bonhoeffer identifies the paradox: 'Our activity must be visible, but never be done for the sake of making it visible.'[30] Combining the visible and invisible aspects of discipleship is partly achieved by showing that it is to be visible to others in good works, but invisible to the disciple. Obedience has to be purely spontaneous and reflective and therefore effective in achieving self-denial, the death of the old man.[31]

Bonhoeffer is aware of the difficulties of the Sermon on the Mount: to hold together the visible and invisible, to insist that the extraordinary has to be done, is to create problems. His response was optimistic: all these problems could be overcome; or rather, were already overcome in Christ: 'Jesus does not tell us what we ought to do, but cannot; he tells us what God has given us and promises still to give.' All depended on the reality of God and his gift of discipleship.

THE COMMUNITY

The breach is merely the necessary condition always attached to the positive blessing given to disciples. They have everything through the Mediator 'with persecutions',[32] and their reward is the fellowship of the church. Thus discipleship means life together. Community is greatly desired, with natural and spiritual longing: 'the physical presence of other Christians is a source of incomparable joy and strength'; but it is a privilege which disciples of the Lord who died alone may not take for granted as a right. For his seminarians, who experienced the loneliness of being 'illegals' on the edge of society, the ordered life together was strange and sometimes burdensome, but often enlivening, soul-saving. Christian community requires special discipline; its life is to be ordered so that members share in and manifest the reality of life in Christ.

Repeatedly Bonhoeffer draws attention to the difference made to community when it is constituted by the mediation of Christ, expressed through a common discipline and worship.[33] 'The basis of spiritual community is truth; the basis of emotional community is desire.' Direct access to other people is never good. 'Within the spiritual community there is never . . . an "immediate" relationship of one to another. However, in the self-centred community there exists a profound, elemental emotional desire for community, for direct contact with other human souls.' In Christian community, there is a distance which means freedom for each, not alienation. The day together requires a capacity to live thankfully with others as they are and not to destroy community by working with what we wish or imagine others to be. The life together involves service: and service means living so as to build up community and to serve the other. Striving to be the greatest must be curbed. Community life requires that the natural struggle for self-justification through judging others is given up. Talk must be controlled from this point of view. The diversity of the community should be enjoyed and the will and honour of others respected. 'Whoever cannot be alone should beware of community: whoever cannot stand being in community should beware of being alone.' The day alone is sustained by the sense of belonging to community even when it is hidden. The day together cannot be guaranteed to alternate comfortingly with 'the day alone'; community depends on grace and intelligent hard work, when opportunity is given. Often, there is no chance for bodily life together. Bonhoeffer evidently valued the experience of genuine Christian community as something that might only be given once in a lifetime.[34] With and without community, Christians must live by faith in God's gift.

At the heart of the community was the forgiveness of sins, which was not restricted to the hidden privacy of the day alone. Confession to a brother, as to Christ, gave objectivity to the confession of sin and to its absolution. 'In confession there takes place a breakthrough to community' and 'to the cross',35 thus ending both the loneliness and the pride of sin. There is the breakthrough to new life and to assurance. Without confession, community rests on what pious believers have in common, but not on the reality of what people are, as sinners. Christ's presence ends pretence – but it is not presence as idea or feeling. Christ is present in the action of one person with another. Not as something above the community, or as an interpretation of it, but as part of its action, the content of its life, and then, not as occasional crisis management, but as part of its routine daily discipline, its accepted and understood way of life. Confession to a brother is an action in which community is both made (at the point of confronting what unmakes community) and comes into the light to be understood. 'When I go to another believer to confess, I am going to God.'

THE WORD OF GOD

The day together includes prayer and hearing the Bible. The community knows how to listen; its silence before the word is a form of aloneness as well as of community.36 The direct and total relation with the Lord depended on hearing the call and obeying. This was not to be achieved by the physical presence of the Lord; or by any enthusiastic religious experience – the lordship of Jesus was not accomplished by emotional power.

The Bible is the Lord's voice. The call to discipleship, the command, is not heard in the empty silence or in the depths of an individual's being; it speaks in the Bible. It is external to the disciple, standing over against him as a real other. Its objectivity can challenge, cut across and change the disciple, because the word is not his mental production, nor does it automatically suit his tastes. Because of its content, the Bible has specific capacity to save: it is centred on the Christ and the cross. The cross is the place where God suffers contradiction by humanity, but also maintains his uncomfortable, non-negotiable word – to accept the crucified as Lord implies a constant practice of yielding to commands which conflict with one's desires and ambitions. To hear the word is converting.

Such a word needs to be listened to constantly, repeatedly, and so within a supportive and educative discipline. It cannot be absorbed in an instant: that will not enable effective action. The word of God is too big to be taken in a short time – or even in a lifetime's attention. There has to be meditation.

The word is always the word of the living present Lord, addressing the disciple in real life. Consequently, the Bible has to be listened to in a way which allows the Lord to speak. This can happen in meditation, where a small part of the Bible is listened to each day for a week.[37] Taking a short text means that the whole of it can become present in and to the mind of the disciple, who is thus not spending energy getting an intellectual grip on the text, as is inevitable with larger texts, which have to be analysed and summarised and even then cannot be directly listened to in one concentrated action. The tools of scholarship, such as dictionaries and commentaries, were excluded (though used at other times) so that the meditator was protected from the temptations to enlarge learning and to exercise manipulative power over the text, thereby evading the personal address by the Lord through the text. Meditation is not the time for the preparation of sermons: it is an act between Lord and disciple alone, which properly has no intention beyond that relation because there is nothing behind or beyond God. Here is an exercise in which the Ultimate is met. Bonhoeffer told his students that if their minds wandered, they should intercede for whoever came into their thoughts – but they should beware lest their intercessions become another means of taking flight from 'the most important thing: prayer for our own soul's salvation'.[38] The disciple is thereby distinguishable from the theologian. In meditation, the text escapes scholarly manipulation, ecclesiastical exploitation, or the powerlessness of a sacred text read but not heard.

The Lord speaks in and through the Bible, as the Other commanding. But there was more. The disciple prays. What he says must be the voice of his heart, the real person in truth, but not the voice of a person alienated and different from the Lord. The true voice of prayer is the voice of Christ. Prayer is thus informed and given words by the Bible, which, as a whole, is God speaking his word, in and as Christ. How concretely Bonhoeffer took this Christocentric way of reading the whole Bible, and how practically he applied it to praying, can be seen in *Prayerbook of the Bible*. 'God's speech in Jesus Christ meets us in the Holy Scriptures.' Yet Bonhoeffer acknowledges that the Psalms constitute a book of prayers, which are *human* speech. These prayers are nevertheless really God's word, because they are prayed by Jesus Christ, who teaches us to pray. 'Only in and with Jesus Christ can we truly pray.'[39] Bonhoeffer took this Christocentrism to strange, perhaps unnecessary but typical lengths when David's authorship of the Psalms was argued for as a ground for referring the Psalter to Christ. More indispensable was the contention that as Christ is fully human, so the full human range of the Psalms could be prayed by and through Christ. As the One who took our sins on himself, Christ prays even the penitential Psalms; and the Psalms of vengeance on enemies can only be prayed by the Son of God who bore the vengeance of God against his enemies. Christian pacifism controls exegesis here as Bonhoeffer's traditional Lutheranism does in other places. In these seminary texts, he is evidently determined to be a Christian, even when treating the Old Testament – neither then nor later did he have the time to solve the problems created for the theologian.

POLITICS AND PEACEMAKING

When Bonhoeffer became a Christian, he said, 'I suddenly saw as self-evident the Christian pacifism that I had recently passionately opposed.'[40] This pacifism was a commitment of obedience, not a political judgement. Christ commands peace and commits disciples to preaching peace, which can only be convincing if they are at peace with brothers and neighbours. Grace is cheap if the Christian relies on the forgiveness of sin to cover a breaking of the command not to kill.[41]

Pacifism was the opposite of Nazism – the clearest repudiation of its values, goals and methods; but it could not be turned into a practical politics that would stop Hitler. In the theology of discipleship, Bonhoeffer taught no strategy for effective resistance to Hitler. In *The Cost of Discipleship* he insists that Paul in Romans 13 ('let every soul be in subjection to the higher powers') is talking to Christians, not the state, which has no right to use this text to justify itself.[42] This passage tells the disciple how to behave towards the state, persevering in repentance and obedience. Christians are to do good without any fear or inhibition: that such conduct will receive praise from the good state (where there is one) is merely an 'afterthought'. Disciples, after all, live to God and practise hiddenness: they do not seek worldly praise or depend on it.

It was consistently as a disciple that Bonhoeffer responded to issues raised by politics, or – should we say – the evil debasement of politics achieved by the Nazis. Discussing Matthew 5:38–42,[43] he affirmed the divine institution of retribution to convict and overcome evil, which was executed through the state. The church, however, was not an agent of retribution by force. It had given up political and national status, in order to be the church; it was called to endure aggression patiently. The outcome Bonhoeffer draws from this line of thought is startling: the church was more powerful than the state in dealing with evil. According to Jesus, 'the right way to requite evil is not to resist it'.[44] 'When the last ounce of resistance is abandoned', evil meets an opponent which is more than a match for it, and becomes a spent force. What kind of victory does such non-resistance win?

Is it simply a spiritual victory, before God, in the hiddenness of the disciple's life? Chapter 30, on the visible community, refutes that interpretation, but not by arguing that the church's way might have the power to stop evil in the world. Rather, it is envisaged that the church will persist in prayer and righteous action, 'opening its mouth for the dumb', in a world becoming 'one hundred per cent non Christian', until it is deprived of its last inch of space on earth and the end of the world is near. Thus, the church fulfils its calling of taking on the form of its suffering Lord. The church overcomes evil by becoming one with the Lord, not by bringing about a world free of evil.

Bonhoeffer's treatment of political issues in this period was thus entirely an aspect of his discipleship. And in the end, it was discipleship which freed him from the command not to kill which inhibited resistance to Hitler – for the disciple is led by the call of Jesus Christ, who sets people free from the law for responsible action.[45] Killing in war may be necessary to restore the authority of life, but even so, there is objective guilt for the breaking of the commandment. If this guilt is acknowledged, then the law may be hallowed even in its being broken. Acknowledging guilt involves more than churchly confession; it can be done by living before God, fully in the world, accepting that those who take the sword, even rightly, shall perish by the sword (Matthew 26:52). Bonhoeffer's concern was to be responsible to the Lord in every complexity of action; it was discipleship that made sense of life for him and which set him the problems he thought about to the end. The disciple who uses force has to accept the perishing that comes upon the sword user. In accepting and not resisting, not trying to justify one's own using the sword by comparison with others, by recognising that the whole action takes place within the sphere of evil and as a playing out of evil, even though it is free and responsible action for the good, the sufferer overcomes evil finally. This victory is accomplished when the sufferer in penitence does not give an ounce of resistance to the effects of evil coming back upon himself, but accepts the truth of God's judgement in it. Evil is not overcome by virtue of the uncomplaining suffering, but by God's forgiveness of sins, which, in such circumstances, is certain but not cheap. Participating actively in the history of evil, the disciple confesses public sin as his own, so that all falls on him.[46] Thus the confession of sin and the pronouncement of absolution comes out of the secluded monastic seminary into the history of the world. The depth of Bonhoeffer's view of discipleship is plumbed here: the disciple shares with the Lord in bearing the sin of the world and in the realisation of forgiveness.

The point of discussing this political side of Bonhoeffer's discipleship is not merely to eschew any presentation of him as an effective resister of Hitler. At one level, only effective resistance had any worth – Hitler and all his works were not an item for discussion, as though there were pros and cons, but simply needed stopping. And Bonhoeffer, like all others who dissented from Hitler and even resisted, failed to stop him at the right time; failed inevitably, as all the good people were bound to do on their own. Hitler was only to be stopped when his own hates and fears and megalomaniac maladroitness in international relationships brought down upon his Reich the combined powers of American and Soviet Empires. Bonhoeffer had no credible plan by which to resist Hitler, though he clearly had the will and the moral insight – and he had a theology and ethics which could enlighten the Allies who finally destroyed Hitler, only to find themselves holding in their hands, in the name of righteousness and peace, the same sort of universally destructive sword which Hitler had wielded, and the same godless, if often piously argued, acceptance of the principle that the world can only be ordered by violence. Bonhoeffer's discipleship, which is essentially obedience to, and faith in, the one Lord Jesus Christ, offers no escape from such politics in this present world. If Bonhoeffer were ever a political pacifist, he was mistaken. But his pacifism was not a political programme or device, but a correlate of faith, which came into play in a discipleship to which all are called, and in which they may live by not resisting the evil they are caught up in as agents. That way of non-resistance meant accepting death and defeat as judgement on the way that has been taken and looking beyond it with trust in God's forgiveness and in hope for the next generation.[47]

Bonhoeffer opposed Nazism in part out of the resources of the German-Prussian tradition of a legal state and a humane ethics. What Bonhoeffer did not have was any great sense, derived from experience, of a kind of politics where violence was minimised and where discussion as a way of dealing with differences was more important than authority as a way of ensuring order in society. Bonhoeffer is not to be blamed for this lack of experience – even Britain and the USA, which he experienced briefly in the early thirties, offered at best limited examples of liberal democracy working well. His criticism of the idea of Leadership (*Führerprinzip*) was dependent on his strong concept of responsibility in office, not on any awareness of the powers of pluralist politics to make leaders accountable and occasionally modest. Bonhoeffer shared in many ways, though never with irrational abandon, the culture through which the phenomenon of Hitler was built up. Hitler's appeal lay partly in his command to disciples to follow – if that kind of demand for total commitment was as such necessarily a source of evil, it was a dangerous perversion which Bonhoeffer failed to identify. He opposed one discipleship to another. His way was different from Hitler's because Jesus Christ was, in Bonhoeffer's exposition and practice, evidently a quite different Lord. But it was a battle between Lords – not between an authoritarian conception of society and a liberal democratic one. Thus for many who in the last fifty years have most read Bonhoeffer, there is much to disturb and embarrass. For Bonhoeffer has nourished the souls not of conservatives and authoritarians, but of liberal and humanist Christians. The nourishment, the companionship on the way, is genuine – but it should never be forgotten that Bonhoeffer offers this nourishment from sources and by routes which are strange to his Western liberal devotees. Perhaps they are not entitled to the nourishment they get if they cannot digest the roots and orientation of what he offers. Above all, he spoke consistently as a disciple, in a fellowship of disciples. He worked in the world which was mediated to him through the only relation, with Jesus Christ, which he believed could and should be a direct, immediate relation. He rested his whole being, including the worth of his ideas, on the truth of Jesus Christ as the Lord and Son of God. That was a truth he yielded to as a disciple who obeys the call; he explained it with no rational apology but lived it to the end in faith. Attempting to make sense and use of Bonhoeffer, outside of a discipleship like and with his, will result in serious misreading.

Notes

1 E. Bethge, *Dietrich Bonhoeffer: Theologian, Christian, Contemporary* (London: Collins, 1970); D. Bonhoeffer, *Illegale Theologenausbildung: Finkenwalde 1935–1937, Dietrich Bonhoeffer Werke*, vol. xiv (Gütersloh: Chr. Kaiser/ Gütersloher Verlagshaus, 1996), pp. 112–14, 144.

2 See Wedding Sermon, in D. Bonhoeffer, *Letters and Papers from Prison: The Enlarged Edition* (London: SCM, 1971); 'Vocation', in 'History and Good', in D. Bonhoeffer, *Ethics* (New York: Macmillan, 1965) and chapter 30 in D. Bonhoeffer, *The Cost of Discipleship* (New York: Macmillan, 1960).

3 Letter to Rüdiger Schleicher in Bonhoeffer, *Illegale Theologenausbildung: Finkenwalde*, p. 145.

4 D. Bonhoeffer, *Letters and Papers from Prison: The Enlarged Edition* (New York: Macmillan, 1972), p. 347.

5 ibid., pp. 369–70.

6 Bethge, *Dietrich Bonhoeffer: Theologian, Christian, Contemporary*, p. 159; D. Bonhoeffer, *Life Together; The Prayerbook of the Bible, Dietrich Bonhoeffer Works*, vol. v, trans. D. W. Bloesch and J. H. Burtness (Minneapolis: Fortress Press, 1996), pp. 125, 133.

7 Bonhoeffer, *Cost of Discipleship*, p. 49.

8 Letter to Rüdiger Schleicher, in Bonhoeffer, *Illegale Theologenausbildung: Finkenwalde*, p. 145.

9 Luther's protest against indulgences had been a struggle for proper respect for God's grace, against an easy pastorally or financially motivated perversion of it. Bonhoeffer updates that Lutheran argument.

10 See chapter 3 in Bonhoeffer, *Cost of Discipleship*.

11 Letter of 21 July 1944 in Bonhoeffer, *Letters and Papers from Prison* (1971), pp. 369–70.

12 Bonhoeffer, *Cost of Discipleship*, p. 71.

13 Bethge, *Dietrich Bonhoeffer: Theologian, Christian, Contemporary*, p. 512.

14 See 'The Preparing of the Way', in Bonhoeffer, *Ethics*.

15 Bonhoeffer, *Cost of Discipleship*, p. 54.

16 'Powers for Good', in Bonhoeffer, *Letters and Papers from Prison* (1972), p. 400.

17 G. Bell, *Brethren in Adversity*, Church of England Record Society 4 (Boydell, 1997), pp. 84–5.

18 A. Schweitzer, *The Quest of the Historical Jesus* (London: A. & C. Black, 1936), p. 401.

19 Bonhoeffer, *Cost of Discipleship*, p. 48.

20 ibid., chapter 5.

21 ibid., chapter 28.

22 ibid., p. 162.

23 ibid., p. 113.

24 ibid., p. 137.

25 ibid., chapter 13.

26 ibid., p. 135.

27 Bonhoeffer, *Letters and Papers from Prison* (1972), p. 348.

28 Bonhoeffer, *Cost of Discipleship*, chapter 7.

29 ibid., p. 106.

30 ibid., p. 141.

31 ibid., pp. 144, 146.

32 ibid., chapter 5.

33 Bonhoeffer, *Life Together; Prayerbook of the Bible*, pp. 39ff.

34 ibid., p. 47.

35 ibid., p. 110.

36 ibid., p. 84.

37 Bonhoeffer, *Illegale Theologenausbildung: Finkenwalde*, p. 144.

38 'Instructions in Daily Meditation', circular letter 1936, in D. Bonhoeffer, *Meditating on the Word* (Cambridge: Cowley, 1986), p. 33.

39 *The Prayerbook of the Bible*, in D. Bonhoeffer, *Gemeinsames Leben; Das Gebetbuch der Bibel, Dietrich Bonhoeffer Werke*, vol. v (Munich: Chr. Kaiser Verlag, 1987), pp. 155–7.

40 A letter to E. Zinn in Bethge, *Dietrich Bonhoeffer: Theologian, Christian, Contemporary*, p. 155.

41 ibid., p. 159.

42 Bonhoeffer, *Cost of Discipleship*, p. 236.

43 ibid. See section on 'revenge' in chapter 12.

44 ibid., p. 127.

45 Bonhoeffer, *Ethics*, p. 261.

46 ibid., Part 1, chapter 3 on guilt, justification and renewal.

47 'The Death of Moses', poem in Bonhoeffer, *Letters and Papers from Prison* (1971).

10 Church, state and the 'Jewish question'

RUTH ZERNER

The church is the church only when it is for others.[1]

Civil courage, in fact, can grow only out of the free responsibility of free men . . . a person's inward liberation to live a responsible life before God is the only real cure for folly.[2]

In these words of Dietrich Bonhoeffer we glimpse the creative centre of his paradigm for human behaviour within the church and the state. Through essays, letters and books he explored both traditional and experimental patterns of relating the church which he served to the state, especially the German state during the rule of Adolf Hitler and the Nazis (1933–45). Bonhoeffer's institutional vision, initially focused intellectually and geographically on central Europe, impelled him, particularly during his imprisonment (1933–45), into an expansive love for the world, 'the whole of human life in all its manifestations'.[3]

The Canadian theologian Douglas John Hall discerns Bonhoeffer's 'theology of world-orientation' most vividly in the letters and papers penned in his Tegel prison cell. For Hall this Tegel theology constituted 'a fundamental break with the other-worldliness and world-ambiguity of conventional Christianity'.[4] Yet, at the start of his career, Bonhoeffer had already displayed sensitivity towards the struggles of marginal groups in society (blacks in New York City and poor, troubled teenagers in Berlin), revealing his unwillingness to retreat from reality, even during the early 1930s.[5] As soon as the Nazis began anti-Semitic persecution in April 1933, Bonhoeffer was one of the first Christian theologians to focus on the Jewish issue as central in the church struggle (*Kirchenkampf*), both within the German Evangelical (Protestant) Church itself and in its fight against Nazi control.

BONHOEFFER AND THE JEWS

Born to privilege in a family of aristocratic and upper-middle-class lineage, rich in professional distinctions and achievements, Dietrich Bonhoeffer was an insider who became an outsider in his own land. He moved from clerical opposition to Hitler's attacks on the churches to political conspiracy, when he joined his brother-in-law Hans von Dohnanyi and other relatives and friends in clandestine anti-Nazi resistance activities, which culminated in the unsuccessful attempt of 20 July 1944 to kill Hitler. As persons of conscience, Dohnanyi and Bonhoeffer participated in a rescue operation which succeeded in the 1942 smuggling of fourteen people, Jewish and of Jewish descent, into Switzerland. Investigation of alleged irregularities connected with this rescue mission triggered the Gestapo's 1943 arrest of Bonhoeffer, who was executed by the Nazis in 1945. Shortly before his two-year incarceration, Bonhoeffer sketched for his fellow conspirators and his family the reversal in status and new insights which ten years under Nazi oppression and genocidal leadership had yielded:

The View from Below
We have for once learnt to see the great events of world history from below, from the perspective of the outcast, the suspects, the maltreated, the powerless, the oppressed, the reviled – in short from the perspective of those who suffer.[6]

The suffering of Jews in Hitler's Germany began in April 1933 with words and actions: the economic boycott of 1 April of Jewish businesses and the 'Law for the Re-establishment of the Professional Civil Service' of 7 April, with its infamous 'Aryan clause'. Article 3 of this law called for the retirement of all civil-service officials of 'non-Aryan descent', with the exception of those 'who were already in service on 1 August 1914, or who fought in the world war at the front for the German Reich, or who fought for its allies, or whose fathers or sons were killed in the world war'.[7] In the months and years that followed, the Aryan clause was extended to all major fields of professional study and practice, effectively excluding Jews from Germany's leading professions.

Particularly concerned about this prohibition as applied to baptised Jews (Jewish Christians) who were ministers of the Protestant Church, Bonhoeffer helped formulate tracts and statements opposing the intrusion of the Aryan legislation into the church. Battling against pro-Nazi German Christians who demanded that the Aryan clause be applied to Protestant clergy, Bonhoeffer stridently insisted:

Pastors are not state officials. Hence official regulations cannot be
applied to them under any circumstances. Concerning admission to
the ministry, as to other church positions, only ecclesiastical
viewpoints are decisive, i.e., right doctrine, Christian conduct, and
spiritual endowments alone qualify for the ministry. It is therefore an
ecclesiastical impossibility to exclude, as a matter of principle, Jewish
Christian members from any offices of the Church . . . With the
exclusion of Jewish Christians from the communion of worship, he
who realises the nature of the Church must feel himself to be excluded
also . . . On a church whose substance, whose essential nature has been
violated, the blessing of God can no longer rest – despite the honest
and best intentions of individual members.[8]

Appealing to the ministers of the Old Prussian Union within the Protestant Church, Bonhoeffer warned that the Aryan paragraph was a "*status
confessionis*" for the Church . . . A Christian Church cannot exclude from its
communion a member on whom the sacrament of baptism has been
bestowed, without degrading baptism to a purely formal rite to which the
Christian communion that administers it is indifferent.'[9] Despite Bonhoeffer's plea, in September 1933 the Prussian Synod enacted the Aryan paragraph, causing consternation and alarm in clerical and lay circles.

German Protestant opposition to such Nazi attempts at *Gleichschaltung*
(synchronisation or co-ordination) led to the formation in 1933 of the
Pastors' Emergency League by one-third of the German Protestant clergy. By
January 1934 this group reached its high point with 7,036 members (out of a
total of 18,000 clergy).[10] The leaders of the Pastors' Emergency League,
spearheaded by the dynamic Dahlem, Berlin preacher Martin Niemöller,
rejected the established Protestant Church (Reichskirche) and formed the
Confessing Church in 1934. Unique and complex in its organisation, the
Confessing Church (Bekennende Kirche) included active lay leadership.
According to the American church historian Ernst Christian Helmreich:

Pastors may well have been instrumental in its formation and
furnished its leadership, but as it developed it was far from being a
mere 'pastors' church'. It was rooted in and supported by the people,
the members of the congregation . . . there always remained a loyalty
to the concept of a Confessing Church – a group of Christians and
churches who could and would not accept the religious ideas and
religious policies of the Nazi rulers, and who sought to preserve the
purity of the gospel.[11]

Committed to the Confessing Church and stridently opposing the Aryan clause, which applied to persons who had at least one full Jewish grandparent, Bonhoeffer was touched personally by this legislation; it applied to his twin sister's husband, Gerhard Leibholz, and to his close friend and colleague, Pastor Franz Hildebrandt. Both of these men were baptised Christians of Jewish ancestry, whose careers in Germany would be ended by this Nazi edict. Eventually Leibholz, a constitutional lawyer, and Hildebrandt fled to Great Britain. Bonhoeffer himself escaped the church turmoil within Germany from the end of 1933 to 1935, when he served as pastor for a German-speaking congregation in London.

Although unequivocal in his stand against the exclusion of baptised Jews from the Christian ministry, Bonhoeffer penned several equivocal and problematic paragraphs in his first essay concerning church responses to the state's Jewish policies. Bonhoeffer completed this document, 'The Church and the Jewish Question', on 15 April 1933.[12] As one of the first Christian theologians to sense the crucial centrality of Nazi anti-Semitism for Christian communities, Bonhoeffer clearly separated the Christian church's attitude towards the new political problems of Jews in general from the special problems of baptised Jews within the Christian church. Moreover he thrust the entire Jewish policy first against the backdrop of church–state relations and then against a wider historical and eschatological horizon. In neither framework are his arguments convincing or compatible with contemporary, post-Holocaust political and theological perspectives.

> Without doubt the Jewish question is one of the historical problems which our state must deal with, and without doubt the state is justified in adopting new methods here . . . The church cannot in the first place exert direct political action, for the church does not pretend to have any knowledge of the necessary course of history. Thus even today, in the Jewish question, it cannot address the state directly and demand of it some definite action of a different nature . . . It is not the church, but the state, which makes and changes the law.[13]

A self-conscious heir of Martin Luther, Bonhoeffer held that 'the Church of the Reformation has no right to address the state directly in its specifically political actions. It has neither to praise nor to censure the laws of the state, but must rather affirm the state to be God's order of preservation in a godless world.'[14] Bonhoeffer, however, reserved to Christian individuals and to humanitarian associations the right to accuse the state of offences against morality. But for Bonhoeffer, the church was not included among 'humanitarian associations'.[15]

According to Bonhoeffer, 'the true church of Christ . . . will never intervene in the state in such a way as to criticise its history-making actions, from the standpoint of some humanitarian ideal'. He grounded this position in the church's recognition of 'the absolute necessity of the use of force in this world', including 'the "moral" injustice of certain concrete acts of the state'.[16] Bonhoeffer, reared in the intellectual traditions of the Reformation legacy and German organic political theories of state, is putting forward theses which are not unique. Influenced by reason of state concepts traced by the German historian Friedrich Meinecke back to Machiavelli, Bonhoeffer here articulates traditional, realistic ideas about state actions (*Realpolitik*).[17]

Yet, there remains a puzzling tension in Bonhoeffer's April 1933 description of the almost mystical link between church and state; he suggests that the state receives its 'peculiar rights' from the Christian proclamation and faith and that 'only the church, which bears witness to the coming of God in history, knows what history, and therefore what the state is'. Indeed he argues that the church 'alone testifies to the penetration of history by God in Christ and lets the state continue to make history'.[18] At the same time he claims that a state which 'includes within itself a terrorised church has lost its most faithful servant'.[19] On the one hand, the church 'lets' the state make history, and on the other hand, the church is the 'most faithful servant' of the state. Such apparently contradictory characterisations help one to understand why scholars like Franklin H. Littell have concluded that Bonhoeffer's 'inadequate understanding of the nature of the church was the most tragic element in his eventual martyrdom'.[20]

In Bonhoeffer's essay the most painful and problematic section for both Jews and many post-Holocaust Christian thinkers is a string of sentences recapitulating traditional Christian teachings on: deicide, the cursed Jews, the rejected people, the Jewish problem, the suffering people 'loved and punished by God', and the final homecoming 'in the conversion of Israel to Christ'.[21] For contemporary Jewish leaders and thinkers the following statement by Bonhoeffer still offends:

> Now the measures of the state towards Judaism in addition stand in a quite special context for the church. The church of Christ has never lost sight of the thought that the 'chosen people', who nailed the redeemer of the world to the cross, must bear the curse for its action through a long history of suffering.[22]

When the United States Holocaust Memorial Museum held a ceremony on 29 May 1996 honouring Dietrich Bonhoeffer and Hans von Dohnanyi as righteous Gentiles, who helped to save Jews, the invitation included the following: 'Although repudiating Nazism, Bonhoeffer also expressed the anti-Jewish bias of centuries-old Christian teaching.'[23] While Bonhoeffer did not invent any of these categories or concepts, he uncritically quoted some of the earlier exponents of condescension, if not contempt, towards Jews.[24]

Refusing to succumb to 'cheap moralising', Bonhoeffer later in 1933 focused on restraining popular attitudes of revenge and contempt towards Jews. He participated in framing resolutions at two church conferences, both revealing unwillingness to capitalise on traditional Christian condemnation of Jews: 'No nation can ever be commissioned to avenge on the Jews the murder at Golgotha.'[25] 'We especially deplore the fact that the state measures against the Jews in Germany have had such an effect on public opinion that in some circles the Jewish race is considered a race of inferior status.'[26] Moreover Bonhoeffer did not go as far as other Confessing Church leaders, like Walter Künneth and Martin Niemöller, in reinforcing popular stereotypes of Jews.[27]

I think that had Bonhoeffer survived the war, one of the platforms in his 'reconstruction of Christian life in Germany after the war',[28] a challenge he anticipated in 1939, would have been a radical rethinking of teachings about Jewish people, past and present. His students and theological heirs in post-war Germany have taken the lead in the creative dismantling of the Christian legacy of anti-Judaism and its historical consequences.[29] Therefore, it is probable that Bonhoeffer would have done likewise. Indeed the courageous, feisty leader of the Confessing Church, Martin Niemöller, who admitted in court in 1938 that he came from an anti-Semitic past and tradition, 'returned home after eight years' imprisonment as a completely different person'. Held as Hitler's personal prisoner from 1937 to 1945, Niemöller in the post-war era 'jettisoned much that had been traditionally taught in Christendom about the Jews'.[30]

Despite Bonhoeffer's nod to traditional Christian perspectives on Jews, he displayed glimpses of unconventional, extreme risk-taking in his suggestions for future church action towards the state, especially when the state endangers the Christian proclamation, thereby negating the state itself (according to Bonhoeffer). Beyond simply asking the state whether it is bringing about law and order, i.e. whether its actions are legitimate, Bonhoeffer sketches two other alternatives, including aid to the victims of state action: 'The church has an unconditional obligation to the victims of any ordering of society, even if they do not belong to the Christian community.' He views this as the church serving 'the free state in its free way'. But the radical possibility which foreshadows his later involvement in the anti-Nazi resistance movement is the third one:

> not just to bandage the victims under the wheel, but to put a spoke in the wheel itself. Such action would be direct political action, and it is only possible and desirable when the church sees the state fail in its function of creating law and order.[31]

As Bonhoeffer expounds on the type of situation in which the church might try to jam the spokes of the wheel, he focuses on internal, ecclesiastical issues, not the suffering of outsiders. His concern is primarily for baptised Jews; the third option would arise if the state intervened in 'the character of the church', by the forced exclusion of baptised Jews from the congregation or by the prohibition of mission to the Jews. Ironically, the very issue which today offends many Jewish leaders (for whom targeting Jews for conversion is a form of spiritual genocide) was, in the context of Nazi attempts to purge the churches of persons of Jewish lineage, a cherished freedom. State inroads into these internal affairs of the church would constitute a *status confessionis*, a challenge to the fundamental contours of the faith (the confessions). But only an 'Evangelical Council' might decide on the necessity of direct political action by the church.[32] Bonhoeffer's closest friend and peerless biographer, Eberhard Bethge, admits that in this essay 'Bonhoeffer still spoke a theological language that did not admit of an humanitarian-liberal policy.' Yet Bethge finds a few germs of democratic thought in Bonhoeffer's suggestion that a strong state needs opposition.[33]

Bonhoeffer's brother-in-law Hans von Dohnanyi rocketed to the highest ranks of the civil service within the Ministry of Justice during the Weimar years; in the first period of Hitler's reign Dohnanyi began compiling a 'Chronicle of Shame', detailing the criminal actions of Nazi Party leaders. By 1938 Dohnanyi was the only lawyer in the Ministry of Justice who was willing to join in conspiratorial plans to overthrow the Nazi regime, and later he helped to initiate the daring undercover operation which rescued fourteen persons, Jewish and of Jewish descent, in 1942. Carried out under the instructions of Admiral Wilhelm Canaris, head of the *Abwehr* (military intelligence), for which Dohnanyi and Bonhoeffer worked in the early 1940s, 'Operation 7' succeeded in smuggling fourteen Jewish individuals into Switzerland. However, alleged irregularities connected with this project alerted the Gestapo and led to the 1943 arrest of both Dohnanyi and Bonhoeffer. Thus, they were arrested as insiders who had secretly aided outsiders in their attempt to flee persecution. At the time of his arrest, Bonhoeffer was no longer working for the Confessing Church; in fact, his name had been taken off the prayer list. Dohnanyi had helped him to obtain a position in the *Abwehr*, ostensibly to provide intelligence concerning foreign churches; in actuality, he was a double agent, carrying messages from the anti-Nazi German resistance movement to the British.

In his thorough analysis of 'Operation 7', the German scholar Winfried Meyer cites a contemporary who criticised Dohnanyi for allowing an act of charity, saving Jews, to deflect him from the primary aim of overthrowing the Nazis. Dohnanyi explained it as 'the obligatory path of a decent human being'.[34] Thus both Dohnanyi and Bonhoeffer emerge as forerunners of contemporary human-rights activists, providing paradigms for people of conscience struggling to find words and ways to express their concern for those caught in the grip of oppressive political systems.

Just as Dohnanyi compiled a chronicle of shame, I would like to outline a 'chronicle of compassion and courage', encapsulating Bonhoeffer's action on behalf of the main targets of Nazi persecution, tormenting and annihilation:

> Bonhoeffer's foresight in being one of the first to focus on the Jewish issue as central in the church struggle;
>
> vigorous, unrelenting opposition to the Aryan clause;
>
> undeviating comfort and support for pastors of Jewish descent and for Gerhard Leibholz, a Jewish-Christian lawyer married to his twin sister Sabine, as they fled to England;
>
> the April 1933 proposal that the Christian church should aid the victims of state action 'even if they do not belong to the Christian community',[35] his anticipation in 1933 that a time might come when direct political action might be necessary 'not just to bandage the victims under the wheel', but to jam the spokes of the wheel itself;[36]
>
> assistance to Jewish refugees in London and later in Germany, especially in 'Operation 7';
>
> travel abroad to communicate plans of the anti-Nazi conspiracy to his British ecumenical contact, George K. A. Bell, Bishop of Chichester, who in turn informed his government;
>
> the dramatic admonitions: 'Only he who cries out for the Jews may sing Gregorian chant';[37] 'If the synagogues burn today, the churches will be on fire tomorrow';[38] 'An expulsion of the Jews from the West must necessarily bring with it the expulsion of Christ. For Jesus Christ was a Jew';[39] 'Christians in Germany will face the terrible alternative of either willing the defeat of their nation in order that Christian civilisation may survive, or willing the victory of their nation and thereby destroying our civilisation.'[40]

Part of the plot to take Hitler's life, Bonhoeffer acknowledged his loss of innocence for participation in planning assassination, as well as the historic guilt of the church, which was 'silent when she should have cried out because the blood of the innocent was crying to heaven ... She is guilty of the deaths of the weakest and most defenceless brothers of Jesus Christ.'[41]

BONHOEFFER ON CHURCH AND STATE

Although certain themes, such as Christology and community, are continuing leitmotifs in Bonhoeffer's writings, his intellectual life was hardly rigid or static. On the contrary, a stretching and elaboration of the central core continued until the end. Flexibility and fluidity were especially evident in his ability to rephrase, re-evaluate or re-examine complexities and contradictions. While accepting the historical legacy of his time and place, he chiselled changes wherever necessary. The synthesis that shaped his *Staatsgedanken* (ideas about the state) included: themes from the sixteenth-century Reformation, the tradition of German organic political theories of the nineteenth century, and the striving for community and wholeness so evident in his generation (of the Weimar era).[42] Although refinements and nuances in his political thought are particularly evident in *Ethics*, Bonhoeffer's greatest gifts remained those of a synthesiser, not an innovator in ideas about the state.

In his 1932/3 lectures and essays Bonhoeffer sketched church–state relations that should never evolve into a penetration of one by the other; he defined a mutual recognition of limits and a continuing balance of tensions. Authority, force and the preservation of order belonged to the realm of the state. Despite his inconsistent use of terms like 'communities' and 'orders of preservation', Bonhoeffer's words called for obedience to God in the church and in the state. Clearly he depended on Reformation teachings on church and state during this period.

New emphases appeared in Bonhoeffer's radio address 'The Leader and the Individual in the Younger Generation', which he delivered on 1 February 1933. In the concluding paragraph (which was never aired) Bonhoeffer warned of leaders or offices which 'set themselves up as gods', thereby mocking God and the individual who stands alone before him. 'Alone before God, man becomes what he is, free and committed in responsibility at the same time.'[43] This note modifies Bonhoeffer's tendency towards anti-individualistic statements. On the other hand, it is in keeping with the German spiritual and intellectual traditions of 'inner freedom' for the individual, which may accompany external conditions of subservience and servitude.

Freedom might then be found in conformity rather than in resistance to state power.[44]

Although some of Bonhoeffer's sermons in London (1933–5) warned of the dangers of the worship of power, his 1937 book *The Cost of Discipleship* emphasises the importance of obeying power, whether the state is good or bad. Still clinging to the framework of Reformation church–state teachings in 1939, Bonhoeffer compared American and European church–state attitudes, criticising the continuing impact of the American churches upon the state.[45]

The most thorough and systematic survey of Bonhoeffer's political ideas is found in *Ethics*, a master work that he was crafting in the early 1940s. Although never completed, it provides fresh terminology and new distinctions. At the same time, it synthesises the currents found in his earlier works: German Reformation, nineteenth-century German organic, and Weimar legacies. Attempting to clarify his earlier terms 'community' and 'order', Bonhoeffer suggests a new expression: 'mandates'. But he sharply limits the application of the label 'mandate' to four (and occasionally five) groupings: marriage and the family, labour, government, church, and culture (including 'aesthetic existence' – art, friendship and play).[46]

Bonhoeffer also distinguishes between 'state' and 'government'. For his purposes 'government' now becomes the more useful 'New Testament' concept, replacing his previous reliance on 'state'.[47] According to Bonhoeffer's definition, 'government' is 'a power which comes down from above, no matter whether it discharges its office well or badly'; it refers only to the rulers, not to the ruled. Only government, not state, can have a theological application. Hence Bonhoeffer's mandates include government rather than state, because the mandate refers to 'a divinely imposed task'.[48] Obedience is owed to the government until the government compels Christians to offend against the divine commandment. Thus the new distinction provides an intellectual justification for opposition activity by a person of Christian conscience. This leaves room for an individual to reject a particular government, while still being loyal to the nation-state.

Individuals in Bonhoeffer's scheme have more latitude for action than the church. Although Bonhoeffer's balanced synthesis avoids the extremes of German statism, he is caught between a group-orientated, communal approach and the individualism which might be needed to overcome the corruption of and by groups. 'Free, responsible' individuals might find themselves forced to act outside the communities of church and state. Although Bonhoeffer criticised the excessive individualism found in the West, his system did not clearly indicate how individuals would function against the evils of totalitarian governments. For Bonhoeffer, family and friendship remained as sustaining 'mandates'. But is that adequate?

While in prison Bonhoeffer outlined a book about Christianity and the real meaning of the Christian faith. His conclusions are startling, tantalising and revolutionary:

> The church is the church only when it exists for others. To make a start, it should give away all its property to those in need. The clergy must live solely on the free-will offerings of their congregations, or possibly engage in some secular calling. The church must share in the secular problems of ordinary human life, not dominating, but helping and serving.[49]

He stressed the transforming encounter with Jesus Christ and the power of human example rather than abstract argument.[50] Not only the intensity of his prison experiences, but also his memories of congregational life in the United States must have influenced some of his dramatic suggestions. In the prison letters and papers, Tiemo Rainer Peters perceives that for Bonhoeffer church and world are no longer so sharply separated, but are more closely linked in mutual dialectical tension.[51]

CONCLUDING REFLECTIONS

Bonhoeffer Bio

> A theological de Tocqueville
> explorer, man of action
> man of words, 'renewed,
> transfigured, in another pattern'.[52]

This poem emerged as a distillation of Bonhoeffer's legacy for politics and faith traditions; it came to me as a mini-summary of the ingredients in my study of Bonhoeffer's concepts on church, state and the Jewish 'problem' (a word he used, which might be questioned today). Indeed the power of Bonhoeffer's legacy lies in its malleability; it can be reshaped, moulded and adapted to diverse times and places. After chipping off some of his inherited concepts, especially those traditional Christian teachings of contempt towards Jews and their history, we can uncover some gleaming treasures. Like Bonhoeffer, T. S. Eliot's creativity during the Second World War sought new byways, often fragmentary, but glistening. In *Four Quartets*, poems composed in war-time, Eliot explores and beseeches his past and that of his country, visiting Little Gidding's graveyard and his nation's history. He concludes that 'what you thought you came for is only a shell, a husk of meaning from which the purpose breaks only when it is fulfilled . . . the purpose is beyond the end you figured and is altered in fulfilment'.[53] Eliot's insight applies to the legacy of Bonhoeffer's words, encased in the 'husk of meaning' of his life and era, but finding new fulfilment and purpose wherever they are read world-wide.

That purpose has been altered or adapted, whether the words have been applied to liberation theology in Latin America, to the civil-rights movement in North America, or to the anti-apartheid struggles in South Africa. Words Bonhoeffer penned in prison or before have evolved a life of their own, which he could hardly have anticipated. New patterns emerge, not just for his words, but also for the paradigm of his actions. He and the other anti-Nazi German resisters have become prototypes of contemporary human-rights activists.

Moreover, Bonhoeffer's 'world-orientation' and capacity for action may be compared to the categories of action and love for the world found in the later writings of Hannah Arendt, Jewish political philosopher and refugee from Nazi Germany. In *The Human Condition* Arendt's sensitivity to the legacy of Jesus of Nazareth leads her to conclude that Jesus' insights into the 'miracle-working faculty of man' in action can be compared 'in their originality and unprecedentedness with Socrates' insights into the possibilities of thought'. For Arendt the faculty of action provides 'an ever-present reminder that men, though they must die, are not born in order to die but in order to begin'.[54] She links freedom with action, 'the spontaneous beginning of something new'.[55] While admitting that we may begin something new and not be able 'to control or even to foretell its consequences',[56] Arendt does not advocate retreat from action into passivity, because of the inherently unpredictable course of action. Instead she heralded the French resistance to Hitler and the Hungarian revolt of 1956; in the words of Margaret Canovan, Hannah Arendt recognised that these individuals

> had the courage to stop behaving in a routine manner, to step forward
> from their private lives to create a public space and to act within it in
> such a way that, while the memory of their actions lasts, the human
> world can never again be as if they had not existed. In doing so,
> according to Hannah Arendt, they rediscovered the truth known to the
> Greeks, that action is the supreme blessing that bestows significance
> upon individual human life.[57]

One can only speculate that Hannah Arendt, with her emphasis on 'the genuine experience of and love for the world' and on free action, as well as the human capacity for thought,[58] might have found much in common with Bonhoeffer, had she studied his works and actions. Her ideas resonate with Bonhoeffer's analysis of free responsibility and civic courage; she would probably have placed his activities in the German resistance movement within her category of action in the public space. Arendt, like Bonhoeffer, stresses the link between action, forgiveness and freedom: 'Without being forgiven, released from the consequences of what we have done, our capacity to act would, as it were, be confined to one single deed from which we could never recover.'[59] She perceives the freedom found in Jesus' teachings on forgiveness.

Bonhoeffer understood the need for action in the public sphere so commended by Arendt. Concluding his lament for the dearth of civil courage in Germany, Bonhoeffer claimed that the German

> could not see the need for free and responsible action, even in opposition to his task and calling; in its place there appeared on the one hand an irresponsible lack of scruple, and on the other a punctiliousness that never led to action. Civil courage, in fact, can grow only out of the free responsibility of free men. Only now are the Germans beginning to discover the meaning of free responsibility. It depends on a God who demands responsible action in a bold venture of faith, and who promises forgiveness and consolation to the man who becomes a sinner in that venture.[60]

A talented teacher, courageous citizen, and an explorer of places and ideas, Bonhoeffer may appropriately be termed a theological de Tocqueville – perceptive, prophetic, aristocratic in temperament, suspicious of the masses and sensitive to the realities of his time and place. Like Alexis de Tocqueville, Bonhoeffer deftly diagnosed the pathology of power and obedience; during the Nazi years Bonhoeffer experienced the truth of de Tocqueville's analysis:

> Men are not corrupted by the exercise of power or debased by the habit of obedience, but by the exercise of a power which they believe to be illegitimate, and by obedience to a rule which they consider to be usurped and oppressive.[61]

A man of balanced tensions, Bonhoeffer respected both the boundaries and the power of church and state, freedom and obedience, thought and action, transgression and forgiveness, the individual and the community. Although he was isolated in a prison cell for two years, his commitment to family and friends, social vision and love of the world intensified. He came to understand a 'profound this-worldliness, characterised by discipline and the constant knowledge of death and resurrection'. The day after the failure of the plot of 20 July 1944 to kill Hitler, Bonhoeffer shared his inward liberation and his witness to the world: 'it is only by living completely in this world that one learns to have faith'.[62]

Notes

1 D. Bonhoeffer, *Letters and Papers from Prison: The Enlarged Edition* (New York: Macmillan, 1971), p. 382.
2 ibid., pp. 6, 9.
3 ibid., p. 342.
4 D. J. Hall, 'Ecclesia Crucis: The Disciple Community and the Future of the Church in North America', in *Theology and the Practice of Responsibility: Essays on Dietrich Bonhoeffer*, ed. W. W. Floyd, Jr and C. Marsh (Valley Forge: Trinity Press International, 1994), p. 67.
5 R. Zerner, 'Bonhoeffer's American Experiences: People, Letters, and Papers from Union Seminary', *Union Seminary Quarterly Review*, 31 (4) (Summer 1976), 261–82. Fascinated by black Baptist communities in the United States in 1930/1, Bonhoeffer taught a boys' class at the Abyssinian Baptist Church in Harlem. For his ministry among working-class youth in Berlin, see E. Bethge, *Dietrich Bonhoeffer: Man of Vision, Man of Courage* (New York: Harper & Row, 1967), pp. 109–10, 113–14.
6 Bonhoeffer, *Letters and Papers from Prison*, p. 17.
7 *Documents on Nazism, 1919–1945*, ed. J. Noakes and G. Pridham (New York: Viking Press, 1975), pp. 229–30.
8 *Die mündige Welt V: Dokumente zur BonhoefferForschung, 1928–1945*, ed. J. Glenthøj (Munich: Chr. Kaiser Verlag, 1969), p.104.
9 ibid.
10 E. C. Helmreich, *The German Churches Under Hitler: Background, Struggle and Epilogue* (Detroit: Wayne State University Press, 1979), pp. 146–8, 158, 492. Numbering about six thousand members by the end of 1933, the Pastors' Emergency League experienced a decline in membership during 1934, when large numbers of Protestant pastors from Bavaria, Hanover and Württemberg withdrew. 'This left a membership of 5,256, which remained relatively unchanged in the following years', ibid., pp. 147, 156.
11 ibid., p. 168.
12 D. Bonhoeffer, *No Rusty Swords: Letters, Lectures and Notes, 1928–1936, Collected Works of Dietrich Bonhoeffer*, vol. 1 (London: Collins, 1965), pp. 221–9.
13 ibid., pp. 223–4.
14 ibid., p. 222.
15 ibid., p. 223.
16 ibid.
17 This is developed in detail in my essay 'Dietrich Bonhoeffer's Views on the State and History', in *A Bonhoeffer Legacy: Essays in Understanding*, ed. A. J. Klassen (Grand Rapids: Eerdmans, 1981), pp. 131–57.

18   Bonhoeffer, *No Rusty Swords*, pp. 225, 222–3.

19   ibid., p. 225.

20   F. H. Littell, 'The Churches and the Body Politic', *Daedalus*, 96 (1) (1967), 23.

21   Bonhoeffer, *No Rusty Swords*, pp. 226–7.

22   ibid., p. 226.

23   Invitation to 'The Legacy of Hans von Dohnanyi and Dietrich Bonhoeffer', 29 May 1996, 6 p. m., at the United States Holocaust Museum, Washington, D.C., p. 2.

24   Bonhoeffer quotes S. Menken, 1795, 'When the time comes that this people humbles itself and penitently departs from the sins of its fathers to which it has clung with fearful stubbornness to this day, and calls down upon itself the blood of the Crucified One for reconciliation, then the world will wonder at the miracle that God works', Bonhoeffer, *No Rusty Swords*, p. 226. But Bonhoeffer refused 'cheap moralising' and claims that as the church 'looks at the rejected people, it humbly recognises itself as a church continually unfaithful to its Lord', ibid., p. 227.

25   The first draft of the Bethel Confession, 26 August 1933, in Bonhoeffer, *No Rusty Swords*, p. 241.

26   E. Bethge, *Dietrich Bonhoeffer: Man of Vision, Man of Courage*, p. 201.

27   See the examples cited in R. Zerner, 'German Protestant Responses to Nazi Persecution of the Jews', in *Perspectives on the Holocaust*, ed. R. L. Braham (Boston, Mass.: Kluwer-Nijhoff, 1983), pp. 60–3.

28   D. Bonhoeffer, *The Way to Freedom: Letters, Lectures and Notes, 1935–1939, Collected Works of Dietrich Bonhoeffer*, vol. II (London: Collins, 1966), p. 246.

29   Zerner, 'German Protestant Responses to Nazi Persecution of the Jews', pp. 64–6. See also Asta von Oppen, *Der unerhörte Schrei: Dietrich Bonhoeffer und die Judenfrage im Dritten Reich* (Hanover: Lutherisches Verlagshaus, 1996).

30   J. Bentley, *Martin Niemöller: 1892–1984* (New York: Macmillan, 1984), pp. 166, 165.

31   Bonhoeffer, *No Rusty Swords*, p. 225.

32   ibid., pp. 225–6.

33   Bethge, *Dietrich Bonhoeffer: Man of Vision, Man of Courage*, p. 207.

34   W. Meyer, *Unternehmen Sieben: Eine Rettungsaktion für vom Holocaust Bedrohte aus dem Amt Ausland/Abwehr Oberkommando der Wehrmacht* (Frankfurt-on-Main: Verlag Anton Hain, 1993), p. 458.

35   Bonhoeffer, *No Rusty Swords*, p. 225.

36   ibid.

37   Bethge, *Dietrich Bonhoeffer: Man of Vision, Man of Courage*, p. 512.

38   *I Knew Dietrich Bonhoeffer: Reminiscences by his Friends*, ed. W. Zimmermann and R. G. Smith (London: Collins, 1973), p. 150.

39   D. Bonhoeffer, *Ethics* (New York: Macmillan, 1965), p. 90.

40   Bonhoeffer, *The Way to Freedom*, p. 246.

41   Bonhoeffer, *Ethics*, pp. 113–14.

42   See Zerner, 'Dietrich Bonhoeffer's Views on the State and History', pp. 147–50.

43   Bonhoeffer, *No Rusty Swords*, pp. 203, 204.

44   The Teutonic tendency to combine spiritual independence and secular submission to an authoritarian state has been traced in L. Krieger, *The German Idea*

   of Freedom: History of a Political Tradition (Boston, Mass.: Beacon Press, 1957), pp. 65, 80.

45 Klassen, *A Bonhoeffer Legacy*, pp. 143–4.

46 Bonhoeffer, *Ethics*, pp. 207, 286, footnotes on pp. 286–7, 329; also Bonhoeffer, *Letters and Papers from Prison*, pp. 192–3.

47 Bonhoeffer, *Ethics*, pp. 332–3.

48 ibid., pp. 207, 210–11, 332, 338, 342–3.

49 Bonhoeffer, *Letters and Papers from Prison*, pp. 382–3.

50 ibid., pp. 381, 383.

51 T. R. Peters, *Die Präsenz des Politischen in der Theologie Dietrich Bonhoeffers* (Munich: Chr. Kaiser Verlag, 1976), pp. 89–90, 194–5.

52 My own poem. The final phrase of the poem comes from the last stanza of T. S. Eliot, 'Little Gidding', *The Complete Poems and Plays, 1909–1950* (New York: Harcourt, Brace and Company, 1958), p. 142.

53 ibid., p. 139.

54 H. Arendt, *The Human Condition* (New York: Doubleday, 1959), p. 222.

55 ibid., p. 210.

56 ibid., p. 211.

57 M. Canovan, *The Political Thought of Hannah Arendt* (New York: Harcourt Brace Jovanovich, 1974), p. 65.

58 Arendt, *The Human Condition*, p. 297.

59 ibid., p. 213. Arendt states that 'the freedom contained in Jesus' teachings of forgiveness is the freedom from vengeance' (p. 216). She points out that 'trespassing is an everyday occurrence which is in the very nature of action's constant establishment of new relationships within a web of relations, and it needs forgiving, dismissing, in order to make it possible for life to go on by constantly releasing men from what they have done unknowingly. Only through this constant mutual release from what they do can men remain free agents, only by constant willingness to change their minds and start again can they be trusted with so great a power as to begin something new' (ibid.).

60 Bonhoeffer, *Letters and Papers from Prison*, p. 6.

61 A. de Tocqueville, *Democracy in America* (New York: Vintage Books, 1958), p. 9.

62 Bonhoeffer, *Letters and Papers from Prison*, p. 369.

11 The ethics of responsible action

LARRY RASMUSSEN

As a Christmas gift to his brother-in-law Hans von Dohnanyi, fellow member of the conspiracy Hans Oster, and his closest friend Eberhard Bethge, Bonhoeffer penned an essay at the turn of the year 1942–3. Entitled 'After Ten Years', it was an account of lessons learnt in opposing Nazism across the decade following Hitler's rise to power in January 1933. Bonhoeffer speaks of feeling 'no ground under our feet' and of the shared experience that these friends straddled a 'turning-point in history', an epochal break in time. They had landed in that awkward place history sometimes serves up when 'every available alternative seem[s] equally intolerable' yet the shape of the future cannot be discerned. The way forward is not visible, even to the sage.[1]

The subsection 'No ground under our feet' is followed by 'Who stands fast?' Bonhoeffer leads off with a blunt report: 'The great masquerade of evil has played havoc with all our ethical concepts.' Then he catalogues standard moral options generations have trusted, only to describe their destruction in the West as that had come to murderous expression under fascism. Appeals to 'reason', to 'moral fanaticism' (principled single-mindedness), to 'conscience' and to the paths of 'duty', 'freedom' and 'private virtuousness' had all crumbled as sure guides for living amidst turmoil and crisis. Furthermore, they had failed, not for the unthinking, or the willing followers of historical drift, but precisely for morally sensitive, humane and educated Germans. On these traditional moral grounds none had stood fast. Only the person ready to sacrifice these in deference to 'obedient and responsible action in faith and in exclusive allegiance to God', Bonhoeffer concludes, only the one 'who tries to make his whole life an answer to the question and call of God', can live upright in the unsteady space between lost certainties and unknown futures. 'Where are these responsible people?', he asks as he closes this section.[2] Hardly a throwaway line, it anticipates the weighty query later in the essay, 'Are we still of any use?'[3]

Despite the tinge of despair in these questions, Bonhoeffer's answer is that there are indeed 'responsible people' and they are 'of use'. So the Christmas reflections continue, with caution to fellow resisters not to take to the field in the manner of Don Quixote and think that 'going down fighting like heroes in the face of certain defeat' is in fact heroic at all. Neither should they relate to the inexorable events of history with 'barren criticism' or 'equally barren opportunism'. Rather, 'the ultimate question for a responsible man to ask is not how he is to extricate himself heroically from the affair, but how the coming generation is to live'. It is only from this question, 'with its responsibility toward history', that fruitful solutions might arise.[4]

Two matters push to the fore in this reflection. The first is Bonhoeffer's conviction, made compelling by his experience, that the inherited moral grounds of modernity in the West are effectively spent. Even the moral treasures he himself depended upon will have to find some refuge other than their usual appeals. Their foundations are gone, their formulations impotent, their effective cultural power dissipated. The second is his continual appeal to 'responsibility', 'responsible action', 'responsibility toward history', and 'responsible people' as somehow the locus for thinking beyond present failures. A new account of the Christian life, centred in responsibility and built up from the living of it during a long period of forced social experimentation and conversion of heart and mind, is necessary. Bonhoeffer's *Ethics*, its completion frustrated by his arrest, begins this critical work.

We turn first to the meaning of a 'turning-point in history' for ethical foundations, then to Bonhoeffer's constructive response.

INHERITANCE AND DECAY

The murderous events in Europe in the 1930s and 1940s revealed the ruin of inherited cultural, religious and intellectual frameworks. Moral and ethical frameworks were part and parcel of these. Still, the inadequacy of past ethical bases and formulations did not originate with the triumph of Nazism, even when the flames of war and Holocaust made the failure starkly manifest. Bonhoeffer was convinced well before the 1940s that traditional ethical systems in the Christian West were bereft of power to combat the century's evils. Already in 1932 this young German professor was attracted to Mahatma Gandhi because he sensed that a kind of exhaustion had befallen Western Christian spirituality and ethics. 'Christianity in other words and deeds'[5] might be discovered, by contrast, in Gandhi and the East.

'Christianity in other words and deeds' included fashioning a resistance community and learning non-violence as a way of life. These were subjects vital to Bonhoeffer's understanding of the Christian moral life in the 1930s as he sought to give leadership in the Confessing Church. The ways of costly grace as commanded by Jesus in the Sermon on the Mount needed to find corporate ecclesial expression. A gospel ethic is inseparable from the life of the community and its concrete practices.

Yet Bonhoeffer's judgement about 'the havoc' wreaked upon 'all our ethical concepts' was more than a conviction about Christian ethics in particular, and specifically German Protestant ethics. Bonhoeffer was convinced of a cultural crisis in the West which deeply affected civilisation as a whole. Rabid anti-Semitism was one sure mark. 'An expulsion of the Jews from the west', he wrote at the height of Hitler's power and popularity in 1940, 'must necessarily bring with it the expulsion of Christ. For Jesus Christ was a Jew.'[6] For one who confessed Jesus Christ as the 'centre of history' and the source of a certain historical unity in the West, the 'expulsion of the Jews' marked a spiritual and moral sickness unto death.

An earlier address at the Institute of Technology in Berlin in 1932 makes the same case differently. Here Bonhoeffer contrasts the way of Gandhi and India with 'Euro-American civilisation'. India's is a 'history of suffering', the West's is 'a history of war'. 'War and industry', or 'the machine and war', are the very elements of self-identity and problem-solving in the West, Bonhoeffer says. When he asks about the spiritual and intellectual sources of this aggressive cultural self-assertion, he concludes that it is grounded in efforts by the West 'to turn nature to its service'. 'Human conquest of nature is the foundational theme of Euro-American history', he declares without qualification. Not stopping there, he says that conquest directed at nature is levelled 'against human beings' as well. '[European] life in its essence means "to kill"' is his abrupt and blunt conclusion.[7]

Note that Bonhoeffer says 'European' and 'Euro-American' civilisation, and not simply 'German'. In a manuscript for *Ethics* written a decade later, this is analysed in the subsection 'Inheritance and Decay'. We must take time with these pages, since here Bonhoeffer, now caught in the horror of Hitler's war and participating in the conspiracy as a matter of 'responsibility towards history' for future generations, shows why Christian ethics in the West requires a wholly new beginning.

The fate of Christian ethics in the West certainly does include Germany, in Bonhoeffer's analysis. His thinking is always contextual and concrete and he has Germany uppermost on his mind, though not its immediate history only. The present Nietzschean 'revolt of the natural against grace' was prepared by the German Reformation itself, and found a home in German theology. Nazism glorified elements of a *pre*-Christian Germanic past as well. This paganism, rooted in a Germanic sense of nature, can still be detected, Bonhoeffer says, as a matter of 'national character, or, if one prefers it so, as race'.[8] This legacy is not the chief reason for the specifically *Christian* deformation, however. That has to do with ethics in the course of the Reformation, the Enlightenment and secularisation.

Bonhoeffer records what he judges to be a misunderstanding of a cornerstone in Lutheran social ethics, Luther's teaching on the two kingdoms. An 'emancipation and sanctification of the world and of the natural' occurred via this teaching, a teaching about God's presence and rule in different ways in different social domains. 'Government, reason, economics and culture' were reckoned quasi-autonomous zones of human responsibility in a division of churchly and civic duties. The Reformation was thus celebrated 'as the emancipation of man in his conscience, his reason and his culture and as the justification of the secular as such'.

Such emancipated reason and responsibility prepared the way for Enlightenment secularity. In some key respects, Bonhoeffer is a sharp critic of the Enlightenment, not least its French expression. Here, on Catholic rather than Protestant ground, new-found freedom joined with revolutionary terror. 'The cult of reason, the deification of nature, faith in progress and a critical approach to civilisation, the revolt of the bourgeoisie and the revolt of the masses, nationalism and anti-clericalism, the rights of man and dictatorial terror' all erupted chaotically in the Enlightenment's proud announcement that history had begun anew at the hands of unshackled human beings.[9]

Bonhoeffer also chides secular European Enlightenment ethics for its vaunted universalism. It claimed to be a cosmopolitan ethic whose principles – supposedly expressing universal human nature – transcended contingencies of time, place, culture, ethnicity and class. The ethical, 'in this sense of the formal, the universally valid and the rational', carried 'no element of concretion', Bonhoeffer writes. This leads to 'the total atomisation of human society and of the life of the individual, in unlimited subjectivism and individualism'. Bonhoeffer could hardly have foreseen how precisely his analysis in the 1940s would describe dominant Western moral patterns at century's end:

> When the ethical is conceived without reference to any local or
> temporal relation, without reference to the questions of its warrant or
> authority, without reference to the concrete, then life falls apart into

an infinite number of unconnected atoms of time, and human society resolves itself into individual atoms of reason.[10]

Then only moral fragments remain, themselves justified by appeals to no more than autonomous freedom and individual or group preference. Values become matters of changing tastes and preferences. Such utter subjectivism can scarcely serve as sufficient grounds for a viable, coherent social ethic.

At the same time, this sharp critic of European Enlightenment ethics is also its measured champion. The revolt of reason against the chaperonage of church and state, and against their complicity in social and economic oppression, was justified, Bonhoeffer argues. Not least, the unfettered pursuit of truth and intellectual honesty in all things, 'including questions of belief', is a genuine and lasting achievement of emancipated reason. 'It has ever since been one of the indispensable moral requirements of western man.'[11]

Those moral requirements include, he goes on, another fruit of Enlightenment ethics, namely human rights. Human rights are rooted in the ascription of liberty, equality and respect to every human being as a condition of human fulfilment and what Bonhoeffer calls 'natural life'. As such, they are not subject to the veto of any government, Hitler's included.

In short, the untrammelled pursuit of truth and basic rights with an unconditional and universal reach are moral treasures to be guarded, Bonhoeffer is convinced. That they were won in battles fought against conservative patriotic forces allied with the churches does not escape him. One measure of the churches' moral indolence is that Bonhoeffer himself is among the very first Protestant theologians to claim human rights as essential to Christian ethics.[12]

Yet things went terribly wrong, and Enlightenment secularity contributed to it. Bonhoeffer the measured defender of Western emancipated reason becomes the witness to state and cultural crime on a massive scale. Humanity in Europe and its neo-European extensions around the world used 'emancipated' reason to proclaim itself the master and sovereign of its own fate. It trumpeted its own autonomy in an expansionist journey of idolatrous confidence in progress and conquest, elaborated as an ethic of Christian and/or secular responsibility for sharing a superior civilisation. In an elaboration of themes voiced in the 1930s, but now discussed in *Ethics* notes of the 1940s, Bonhoeffer reiterates the Western aim to be independent of nature. Enlightenment reason pursued a 'technical science of the modern western world' that sought not 'service' but 'mastery'. This is 'a new spirit', he writes, 'the spirit of the forcible subjugation of nature beneath the rule of the thinking and experimenting man'. The outcome is technology as 'an end in itself' 'with a soul of its own'. Its symbol 'is the machine, the embodiment of the violation and exploitation of nature'.[13] A few years later and writing from prison, Bonhoeffer will say that Western technical and organisational triumphs have been so extraordinary that 'human beings have managed to deal with everything, only not with themselves'. 'The spiritual force is lacking' to protect us from the menace of our own organisation,[14] he says in a comment that echoes the earlier conviction of moral and spiritual exhaustion in the West.

Nevertheless, there is no going back behind the Enlightenment to some pre-modern state. Thus everything will still 'turn on human beings' and the uses of the considerable and dangerous powers of modernity.[15] Ours is a 'world-come-of-age', as a measure not of accomplished moral maturity but of moral responsibility for the powers in our hands. There is no depositing the responsibility for what happens somewhere else, including with God. God will not plug the gaps or be the rescuer, the *deus ex machina*. Rather, all turns 'on human beings'. This renders Bonhoeffer's own questions all the more poignant: where are 'the responsible people' of 'world-come-of-age consciousness' for such tasks, and what account of responsibility, being built upon what foundations, will guide them when there is little 'ground under our feet'?

Yet the treatment of nature is not Bonhoeffer's preoccupation. Western treatment of nature is but an instance of the sovereign sway of idolatrous human powers parading mastery on a grand scale. In Bonhoeffer's own lifetime this sovereign swagger means, concretely, the rise of fascist 'vitalism' as an arrogant, death-dealing idolisation of life.

Fascist vitalism, with its slogan of 'Blood and Soil' (*Blut und Boden*), may seem the utter opposite of the Enlightenment's transcendent, cosmopolitan principles. In crucial ways it was, and Bonhoeffer testifies to the Confessing Church's unexpected experience of protecting Enlightenment values against Nazi tribalism. The irony does not escape him, since, as we noted, those very appeals to reason, to human rights, to human dignity and self-determination had served, in the previous century, 'as battle slogans against [a reticent] church'. But now, in an alliance of Christians and morally sensitive secular Germans of the Enlightenment, Enlightenment values countered the fascist 'deification of the irrational, of blood and instinct, of the beast of prey in man'.[16] These values found their refuge, protection and justification in the Christ who suffers for the sake of justice, truth, human decency, and freedom. This Jesus, Bonhoeffer says, gives his support to all who suffer for any just cause. And those who did so in the 1930s in Germany were instinctively drawn from varied quarters to a church who proclaimed the crucified one and suffered with him in opposing fascist ways.[17]

Yet that Christian and secular humanist alliance of dissent and resistance did not succeed. Vitalism triumphed. The identity and morality of a whole people (*das Volk*) drew deeply from mysterious forces they shared with the 'blood and soil' of the forests, mountains, sea, and this people's own mythical past. Moral absolutes supposedly rooted in the natural order only awaited their realisation by a superior race who held the right to wield those absolutes in battles of strength against strength. Such a reborn Aryan nation, leaders and followers both said, merited undivided loyalty and the suspension of critical judgement for a season of overdue and destiny-ridden empire-building.

This glorification of the irrational and subordination of critical reason to exuberant tribalism appears to bear no connection to Enlightenment ethics whatsoever. In some ways Nazi vitalism's most obvious link to the Enlightenment is precisely as a virulent *re*action to the passionlessness of its principles and its veiled disdain for the residues of tribalism and place. But in Bonhoeffer's assessment there is a profound – and profoundly disturbing – link, a link so essential that it spells the shaking of Western ethical foundations.

Vitalism, Bonhoeffer says, absolutises a genuine insight, namely that 'life is not only a means to an end but an end in itself'. This premise it shares with the very Enlightenment ethic that grounds human rights. Yet fascism renders this truth in such a way that 'life which posits itself as an absolute, as an end in itself, [becomes] its own destroyer'.[18] In related fashion, human beings – some humans far more than others, in a racist theology of '*das Volk*' – take on the stature of those larger-than-life, dynamic human beings who fashion history with the power of their own charisma and self-assertion. The strong, virile and industrious lead the way. They command and demand respect and obedience.

The absolutising of life and idolisation of the human go hand-in-hand with the idolisation of death, Bonhoeffer argues. He does so in a description of Nazism penned when Hitler was most popular. Note especially how the last line quoted below accords with the themes of mastery, a new humanity, and a new age trumpeted, not just in reborn Germany, but in the Enlightenment tradition more broadly, a tradition which assumed its own cultural superiority.

Boastful reliance on earthly eternities [blood and soil] goes side by side with a frivolous playing with life. A convulsive acceptance and seizing hold of life stands cheek by jowl with indifference and contempt for life. There is no clearer indication of the idolisation of death than when a period claims to be building for eternity [the Thousand-Year Reich] and yet life has no value in this period, or when big words are spoken of a new man, of a new world and of a new society which is to be ushered in, and yet all that is new is the destruction of life as we know it.[19]

In sum, Bonhoeffer taps a deep and common Western theme he finds lethal, namely *mastery that knows no limits as undertaken by autonomous humans in the name of freedom without constraint.* Thus do we experience 'the twinning of freedom and terror', 'the upsurge of a terrible godlessness in human presumptions of god-likeness',[20] the deification of humans who end up despising those who do not conform to their image. Neither fascist vitalism nor the Enlightenment tradition nor, we might add, Bolshevism and innumerable ideologies of conquest and colonialism understood the havoc wreaked by all totalising ideologies, by all ways of life that recognise no limits as they wield heightened human power.

Bonhoeffer's counter is to underline our finitude and creatureliness and to advocate the way of faith. In the way of humble faith, the creature 'takes of life what it offers, not all or nothing'. Neither 'cling[ing] convulsively to life nor cast[ing] it frivolously away . . . one allows to death the limited rights it still possesses'.[21] The way of Jesus Christ is a humbler, more vulnerable and compassionate way than the arrogance of dominant, limitless Western ethics in its multiple forms. At the same time the suffering God *affirms* human powers and responsible use of them as creaturely powers in a precarious 'world-come-of-age'.

This last remark jumps ahead towards Bonhoeffer's constructive response to the moral ruin of Western, or Euro-American, ethical foundations. Before joining him there, we should note the influential intellectual construct in ethics that hovers in the background for Bonhoeffer. Western ethical theory did not create the ethos Bonhoeffer finds destructive of body and soul, but it abetted that ethos.

For modern Western ethics the self-sufficient human subject and his or her practical reason sits at the centre of the moral universe. The God-centredness of the Middle Ages and the Reformation was abandoned by modernity as the moral horizon. The thinking, judging, experimenting human subject replaced God as the focus of ethical theories. In the classic statement of Enlightenment autonomy (Immanuel Kant's), freedom consists in giving oneself the law. That is, the human agent takes the measure of morality, and practical moral reasoning proceeds *etsi deus non daretur* – as if

God, or any other transcendent moral authority, did not exist. The autonomous self, individually and collectively, defines its own interests and values. It legislates its own morality, subject to the same action by others.

When such moral notions join the idolisation of progress – or other ideologies of historical process and destiny such as Nazis and communists held – then the ethics of the Sovereign Self underwrites and embodies modernity's ethos of mastery. The killing fields of the First and Second World Wars, the Holocaust, racism and the colonisation of non-Western peoples and cultures, all these expose, not deviance from essentially sound moral foundations, but faultlines at the base itself. Even when Bonhoeffer, the nuanced appraiser of the Enlightenment tradition, sought to hold on to and affirm human agency, powers, rights and responsibilities, he knew that he was looking at the moral bankruptcy of the Christian West. 'No ground under our feet' and 'Are we still of any use?' sum it up well.[22]

In other words, just as the anti-Semitism that issued in the horror of the Holocaust did not first appear with the Nazis and Germany, but went centuries deep and spanned a continent and more, so also the Achilles' heel of Western moral traditions, including Christian ones, was not a consequence of events in the 1930s and 1940s alone. Those traditions went deep and were widely held. The Holocaust and the war exposed, but did not create, civilisation-wide moral corruption. Even when one strand of that moral heritage could still be drawn upon to combat the injustice in another, such as Christian motivation for saving Jews or Enlightenment counters to Nazi glorification of blood and soil, the larger framework showed itself too rotted to serve as the ethical frame for the coming age. Whatever moral tradition is appealed to – whether balanced reason, single-minded principles, conscience, autonomous freedom, or private virtuousness – is impotent even for standing fast, not to say constructing an adequate moral base for the future.

There are other reasons why Bonhoeffer judges that a new basis for Christian ethics in the West is necessary, and further elements of analysis are scattered throughout his writings, including those for *Ethics*. But the foregoing will have to suffice, both to register his judgement and to introduce some of the strands of thought and experience that led to it.

RECONSTRUCTION OF CHRISTIAN ETHICS IN THE WEST

So how does Bonhoeffer respond? When he seeks to understand his own convulsive experience and reconstruct Christian ethics on a new basis, he does not, in the first instance, use the works of leading philosophers and ethicists or appeal to standard traditions of moral theory. A few of those thinkers are on his reading list, but they make no appearance in his manuscripts for *Ethics*. Rather, he turns to what might be deemed 'cultural critics', whether from literature, philosophy, history or theology. Thus Kierkegaard, Jaspers, Spengler, Dostoevsky, Cervantes, Balzac, Stifter, Nietzsche, Montaigne and Barth appear.[23] Bonhoeffer's reading is but one more indication that he senses a crisis in civilisation centuries deep. Any proposed Christian ethic will have to show its mettle in the light of that diagnosis.

The notes for *Ethics* give further evidence of this assessment. Note 1 proposes a title for Bonhoeffer's undertaking as a whole.[24] It reads: 'Foundation and Construction of a Future World (Reconciled with God): A Tentative Christian Ethic'. In parentheses is the phrase 'a united West'. Themes are then listed under two major divisions, 'Foundations' and 'Construction'.

A later possible title runs in much the same vein: 'Preparing the Way and Entry'.[25] Regrettably, the work was never prepared as a whole, and what we have as the book *Ethics* is a posthumous collection of Bonhoeffer's unfinished efforts, written while awaiting travel assignments for the conspiracy. None of the drafts are wholly finished, only one was redrafted, and none satisfied Bonhoeffer. The ones we do have were rescued from their hiding place inside gas masks buried in his parents' garden.[26]

Yet the unfinished character of *Ethics* is more a measure of circumstances in Bonhoeffer's life – his arrest and imprisonment – than a measure of his investment. He would confess from prison in mid November 1943: 'I've reproached myself for not having finished my *Ethics* (parts of it have probably been confiscated), and it was some consolation to me that I had told you the essentials, and that even if you had forgotten it, it would probably emerge again indirectly somehow. Besides, my ideas were still incomplete.'[27] Or, in the reflective mood of a month later: 'I sometimes feel as if my life were more or less over, and as if all I had to do now were to finish my *Ethics*.'[28]

All this said, we can still detect his direction and follow his thought. Again, and just as above, we cannot offer a full analysis and exposition. But we can supply essentials that offer a sense of Bonhoeffer's mind. In this case, we shall speak of 'Foundations' (his term) in view of his discussion of 'reality' and of 'Construction' (also his term) in the light of the theme of 'responsibility'.

Foundational reality

Recall Bonhoeffer's proposed title: 'Foundation and Construction of a Future World (Reconciled with God)'. Bonhoeffer makes a reconciled world the foundation itself. He calls this simply 'reality'. Reality is the world as accepted by God in Jesus Christ. This reality, rather than, say, the sovereign, autonomous human self, is the ontological base for a reconstructed Christian ethic. It is the grounds for Christian moral formation, discernment and action.

A key passage in an *Ethics* manuscript puts it succinctly.

> In Christ we are offered the possibility of partaking in the reality of God and in the reality of the world, but not in the one without the other. The reality of God discloses itself only by setting me entirely in the reality of the world, and when I encounter the reality of the world it is always already sustained, accepted and reconciled in the reality of God.[29]

What Christian ethics is about, then, is straightforward, at least conceptually, namely 'the realisation in our world of the divine and cosmic reality which is given in Christ'.[30] But who is this Christ, and how does his nature determine the nature of worldly 'reality'? In *Letters and Papers from Prison*, Bonhoeffer gives Jesus Christ the title 'the man for others'.[31] But that formulation is deceptively simple, and unless it is understood in the broader sweep of Bonhoeffer's work, it does not of itself disclose the 'relational' understanding of all reality that Bonhoeffer sees in Jesus.

In university lectures in 1933 Bonhoeffer argues that Jesus Christ is 'the centre' of all reality. In this context he discusses the essence of Christ's personhood as 'being-there'. 'He is the centre in three ways, in being-there for men, in being-there for history and in being-there for nature.'[32]

'Being-there-for', or, more precisely, 'being-there-with-and-for', is constitutive of reality as the world reconciled in God. 'Christ is Christ not as Christ in himself', Bonhoeffer writes, 'but in his relation to me. His being Christ is his being *pro me*.'[33] That is, Christ can be thought of *only* in relational terms. 'Being-there-with-and-for' *is* the manner of his existence and presence. Bonhoeffer can thus say that Christ exists '*as* community'. He even makes the rather startling comment that 'it is not only useless to meditate on a Christ in himself, but even godless'.[34] Which is to say, God's very being, too, is relational. To conceive of God and Christ, and reconciled reality itself, other than in relational terms – for humanity, for nature and for history and its meaning – gets things fundamentally wrong from the start.

It is not only Christ's and God's nature that Bonhoeffer understands in relational terms. He understands human nature this way as well. The human self is inherently social. It is formed and fashioned in self–other relationships. The self does not exist first as some independent, given substance that then elects to contract with the world around it. Rather, just as Christ is only Christ 'in community', so, too, are we integrally, not accidentally, social creatures. The self is genuinely human in the 'Thou–I, I–Thou' relationship. 'Being-there-with-and-for-others' defines our true self as much as it does Christ's or God's in Bonhoeffer's description of 'reality' as foundational for Christian ethics.

The same sociality defines the nature of the church, which Bonhoeffer likes to picture as a piece of world exhibiting 'realised' (or reconciled) reality. Here, too, his formulation is deceptively simple: 'The Church is the Church only when it is there for others.'[35] Its nature resides in its orientation with-and-towards others. 'The only way in which the Church can defend her own territory is by fighting not for it but for the salvation of the world',[36] Bonhoeffer writes from prison. In this particular discussion he is reflecting his disappointment in his own church: 'Generally in the Confessing church: standing up for the Church's "cause", but little personal faith in Christ. "Jesus" is disappearing from sight . . . The decisive factor: the Church on the defensive. No taking risks for others.'[37]

In short, a unity permeates Bonhoeffer's understanding of the nature of God in Jesus Christ, human nature and the nature of the church. The unity is being-there-with-and-for-others. This is reconciled reality itself. Through Jesus Christ it is already present in the world as we know it, and it is the foundation for Christian ethics in that world.

But things can and do go terribly wrong. Reality can be violated, and is. Bonhoeffer, appreciating Luther, understands the human dimension of this violation as 'sin' and understands sin as the 'heart-turned-in-upon-itself' (*cor curvum in se*). Turned in upon itself, the human self is cut off, isolated, bound, often lost in constricted and illusory worlds of its own individual and collective fantasies and yearnings (fascist vitalism is but one form of collective deviance from reality in Christ). Only the self in open mutuality with others, the related self, or, we might say with more precision, the self in 'right relation', can touch the transcendent ground of its own being and 'realise' genuine, or true, or restored, 'reality'.

Given all this, the heart of the ethical life for Bonhoeffer is clear: to bring to realisation in the fallen world the world's essential character as a world reconciled in God. This is why 'Reconciled with God' is the parenthesis in Bonhoeffer's title for *Ethics*: 'Foundation and Construction of a Future World (Reconciled with God)'. This is why Bonhoeffer can also state the task of ethics in two different ways that are, in fact, one and the same, namely to 'conform our lives to Christ's form in the world', or 'to realise reality'. 'Realise' is used in the sense of bringing to expression or embodying. Method in ethics moves along the same lines, as we shall see shortly.

Responsibility

Understanding responsibility in Bonhoeffer's ethics – the core theme – requires that we understand that for him the relationship with God is both 'social', or relational, and completely 'this-worldly'. The transcendent is not found in some other world but in the ordinary relationships of which we are a part, the relationships that constitute who we are. Drawing upon Luther's contention that 'the finite bears the infinite', Bonhoeffer goes so far as to say that 'the Thou of the other man is the divine Thou. So the way to the other . . . is also the way to the divine Thou, a way of recognition or rejection.' 'The character of a Thou is in fact the form in which the divine is experienced.'[38]

In other words, because Christ exists 'as community' and is found 'in, with, and under all that is' (also Luther's phrase, used by Bonhoeffer), and because our own formation and fulfilment reside in being with and for others, it is amidst these relationships that we experience transcendence, and it is here that we meet God. And the God we meet is 'the one for others', the one 'for us' (*pro nobis*). Prison notes put it this way:

> Our relation to God is not a 'religious' relationship to the highest, most powerful, and best Being imaginable . . . but our relation to God is a new life in 'existence for others', through participation in the being of Jesus. The transcendent is not infinite and unattainable tasks, but the neighbour who is within reach in any given situation . . . God in human form . . . 'the man for others', and therefore the Crucified, the man who lives out of the transcendent.[39]

Bonhoeffer here is rejecting any Christian ethic which places the relationship to God in a different sphere from our relationship to human beings and the rest of nature, just as he is banishing all other-worldliness from Christian spirituality and ethics. There is one world, and it is already in God. The relational nature of reality-in-God is decisive for Bonhoeffer's understanding of responsibility. 'The I arises only with the Thou; responsibility follows on the claim.'[40] Reality is put together in this way.

But what does this mean? As intimated, the ontological coherence of God's reality and the world's in Christ leads Bonhoeffer to discuss moral action in two ways that are the same: 'conformation to Christ' and action 'in accordance with reality', or 'with due regard for reality'.[41] Method in ethics is thus constructed along the following lines: the Christian, facing a decision, answers the question 'What am I to do?' by first answering the question 'How is Christ taking form in the world?', or, as Bonhoeffer frequently puts it, 'Who is Christ for us today?' The method can just as easily be stated this way: the first question is 'What is the truly real here?', and the second is 'What action on my part accords with this reality?'

The questions are the same because of Bonhoeffer's identification of the world-in-Christ with reality. Thus he says straightforwardly: 'Christian ethics enquires about the realisation in our world of the divine and cosmic reality which is given in Christ.'[42]

Responsibility in the first instance, then, is the basic answering (*Verantwort-ung*)[43] of a person to life itself, the fundamental response of one's own life to life as constituted in and by relationships. Responsibility is an overall life-orientation affecting all particular actions and specific responsibili*ties*. To use Bonhoeffer's terms: responsibility is 'the total and realistic response of man to the claim of God and of our neighbour'.[44]

This 'total and realistic response' is not an abstraction for Bonhoeffer, however general it may be as a definition. Responsibility is concrete, part of an ethic that can be described as relational and contextual. That is, while reality is one, it is dynamic and has a history. And while Christ is the same today, yesterday and for ever, the form of Christ in the world varies through time, by circumstance and by culture. Christian ethics is 'a matter of history' and 'a child of the earth',[45] to cite the early Bonhoeffer. The ethical, and responsibility with it, is tied to definite times and places.

As such, moral discernment is an ongoing requirement. 'What can and must be said is not what is good once and for all, but the ways in which Christ takes form among us here and now.'[46] We must always be asking, as Bonhoeffer does, 'Who is Christ for us today?' Asking this – and answering – means immersion in the life of the Christian community. It is the responsibility of that community to garner insight into the forms Christ takes among us now and articulate them for the wider world and the exercise of responsibility there. Beyond theological insight, moral discernment also means an informed empirical knowledge of the situation in which Christians decide and act. Moral credibility and authority require this well-informed knowledge of the ever-changing context of decision. 'The word of the church to the world', Bonhoeffer once wrote,

> must encounter the world in all its present reality from the deepest
> knowledge of the world, if it is to be authoritative. Out of this
> knowledge the church must here and now be able to speak the Word

of God . . . in the most concrete way. The church must not preach timeless principles, however valid, but only commands which are valid today. To us God is 'always' *God today*.[47]

'To us God is "always" *God today*' – a more succinct way of stating the relational and contextual character of a Christian ethic is hardly possible. It is relational and contextual in a double sense. Christians make decisions in a particular *theological* context, namely with a view to reality as the world reconciled in Christ. And decisions are made in a particular (and changing) *historical* context, knowledge of which is indispensable for discerning actions in accord with Christ's present form.

Mandates

A logical question, given what has been said thus far, is whether Christ's form 'here and now' is so separated from Christ's form 'there and then' that Bonhoeffer's relational, contextual ethic renders each ethical decision a case unto itself, in effect rendering the ethic relativistic, even atomistic. The answer is 'no'. A couple of elements in Bonhoeffer's discussion in the *Ethics* manuscript will suffice to show how responsibility is structured over time and across societies and cultures.

We have already touched upon one of them. 'Natural life is formed life', he writes in an unfinished draft.[48] Natural life is formed life because God-in-Christ entered into life, placing life in the service of other life and rendering life, Bonhoeffer says, 'its own physician'. Through that ongoing incarnation, natural life becomes the 'penultimate' – life as we have it in front of us, but as open to Christ. The penultimate is directed towards the 'ultimate' (reality reconciled in God). 'Natural life' is not, then, nature as such, but an ongoing common life for which it makes sense to talk, for example, of universal moral claims and duties that stretch across time and space. It is in this connection that Bonhoeffer speaks of human rights as one expression of life's requirements for human well-being. While Bonhoeffer does not ground the rights of natural life in the Enlightenment doctrine of human nature, he does affirm the efforts of the Enlightenment to give voice to just such rights as universal rights. Of special interest is his argument for bodily rights as foundational for the realisation of any other rights. 'Bodiliness and human life belong inseparably together',[49] he argues. We *are* our bodies, ourselves.[50]

No doubt the realities of Nazism loom large here (and remember that Bonhoeffer's ethics are always concrete and contextual, even when talking of universal rights). The Nazis' utter subordination of human bodies to racist ideology elicits a response on Bonhoeffer's part that opposes any justification for torture, for the deprivation of liberty, for rape and for most cases of euthanasia and abortion.

The 'mandates' are another instance of structured moral responsibility in his relational, contextual ethic. They, too, reflect Bonhoeffer's insistence on the oneness of reality in the penultimate and ultimate, and the orientation of our responsibilities in the former by the act of God in the latter (a world reconciled in Christ). We are not born into an undifferentiated maze of atomised events and relations. Rather, we are formed in the 'mandates'. The mandates are community structures such as family, economic life, citizenship and the state, the church, circles of friendship, etc. Such formation in these social structures, running its own course as part of natural life and the penultimate, pushes us to be-with-and-for-others. So from birth to death we find ourselves amidst a corporate life filled with obligations, opportunities and responsibilities that reflect the requirements of life together. As these requirements are lived out, responsibility is both learnt and exercised. Basic moral formation takes place in this manner, and much of the moral life itself is lived in the rather unguarded and unselfconscious way that happens by virtue of being a good friend, spouse, citizen, church member, employer or employee. In a section of *Ethics* in which Bonhoeffer talks of this ordering of life under the rubric of the command of God as 'permission to live', he says that just such common arrangements as these allow

> the flood of life to flow freely. It lets man eat, drink, sleep, work, rest, and play. It does not interrupt him. It does not continually ask whether he ought to be sleeping, eating, working or playing, or whether he has some more urgent duties. The self-tormenting . . . question regarding the purity of motives, the suspicious observation of oneself, the glaring and fatiguing light of incessant consciousness, all these have nothing to do with the commandment of God, who grants liberty to live and to act.[51]

This structured and communal ordering of reality is not static. In fact, Bonhoeffer chose the word 'mandates' in self-conscious opposition to teachings in Lutheran ethics on the 'orders of creation' and 'orders of preservation'. The latter were being used by German theologians in a conservative fashion that played ever-so-nicely into a German way of life the Nazis could appropriate, and did. In the domain of traditional family values, for example, *Kinder, Küche, Kirche* – 'Children, Kitchen, Church' – named women's contributions to the German nation. Rather, the mandates are dynamic historical forms, structures of time and place that give form to ongoing responsibilities and act as the media of moral formation itself. What truly defines them is not the continuity of unchanging 'orders', but their structuring of our existence so that it is for one another. When they do not do this, they are no longer God's mandates.

Bonhoeffer knew about such failure. He lived when the state no longer served its mandated purpose but turned tyrannical and deadly, idolising death in the name of life. Thus his thoughts on responsibility as the normal duties of life in community do not end with discussion of rights and the natural life, or the mandates. There is also the specific case of the ethical breakthrough as the exceptional, or boundary-line, case. This he discusses as 'the deed of free responsibility'.

The deed of free responsibility

'Times between times', times of epochal breaks in history, times when the usual structures and moral patterns no longer hold or work well, are particularly in need of 'free responsibility'. Such deeds undertake courageous ventures that *simultaneously* transgress accustomed boundaries *and* conform to the form of Christ in the world (reality). Reflecting his own experience of the need for just such bold responsibility in the conspiracy, Bonhoeffer writes that there sometimes comes a point in the course of history 'where the exact observance of a formal law of a state . . . suddenly finds itself in violent conflict with the ineluctable necessities of the lives of men'. At this point, 'responsible and pertinent action leaves behind it the domain of principle and convention, the domain of the normal and regular, and is confronted by the extraordinary situation of ultimate necessities, a situation which no law can control'.[52]

The Christmas essay with which we began, 'After Ten Years', has a poignant discussion of this. Bonhoeffer speaks initially of the bravery and self-sacrifice of Germans, together with their willingness to subordinate personal wishes and ideas to the tasks to which they have been called. This is not a matter of servility and fear, he says, but a genuine sense of a call in these tasks and a vocation in this freely offered obedience. 'Calling and freedom' are, in fact, 'two sides of the same thing'[53] in this widely practised ethic. But Germans did not see soon enough that such willing sacrifice could be exploited for evil ends. 'The man of duty will in the end have to do his duty by the devil too', he says.[54] Germans, 'still lack[ing] something fundamental', could not see 'the need for free and responsible action, even in opposition to [their] task and calling'. Such oppositional and transgressive civil courage 'could grow only out of the free responsibility of free men'.[55]

The mandates, then, are dynamic orderings of community that give form to responsibility in society over time. They let life 'flow freely' without an overburdening of the ethical, on the one hand, and the atomisation of the moral life, on the other. Yet the mandates are the penultimate (as proximate responsibilities) in view of the ultimate (reality as the world in God). When they fail to care for the nurture and protection of life, but instead turn against it, as the Nazi state did, they are no longer God's mandates and they must be reformed. Doing so may well require that special case of the deed of free responsibility that sets itself against current, even entrenched, social institutions and practices and at the same time strikes a blow for life as understood vis-à-vis reality in Christ.

Thus what 'we have experienced and learnt in common these years',[56] Bonhoeffer writes for his friends, is both the discovery of free responsibility and a God whose concrete command is freedom, permission, liberty to live. He adds, in anything but an afterthought, that it is also the discovery of a God whose promise is forgiveness and consolation to those who incur guilt in the risky and unpopular deeds of free responsibility.

I have not surveyed all of Bonhoeffer's manuscripts for *Ethics*, or traced the many ways in which the theme of responsibility both precedes and follows upon the interrupted years he gave to *Ethics*. Instead I have endeavoured to show the circumstances, history and signs of the time which led to his conviction that a Christian ethic on a wholly new basis was necessary in the West. I have tried to sketch his effort to articulate that new basis in a presentation of reality as the world reconciled in God. His formulations here break both with the traditions of Christian ethics he knew and with the secular Enlightenment's moral centre in the Sovereign Self. I have also made an effort to track the theme of responsibility as a way to follow his thinking on a central ethical notion for this new ethic. The fact is, we have only drafts of key notions and directions from Bonhoeffer for *Ethics*. None the less, Bonhoeffer's efforts remain fruitful and suggestive for us. What he knew we need remains needed: a new account of responsibility, and the institutions for it, in the world as a single and complex, but endangered reality, its fate in the hands of far-reaching and cumulative human power. The task before Bonhoeffer thus remains the task before us, just as his question to his friends is also ours: 'The ultimate question for a responsible man to ask is not how he is to extricate himself heroically from the affair, but how the coming generation is to live. It is only from this question, with its responsibility towards history, that fruitful solutions can come.'[57]

Notes

1 The direct quotations are from the subsection, 'No Ground under our Feet', in D. Bonhoeffer, *Letters and Papers from Prison: The Enlarged Edition* (New York: Macmillan, 1972), pp. 3–4.

2 ibid., pp. 4–5.

3 ibid., pp. 16–17.

4 ibid., pp. 6–7.

5 Dietrich Bonhoeffer, 'Brief an Helmut Roessler', in D. Bonhoeffer, *Ökumene: Briefe Aufsätze Dokumente 1928–1942, Gesammelte Schriften*, vol. 1 (Munich: Chr. Kaiser Verlag, 1958), p. 61 (trans. mine).

6 D. Bonhoeffer, *Ethics* (New York: Macmillan, 1965), p. 90.

7 The quotations are from Dietrich Bonhoeffer, 'Das Recht auf Selbstbehauptung', in D. Bonhoeffer, *Theologie Gemeinde: Vorlesungen Briefe Gespräche 1927–1944, Gesammelte Schriften*, vol. iii (Munich: Chr. Kaiser Verlag, 1960), pp. 262–3.

8 Bonhoeffer, *Ethics*, p. 92.

9 ibid., pp. 96–7.

10 ibid., pp. 272–3.

11 ibid., p. 96.

12 ibid., 'The Right to Bodily Life', pp. 155ff.; also the discussion of rights, pp. 99–100.

13 ibid., p. 98.

14 'Outline for a Book', in Bonhoeffer, *Letters and Papers from Prison*, p. 380.

15 ibid.

16 Bonhoeffer, *Ethics*, p. 55.

17 ibid., p. 59.

18 ibid., p. 149.

19 ibid., pp. 78–9.

20 These are Jean Bethke Elshtain's words, interpreting Bonhoeffer. See her chapter in *Bonhoeffer for a New Day: Theology in a Time of Transition*, ed. J. de Gruchy (Grand Rapids: Eerdmans, 1997), p. 225.

21 Bonhoeffer, *Ethics*, p. 79.

22 The phrase from 'After Ten Years' with which we began this section.

23 This is one of the many insights in the important treatment of Bonhoeffer's ethics done by Hans Pfeifer, 'Ethics for the Renewal of Life: A Reconstruction of its Concept', in de Gruchy, *Bonhoeffer for a New Day*, p. 141. Pfeifer's essay is important for the entire discussion above, and especially for the constructive response of Bonhoeffer to the need for a new ethic.

24 See note 1 in I. Toedt, *Zettelnotizen für eine 'Ethik'* (Munich: Chr. Kaiser Verlag, 1993), pp. 47–8.

25 ibid.

26 'How the Prison Letters Survived', in E. Bethge, *Friendship and Resistance: Essays on Dietrich Bonhoeffer* (Geneva: WCC, 1995), pp. 38–57.

27 'Letter of 18 November 1943', in Bonhoeffer, *Letters and Papers from Prison*, p. 129.

28 'Letter of 15 December 1943', ibid., p. 163.

29 Bonhoeffer, *Ethics*, p. 195.

30 ibid., p. 195.

31 'Outline for a Book', in Bonhoeffer, *Letters and Papers from Prison*, p. 382.

32 D. Bonhoeffer, *Christ the Centre*, trans. E. H. Robertson (New York: Harper & Row, 1978), p. 62.

33 ibid., p. 47.

34 ibid., p. 48.

35 'Outline for a Book', in Bonhoeffer, *Letters and Papers from Prison*, p. 382.

36 ibid., p. 202.

37 ibid., p. 381.

38 D. Bonhoeffer, *The Communion of Saints* (New York: Harper & Row, 1963), pp. 36–7.

39 'Outline for a Book', in Bonhoeffer, *Letters and Papers from Prison*, pp. 381–2.

40 Bonhoeffer, *The Communion of Saints*, p. 33.

41 Bonhoeffer, *Ethics*, p. 241.

42 ibid., p. 195.

43 *Antwort* is the German for 'answer', and *Verantwortung* is responsibility as 'answering to'.

44 Bonhoeffer, *Ethics*, p. 245.

45 From an early lecture by Bonhoeffer on 'Basic Questions in Christian Ethics', given in Barcelona in 1929, published in Bonhoeffer, *Theologie Gemeinde*, p. 56.

46 Bonhoeffer, *Ethics*, p. 85.

47 D. Bonhoeffer, *No Rusty Swords: Letters, Lectures and Notes, 1928–1936, Collected Works of Dietrich Bonhoeffer*, vol. I (New York: Harper & Row, 1965), pp. 161–2.

48 Bonhoeffer, *Ethics*, p. 149.

49 ibid., p. 156.

50 ibid., p. 183.

51 ibid., p. 283.

52 ibid., p. 238.

53 'After Ten Years', in Bonhoeffer, *Letters and Papers from Prison*, p. 6.

54 ibid., p. 5.

55 ibid., p. 6.

56 ibid., p. 3.

57 ibid., p. 7.

12 Christianity in a world come of age

PETER SELBY

> One may ask whether there have ever before in human history been
> people with so little ground under their feet.[1]

It is not uncommon to find that the best-known writings of an author are the
most difficult to examine. Familiarity produces its own 'readings' of a text,
an audience already clear what its central content amounts to, and certainly
clear about any impact the text may have made on them personally. Unlike
some of Dietrich Bonhoeffer's earlier texts, the *Letters and Papers from
Prison*[2] have a place in the life of many who, perhaps as a result, come to
want to study him further. It is *Letters and Papers from Prison* that are the
home of those evocative phrases, 'a world come of age', 'the religious *a
priori*' and 'religionless Christianity', and therefore it is in *Letters and Papers
from Prison* that those who have sought Bonhoeffer's support for their
agenda for the interpretation of the Christian faith so as to take account of
the changed thought patterns of the contemporary world have found it.

In the midst of these theological explorations there are other phrases of
a profoundly evocative quality, such as the reference to God's being 'pushed
out of the world on to the Cross',[3] that have offered themselves for use in the
devotion of many subsequent believers. Here also is an utterly engaging
human story, with its insight into the way in which a particular person
survived in the uncertain, frightening and potentially demoralising circumstances of imprisonment: we learn of his love for and a little of his taste in
music, of the kind of life for which he longed and the way in which he
managed the intense loneliness of his situation. At the heart of the letters is
a warm human being, a passionate lover of life, with enough capacity to
engage his readers (readers he never envisaged), even if they had no
particular interest in theology. We have also now been given access to
another aspect of this compelling human story by the publication of Bonhoeffer's correspondence with his fiancée, Maria von Wedemeyer, herself a

person who emerges with increasing and impressive clarity as a result. Before the publication of *Love Letters from Cell 92*[4] she appears in *Letters and Papers from Prison* only as a person written about, and through the very restrained words of the appendix, 'The Other Letters from Prison',[5] written while their correspondence was still withheld from publication.

It is important for those pursuing an interest in Bonhoeffer's contribution to a present-day theological agenda (the principal concern of this chapter) to recognise that the letters were not always read primarily with that interest in mind. The English title is a translation of the German subtitle, *Briefe und Aufzeichnungen aus der Haft.* The title of the 1970 original German edition was *Widerstand und Ergebung,* suggesting a primary concern with Bonhoeffer's contribution as a model of Christian discipleship, and of the demands of 'resistance and submission' in the uniquely terrifying context of the Third Reich. It should also be recognised that the publication of the correspondence between Bonhoeffer and his fiancée as a separate volume with the designation 'love letters' represents in its own way a direction as to where the editors wish the reader's interest to lie, somewhere quite different from that envisaged by the editor of *Widerstand und Ergebung.*

This awareness of Bonhoeffer as a person who even in the mere fifty years which have elapsed since his death has been subject to a range of different 'readings' should be a warning also to those seeking to make a contemporary assessment of his contribution to continuing theological discussion. For here too the concerns that have predominated in past readings of Bonhoeffer have been many and varied. The choice of 'Christianity in the modern world' as the theme of this chapter, should not beguile us into thinking that there has emerged over the years an agreed 'modern world' to which the prison letters make a theological contribution, or indeed that there would have been agreement on the kind of contribution that would count as 'theological' in character. As we shall see, a large part of the power of the prison letters has lain in that aspect of them that has also been subject to most criticism: their unfinished quality, their often hurried and condensed language, the lack of definition of some of the key terms and the questions which their profound and tantalising reflections leave unanswered.

For those who found themselves greeting the suggestive comments of *Letters and Papers from Prison* with enthusiasm there is also often something of a sense of anti-climax. The point at which Bonhoeffer became an inescapable influence in the English-speaking world was the publication of John A. T. Robinson's *Honest to God* in 1963. This was the point at which an audience who, if they had heard of Bonhoeffer at all, knew of him as the author of *The Cost of Discipleship*, a book which had been interpreted largely for devotional purposes, became aware of phrases which seemed to accord with the needs of the liberal Christianity of the time. Robinson himself was very well aware that the excerpts from *Letters and Papers from Prison* which he quoted and the phrases to which he gave currency did not present a balanced view of the whole of Bonhoeffer's theology, for he writes, 'I have made no attempt to give a balanced picture of Bonhoeffer's theology as a whole, which cannot be done by concentrating, as I have done, on this final flowering of it',[6] a revealing tribute to what *Letters and Papers from Prison* had meant to him. That first excitement led him, like so many others, to return to earlier parts of Bonhoeffer's writing, particularly the *Christology*, when ten years after *Honest to God* Robinson published his own Christological exploration, *The Human Face of God*.[7] There he recognises in Bonhoeffer a kindred spirit, struggling with the understanding of the person of Christ, in particular with the tradition of Christ's perfect goodness, even if he did not find Bonhoeffer's solution at all satisfactory, and has delved more deeply into the range of his thinking than appeared in the writing of *Honest to God*.[8]

An examination of Bonhoeffer's earlier writing did for Robinson what it has done for many who have read more widely in the Bonhoeffer inheritance, after a first acquaintance with *Letters and Papers from Prison*; namely it underlined the many unresolved issues which they leave. For what is hinted at in the most evocative of the language of the letters turns out to point in a number of different directions, rather than being the sustained affirmation of modernity that first seemed to present itself. This apostle of secular Christianity turns out to be remarkably attached to its central doctrinal inheritance; this protagonist of what came to be celebrated as 'religionless Christianity' is clearly immersed in a tradition of piety and devotion from which he derived enormous sustenance and which echoes with the sounds of a lifetime's spiritual formation; this determined advocate of human autonomy and secular strength is constantly searching for the way of obedience to Christ's claim upon his life; and Bonhoeffer the disciple determined to share the fate of God who suffers at the hands of a godless world shows no sign of the disdain for life and its beauty and delight which sometimes characterises those willing to suffer and die for their faith.

It is no part of the intention of this chapter to gloss over these apparent disjunctions, but on the contrary to see them as the signs of the continuing capacity of the Dietrich Bonhoeffer of *Letters and Papers from Prison* to address humanity in our time. The argument that will be set out here is, in brief, that Bonhoeffer's crucial contribution through *Letters and Papers from Prison* lies in the fact that he dared to see humanity's passing out of the era of 'religion' as, on the one hand, an emancipation and a historical development and, on the other, as a working out of God's purpose revealed in Christ; that therefore discipleship could be truly *worldly* without *accommodation to* the world, and involved living 'before God, without God, as God requires'; that Christ is to be at the centre precisely as and not in spite of God's having been edged out of the world on to the cross. In short, the development of thought called 'coming of age' could be seen as part of a regaining of humanity's whole destiny, part of the Christian vision of what that destiny could be, precisely as Christ expresses it in his continued *presence in* the world without *accommodation to* the world; and finally that Bonhoeffer was able to understand his own and others' participation in the church struggle and in the resistance to Hitler as a working out of humanity's calling as responsible in the world, charged above all to use the capacity to speak in order to be the voice of those who had been deprived of their own right to do so (Proverbs 31:8). Thus the huge variety of different ways in which *Letters and Papers from Prison* has been read are a demonstration not of their ambiguity or inconsistency, but rather of their unusual capacity to bring together aspects of Christianity's engagement with modernity which are too frequently seen as disconnected or even as contradictory.

Before we embark on an examination of the main themes of *Letters and Papers from Prison*, a word is in order about the term 'modernity' as it is used in this chapter, given the currency of the term 'post-modernity' in much discussion at the present time. Bonhoeffer is preoccupied in his prison reflections with what he sees as a major development in human thought, with the passing of the age of 'religion', and with the question that implies for the meaning of Christianity in our time.

> Our whole nineteen-hundred-year-old Christian preaching and theology rest on the 'religious *a priori*' of mankind. 'Christianity' has always been a form – perhaps the true form – of 'religion'. But if one day it becomes clear that this *a priori* does not exist at all, but was a historically conditioned and transient form of human self-expression, and if therefore humanity becomes radically religionless – and I think that that is already more or less the case (else how is it, for example, that this war, in contrast to all previous ones, is not calling forth any 'religious' reaction?) – what does that mean for 'Christianity'? It means that the foundation is taken away from the whole of what has up to now been our 'Christianity', and that there remain only a few

'last survivors of the age of chivalry', or a few intellectually dishonest people, on whom we can descend as 'religious'. Are they to be the chosen few? Is it on this dubious group of people that we are to pounce in fervour, pique, or indignation, in order to sell them our goods? [9]

However sharp we may consider such judgements to be, and in the light of the present situation of religions in the world, however over-simplified his proclamation of the end of religion, his question represents no diminution of his commitment to Christian faith and the communication of it to his contemporaries. For the question that follows only lines after this diagnosis is, 'How can Christ become the Lord of the religionless as well?' His question about the possibility of a 'religionless' form of Christianity, controversial as it is – what he in fact calls for is the non-religious interpretation of biblical concepts – arises from that concern and no other.

So this extract from the letter of 30 April 1944 expresses the passion that excites Bonhoeffer in his prison cell, and defines the 'modernity' with which he is concerned. The development known as 'post-modernity', the abandonment of any quest for an overarching narrative or conceptual framework for the encompassing of reality, does not come within the range of his concern; but what he has to say about the shape of Christianity applies equally – perhaps even more – to the questions raised by post-modernity: the aspect of present-day culture with which he is primarily concerned, the end of 'religion', is the matter to which we shall be attending. As will appear, this has been the most fundamental, and also the most elusive, issue with which *Letters and Papers from Prison* has troubled its readers.

THE END OF RELIGION?

One of the most significant accounts he gives of his meaning is in a passage in his letter of 5 May 1944, where we are assisted by the fact that he specifically contrasts his project with Bultmann's essay on the 'demythologising' of the New Testament.

My view of it today would be, not that he went 'too far', as most people thought, but that he didn't go far enough. It's not only the 'mythological' concepts, such as miracle, ascension, and so on (which are not in principle separable from the concepts of God, faith, etc.), but 'religious' concepts generally, which are problematic. You can't, as Bultmann supposes, separate God and miracle, but you must be able to interpret and proclaim *both* in a 'non-religious' sense. Bultmann's approach is fundamentally still a liberal one (i.e. abridging the gospel), whereas I'm trying to think theologically.[10]

Equally he links his project to, while at the same time distancing himself from, Barth's criticism of religion.

> Barth was the first theologian to begin the criticism of religion, and that remains his really great merit; but he put in its place a positivist doctrine of revelation which says in effect, 'Like it or lump it': virgin birth, Trinity, or anything else; each is an equally significant and necessary part of the whole, which must simply be swallowed as a whole or not at all.[11]

Barth himself was clearly perplexed by Bonhoeffer's account of his positivism of revelation, and in his letter of December 1952 to Landessuperintendent P. W. Herrenbrück expresses the hope that 'in heaven at least he has not reported about me to *all* the angels (including the church fathers), with just this expression'.[12] At the same time he was clearly intrigued by Bonhoeffer's project and also saw it as very different from Bultmann's, for in the same letter he wrote:

> The letters, whatever one may make of their individual sentences . . . are a particular thorn; to let them excite us can only do us all good – for unlike 'demythologising', this is unrest of a spiritual kind.[13]

That this is 'unrest of a spiritual kind' is due to the fact that Bonhoeffer sees the biblical imperative and the requirements of contemporary humanity coming together in the utter necessity of speaking in a non-religious way. For if religion speaks of God

> on the one hand metaphysically and on the other hand individualistically [n]either of these is relevant to the biblical message or to the person of today. Hasn't the individualistic question about personal salvation almost completely left us all? Aren't we really under the impression that there are more important things than that question (perhaps not more important than the *matter* itself, but more important than the *question*!)? I know it sounds pretty monstrous to say that. But isn't this in fact biblical? Does the question about saving one's soul appear in the Old Testament at all? Aren't righteousness and the Kingdom of God on earth the focus of everything, and isn't it true that Romans 3.24ff. is not an individualistic doctrine of salvation, but the culmination of the view that God alone is righteous? It is not

with the beyond that we are concerned, but with this world as created and preserved, subjected to laws, reconciled, and restored.[14]

Clearly such a passage as this leaves many questions unanswered: can one speak of a world 'created and preserved' without some metaphysic? In what sense is the *matter* of personal salvation, which has not ceased to be important, to be distinguished from the *question* of it, which has?

These major issues are clearly still unresolved. Bonhoeffer's language undoubtedly opens him to Hans Schmidt's accusation that his 'trust in the self-sufficiency of autonomous reason was a fateful illusion closely bound to the modern superstition of the myth of belief in science'. His words could therefore abandon human beings 'charged with responsibility for the world to the hopeless circle of abstract reason, or to secondary political causes'.[15] Yet even a person making that charge is bound to make clear that

> Bonhoeffer's leading intention, which was there from the beginning, is not disposed of. There is a clear line to be discerned: to a society which is freeing itself . . . the word of God should once more be so proclaimed that the world would change and renew itself. The ultimate must lay claim to the penultimate once more.[16]

Given the history through which he had lived and was still living, it may not be particularly surprising that Bonhoeffer wished to distance himself from the accommodations of liberal theology. He knew only too well how essential the contribution of Barth had been to the saving of the church from absorption into the culture with which it had been presented. As Ernst Feil says in his study, Bonhoeffer knew very well why he had followed Barth. What is perhaps more remarkable, given that history, is Bonhoeffer's preparedness to risk again dealing with the questions of modernity which had generated liberal theology. It is that double 'following' which represents the particular creative edge of Bonhoeffer's theology, even if taking it seriously has meant releasing him from the 'liberal' reading of him of some decades ago. As Feil puts it:

> It has been argued in some circles that Bonhoeffer's view of religionless Christianity in a world come of age is not as radical, not as exciting, and certainly not as troublesome as many of his alleged followers and opponents believe . . . It must be said that the transformation of the church's form in a new period of our understanding of the world is presumably more radical when the church reacts positively to that process and embraces its heritage in a positive way as well.[17]

HUMAN AUTONOMY

Bonhoeffer's view of the modernity to which Christianity now has to make a new response is most coherently expressed in his letter of 8 June 1944, where he outlines his view of the nature of the historical development. He expresses it uncompromisingly:

> The movement that began about the thirteenth century (I'm not going to get involved in any argument about the exact date) towards the autonomy of man (in which I should include the discovery of the laws by which the world lives and deals with itself in science, social and political matters, art, ethics, and religion) has in our time reached an undoubted completion. Man has learnt to deal with himself in all questions of importance without recourse to the 'working hypothesis' called God. In questions of science, art, and ethics this has become an understood thing at which one hardly dares to tilt.[18]

It is important to interject here that it is only more recently that such words have come to seem generally far too one-sided a description of the progress of human thought and the point at which it has arrived. When Robinson quoted this letter at length,[19] Bonhoeffer's words could far more readily seem an unquestionable assertion than would be the case today, when positivist statements about what science has 'proved' seem far more dubious. We can now see many reasons to doubt Bonhoeffer's statements about the final triumph of secularity, from the rise of religious fundamentalism to some of the reflections of scientists open to the mysteriousness of the scale of the universe and the interaction of forces and the character of subatomic particles. The most challenging assertion Bonhoeffer was to make, however, was that this history which had led to the growth of human autonomy in the fields of science, politics and culture was going to continue to erode the place of 'God' even in those areas of life that had been the arena of religious faith.

> But for the last hundred years or so [this sense of human autonomy] has also become increasingly true of religious questions; it is becoming evident that everything gets along without 'God' – and, in fact, just as well as before. As in the scientific field, so in human affairs generally, 'God' is being pushed more and more out of life, losing more and more ground.[20]

Bonhoeffer is not unaware that some of the self-confidence engendered by this history runs into 'failures and false developments'; but his point is that even these 'do not make the world doubt the necessity of the course that it is taking, or of its development; they are accepted with fortitude and detachment as part of the bargain'. As he proceeds, it becomes clear that he is not vulnerable to the charge of hubris, exulting in a development that is wholly good, but feeling required, for himself and for the church, to face up to the truth about it.

He is dubious about all attempts to avoid the implications of this growth in human autonomy. One of the books he was reading, Weizsäcker's *The World-View of Physics*, brings home to him, he says,

> how wrong it is to use God as a stop-gap for the incompleteness of our knowledge. If in fact the frontiers of knowledge are being pushed further and further back (and that is bound to be the case), then God is being pushed back with them, and is therefore continually in retreat. We are to find God in what we know, not in what we don't know; God wants us to realise his presence, not in unsolved problems but in those that are solved.[21]

Later in the letter of 16 July he returns to the history of human autonomy, which he describes as the 'one great development'. He lists the scientific, political and philosophical giants of Western intellectual development. In a terribly brief sweep he includes Herbert, Montaigne, Bodin and Machiavelli, before coming to Grotius, 'setting up his natural law as international law, which is valid *etsi deus non daretur*, "even if there were no God"'.[22] Again, out of that development, he is able to say,

> It seems that in the natural sciences the process begins with Nicolas of Cusa and Giordano Bruno and the 'heretical' doctrine of the infinity of the universe. The classical *cosmos* was finite, like the created world of the Middle Ages. An infinite universe, however it may be conceived, is self-subsisting, *etsi deus non daretur*. It is true that modern physics is not as sure as it was about the infinity of the universe, but it has not gone back to the earlier conception of its finitude.
>
> God as a working hypothesis in morals, politics, or science, has been surmounted and abolished; and the same thing has happened in philosophy and religion (Feuerbach!). For the sake of intellectual honesty, that working hypothesis should be dropped, or as far as possible eliminated.[23]

It is this survey of intellectual development that leads him to make his passionate appeal for a Christianity appropriate to a new situation:

We cannot be honest unless we recognise that we have to live in the world *etsi deus non daretur.* And this is just what we do recognise – before God. God himself compels us to recognise it. So our coming of age leads us to a true recognition of our situation before God. God would have us know that we must live as men who manage our lives without him. The God who is with us is the God who forsakes us (Mark 15.34). The God who lets us live in the world without God is the God before whom we stand continually. Before God and with God we live without God. God lets himself be pushed out of the world on to the cross. He is weak and powerless in the world, and that is precisely the way, the only way, in which he is with us and helps us. Matt. 8.17 makes it quite clear that Christ helps us, not by virtue of his omnipotence, but by virtue of his weakness and suffering.[24]

This passage is particularly worth quoting because it illustrates so clearly the main contention of this chapter: Bonhoeffer insists *both* on a historical development leading to human autonomy *and* on a gospel impetus to autonomy, both requiring a situation where the *deus ex machina* is replaced by a God who is truly a suffering participant within the life of the world. The passage also makes clear how important it is to note the context from which Bonhoeffer's most evocative phrases come. The slogan-presentation of Bonhoeffer as advocating 'living in the world as though God did not exist' needs to be modified by reference to the meaning the phrase has in Grotius: 'as though God were not a given', i.e. without the 'working hypothesis of God'. That is what enables him to say that it is God who requires us to live in that way.

The historical development Bonhoeffer sketches has not been without resistance and response, as he himself tells us. Even though there has been, as he puts it, surrender on all secular problems, attempts are made to find refuge in the 'ultimate questions' of death and guilt as areas where 'God' is still needed. He insists, in the letter of 8 June 1944 already quoted on p. 233 above, that what is true of the advance of science is also true in relation to the 'wider human problems'. Even to rely on 'ultimate questions' as a place for God leaves God in effect retreating before the advance of human autonomy. His reflection on the ineffectiveness of this apologetic strategy leads him to make one of his best-known and most scathing criticisms of all attempts to salvage a place for Christianity on the basis of the maintenance of 'religion'.

But what if one day [these ultimate questions] no longer exist as such, if they too can be answered 'without God'? Of course, we now have the secularised offshoots of Christian theology, namely existentialist philosophy and the psychotherapists, who demonstrate to secure, contented and happy mankind that it is really unhappy and desperate and simply unwilling to admit that it is in a predicament about which it knows nothing, and from which only they can rescue it. Wherever there is health, strength, security, simplicity, they scent luscious fruit to gnaw at or to lay their pernicious eggs in. They set themselves to drive people to inward despair, and then the game is in their hands.[25]

And in the same letter, he delivers the *coup de grâce* to what he sees as the refusal to face the implications of the history of human autonomy by the churches: it is useless as well as a failure to grant the force of the gospel.

The attack by Christian apologetic on the adulthood of the world I consider to be in the first place pointless, in the second place ignoble, and in the third place unchristian. Pointless, because it seems to me like an attempt to put a grown-up man back into adolescence, i.e. to make him dependent on the things on which he is, in fact, no longer dependent, and thrusting him into problems that are, in fact, no longer problems to him. Ignoble, because it amounts to an attempt to exploit man's weakness for purposes that are alien to him and to which he has not freely assented. Unchristian, because it confuses Christ with one particular stage in man's religiousness, i.e. with a human law.[26]

For, as he remarks in the letter of 8 July, the history of developing human autonomy, the 'displacement of God from the world, and from the public part of human life, led to the attempt to keep his place secure at least in the sphere of the "personal", the "inner", and the "private"', a strategy equally contemptible in his view, a twofold theological error:

First, it is thought that a man can be addressed as a sinner only after his weaknesses and meannesses have been spied out. Secondly, it is thought that a man's essential nature consists of his inmost and most intimate background; that is defined as his 'inner life', and it is precisely in those secret human places that God is to have his domain.[27]

Constantly as Bonhoeffer reflects on these issues, there come together in his mind reflections on the history of human autonomy as simply a develop-ment to which a response has to be made, and theological reflections on the character of the gospel. So his reference to religion as 'a human law' is pressed home in the postscript to his letter of 30 April, where he daringly compares the place of religion in the modern world with St Paul's discussion of circumcision: 'the Pauline question whether *peritomē* [circumcision] is a condition of justification seems to me in present-day terms to be whether religion is a condition of salvation. Freedom from *peritomē* is also freedom from religion.'[28]

It is clear that for Bonhoeffer 'religion' is opposed to autonomy, undermining of human strength and ultimately of the love of life. He reflects, in the postscript just quoted, on his reluctance to talk about God with those who are religious, in contrast with his ability to do so with 'secular' human beings. The contrast lies in the fact that religious people

> speak of God when human knowledge . . . has come to an end, or
> when human resources fail – in fact it is always the *deus ex machina*
> that they bring on to the scene, either for the apparent solution of
> insoluble problems, or as strength in human failure – always, that is to
> say, exploiting human weakness or human boundaries.[29]

Such is the reflection behind his famous poem 'Christians and Pagans',[30] contrasting as it does the 'religious' approach to God in weakness with the Christian response to God, standing by God in his hour of grieving. It is this radical response to the historical development of human autonomy – which is also a demand of the gospel – that constitutes for Bonhoeffer the distinctively Christian, and not at all necessarily religious, way of life.

Bonhoeffer's agenda in *Letters and Papers from Prison*, often presented under the banner 'Christ for a world come of age', sounded immensely creative to so many who came upon it because of the declaration it seemed to make about us and our society. It is good to hear yourself described as mature, and the words seemed to carry that implication. Like all metaphors, it took on a life of its own, as a statement about the end of childish things and the possibility of an end to all kinds of tutelage and humanity's emergence into adult, autonomous living. There is no doubt that much of what is in *Letters and Papers from Prison* can be read in a way that would support that interpretation; when they first reached a wider English-speaking public it was also too easy to forget that a protest for adulthood and against tutelage might mean something very different in the context of Nazi imprisonment. It is in any case worth adding that Bonhoeffer made general statements about the society in which he lived without making any use of what would now certainly be regarded as the essential empirical tools: in one of the earliest collections of essays on Bonhoeffer, the sociologist Peter Berger makes the point that Bonhoeffer's doctoral dissertation *Sanctorum*

Communio is subtitled 'A Systematic Enquiry into the Sociology of the Church' but makes use only of abstract, philosophical methods.[31]

That reading of *die mündige Welt* (the world that is of age) or *die mündig gewordene Welt* (the world that has become of age) as only or primarily to do with adulthood has certainly proved helpful in a number of causes in the general struggle for a church, and a world, that takes seriously the autonomy of persons and resists its own constant tendency to mistrust people's capacity to make their own decisions and come to their own conclusions. But there is without doubt a way in which such a reading can be highly misleading: the metaphor of age and adulthood can be read, if we so wish, as describing a process that is developmental, even inevitable and then (most deceptive of all) irrevocable. In so far as Bonhoeffer is describing a historical development leading to the *Mündigkeit* of the world, that interpretation of his language was to be expected, and was perhaps largely the one in his mind.

Not surprisingly, however, such a view of a historical development leading to 'adulthood' is not one that easily commends itself to societies which have not shared in that intellectual and cultural tradition, as John de Gruchy points out in his reflections on the relation of Bonhoeffer's thought to the life of South Africa in the days of its struggle against apartheid.

> We have not referred at all in this essay to Bonhoeffer's thinking in prison about Christianity in a 'world come of age'. The reason for this is that his earlier writings appear to be more relevant to our present situation. Moreover, there is a sense in which the Enlightenment as an historical event has passed us by at the southern tip of Africa, and therefore we are still a religious rather than a secular society.[32]

Among the most important developments of the decades since Bonhoeffer's death has been the increased consciousness of the cultures of Africa, Asia and Latin America, and therefore of the inappropriateness of allowing the experience of European and North American Christianity to be decisive for the future of Christian faith world-wide. For societies living under oppression, for cultures which have been largely ignored, for vast tracts of the world suffering deprivation of many kinds, for the economically dominated societies which are victims of international indebtedness[33] the notion of humanity's having come of age and of their having gained the human autonomy of which Bonhoeffer speaks and about which those who read him were so excited will be largely incredible.

Yet the metaphor of *Mündigkeit* can make a more profound point. It is rooted in the word *Mund*, 'mouth'; its reference is to the point where someone is a legally responsible person, able to speak for herself and enter into obligations on her own account. In most cases, of course, that point is arrived at through the passing of the years, when a person reaches the age of majority and is not any longer regarded as, to use the Latin metaphor, in-fant, unable to speak. But there are categories besides the young who are denied the right to speak for themselves: the imprisoned and those certified as insane, not to mention the whole list of *Unmenschen*, non-persons who have been the creation of the Third Reich – and not just the Third Reich.

Once we remove the connotations of inevitability and irrevocability from our perception of the human situation in the modern era, the language of a world 'come of age' can hold out, in a contemporary reading and appropriation of the testimony of Dietrich Bonhoeffer, a vision that is both realistic and challenging. We shall not be naïvely blind to the possibility that people, societies and communities will be put back 'under guardianship' willingly or unwillingly, deprived of autonomy and the right to act responsibly, *entmündigt*, as the German would render it, put under administration, reduced to the level where their own decisions count for nothing. Thus understood, the high cost and the tremendous fragility of the declaration that the world is of age come very quickly and clearly before our eyes, as does the great difficulty which human beings have in bearing that reality. Not surprisingly, those who have shared in the inheritance of human autonomy have gained from *Letters and Papers from Prison* primarily the sense of solidarity with one who resisted on behalf of those who had been *entmündigt* in his day, who 'opened his mouth for those who had no voice'.

ETHICAL ACTION AND THE SUFFERING OF GOD

We do well to recall that the estimate of Bonhoeffer's career and contribution remained controversial long after his death. The language of 'exile and martyr', as the title of Bethge's 1975 book has him, complements the words that appear in the title of his classic biography, 'theologian, Christian, contemporary'. What was this man seeking to do and to be as a Christian? Was he a Christian saint determined, as the language of *The Cost of Discipleship* suggests, to live by the Sermon on the Mount? His last recorded words, 'This is the end, for me the beginning of life',[34] conform to the pattern of the Christian tradition of the devout death, and at least initially he was accorded the status of a martyr for the faith, one who died for the truth. Yet here too questions are raised both by his self-understanding and by the related, and much-debated, issue of his 'martyrdom'. Among the papers written to commemorate the sixtieth anniversary of the meeting

Bonhoeffer and other German Evangelical pastors in Britain held in Bradford in 1933 is one by Haddon Willmer on the problem posed for Bonhoeffer study by Bonhoeffer's 'sanctity'. He quotes from the letter Bonhoeffer
wrote on the day on which he learnt of the failure of the plot of 20 July 1944
to kill Hitler:

> [I]t is only by living completely in this world that one learns to have
> faith. One must completely abandon any attempt to make something
> of oneself, whether it be a saint, or a converted sinner, or a churchman
> . . . By this-worldliness I mean living unreservedly in life's duties,
> problems, successes and failures, experiences and perplexities. In so
> doing we throw ourselves completely into the arms of God, taking
> seriously not our own sufferings, but those of God in the world –
> watching with Christ in Gethsemane.[35]

If the quest for sanctity turns out not to be what Bonhoeffer thought
important, it was not long after his death that a debate also ensued about
whether someone complicit in an attempt to assassinate the German Head
of State could properly be designated a martyr. Fifty years of knowing the
evil Hitler represented should not prevent us from seeing the real force of
that question. What has happened, however, is that Bonhoeffer, in what
Willmer calls his 'subsequent posthumous career as a saint', has come to
attract admiration precisely because of, rather than despite, the recognised
ambiguity of his actions. 'Bonhoeffer's status in many circles as one of the
few, perhaps the only, Protestant candidate for sanctity to come out of Nazi
Germany, depends precisely on his willingness to incur guilt politically.'[36] In
fact the letter from which Willmer quotes contains in an earlier paragraph a
clue to the development of Bonhoeffer's thinking over his time in prison:

> During the last year or so I've come to know and understand more and
> more the profound this-worldliness of Christianity. The Christian is
> not a *homo religiosus*, but simply a man, as Jesus was a man – in
> contrast, shall we say, with John the Baptist. I don't mean the shallow
> and banal this-worldliness of the enlightened, the busy, the
> comfortable, or the lascivious, but the profound this-worldliness,
> characterised by discipline and the constant knowledge of death and
> resurrection. I think Luther lived a this-worldly life in this sense.[37]

This is a paragraph which summarises very well almost the whole
burden of his earlier *Ethics* and, written, as has been said, on the day he
heard of the failure of the plot to kill Hitler, it speaks about a 'this-
worldliness' of a very different kind from what later decades came to think

of Bonhoeffer's teaching about a 'this-worldly transcendence'. The debates surrounding Bonhoeffer's Christian praxis are therefore and inevitably debates about the character of Christian engagement. That is as it should be: remembering is not about building monuments to the prophets as an alibi for meeting the challenges of our time, and acknowledging the contribution of a particular Christian person of action means inevitably working at what action is required in our own situation. Rightly *Letters and Papers from Prison* have provoked much reflection on the challenge presented to us by what was done and risked not just by Bonhoeffer, and indeed not just by Christian believers, but by all those in Germany who dared to resist the tide of National Socialism. There was for Bonhoeffer the most intimate link between human autonomy, 'this-worldly holiness' and sharing in the suffering of God. 'How', he asks in the same letter, 'can success make us arrogant or failure lead us astray, when we share in God's sufferings through a life of this kind?'

Writing just two years after Robinson's *Honest to God*, but from the vantage point which Germany provided for an appreciation of Bonhoeffer's meaning, Dorothee Sölle indicts modern atheism no less than religious belief for its insistence that God must answer for the suffering in the world. Quoting Bonhoeffer's comment in the letter of 16 July, 'Man's religiosity makes him look in his distress to the power of God in the world; he uses God as a *Deus ex machina*. The Bible however directs him to the powerlessness and suffering of God; only a suffering God can help',[38] she makes the point that the God 'who is arraigned on behalf of the innocent is really the omnipotent God, the king, the father, and ruler, who is above the world. Modern man rightly indicts this God.'[39] Perhaps in the nineteenth century, suffering was still the 'rock of atheism'; but by contrast, she asserts,

> nothing is so eloquent of God in our own century as his defeat in the world. That God in the world has been, and still is, mocked and tortured, burnt and gassed: that is the rock of Christian faith which rests all its hope on God attaining his identity.[40]

Towards the end of *Letters and Papers from Prison* we find Bonhoeffer's 'Outline for a Book',[41] where he captures in a mere four pages most of the themes we have extracted from the letters. His first chapter was to deal with 'the coming of age of mankind' and the second with 'God and the secular', and the third is a radical call to the church to be Christian. 'The church is the church only when it exists for others.' He meant this not as mere rhetoric, but as a practical programme, involving the giving away of its property. Whether he would have advanced the same proposal at this time we shall never know. What is clear is that the roots of the 'church for others' are to be found all through the letters, in their theology and their ecclesiology, all born out of an experience which he described as having been one of 'incomparable value', for he and his fellow conspirators had

> learnt to see the great events of world history from below, from the perspective of the outcast, the suspects, the maltreated . . . in short from the perspective of those who suffer. The important thing is that neither bitterness nor envy should have gnawed at the heart during this time, that we should have come to look with new eyes at matters great and small . . . that our perception of generosity, humanity, justice and mercy should have become clearer, freer, less corruptible.[42]

Those words make something else clear: Bonhoeffer was well aware that he made his spiritual journey starting out from a position of privilege and relative stability. That is also to make clearer the testimony of the letters. He possessed many identities, and apologised for none of them, whether as German, as professional, as Christian, as Lutheran, as pastor, as theologian. His sacrifice was the loss of things he accounted good, but knew were not the supreme good, which was his understanding of and commitment to *Christ for us.* His surrender of life, and his call to the church to be prepared to do the same, was not the surrender of one who had hated his life, but one who had loved it.

Not many days before a family event he was very sad to miss, Bonhoeffer wrote his 'Thoughts on the Day of the Baptism' of his great-nephew, Dietrich Bethge. It is a piece full of the sense of loss and tragedy, yet also welcoming and loving the new possibilities this baby will face. It values his identity in family and society. But then abruptly he comes to the meaning of the baptism, which was to be the source of the most important identity of all. He remarks that the great words of the Christian proclamation will be spoken over the baby without his understanding them. Yet that, he says, is true for the church too, for whom

> all these things are so difficult and so remote that we hardly dare speak of them. In the traditional words and acts we suspect that there may be something quite new and revolutionary, though we cannot as yet grasp or express it. That is our own fault. Our church, which has been fighting in these years only for its self-preservation, as though that were an end in itself, is incapable of taking the word of reconciliation and redemption to the world.[43]

He then and for that reason issues his famous call to a silent witness, to what elsewhere he calls the only true confession which is the deed which interprets itself, the *arcani disciplina* ('the discipline of the secret'), to prayer and righteous action in the world. He goes on nevertheless to speak in hope of the day when it will be possible to speak again 'a new language, perhaps quite non-religious, but liberating and redeeming as was Jesus' language . . . proclaiming God's peace with humanity and the coming of the Kingdom'. Till then he prays that young Dietrich will live out his baptismal identity as one of those who 'pray and do right and wait for God's own time'.

Bonhoeffer's prison letters are those of a person asking whether he, or his church, could be able, is able, to live that identity, to declare *Christ for us* with integrity, and to value the baptismal identity above all the other profoundly valuable ones we possess, and resist all that makes those a privilege to be defended at others' expense. The enduring quality of *Letters and Papers from Prison* lies, therefore, in the question with which they leave us, of what it is to be part of that inheritance.

It will be best to express that question pictorially, by way of conclusion: another resistance fighter, somewhat younger than Bonhoeffer, part of the 'White Rose' movement based in Munich, was Sophie Scholl. She was executed with her brother Hans, with whom she is commemorated today by the Geschwister Scholl Platz, the square outside Munich University. She confided to her cellmate a dream she had had, and it is recorded by her sister Inge in her account of the movement.[44]

Sophie dreamt that she was climbing a hill, carrying a child in baptism robes. Suddenly and without warning she found herself on the edge of a crevasse. She just had time to deposit the child on the far side before herself plunging into the abyss below.

That day Sophie Scholl was beheaded with her brother. The living out of Christianity in the modern world is the task of those who see themselves as people who are essentially godchildren, beneficiaries of the sacrifice and perception of Bonhoeffer and those like him, spared the abyss they endured and seeking to be prepared for the ones that lie ahead.

Notes

1 D. Bonhoeffer, *Letters and Papers from Prison: The Enlarged Edition* (London: SCM, 1971), p. 3.

2 Quotations from the letters and papers in this chapter are all taken from ibid. This was an expansion of the first English edition (London: SCM Press, 1953), and is a translation of *Widerstand und Ergebung: Briefe und Aufzeichnungen aus der Haft* (Munich: Christian Kaiser Verlag, 1970). I have not made the language of that translation inclusive.

3 Bonhoeffer, *Letters and Papers from Prison*, p. 360.

4 D. Bonhoeffer and M. von Wedemeyer, *Love Letters from Cell 92* (London: HarperCollins, 1993).

5 Bonhoeffer, *Letters and Papers from Prison*, pp. 412–19.

6 J. A. T. Robinson, *Honest to God* (London: SCM Press, 1963), p. 36, n. 1.

7 J. A. T. Robinson, *The Human Face of God* (London: SCM Press, 1973).

8 For example, he quotes Bonhoeffer's observation, 'In his flesh too was the law that is contrary to God's will', and follows it up in a long footnote with Bonhoeffer's far stronger statement that Jesus 'was not the perfectly good man. He was continually engaged in struggle. He did things which outwardly sometimes looked like sin.' But Robinson regards Bonhoeffer's solution to this paradox, one in which Jesus' acts might have been sinful though he himself was not, as unsatisfactory. ibid., pp. 93f., n. 125.

9 Bonhoeffer, *Letters and Papers from Prison*, p. 280.

10 ibid., p. 285.

11 ibid., p. 286.

12 J. A. Phillips, *The Form of Christ in the World: A Study of Bonhoeffer's Christology* (London: Collins, 1967), p. 253; also published in *A World Come of Age: A Symposium on Dietrich Bonhoeffer*, ed. R. G. Smith (London: Collins, 1967), pp. 89–92.

13 ibid.

14 Bonhoeffer, *Letters and Papers from Prison*, p. 286.

15 Smith, *A World Come of Age*, p. 241.

16 ibid., p. 242.

17 E. Feil, *The Theology of Dietrich Bonhoeffer* (Philadelphia: Fortress Press, 1985), p. 203.

18 Bonhoeffer, *Letters and Papers from Prison*, p. 325.

19 Robinson, *Honest to God*, p. 36.

20 Bonhoeffer, *Letters and Papers from Prison*, p. 326.

21 ibid., p. 311.

22 ibid., p. 359.

23 ibid.

24 ibid., p. 360.

25 ibid., p. 326.

26 ibid., p. 327.

27 ibid., p. 345.

28 ibid., p. 281.

29 ibid.

30 ibid., p. 348.

31 *The Place of Bonhoeffer: Problems and Possibilities in his Thought*, ed. M. E. Marty (London: SCM, 1963), pp. 53–79.

32 E. Bethge, *Bonhoeffer: Exile and Martyr*, ed. John de Gruchy (London: Collins, 1975), p. 41.

33 This aspect of the loss of autonomy, occasioned in particular by indebtedness, is one I have dealt with more fully in my book *Grace and Mortgage: The Language of Faith and the Debt of the World* (London: Darton, Longman & Todd, 1997). See also 'Jesus Christ for us Today', in *Bonhoeffer for a New Day: Theology in a Time*

of Transition, ed. J. de Gruchy (Grand Rapids: Eerdmans, 1997).

34 E. Bethge, *Dietrich Bonhoeffer: Theologian, Christian, Contemporary* (London: Collins, 1970), p. 830.

35 From the letter of 21 July 1944, quoted in Haddon Willmer, 'Bonhoeffer's Sanctity as a Problem for Bonhoeffer Studies', in *Celebrating Critical Awareness: Bonhoeffer and Bradford 60 Years on* (London: International Bonhoeffer Society, 1993).

36 ibid., p. 10.

37 Bonhoeffer, *Letters and Papers from Prison*, p. 369.

38 ibid., p. 361.

39 D. Sölle, *Christ the Representative: An Essay in Theology After the Death of God* (London: SCM Press, 1967), p. 150.

40 ibid., p. 151.

41 Bonhoeffer, *Letters and Papers from Prison*, pp. 380–3.

42 ibid., p. 17.

43 ibid., p. 300.

44 I. Scholl, *Die weisse Rose* (Frankfurt-on-Main: Fischer, 1986). See also A. Gill, *An Honourable Defeat* (London: Heinemann, 1994).

13 Prayer and action for justice: Bonhoeffer's spirituality

GEFFREY B. KELLY

Those whose only acquaintance with Dietrich Bonhoeffer is limited to his exciting affirmation about 'Christian secularity' in the prison letters and his inspirational role in the plot to kill Hitler are often astonished to learn that he was also a man of daily, at times childlike, prayer. Some early analysts of Bonhoeffer's theology did, in fact, dismiss his most directly 'spiritual litera-ture', *The Cost of Discipleship* and *Life Together*, as deviations from the exemplary activism that reached crescendo pitch in the anti-Hitler conspir-acy and his goading the churches to responsible action against the state in the *Ethics*. These writings, however, were far from being 'devotional' de-tours. They reflect enduring, faith-filled sources of Bonhoeffer's inner stam-ina, his profound 'spirituality', without which he could never have per-severed in his struggle against Nazism.

Discerning the rhythms of Bonhoeffer's 'spiritual strength', which is the focus of this study, brings us time and again to the intrinsic connection between prayer and action as expressed in his daily meditation on the biblical word, his efforts to form genuine Christian community, and his willingness to be led by God's grace to take Christlike risks to retrieve freedom and justice for a nation under the heel of a cruel dictatorship. These were the 'Powers for Good', to cite a phrase from one of his poems,[1] that steadied him in his resistance to Nazism. They also distinguish his Christ-centred spirituality from false piety and idolatrous religion.

FALSE PIETY AND IDOLATROUS RELIGION

Bonhoeffer's own attunement to what following Jesus Christ demanded made him wary of the pietistic shield behind which many believers hid their infidelity to the gospel. He was gifted with an extraordinary ability to recognise and expose the moral obtuseness and political opportunism that gave the lie to self-serving assertions that Christian faith was congruent with the dictates of Adolf Hitler. Having witnessed the nazification of the churches, Bonhoeffer was angered by the betrayal of the gospel by a so-called Christian society.

Phrases can be found in several of Bonhoeffer's collected writings in which he voices his suspicions that church life and the profession of faith had been cheapened by an easy accommodation to a paganised world. The ecclesiastical endorsements of Nazism's promise for a more law-abiding, orderly society had alerted him to the churches' proclivity for entering into unholy alliances with tainted political systems. Even a seemingly harmless sermon, such as he described in his diary in 1939, could stir up his inner malaise over the church's failure to be Christ to the world. On that occasion Bonhoeffer lamented that a worship service he had attended in a prominent Riverside, New York, church was nothing more than 'a respectable, self-indulgent, self-satisfied religious celebration'. For Bonhoeffer, that service represented the 'sort of idolatrous religion' that 'stirs up the flesh which is accustomed to being kept in check by the Word of God'. He complained that the sermon reeked of 'libertinism, egotism, and indifference'.[2]

Far from being ungracious towards his American hosts, Bonhoeffer's criticisms of that service were consistent with his reproachful attitude towards the churches of Germany. His was an unabashed outspokenness against anything that could erode genuine Christian community and subvert the word of God, whether from the pulpit, the academic podium or in one's daily life. What he missed in that spongy sermon was a biblical focus on Jesus Christ and on the gospel's repudiation of the bloated complacency that had infected Christian churches around the world. He had, likewise, had enough of the American churches' claim that because they were nestled in the 'land of the free', their people enjoyed unparalleled freedoms, including freedom of speech and worship. True enough, if this meant the 'possibility' of unhindered religious activity by the churches, but certainly not if freedom meant that God's word should reverberate with the strongest cadences of judgement, command, forgiveness and liberation. When a church rendered its timid homage to state order and powerful persons in positions of status and wealth by watering down the gospel, this church, whether set in Nazi Germany or 'democratic' America, was 'in chains', no matter how loudly it proclaimed its freedom.[3]

Everywhere Bonhoeffer turned in the 1930s it seemed that an easily led citizenry was content to bask in the Teutonic pride that Hitler was proclaiming to mesmerised audiences all over Germany. They sheltered, not in Jesus Christ, but under the political wings of Hitler's military might and Nazism's promise of unparalleled prosperity and national security. The churches, supposedly representing Jesus Christ, were neither the voice of compassion nor the conscience of their nation in all the crises churned up by Hitler's stifling of individual freedom and dignity. Jesus' Sermon on the Mount had mandated Christians and their churches to serve as levers of spiritual and social regeneration in the world; following Hitler, on the other hand, had, to Bonhoeffer's consternation, left a trail of spiritual degeneration and social iniquity. Churches survived by adroitly separating the sacred side of their activities from the secular, the religious from the profane, retreating behind the protection offered them in political-ecclesiastical concordats or in the security of Luther's doctrine of the two kingdoms.

But Luther's teaching on the relationship between 'the sword and the gospel', state and church, was never intended to be a severance of one from the other, as if one's church and individual faith had to accept without contention whatever a political government decreed. The playing-it-safe tactics of the churches were, in Bonhoeffer's opinion, a dishonouring of the faith in Jesus Christ whom religious people so cheerfully professed to follow. The churches had given the impression to countless believers that it was common prudence to cordon off the demands of their everyday, secularised life from the more rigorous demands made on them as followers of Jesus Christ. And they, in turn, were allowed to prosper so long as they did not question political decisions even if this meant shirking their responsibility to promote justice and to defend human rights in the name of Jesus Christ.

Bonhoeffer was harsh on religious leaders who encouraged such 'thinking in two spheres', keeping the issue of human rights apart from their worship services. He accused them of denying to people 'that community with the world into which God entered in Jesus Christ'.[4] Further, against those who had become adept at splitting their religious from their secular allegiances, Bonhoeffer maintained that, in the reality of Jesus Christ's human solidarity with all peoples, including the hated Jew and the despised socialist, God invests the world with a unity in which one's faith and one's 'worldliness' must be reconciled. The true interpretation of Luther's doctrine of the two kingdoms is that of a mutually supportive yet critical relationship in which Christians may and at times should oppose the secular 'in the name of a better secularity'.[5] Bonhoeffer was aware that interpreting Luther in this way and invoking the example of Christ in 'opposing the secular' could bring down the wrath of the Nazi Empire on the person of faith. The 'cost' of Christian discipleship was the cup of suffering and even an inglorious death in those twentieth-century Golgothas, the Nazi extermination camps.

Throughout his life Bonhoeffer urged the churches to live up to their social responsibilities, to care for the poor, to take risks for the cause of peace, to live daily the Sermon on the Mount, to profess solidarity with the Jews, and even to confront malice in government head-on. Passages stand out in Bonhoeffer's collected writings in which he reminds the churches in many different ways of what he had advanced in an early essay, that 'God wants us to honour God on earth; God wants us to honour God in our fellow man and woman – and nowhere else.'[6] In one memorable sermon on freedom, Bonhoeffer went so far as to preach that genuine Christians, i.e. 'the people who love . . . are the most revolutionary people on earth. They are the ones who upset all values; they are the explosives in human society.' But they are also those 'whom they want to get rid of, whom they declare an outlaw, whom they kill'. Their way 'leads to the cross'.[7] The allusion to Nazi boasts and repression was not lost on his congregants. This was not the time for church leaders to assess cunningly the political advantages and disadvantages of resistance. For Bonhoeffer, the call to follow Christ was stark but clear: self-sacrificing faith and wholehearted solidarity with one's neighbours, particularly those declared 'subhuman' by harsh, vindictive ideologues.

Bonhoeffer's embittered chagrin at his church's reluctance to travel with Christ the way of the cross is evident in several passages from his prison writings. One unforgettable line, for example, was a gauntlet thrown at the church daring it to 'come out of its stagnation . . . and risk saying controversial things, if we are to get down to the serious problems of life'.[8] His disturbing assertion that there would come a time of 'non-religious Christianity' and his call for a 'non-religious interpretation' of biblical concepts are of a piece with his conviction that the churches of Germany had become stagnant ponds of escapist religiosity. Their major concerns seemed to be taken up with dogmatic orthodoxy and shifty platitudes. He was dismayed that these churches had 'little personal faith in Christ'. They were afraid of 'taking risks for others' because they had become unhinged from God's biblical word; and, as a consequence, '"Jesus" [was] disappearing from sight.'[9]

Bonhoeffer spoke, therefore, of a 'non-religious Christianity' in which the church would become, like Christ, a community of service to the oppressed, not a sacralised institution eager to preserve its clerical privileges and maintain its powerful hold over spiritually dependent subjects. To be a true church this community would have to be stirred from its spiritual lethargy and be willing to 'share in the sufferings of God at the hands of a godless world'.[10] In short, the churches had to allow themselves 'to be caught up in the way of Jesus Christ'.[11]

In retrospect, Bonhoeffer's dream of a renewed, Christ-orientated church may have been too upsetting and unreal for the churches and their bourgeois parishioners. Bonhoeffer had taken the Sermon on the Mount seriously; he also wanted to hold the churches to their claims that they were an *alter Christus* to the world. In this lay both his disappointment and his hope. While in prison he longed for the rebirth of Christianity in nations where the gospel's mandate of love for all people had been thwarted. He had come to the sobering conclusion, as we read in his baptismal sermon from prison, that the church, 'which has been fighting in these years only for its self-preservation, as though that were an end in itself', had become 'incapable of taking the word of reconciliation and redemption to humankind and the world'.[12] This was a church that, while proclaiming its allegiance to Jesus Christ, had been paying homage, instead, to Teutonic gods. This church was in need of radical conversion.

THE 'DISCIPLINE OF THE SECRET'

Bonhoeffer was wary of a church rising high from the rubble of the Second World War and once again exerting clerical dominance over a certifiably sinful world. He spoke, therefore, of his misgivings about a future church's scramble to recover its prestige and convince itself that it was without blame for the atrocities of the Hitler years. His statements about the coming of a non-religious Christianity are a caution to the church to convert to Christ and patiently to wait with perseverance in prayer and courage in deeds until it can 'once more be called so to utter the Word of God that the world will be changed and renewed by it . . . It will be a new language, perhaps quite nonreligious, but liberating and redeeming – as was Jesus' language. It will shock people and yet overcome them by its power.'[13] A clue to what kind of 'nonreligious language' both liberates and shocks is given almost immediately when he adds that in the future 'the Christian cause will be a *silent* and *hidden* affair'.[14] In two related passages from letters sent around the same time as the baptismal sermon, he mentions a 'discipline of the secret' (*disciplina arcani*), a reference to a practice of the ancient church that was aimed at safeguarding church integrity against pagan corruption. The first reference brings out some of his intent behind that phrase as Bonhoeffer invokes the 'discipline of the secret' in the context of his asking what meaning worship and prayer will have in a non-religious Christianity.[15]

For Bonhoeffer, religion was never to be equated with faith as God's gift; religion was all too human, flawed, and prone to sin. The religious trappings of faith were never the same as the faith that saves and the genuine holiness that flowed from that faith. Bonhoeffer spoke of the mysteries of faith which had to be protected from profanation. Hence the restoration of the practice of the 'discipline of the secret'.[16] Bonhoeffer was cognisant of the cavalier way the churches had transformed the ultimacy of God into an icon of their own idolatrous making and turned the 'sacred' into empty religious jargon. The words of the churches had lost any claim to credibility in an era of gospel spoliation through the acts of injustice perpetrated by so-called Christians, abetted by their churches.

The question thus became for Bonhoeffer how to prevent Christians and communities of faith from squandering their identity with Jesus Christ in the midst of their involvement with the secular. Discipline was essential but, as in the early church, this was not to be brandished triumphantly before a hostile society or forced upon an unwilling citizenry. A discipline of modesty in claims and humility in action was called for to help the church become liberated from itself, delivered from the stagnation of outmoded forms of religious expression. The church had a mandate to preserve the mysteries of the Christian faith proclaimed by God's word, not with a pathetic defensive frenzy, but with prayer, worship and Christlike example. According to Bonhoeffer, no proclamation of God's perduring goodness in an evil world carries any cogency without this prayer and example. Bonhoeffer's cryptic allusion to the 'discipline of the secret' was intended to preserve this Christ-centred perspective of all vicarious action of the church on behalf of others.[17]

To extrapolate from Bonhoeffer's Christocentric spirituality, Christ is as much the centre of this 'discipline' as he is the structure of all reality and the inspiration behind the responsible life of a Christian. Christians are to pray and worship in a community of believers and thus be strengthened in those attitudes that enable them to serve others who have experienced only destitution and sorrow. If the same Christ-orientated outlook is not shared by everyone, Christians and their churches are, none the less, to continue to trust that the Holy Spirit will eventually give revelatory sound to their prayer and example and bring the church once more to speak God's word effectively to those who are brother and sister to them in Jesus Christ.

The baptismal letter to his godson, which provides so many insights into Bonhoeffer's feelings about this future direction of the church, exposes too the heart of his own Christ-centred spirituality: 'Our being Christians today', he wrote, 'will be limited to two things: prayer and action for justice on behalf of people. All Christian thinking, speaking, and organising must be born anew out of this prayer and action.' The churches, he said, needed a new way of speaking . . . 'Till then the Christian cause will be a silent and hidden affair, but there will be those who pray and act for justice and wait for God's own time. May you be one of them.'[18] Indeed, prayer and action for justice stand out as the most distinctive characteristics of what I have called Bonhoeffer's 'spirituality'. Above all, Bonhoeffer emerges from his writings as a person who, despite his personal flaws, was led by a deep, prayerful faith to undertake great risks to his life in working for the restoration of justice in a society befouled by systemic immorality.

PRAYER AND MEDITATION

It was unfortunate that, when Bonhoeffer was first arrested, the reaction of many of his fellow churchmen was to dismiss him as a mere political agitator who had meddled in matters totally foreign to his faith and ecclesiastical calling. He was not to be included in the church intercessory prayers, despite the peril he was in. After the war, it was smoother for churchmen to catalogue Bonhoeffer's involvement in the conspiracy as a misguided, politically treasonous act than to see in his participation in the resistance a persistent shaming of the churches to represent Jesus Christ more honestly against a particularly noxious tyranny. To accept the challenge of his prison letters and to follow his personal example meant that they would have to sacrifice too many of their clerical privileges. In his *Ethics* he had already summoned the churches to confess their guilt in the violence done to the victims of Nazism's genocide rule.[19] In retrospect, Bonhoeffer's dramatic words of the 'Confession of Guilt' seemed to exact a greater leap of humility and contrition than the churches were willing to acknowledge. Only much later did the issue of Bonhoeffer's Christian witness in and through his actions in the German resistance movement become a matter of admiration and emulation as Christian denominations began reluctantly to examine their consciences and cope with their complicity in the hatreds on which Nazism had fed. The churches began to draw a delayed empowerment from his inspiring words. Though the situations and times have changed, the challenges of Bonhoeffer's life and theology have remained: how does a church relate Christian faith with concrete action to achieve peace and justice in a world rampant with racial, class and sectarian enmity? Or, the equally germane question: how can Christians condition themselves to endure persecution for the cause of justice (Matthew 5: 10)?

If a martyr is a witness to the truth of Jesus Christ, then John de Gruchy's explanation of why Bonhoeffer could link his Christian faith with the unwavering defence of human rights and involvement in the anti-Hitler conspiracy is highly relevant here. 'Bonhoeffer did not seek martyrdom; he pursued the truth as he saw it and was executed because he lived that truth.'[20] And the truth, as Bonhoeffer pursued it, was that God was suffering in the innocent who cried out to be delivered from the daily torments of the death camps. Many passages from Bonhoeffer's collected writings underline his conviction that the task of Christians is, therefore, not to stand on the sidelines in silence or lost in prayerful reverie in the safety of their churches, while violence was being done, resistance to evil crushed, and one's brothers and sisters in Jesus Christ made to suffer. Bonhoeffer knew this from his daily meditation on biblical texts and it was his dedication to prayer, Bethge observed, that kept Bonhoeffer's actions from degenerating into self-righteousness, that infused his spirits with dogged perseverance, and kept his 'doing of justice in line with the truth of the Gospel'.[21] No prayer seemed complete for him without its bonding to prophetic action for justice.

That is why, in a revealing letter to Bethge, Bonhoeffer wrote of just how his practice of personal prayer had helped him integrate into a manageable whole the many conflictual directions his life was taking. At the time he was staying with the Kleist-Retzow family and labouring over an initial draft of his *Ethics*. He wrote,

> I enjoy the daily morning prayers here very much. These prayers compel me to ponder the meaning of the biblical text. Likewise, by reading the Bible, I am led to think a lot about you and your work. The regularly structured day for me means work and prayer. These make it easier for me in my relations with people and protect me from the emotional, physical and spiritual troubles which ensue from a lack of discipline.[22]

Bonhoeffer's adherence to the tandem of work and prayer, which is affirmed here, though springing from an entirely different context, is a counterpart of the action for justice and prayer that he hoped would characterise the church in post-war Germany.

To find out what Bonhoeffer's prayer life was like and, indirectly, what kind of prayer he was alluding to in his baptismal sermon is to explore how personal and community prayer always held a special place in his priorities. He once declared from the Monastery of Ettal, where he had been sequestered for the German resistance, that, for him, 'a day without morning and evening prayers and personal intercessions was actually a day without meaning or importance'.[23] So convinced was Bonhoeffer of the power of prayer to hold the various threads of one's otherwise scattered life together that he insisted on incorporating daily prayer and meditation into the training of the Confessing Church's seminarians at Finkenwalde. Their communal life was structured into a balance of coursework, study, meals, worship, mutual service, leisure and sports. But at the centre of their spiritual formation was their opening and ending the day in prayer and their practice of daily meditation on biblical texts.

This daily meditative prayer, dubbed 'Bonhoeffer's way', was an unexpected and, at first, misunderstood aspect of their preparation for ordination. There were even jokes about the 'unevangelical monasticism' that Bonhoeffer was imposing on these young ordinands. When they complained to him about this, following a protracted absence from the community, he did not back off from maintaining the practice as part of their seminary routine. Instead, he suggested that once a week they hold a communal service with public reflections on given scriptural texts. He himself took the lead by sharing his own meditative prayer with the seminarians. Gradually their opposition waned and they began to appreciate with him what the daily meditation was all about. They were to consider themselves personally gifted by the word spoken to nourish their own faith, strengthen them in their ministry and empower them to preach the gospel with greater conviction. Bonhoeffer knew from his own experience that Christian ministers had to 'enter into a daily, personal communion with the crucified Jesus Christ' whose voice would come to them 'directly from the cross . . . where Christ is so present to us that frankly he himself speaks our word, there alone can we banish the dreadful danger of pietistical chatter'.[24]

Later he introduced his seminarians to the practice, then customary in the communities of the Moravian Brethren, of meditating on the daily *Losungen*, or brief texts drawn from the Scriptures. Several times in the years that followed their Finkenwalde experience Bonhoeffer would call their attention to these texts for the day. For his Christmas 1937 letter to the ordinands now labouring in collective pastorates, for example, he painstakingly transcribed reflections on the 'Daily Texts' from Christmas Eve until New Year's Eve. This was to be his Christmas gift in lieu of a copy of his recently published book, *The Cost of Discipleship*, which he was unfortunately unable to send to each of them.[25] He kept up these reminders of their life together in Finkenwalde and, though their community had been shut down by the Gestapo, he encouraged his seminarians to continue their practice of reflecting on the texts for the day.[26] While in prison he wrote that meditation on the *Losungen* had opened up a world of meaning for him.[27]

Even after the Gestapo had caused the dispersal of the seminarians, Bonhoeffer preserved a semblance of their community life through circular letters that offered the weekly texts for their reflection. In one such letter at the height of the war he urged them again not to abandon the practice of daily meditation. He shared with them his conviction that 'daily, quiet attention to the Word of God . . . even if it is only for a few minutes' was the 'focal point of everything which brings inward and outward order into [their] life' now fragmented by the war. It was their daily meditation, in fact, that preserved the unity of their lives from their baptism to their confirmation and ordination. 'It keeps us', he concluded, 'in the saving community of our congregation, of our brothers and sisters, of our spiritual home.'[28] To the seminarians these words brought back their memories of Bonhoeffer's own instructions on the importance of daily prayer.

His biographer informs us, too, that Bonhoeffer taught his seminarians how to pray by his personal example as well as by his classroom instructions. He often took responsibility for the extemporised prayers of the community. These included prayers of thanksgiving for all of God's gifts, not the least of which was their community life together, intercessory prayers for the Confessing Church, especially the imprisoned pastors, prayers of forgiveness for their failings in ministry, and even prayers for their enemies. Bonhoeffer's method was to pray aloud from his heart and to encourage all to share their thoughts with the others and thus to enrich their mutual faith and enhance their sense of community. This was an indirect mode of teaching prayer, the like of which, as the then seminarian Bethge points out, 'we had never had before'.[29] Another of the seminarians spoke of how Bonhoeffer's

> love of Jesus, especially in the figure of the humiliated one, of the earthly Jesus in the Christ of faith came through in Bonhoeffer's extemporised prayers. Here was the very heart and core of the existence of this highly intellectual Christian; we felt it in the improvised prayers of the morning and evening devotions; they sprang from the love of the Lord and of his brethren.[30]

Both for himself and his seminarians Bonhoeffer stressed the need to allow the word of God to speak to them daily. 'Pastors', he insisted, 'must pray more than others [because] . . . they have more to pray about.' This statement comes from an essay he wrote to support the practice of daily meditation at the seminary. Under the rubric of 'Why do I meditate?' Bonhoeffer replied that 'prayer is the first worship of the day'.[31] His words, sent as part of a circular letter to the seminarians in 1936, would return in his book, *Life Together*, where he stipulated that their

> life together under the Word begins at an early hour of the day with a worship service together. A community living together gathers for

praise and thanks, Scripture reading, and prayer. The profound silence of morning is first broken by the prayer and song of the community of faith. After the silence of the night and early morning, hymns and the Word of God will be heard all the more clearly. Along these lines the Holy Scriptures tell us that the first thought and the first word of the day belong to God.[32]

Fittingly, the evening prayers were to be the community's final word before the night's repose. Bonhoeffer and his ordinands closed the day as they began it: with praying the Psalms, a reading of Scripture, a hymn and a concluding prayer together. Among the various intentions that Bonhoeffer brought to the forefront of that prayer were God's blessing on their day, peace in the world, intercessions for those in need, especially fellow pastors, the poor, miserable and lonely, the sick and dying, and even enemies. Bonhoeffer turned their attention also to the need for forgiving one another's sins, particularly the sins of omission and the sins that hurt a fellow brother or sister. He made it the rule of his life and of the community to seek healing for every division. No one, he said, should 'go to bed with an unreconciled heart'. That reconciliation, he pointed out, was essential if the community was ever to be renewed in the love of Jesus Christ and of one another.[33]

Bethge notes in his recollections of those seminary days that Bonhoeffer seemed to put his soul into their community worship. Bonhoeffer was convinced that to form a truly Christian community they had to develop a prayerful relationship with God and be led by God's word. For this to happen, he felt that praying the Psalms, both in solitude and in common, was crucial. Why that was so can be seen in one of his highly informative citations from Luther to the effect that the Psalms made other prayers seem bloodless; and in another revealing statement, he said that 'those other easy, little prayers' lacked the 'power, passion, and fire' that could be experienced in the Psalter.[34]

In several passages from the collected writings one can appreciate that, through the Psalms, Bonhoeffer seemed to encounter both the presence of God and the connection between God's word and everyday happenings. His biographer illustrates this through a scrutiny of Bonhoeffer's jottings in the Bible he used for prayer and meditation. To show Bonhoeffer's prayerful sensitivity to the plight of the Jews, for example, Bethge calls attention to Bonhoeffer's marginal notes at Psalm 74:8. Bonhoeffer had written '9.11.38' (9 November 1938), the date of Crystal Night, in which synagogues were burnt, Jewish shops broken into, and Jews brutalised. The text reads: 'They say to themselves, "Let us plunder them." They have set afire all the houses of God in the land.' The following two verses are also marked with a stroke of his pen and an exclamation point: 'Our signs we do not see; there is no longer a prophet to preach; there is nobody among us who knows how long. How long, O God, shall the foe blaspheme? Shall the enemy revile thy name forever?'[35] Later Bonhoeffer incorporated his reactions to Crystal Night in a circular letter to his former seminarians now occupied with their own parish ministries. 'During the past few days', he wrote, 'I have been thinking a great deal about Psalm 74, Zechariah 2:12 (2:8 "he who touches you touches the apple of his eye!"), Romans 9:4f. (Israel, to whom belongs the sonship, the glory, the covenant, the law, the service, the promises); Romans, 11:11–15. That takes us right into prayer.'[36] This was a typical illustration of the way Bonhoeffer prayed the Psalms and meditated on them as God's word for any given situation and unforeseen eruptions in one's ordinary life, in this case one of the most traumatic moments in Nazi Germany's vicious persecution of the Jews.

These verses from the Psalms show, too, that for Bonhoeffer, praying the Psalms was never to be isolated from the everyday side of one's life and ministry. He was asking his seminarians to ponder the passages in question and to consider God's own word, not the discredited teaching of contempt, but the love and concern for the Jewish people whom God had never really repudiated. In meditating on those verses, Bonhoeffer was also alluding to the sufferings of God in the Jews. Bonhoeffer had taught his seminarians to pray the Psalms with Jesus Christ; in Crystal Night they could cry out with Jesus in the person of their Jewish brothers and sisters, 'How long, O God, shall the foe blaspheme? Shall the enemy revile thy name forever?'

This practical dimension of the Psalms helps explain why Bonhoeffer cherished them as his principal form of prayer. Above all, the Psalms enabled him to cope with his own shifting moods amid all the vicissitudes of his ministry, including his imprisonment. The Psalms taught him that God was near in all the sorrows and joys, successes and disappointments that had marked his own days. It came, therefore, as no surprise to the seminarians who followed his lessons and shared his community life that he would insist on integrating the Psalms into their regular community worship. 'The prayer of the Psalms', he told them, 'teaches us to pray as a community.'[37] Even during the most dismal days in Tegel Prison, he could send these words to his parents: 'I read the Psalms every day, as I have done for years; I know them and love them more than any other book.' In that same letter he told his parents that he derived spiritual solace from the Bible's answer to a prisoner's anguish over the apparent meaninglessness of his captivity.

Psalm 31, in particular, helped him to concede that his life was still con-signed to God: 'My time is in your hands' (verse 15), he prayed, though Psalm 13 permitted him, none the less, to air his impatience and demand an answer to the agonising question: 'How Long, O Lord?'[38] The Psalms were for him the prayer of Jesus Christ, who, as Bonhoeffer claimed, perhaps paraphrasing Augustine's *Deus intimior intimo meo* (God is more intimate to me than I am to myself), 'knows us better than we know ourselves'.[39]

It was predictable, therefore, that the prayers Bonhoeffer composed for his fellow prisoners were filled with the spirit of the Psalms. Their constant theme was trust in God's love and acceptance of whatever God has permit-ted in their regard. 'Whatever this day may bring', he prayed, God's 'name be praised.' He commended into God's hands at close of day his loved ones and fellow prisoners, even their warders, as well as his own person. He asked for strength to bear what God might send and the courage to over-come their fears. In the all-pervasive distress of prison life, he would say to God: 'I trust in your grace and commit my life wholly into your hands. Do with me according to your will and as is best for me. Whether I live or die, I am with you, and you, my God, are with me.'[40] These prayers, which were circulated illegally among the cells, manifest many of the insights that helped guide Bonhoeffer's own actions on behalf of peace and freedom and exude his concern for Christian community even in prison. In effect, Bonhoeffer was trying 'to bring everyone in the sprawling prison of Tegel with whom he was able to make some kind of contact, by his own example, into the field of force from which he drew his own strength'.[41] A fellow conspirator and prisoner who survived the war has given this account of Bonhoeffer's solicitude for the spiritual well-being and morale of those around him. 'To the very end', he wrote, 'Bonhoeffer took advantage of [their] condition by arranging prayer services, consoling those who had lost all hope, and giving them fresh courage. A towering rock of faith, he became a shining example to his fellow prisoners.'[42] One student of Bonhoeffer's spirituality has remarked that a perusal of his prayers in prison made him begin 'to realise with new appreciation the source of Bonhoeffer's spiritual stamina and vitality – his constant, daily, childlike relationship to God'.[43]

That 'childlike relationship' also took on the form of a strong sense of solidarity with his family, friends, fellow ministers, co-conspirators, and even the victims of Nazism. 'The physical presence of other Christians', he wrote, 'is a source of incomparable joy and strength to the believer.'[44] But, whether they were physically present or close to him in prayers and reflections, Bonhoeffer experienced intense comfort from the thought that they were all 'in a community that sustains [them]'. These words from one of his farewell letters to Bethge come just before his powerful confession of faith: 'In Jesus God has said Yes and Amen to it all, and that Yes and Amen is the firm ground on which we stand.'[45]

This was a solidarity that helps explain another important aspect of Bonhoeffer's faith in prayer: his belief in the power of intercession. His own refined sense of solidarity with family, friends, seminarians and even co-conspirators fitted naturally into his appreciation of the need for intercessory prayers. They were united by ties of love, faith, compassion and the dangers of their resistance to Nazism, to be sure. But, however far apart physically, they had been brought together by their communion in Jesus Christ and God's gift of a common faith, whether consciously or unconsciously, moving them to remember each other in their prayers and to intercede for one another with the Lord. Nowhere does Bonhoeffer assert the importance of intercession within a Christian community more than in his blunt assertion to the community of ordinands in Finkenwalde: 'A Christian community either lives by the intercessory prayers of its members for one another or the community will be destroyed.' Bonhoeffer valued their intercessory prayer as 'the purifying bath into which the individual and the community must enter every day'. [46] Bonhoeffer knew that to pray for the other achieved what was often considered nearly impossible among people cast together by all the unpredictable directions one's life could take. In this prayer, enemies could be forgiven, burdens lightened and sorrows alleviated.

Separated from his family and friends and denied the visible support of the Confessing Church while in prison, Bonhoeffer was strengthened, none the less, by the thought of his being remembered in the prayers offered on his behalf. He was not ashamed to ask Bethge to promise that they

> remain faithful in interceding for each other . . . And if it should be
> decided that we are not to meet again, let us remember each other to
> the end in thankfulness and forgiveness, and may God grant us that
> one day we may stand before [God] praying for each other and joining
> in praise and thankfulness.[47]

Their union in prayer was more than a mere leap of empathy. If Bonhoeffer was able to persevere in his anti-Nazi resolve, this was due in large part to the continual inspiration he derived from Bethge's friendship and prayerful support. 'Please don't ever get anxious or worried about me, but don't forget to pray for me', he pleaded in one of his final letters. He then added:

> I'm sure you don't! I am so sure of God's guiding hand that I hope I
> shall always be kept in that certainty. You must never doubt that I'm

travelling with gratitude and cheerfulness along the road where I'm being led. My past life is brim-full of God's goodness, and my sins are covered by the forgiving love of Christ crucified.[48]

In the intensity of such a friendship and mutual prayer Bonhoeffer's concern for personal survival and the safety of his loved ones yielded to the quiet confidence in God's protection that made his eventual death an act of faith and resignation to what God was permitting. He prays this sentiment in a moving stanza from his poetic hymn, 'The Powers for Good', 'But should you tend your cup of sorrow,/ To drink the bitter dregs at your command,/ We accept with thanks and without trembling,/ This offering from your gracious, loving hand.'[49] Even as he attempted to cope with his own inability to overcome the fate awaiting him and his friends in the conspiracy, he incorporated lines into his poem on freedom that express the need to 'step out of [his] anguished waverings' and 'calmly and trusting . . . surrender [his] struggle to more powerful hands'.[50] Those 'more powerful hands' he had alluded to earlier in a letter to Renate and Eberhard Bethge in the context of having his efforts to shape the destiny of others 'suddenly cut off' and with feelings of helplessness invading his equilibrium, hoping not to lose sight of their belief that their 'life has now been placed wholly in better and stronger hands'.[51]

The attitude expressed here would be refined in the letter of 21 February 1944. There he tells Bethge that he must both confront and submit to his 'fate', but all in its proper time. The problem for him was how to find God in the quite neutral zone of what is judged to be his 'fate'. He concludes that no one can define abstractly the boundary between resistance and submission; only his faith could give him enough elasticity of decision and action to 'stand [his] ground in each situation'.[52] After the failure of the conspiracy of 20 July 1944, his writings increasingly attest to the 'submission' in faith to whatever God would permit, given that his efforts to deliver his nation and the victims of Nazism from their sufferings were now consigned to God's more powerful wisdom and control. Prayer in such circumstances led him more and more to faith in God's providential care despite the nagging realisation that suffering, even death, was to be his fate. Just eight days after the failed assassination attempt, he wrote that, '[I]n suffering, the deliverance consists in our being allowed to put the matter out of our own hands into God's hands.'[53] His act of faith in that deliverance accords with his insistence in his book on Christian discipleship that to follow Christ was to give oneself over to the cross that is the destiny of those who brave persecution for the sake of justice. Such a death was, in fact, not the end of everything but the full blossoming of a Christian's communion with Jesus Christ.[54]

ACTION FOR JUSTICE AND PEACE

Prayer, however heart-warming and fervent, is not the sole structure of a Christian community. As Bethge has observed, Bonhoeffer was equally convinced that, without being connected to concrete action for justice, prayer could deviate into pietistic self-sufficiency and a vapid otherworldliness.[55] His spirituality pivots on an undaunted imitation of Jesus Christ as well as on the trustful prayer of a Christian. Bonhoeffer speaks of the world itself having reached a certain maturity with regard to solving the problems of ordinary life. But he is also aware that a truly mature faith can be attained only when one's love of neighbour transmutes into a ministry of peace and justice against those who thrive on belligerence and exploitation. The Christians of the post-Hitler future, as Bonhoeffer envisioned it, had to be persons whose daily prayer was conjoined to the practical deeds necessary in order to foster justice where people had experienced only pain and oppression. This was the path the Christian churches had to travel if they were to regain their credibility in a world grown sceptical of religious solutions to seemingly impossible problems. For Bonhoeffer, the only credible faith was that inspirited by compassion and shaped in service.

Although there is no one answer to what is intended by the 'action for justice' to which he referred in his baptismal sermon, three directions seem consistently to emerge from his writings. Bonhoeffer advocates an unabashed solidarity with the oppressed, concrete steps to liberate the victims of unjust societies, and the willingness to suffer for the sake of Christ, all related to what for him was the 'costly grace' of following Jesus Christ. In this last section we shall consider each of these in order, beginning with Bonhoeffer's emphasis on the church's vocation to enter into solidarity with the 'least' of God's people and to proclaim their dignity in the face of the indignities to which they had been subjected.

Solidarity

Those looking for inspiration in fighting the forces of racist and classist oppression in the world often cite a dramatic passage from Bonhoeffer's Christmas 1942 exhortation to his fellow conspirators and family. In that essay, entitled 'After Ten Years', he tells them of the need to appraise the happenings of history, not so much from the commanding position of the powerful few who exert control over the destinies of the masses, but with the eyes of the victims. The conspirators were privileged 'to see the great events of world history from below, from the perspective of the outcast, the suspects, the maltreated, the powerless, the oppressed, the reviled – in short, from the perspective of those who suffer'.[56] These words, penned shortly before his arrest by the Gestapo, do not indicate a sudden turn in his life's journey. As early as 1928, when he had to deal with the raw poverty of his people for the first time, he took pains to remind his parishioners that Jesus Christ was among them in the faces of the grubby poor. That continued presence in the Christ living in the least of his brothers and sisters was not something that a church could ignore in order to cater to the whims of the well-to-do. Indeed, the Christ Christians are to honour is one who, according to Bonhoeffer, upsets the snobbish values of society by proclaiming 'the unending worth of the apparently worthless and the unending worthlessness of what is apparently so valuable'.[57] To discover Jesus Christ in the hard-nosed societies of that day later became one of the most disturbing challenges to his students at the University of Berlin. Bonhoeffer insisted that Jesus had entered our world 'in such a way as to hide himself in it in weakness and not to be recognised as God-man'. Jesus did not wear 'kingly robes'; instead, 'he goes incognito, as a beggar among beggars, as dying among the dying'.[58] This sensitivity to the contemporaneous presence of Jesus Christ among the dispossessed of a nation is a focal point for what Bonhoeffer would demand of the church of the future. Christians had to affirm Jesus in the weakest of their brothers and sisters. In his *Ethics* he took that issue of solidarity in Christ with the oppressed to an ultimate conclusion: those who persecuted the Jews were complicit in the deaths of 'the weakest and most defenceless brothers and sisters of Jesus Christ'.[59]

Such solidarity with the oppressed was not something foreign to church teaching over the centuries. But Bonhoeffer's vision sharpened the focus for a church that had so obviously been unwilling to stand up for anyone or anything but its own survival. Solidarity was to be with none other than Jesus Christ himself now suffering in the 'incognito' of six million Jews, countless other so-called *Untermenschen*, and political opponents, in a word, all those destined for enslavement and elimination in Hitler's mad scheme to create a racially pure, Teutonic millennium. 'Those who are now attacking the least of the people', he told his seminarians, 'are attacking Christ.'[60] For Bonhoeffer, following Christ along the way of the cross required no less of the church than embracing God's own vulnerability in caring for those whom vicious political leaders had made an object of contempt.

Deeds of justice

Solidarity with the oppressed is, however, only a first stage in the mission of Christians to help create a just society. Bonhoeffer was known among friends and enemies alike as an irrepressible agitator in church circles, urging religious leaders to accept responsibility for those victimised by repressive public policies and to take effective means to protect these 'little ones'. He was disturbed by the troubling trend of churches to trot out their wobbly generalities when prophetic outrage and quick action were called for. In prison, with the failure of the plot of 20 July 1944 hanging over him, he points again to what Christians and their churches needed to do in order to liberate their nation from its enthralment to Adolf Hitler. In a dramatic outburst in his now famous poem 'Stations on the Way to Freedom', he alleges that freedom can, indeed, become a reality for them, though 'Not [through] what fancies the mind, but what is braved in the bold deeds of justice; /... Not through ideas soaring in flight, but only through action'.[61]

Here we see the practical bent of Bonhoeffer's having spurred the churches to accomplish something palpable to stop the evil that had created misery among so many innocents, stigmatised in the eyes of Nazi overlords as less than fully human. Neither endless rumination about what fanciful courses to take nor dreaming of what to do without ever doing it will ever make a difference in the precarious situation of the victims awaiting their fate in the death camps. Only vigorous, courageous action could make that difference. Conceding that Christians are not replicas of Jesus Christ himself, Bonhoeffer none the less insisted to his fellow conspirators that if they wanted to be genuine Christians, they had to 'share in Christ's largeheartedness by acting with responsibility and in freedom when the hour of danger comes, and by showing a real compassion that springs, not from fear, but from the liberating and redeeming love of Christ for all who suffer'. The final words of that portion of his exhortation to the conspirators are an unmistakable judgement on the need to stop dallying and begin to act: 'Mere waiting and looking on is not Christian behaviour. Christians are called to compassion and action.'[62]

Bonhoeffer's efforts to push the church to defend the Jews had their counterpart in his agitation on behalf of world peace even while his own flag-waving nation was revelling in its dreams of being led to greater military glory. Here, too, he charged the churches with the responsibility to 'speak out so that the world, though it gnash its teeth, will have to hear, so that the people will rejoice because the church of Christ in the name of Christ has taken the weapons from the hands of their sons, forbidden war, proclaimed the peace of Christ against the raging world'.[63] Peace, he told that gathering of ecumenical delegates, 'was the great venture'. Few pacifists this century have matched the passion of Bonhoeffer's untiring efforts in that sermon to persuade church leaders to use moral suasion to achieve peace and justice in a world that, as he had observed, was bristling with weapons.[64] Their failure to do so is behind his scathing accusation that the churches were by their silence 'guilty of the decline in responsible action, in bravery in the defence of a cause and in willingness to suffer for what is known to be right'. They had 'witnessed the lawless application of brutal force, the physical and spiritual suffering of countless innocent people, oppression, hatred and murder, and . . . not found ways to hasten to their aid'.[65]

The implications of this 'Confession of Guilt' on the part of the churches is clear for the kind of action Bonhoeffer was expounding in his *Ethics*: the churches had to '*find ways*' to alleviate the sufferings of 'countless innocent people'. They were not relieved of their duty to act for the sake of justice. Nor were they permitted the excuse of obeying the law or valuing their directly spiritual mission over the practical problem of defending people against the state for fear of losing their livelihood or, in the atmosphere of the dictatorship, what was worse, their reputation for love of country. As Bonhoeffer put it to his seminarians in one of his most challenging lectures on following Christ, Christians had even to 'cast away the most priceless treasure of human life, their personal dignity and honour'.[66]

Suffering

The church, Bonhoeffer insisted, is the church only when it is willing to suffer for those who were being victimised by the ruthless government that had come to dominate their lives. In prison Bonhoeffer took comfort from reading Mark 15:34, where the dying Jesus cries out in near despair from the cross: 'My God, my God, why have you abandoned me?'[67] Like their saviour, Christians cannot flee from responsibility for the least of their brothers and sisters in whom God has become vulnerable. If they are to conform to Jesus Christ, those who spend their energies for the oppressed of this world cannot expect some sensational divine rescue or some miraculous intervention to force justice on an unwilling world. Bonhoeffer goes so far as to confess that, 'God even lets God be pushed out of the world on to the cross. God is weak and powerless in the world, and this is precisely the way, the only way, in which God is with us and helps us . . . Christ helps us, not by virtue of his omnipotence, but by virtue of his weakness and suffering.'[68]

That 'help' is God's gift of faith. God does not offer Christians a rational, logically ordered answer to the why of their afflictions. God suffers with them. Hence, Bonhoeffer accepted the scriptural reality that 'only the suffering God can help'.[69] That 'help' is the graced assurance that the downtrodden are not alone in their misery. God in Christ will not offer glib, evasive explanations for the agonising problems faced by those whose lives have been menaced by the murderous forces of twentieth-century evil. God chooses to suffer with those who suffer, all the while raising up prophets of hope who are spiritually empowered to free God's people from their captivity. Those, like Bonhoeffer, whose destiny it is 'to share the sufferings of Christ to the final and fullest extent'[70] had realised that God bears their pain and rejection.[71] This faith in God's vulnerability and compassion is at the core of Bonhoeffer's theology of the cross and of what he would necessarily include in that 'action for justice' that would offer a liberating solace for those wounded by malevolence beyond their control. These are God's special children who sigh for the God who listens to their cries and for Christians who will reach out to them in compassion and act to alleviate their pain.

Bonhoeffer's theology of a future church that combines prayer with action for justice is itself interlocked with the concrete problems faced by people deprived of their civil rights in today's world. In their suffering they long for the prophetic word of God's solidarity with them in their troubles and practical action on their behalf. To accept a status quo that favours those in power and affluence and to counsel patience when human rights are being violated was rejected by Bonhoeffer as an infidelity to the gospel and a turning away of Jesus Christ in the 'least' of his brothers and sisters.

Notes

1 D. Bonhoeffer, *Letters and Papers from Prison: The Enlarged Edition* (New York: Macmillan, 1972), p. 400.
2 G. Kelly and F. B. Nelson, *A Testament to Freedom: The Essential Writings of Dietrich Bonhoeffer* (San Francisco: Harper & Row, 1990), p. 470.
3 ibid., p. 524.
4 D. Bonhoeffer, *Ethics* (New York: Macmillan, 1965), p. 200 (translation slightly altered).
5 ibid., p. 199.
6 'Thy Kingdom Come', in Kelly and Nelson, *A Testament to Freedom*, p. 92.
7 ibid., p. 206.
8 Bonhoeffer, *Letters and Papers from Prison*, p. 378 (translation slightly altered).
9 ibid., p. 381.
10 ibid., p. 361.
11 ibid.
12 Kelly and Nelson, *A Testament to Freedom*, p. 505.

13 Bonhoeffer, *Letters and Papers from Prison*, p. 300 (translation slightly altered).

14 ibid. (my italic).

15 ibid., p. 281.

16 ibid., p. 286.

17 The analysis of the 'discipline of the secret' presented here is drawn from my book G. B. Kelly, *Liberating Faith: Bonhoeffer's Message for Today* (Minneapolis: Augsburg Publishing House, 1984), pp. 133–8. For a more detailed study of this aspect of Bonhoeffer's theology, see J. W. Matthews, 'Responsible Sharing of the Mystery of Christian Faith: Disciplina Arcani in the Life and Theology of Dietrich Bonhoeffer', *Dialog*, 25 (1) (Winter 1986), 19–25.

18 Kelly and Nelson, *A Testament to Freedom*, p. 505. Translation altered from Bonhoeffer, *Letters and Papers from Prison*, p. 300.

19 'Confession of Guilt', in Bonhoeffer, *Ethics*, pp. 110–16.

20 John de Gruchy, 'Bonhoeffer in South Africa', in E. Bethge, *Bonhoeffer: Exile and Martyr*, ed. John de Gruchy (London: Collins, 1975), p. 27.

21 E. Bethge, *Prayer and Righteous Action* (Belfast: Christian Journals Ltd, 1979), pp. 26–7.

22 D. Bonhoeffer, *Kirchenkampf und Finkenwalde: Resolutionen Aufsätze Rundbriefe 1933–1943, Gesammelte Schriften*, vol. II (Munich: Chr. Kaiser Verlag, 1959), p. 376 (author's translation).

23 ibid., p. 398 (author's translation).

24 D. Bonhoeffer, *Theologie Gemeinde: Vorlesungen Briefe Gespräche 1927–1944, Gesammelte Schriften*, vol. III (Munich: Chr. Kaiser Verlag, 1960), p. 43 (author's translation).

25 Bonhoeffer, *Kirchenkampf und Finkenwalde*, pp. 524–30.

26 See, for example, D. Bonhoeffer, *Auslegungen Predigten: Berlin London Finkenwalde 1931–1944, Gesammelte Schriften*, vol. IV (Munich: Chr. Kaiser Verlag, 1961), pp. 588–96, for Bonhoeffer's reflections on the texts for Pentecost, Pentecost Tuesday and for 7 and 8 June 1944.

27 See Bonhoeffer, *Letters and Papers from Prison*, p. 176. This section is drawn in large part from my 'Editor's Introduction', D. Bonhoeffer, *Life Together; The Prayerbook of the Bible, Dietrich Bonhoeffer Works*, vol. V, trans. D. W. Bloesch and J. H. Burtness (Minneapolis: Fortress Press, 1996), pp. 14–15. On Bonhoeffer's use of the 'Daily Texts', see especially F. B. Nelson, 'Bonhoeffer and the Spiritual Life: Some Reflections', *Journal of Theology for Southern Africa*, 30 (March 1980), 34–8.

28 'Letter of March 1, 1942', in Kelly and Nelson, *A Testament to Freedom*, p. 457 (translation slightly altered).

29 'Der Ort des Gebets im Leben und Theologie Dietrich Bonhoeffers' ('The Place of Prayer in the Life and Theology of Dietrich Bonhoeffer', in E. Bethge, *Bekennen und Widerstehen: Aufsätze – Reden – Gespräche* (Munich: Kaiser Verlag, 1984), p. 163.

30 Wilhelm Rott, 'Something Always Occurred to Him', in *I Knew Bonhoeffer: Reminiscences by his Friends*, ed. W. Zimmermann and R. G. Smith (London: Collins, 1966), p. 134.

31 Bonhoeffer, *Kirchenkampf und Finkenwalde* (my translation).

32 Bonhoeffer, *Life Together; Prayerbook of the Bible*, p. 51.

33 ibid., pp. 78–9.

34 See my 'Editor's Introduction' to *Prayerbook of the Bible*, ibid., p. 147.

35 These biblical quotations are taken from Bethge's essay 'Dietrich Bonhoeffer and the Jews', in *Ethical Responsibility: Bonhoeffer's Legacy to the Churches*, ed. J. D. Godsey and G. B. Kelly (New York: Edwin Mellen Press, 1981), pp. 74–5.

36 D. Bonhoeffer, *Kirchenkampf und Finkenwalde*, p. 544 (author's translation).

37 Bonhoeffer, *Life Together; Prayerbook of the Bible*, p. 57.

38 Bonhoeffer, *Letters and Papers from Prison*, pp. 39–40.

39 *Prayerbook of the Bible*, in Bonhoeffer, *Life Together; Prayerbook of the Bible*, p. 160.

40 Bonhoeffer, *Letters and Papers from Prison*, pp. 139–43.

41 J. C. Hampe, *Prayers from Prison* (Philadelphia: Fortress Press, 1979), p. 45.

42 F. von Schlabrendorff, *The Secret War Against Hitler* (London: Hodder & Stoughton, 1966), p. 324.

43 Nelson, 'Bonhoeffer and the Spiritual Life', p. 36.

44 Bonhoeffer, *Life Together; Prayerbook of the Bible*, p. 29.

45 ibid., p. 391 (translation slightly altered).

46 ibid., p. 90.

47 Bonhoeffer, *Letters and Papers from Prison*, p. 131.

48 ibid., p. 393.

49 Kelly and Nelson, *A Testament to Freedom*, p. 522 (author's translation).

50 From 'Stations on the Way to Freedom', ibid., p. 516 (author's translation).

51 Bonhoeffer, *Letters and Papers from Prison*, p. 190.

52 ibid., pp. 217–18.

53 ibid., p. 375.

54 See D. Bonhoeffer, *The Cost of Discipleship*, p. 99.

55 Bethge, *Prayer and Righteous Action*, pp. 26–7.

56 Bonhoeffer, *Letters and Papers from Prison*, p. 17.

57 Kelly and Nelson, *A Testament to Freedom*, p. 196.

58 D. Bonhoeffer, *Christ the Centre*, trans. E. H. Robertson (New York: Harper & Row, 1978), p. 197.

59 Bonhoeffer, *Ethics*, p. 114 (translation slightly altered).

60 Bonhoeffer, *Cost of Discipleship*, p. 341.

61 Kelly and Nelson, *A Testament to Freedom*, p. 515 (author's translation).

62 D. Bonhoeffer, *Letters and Papers from Prison*, p. 14 (translation slightly altered).

63 Kelly and Nelson, *A Testament to Freedom*, pp. 228–9.

64 See ibid., p. 104. This claim was made in the context of an ecumenical conference at Gland, Switzerland, in which Bonhoeffer condemned the idolatry of 'national security'. In the sermon noted above, Bonhoeffer declared that 'the world is choked with weapons'.

65 Bonhoeffer, *Ethics*, pp. 114–15.

66 Bonhoeffer, *Cost of Discipleship*, pp. 124–5.

67 Bonhoeffer, *Letters and Papers from Prison*, pp. 337, 360.

68 ibid., pp. 360–1 (translation slightly altered).

69 ibid.

70 Bonhoeffer, *Cost of Discipleship*, p. 98.

71 See my article, 'Sharing in the Pain of God: Dietrich Bonhoeffer's Reflections on Christian Vulnerability', *Weavings: A Journal of the Christian Spiritual Life*, 8 (4) (July–August 1994), 6–15.

Select English bibliography

Bethge, E. *Dietrich Bonhoeffer: Theologian, Christian, Contemporary.* London: Collins, 1970.

Bonhoeffer: Exile and Martyr. London: Collins, 1975.

Bonhoeffer: An Illustrated Introduction. London: Collins, 1979.

Prayer and Righteous Action. Belfast: Christian Journals Ltd, 1979.

Friendship and Resistance: Essays on Dietrich Bonhoeffer. Geneva: WCC, 1995.

Bethge, E., Bethge, R. and Gremmels, C. *Dietrich Bonhoeffer: A Life in Pictures.* Philadelphia: Fortress Press, 1986.

*Bonhoeffer, D. *Temptation.* New York: Macmillan, 1955.

The Cost of Discipleship. New York: Macmillan, 1960.

Sanctorum Communio: A Dogmatic Enquiry into the Sociology of the Church. London: Collins, 1963.

Ethics. New York: Macmillan, 1965.

No Rusty Swords: Letters, Lectures and Notes, 1928–1936, Collected Works of Dietrich Bonhoeffer, vol. i. New York: Harper & Row, 1965.

The Way to Freedom: Letters, Lectures and Notes, 1935–1939, Collected Works of Dietrich Bonhoeffer, vol. ii. London: Collins, 1966.

Letters and Papers from Prison: The Enlarged Edition. New York: Macmillan, 1972.

True Patriotism: Letters, Lectures and Notes, 1939–1945, Collected Works of Dietrich Bonhoeffer, vol. iii. London: Collins, 1973.

Christ the Centre. New York: Harper & Row, 1978.

Fiction from Prison: Gathering up the Past. Philadelphia: Fortress Press, 1981.

Spiritual Care. Philadelphia: Fortress Press, 1985.

Meditating on the Word. Cambridge: Cowley, 1986.

Act and Being: Transcendental Philosophy and Ontology in Systematic Theology, Dietrich Bonhoeffer Works, vol. ii. Minneapolis: Fortress Press, 1996.

Life Together; The Prayerbook of the Bible, Dietrich Bonhoeffer Works, vol. v. Minneapolis: Fortress Press, 1996.

Creation and Fall: A Theological Exposition of Genesis 1–3, Dietrich Bonhoeffer Works, vol. iii. Minneapolis: Fortress Press, 1997.

Bonhoeffer, D. and von Wedemeyer, M. *Love Letters from Cell 92.* London: Harper-Collins, 1993.

Bosanquet, M. *The Life and Death of Dietrich Bonhoeffer.* London: Hodder & Stoughton, 1968.

Burtness, J. H. *Shaping the Future: The Ethics of Dietrich Bonhoeffer.* Philadelphia:

Fortress Press, 1985.

Clements, K. *A Patriotism for Today: Love of Country in Dialogue with the Witness of Dietrich Bonhoeffer*. London: Collins, 1986.

What Freedom? The Persistent Challenge of Dietrich Bonhoeffer. Bristol: Bristol Baptist College, 1990.

Day, T. I. *Dietrich Bonhoeffer on Christian Community and Common Sense*. New York: Edwin Mellen Press, 1982.

de Gruchy, J. *Bonhoeffer and South Africa: Theology in Dialogue*. Grand Rapids: Eerdmans, 1984.

Dietrich Bonhoeffer: Witness to Jesus Christ. London: Collins, 1987.

(ed.) *Bonhoeffer for a New Day: Theology in a Time of Transition*. Grand Rapids: Eerdmans, 1997.

Dumas, A. *Dietrich Bonhoeffer: Theologian of Reality*. New York: Macmillan, 1971.

Fant, C. E. *Bonhoeffer: Worldly Preaching*. New York: Crossroad, 1990.

Feil, E. *The Theology of Dietrich Bonhoeffer*. Philadelphia: Fortress Press, 1985.

Feil, E. *Bonhoeffer Studies in Germany: An Overview of Recent Literature*, Philadelphia: International Bonhoeffer Society, 1997.

Floyd, W. W., Jr. *Theology and the Dialectics of Otherness: On Reading Bonhoeffer and Adorno*. Baltimore: University Press of America, 1988.

Floyd, W. W., Jr. and Marsh, C. (eds.) *Theology and the Practice of Responsibility: Essays on Dietrich Bonhoeffer*, Valley Forge: Trinity Press International, 1994.

Glazener, M. *The Cup of Wrath: The Story of Dietrich Bonhoeffer's Resistance to Hitler*. Macon, Ga.: Smyth & Helwys, 1992.

Godsey, J. D. *The Theology of Dietrich Bonhoeffer*. London: SCM, 1960.

Godsey, J. D. and Kelly, G. B. eds., *Ethical Responsibility: Bonhoeffer's Legacy to the Churches*. New York: Edwin Mellen Press, 1981.

Green, C. *Bonhoeffer: A Theology of Sociality*. Grand Rapids: Eerdmans, 1999.

Huntemann, G. *The Other Bonhoeffer: An Evangelical Reassessment of Dietrich Bonhoeffer*. Grand Rapids: Baker Books, 1993.

Kelly, G. B. *Liberating Faith: Bonhoeffer's Message for Today*. Minneapolis: Augsburg Publishing House, 1984.

Kelly, G. B. and Nelson, F. B. *A Testament to Freedom: The Essential Writings of Dietrich Bonhoeffer*. New York: HarperCollins, 1990.

Klassen, A. J. (ed.) *A Bonhoeffer Legacy: Essays in Understanding*. Grand Rapids: Eerdmans, 1981.

Kuhns, W. *In Pursuit of Dietrich Bonhoeffer*. London: Burns & Oates, 1967.

Kuske, M. *The Old Testament as the Book of Christ: An Appraisal of Bonhoeffer's Interpretation*. Philadelphia: Westminster, 1976.

Leibholz-Bonhoeffer, S. *The Bonhoeffers: Portrait of a Family*. London: Sidgwick & Jackson, 1971.

Lovin, R. W. *Christian Faith and Public Choices: The Social Ethics of Barth, Brunner and Bonhoeffer*. Philadelphia: Fortress Press, 1984.

Marsh, C. *Reclaiming Dietrich Bonhoeffer: The Promise of his Theology*. New York: Oxford University Press, 1994.

Marty, M. E. (ed.) *The Place of Bonhoeffer: Problems and Possibilities in his Thought*. New York: Association Press, 1962.

Moltmann, J. and Weissbach, A. *Two Studies in the Theology of Dietrich Bonhoeffer*.

New York: Charles Scribner's Sons, 1967.

Ott, H. *Reality and Faith: The Theological Legacy of Dietrich Bonhoeffer*. London: Lutterworth, 1971.

Pangritz, A. *Karl Barth in the Theology of Dietrich Bonhoeffer*. Grand Rapids: Eerdmans, 1998.

Peck, W. J. (ed.) (1987) *New Studies in Bonhoeffer's Ethics*, Toronto Studies in Theology, vol. 30. New York: Edwin Mellen Press, 1987.

Pejsa, J. *To Pomerania in Search of Dietrich Bonhoeffer*. Minneapolis: Kenwood Publishing, 1995.

Phillips, J. *The Form of Christ in the World: A Study of Bonhoeffer's Christology*. London: Collins, 1967.

Rasmussen, L. *Dietrich Bonhoeffer: Reality and Resistance*. Nashville: Abingdon, 1972.

  Dietrich Bonhoeffer: His Significance for North Americans. Minneapolis: Fortress Press, 1990.

Reist, B. A. *The Promise of Bonhoeffer*. Philadelphia: Lippincott, 1969.

Robertson, E. H. *The Shame and the Sacrifice: The Life and Teaching of Dietrich Bonhoeffer*. London: Hodder & Stoughton, 1987.

Scholder, K. *The Churches and the Third Reich*. 2 vols. Philadelphia: Fortress Press, 1988.

Smith, R. G. *A World Come of Age: A Symposium on Dietrich Bonhoeffer*. London: Collins, 1967.

Wind, Renate *Dietrich Bonhoeffer: A Spoke in the Wheel*, 1992. London: SCM, 1992.

Woelfel, J. *Bonhoeffer's Theology: Classical and Revolutionary*. New York: Abingdon, 1970.

Wüstenberg, R. K. *A Theology of Life: Dietrich Bonhoeffer's Religionless Christianity*. Grand Rapids: Eerdmans, 1998.

Zimmermann, W. and Smith, R. G. (eds.) *I Knew Bonhoeffer: Reminiscences by his Friends*. London: Collins, 1966.

*For publishing details of the new translations of Bonhoeffer's writings see chapter 4.

Index of names

Althaus, Paul, 163
Arendt, Hannah, 201–2
Aristotle, 74, 113
Athanasius, 121
Atkinson, Henry, 155
Augustine of Hippo, 116, 258

Barth, Karl, 19, 29 32, 40, 43, 53, 58, 61–5, 67, 73, 76–7, 79, 100–2, 114–15, 122, 134, 154–5, 163, 215, 231
Bell, George, 33–4, 40, 44, 81, 84, 86, 156–9, 170–1, 175, 197
Berger, Peter, 237
Bergraav, Bishop Eivind, 40
Best, Payne, 44, 86
Bethge, Eberhard, 22, 26, 30–1, 33, 36–7, 43–4, 50, 57, 61–2, 64, 72, 77, 82–3, 85–7, 88, 93, 96–8, 103, 136, 196, 206, 239, 256, 258, 260–1
Bethge, Renate, 25–6, 87, 260
Bismarck, Otto von, 3, 17
Bodin, Jean, 234
Bonhoeffer, Christel, 23
Bonhoeffer, Friedrich von, 23
Bonhoeffer, Grete, 67
Bonhoeffer, Julie Tafel, 23, 25–6
Bonhoeffer, Karl, 23–5, 43, 50
Bonhoeffer, Karl-Friedrich, 23–4, 27, 38, 67, 81
Bonhoeffer, Klaus, 23–4, 43, 66, 127
Bonhoeffer, Paula von Hase, 23–5
Bonhoeffer, Sabine, 23–4, 82, 197
Bonhoeffer, Susanne, 23–4
Bonhoeffer, Ursula, 23, 27
Bonhoeffer, Walter, 23, 154
Brahms, Johannes, 27
Bruning, Heinrich, 13, 15-16
Brunner, Emil, 29
Bruno, Giordano, 234
Buber, Martin, 51
Bullock, Alan, 16
Bultmann, Rudolf, 52, 102, 230–1

Calvin, John, 63
Canaris, Wilhelm, 39, 196
Canovan, Margaret, 201
Cervantes, Miguel de, 215
Chung Hyun Kyung, 104
Churchill, Winston, 40
Conway, John, 169
Crossman, Richard, 170

de Gruchy, John, 238, 252
Deissmann, Adolf, 19
Dellbrück, Hans, 43, 51
Dickinson, Willoughby, 155
Dilthey, W., 43, 66, 129
Dohnanyi, Hans von, 37, 39–40, 44, 127, 191, 194, 196–7, 206
Dostoevsky, Feodor, 215
Dumas, André, 101
Durkheim, Emil, 74

Ebeling, Gerhard, 102
Ebert, Fritz, 11–12
Eden, Anthony, 40
Eliot, T. S., 200–1
Euripides, 27

Feil, Ernst, 99–101, 232
Feuerbach, Ludwig, 234
Fisher, Frank, 29
Floyd, Wayne, W., Jr, 101
Freud, Sigmund, 66

Gandhi, Mahatma, 81, 118, 157, 169, 207–8
Gehre, Ludwig, 44
Godsey, John, 100
Goethe, Johann Wolfgang von, 27
Green, Clifford, 63
Grisebach, Eberhard, 116
Groener, Wilhelm, 12
Grotius, Hugo, 235

Index of Scripture references

Index of subjects